A WORLD BANK COUNTRY STUDY

Ecuador Poverty Report

The World Bank
Washington, D.C.

World Bank Country Studies are among the many reports originally prepared for internal use as part of the continuing analysis by the Bank of the economic and related conditions of its developing member countries and of its dialogues with the governments. Some of the reports are published in this series with the least possible delay for the use of governments and the academic, business and financial, and development communities. The typescript of this paper therefore has not been prepared in accordance with the procedures appropriate to formal printed texts, and the World Bank accepts no responsibility for errors. Some sources cited in this paper may be informal documents that are not readily available.

The World Bank does not guarantee the accuracy of the data included in this publication and accepts no responsibility whatsoever for any consequence of their use. The boundaries, colors, denominations, and other information shown on any map in this volume do not imply on the part of the World Bank Group any judgment on the legal status of any territory or the endorsement or acceptance of such boundaries.

The material in this publication is copyrighted. Requests for permission to reproduce portions of it should be sent to the Office of the Publisher at the address shown in the copyright notice above. The World Bank encourages dissemination of its work and will normally give permission promptly and, when the reproduction is for noncommercial purposes, without asking a fee. Permission to copy portions for classroom use is granted through the Copyright Clearance Center, Inc., Suite 910, 222 Rosewood Drive, Danvers, Massachusetts 01923, U.S.A.

The complete backlist of publications from the World Bank is shown in the annual *Index of Publications*, which contains an alphabetical title list (with full ordering information) and indexes of subjects, authors, and countries and regions. The latest edition is available free of charge from the Distribution Unit, Office of the Publisher, The World Bank, 1818 H Street, N.W., Washington, D.C. 20433, U.S.A., or from Publications, The World Bank, 66, avenue d'Iéna, 75116 Paris, France.

Cover photo courtesy of the World Bank and Edwin Huffman.

ISSN: 0253-2123

Library of Congress Cataloging-in-Publication Data

Ecuador poverty report.
      p.   cm. — (A World Bank country study)
    Includes bibliographical references.
    ISBN 0-8213-3665-7
    1. Poverty—Ecuador.   2. Poverty—Government policy—Ecuador.
I. Series.
HC204.P6E28   1996
362.5'09866—dc20
                                      96-21991
                                      CIP

CONTENTS

Basic Indicator Table

General

Area, land	sq km	283,600
Population, 1994	thousands	11,220
growth rate	percent per annum	2.0
density, 1994	per sq km	39.6

Social Indicators

literacy rate, 1994[a]	population age 15 and over	88
primary school enrollment, 1994[a]	percent of relevant population	92
secondary school enrollment, 1994[a]	percent of relevant population	54
under five mortality, 1992	per 1000 births	64
maternal mortality rate, 1992	per 100,000 births	170
unattended births urban, 1992	percent	70
unattended births rural, 1992	percent	20
tuberculosis vaccination, 1994[a]	percent of children below five	95
measles vaccination, 1994[a]	percent of children below five	92
polio vaccination, 1994[a]	percent of children below five	91
difteria vaccination, 1994[a]	percent of children below five	78
population per physician, 1990		957
health insurance (IESS), 1994[a]	percent of pop. covered	11
malnutrition, global, 1990	percent of children below five	34
malnutrition, chronic, 1990	percent of children below five	45
vulnerability incidence, 1994[a]	percent	52
poverty incidence, 1994[a]	percent	35
extreme poverty incidence, 1994[a]	percent	15
consump. of bottom 40%, 1994[a]	percent of total consumption	16
consump. of top 20%, 1994[a]	percent of total consumption	50

Economic

GNP per capita, 1994	$US	1299
GDP growth, 1994	percent	4
agriculture, 1994	percent of GDP	12
inflation, 1994	percent (end of period)	25
budget balance, 1994	percent of GDP	0.5
current account	percent of GDP	-4.9

[a]   From Living Standard Measurement Survey (SECAP 1994).

Currency Equivalents
Currency Unit - Sucre (S/.)

US$1.00 = S./ 3217 (July 31, 1996)

Government FISCAL YEAR
January 1 to December 31

Acronyms and Abbreviations

BEV	Banco Ecuatoriano de Vivienda (Ecuadoran Housing Bank)
BNF	Banco Nacional de Fomento (National Bank for Development)
CONADE	Consejo Nacional para el Desarrollo (National PlanningCouncil)
EB/PRODEC	Educación Básica - Proyecto de Educación (Basic Education Project)
FASBASE	Proyecto de Fortalecimiento y Ampliación de Servicios Básicos de Salud en Ecuador (Basic Primary Health Project)
FISE	Fondo de Inversión de Emergencia (Emergency Social Fund)
IDB	Inter-American Development Bank
IESS	Insituto Ecuatoriano de Seguridad Social (Ecuadoran Social Security Institute)
IMF	International Monetary Fund
INDA	Instituto Nacional de Desarrollo Agrícola (National Institute of Agricultural Development)
INEC	Instituto Nacional de Estadística y Censo (National Institute for Statistics and Census)
INECEL	Instituto Ecuatoriano de Electrificación (Ecuadoran Electricity Company)
INNFA	Instituto Nacional de la Juventud y de la Familia (National Institute of Children and the Family)
JNV	Junta Nacional de Vivienda (National Housing Board)
LSMS	Living Standard Measurement Survey
NGOs	Non-Governmental Organizations
ORI	Operación de Rescate Infantil (Operation Child Resuce)
RQA	Rural Qualitative Assessment
SECAP	Servicio Ecuatoriano de Capacitación Profesional (Ecuadoran Training Council)
USAID	U.S. Agency for International Development

Acknowledgments

The *Ecuador Poverty Report* is a product of the Country Department III, Latin America and the Caribbean Region. It was prepared by a team led by Jesko Hentschel and is based on two missions to Ecuador in May and October of 1994. The *Poverty Report* team comprised Alexandra Cox Edwards, Julie van Domelen, Peter Lanjouw, Haeduck Lee, Donna MacIsaac, Caroline Moser and Martin Rama. Robert Ackland contributed to the aggregation and valuation of consumption data, Armando Godinez to the targeting analysis of social programs, Surajit Goswami to the agricultural policy analysis, and Will Waters and Anna Webb to the *Rural Qualitative Assessment*. Staff from the 'Central Ecuatoriana de Servicios Agrígolas' and 'Desarollo y Autogestión' conducted household interviews in seven rural communities for the *Rural Qualitative Assessment*. Background papers for the Report were prepared by Wilma Freire and Will Waters (nutrition), José Sanchez-Parga (indigenous peoples) and the Centro de Planificación y Estudios Sociales (gender issues). Norman Hicks (Lead Economist) participated in the two missions and led the policy dialogue with the Government on expenditures in the social sectors, the gas subsidy and the direct voucher schemes. Margarita Caro processed a large part of this document.

Thanks are due to many commentators and advisors in Ecuador, the World Bank and other international organizations, among them Renán Cisnero, Juan-José Illingworth, Paul Isenman, Guillermo Jauregui, Jeffrey Hammer (peer reviewer), Dan Morrow, Martin Ravallion (peer reviewer), Rafael Urriola and Rob Vos. Special thanks to Eduardo Somensatto -- only his continued advice and support made this study possible.

Financial support from the Dutch Government for several background papers and the *Rural Qualitative Assessment* is gratefully acknowledged. UNICEF contributed six community case studies to the *Rural Qualitative Assessment*.

Introduction and Executive Summary

Ecuador is a poor country, measured by the number of people who cannot afford to purchase a basic basket of goods. Although the oil boom of the 1970s led to unprecedented growth, poverty remains pervasive. The distribution of wealth is highly skewed, and close to four million Ecuadorans, about thirty-five percent of the population, live in poverty. Another seventeen percent are vulnerable to poverty. One and a half million Ecuadorans live in extreme poverty and cannot meet their nutritional requirements even if they spend everything they have on food. Poverty is higher in rural areas, where two out of three poor people live.

The characteristics of rural and urban poverty are quite different. Rural poverty is associated with lack of education, little access to land, a low degree of market integration, and lack of employment in the vibrant off-farm rural sector. Further, poverty among the many indigenous people, who live predominantly in the rural Sierra and the Amazon region, is much higher than for the non-indigenous population. This population group also shows alarming levels of malnutrition and child mortality and has much less education than the non-indigenous population. Urban poverty, which affects one and a half million people, is linked to a somewhat different set of variables, which vary by region. For example, while basic service provision has reached the poor in the urban Sierra, many poor in the urban Costa are without a functioning water supply or sewage system. But the poor in various urban areas also have some characteristics in common. These are, again, low educational achievement, informal sector employment, rented -- instead of owned -- housing, and low rates of labor force participation by the spouse of the household head.

Because of the lack of progress in reducing both urban and rural poverty, it is clear that Ecuador must seriously rethink its approach to these problems. It is generally agreed that the multitude of existing social programs need to be better coordinated as many are overly centralized today and often duplicate rather than complement each other. The poor do not have access to social security, public primary health care is almost nonexistent, and nutritional programs reach only 6 percent of poor children below the age of five. The subsidies that do exist, even for education, cater mainly to the wealthy.

This Report aims to help the Government and others to identify key aspects of a new poverty reduction strategy and possible options or first-best alternatives for policy interventions. Actual blueprints for reforms, and programs, however, will need to be worked out with all concerned parties, including the poor as the target group.

Components of a Poverty Reduction Strategy

This Report argues that a successful poverty reduction strategy can be based on the following components: basic nutrition and health programs for the poor; an effort to strengthen the assets of the poor; and support for a strong and stable demand for labor. The first two components, in particular, will require public resources. Hence, resource mobilization is an essential part of Ecuador's poverty reduction strategy.

Sustained labor-intensive macroeconomic growth is the single most important condition for poverty reduction because it creates employment opportunities and higher incomes for the poor while providing the public sector with much needed resources to support social programs and targeted interventions, without crowding out private initiative and investment. In addition, international experience has shown that it is much more difficult for the poor to protect their income and wealth in a low-growth environment. If the country were able to raise the per capita growth rate of around one percent to reach three percent for five years, poverty could be reduced from 35 to 26 percent. However, growth by itself is by no means sufficient for reducing poverty -- especially for addressing the non-income aspects of poverty, particularly lack of access to basic social services. In addition, poverty reduction from faster growth could be partly or completely offset if inequality increases. If the share of the bottom 40 percent of the population in total consumption were to fall from the current 16 percent to 10 percent, poverty would increase to 40 percent in five years despite a three percent per capita growth rate.

Financing Social Programs and Targeted Interventions. Financing of improved or expanded poverty programs, as suggested below, must take place within a sound, sustainable macroeconomic framework. This means that tough choices must be made in order to maintain fiscal discipline. Not all of the programs mentioned below can be implemented at the same pace. However, Ecuador could raise substantial resources by eliminating or reducing several subsidies, tax evasion, and tax exemptions, which would enable it to finance social programs and targeted interventions while maintaining fiscal balance. For example, achieving a cost recovery rate of one half for higher education could finance a 40 percent increase in expenditures on primary or a 35 percent increase of expenditures on secondary education, which would benefit the poor. Targeting the subsidy on electricity use through a lifeline rate to the light users (many of who are poor) could generate resources equivalent to the entire 1993 budget of the Ministry of Health.

Basic Nutrition and Health Program. Nutrition programs for malnourished children and a basic health program for the poor are preconditions for a successful strategy to help poor people out of poverty -- and for Ecuador to advance as a country. Any investments in education or infrastructure will bring a significant return only if people are healthy and well-nourished enough to be able to take advantage of these investments.

Strengthening the Assets of the Poor. The main assets of the poor in Ecuador are labor, land, and housing. The key to increasing the productivity and use of labor is to improve primary education, expand access to secondary education, and increase female participation in the labor force. Increasing poor farmers' access to land would not only decrease poverty but could also raise land productivity in large parts of the Ecuadoran agricultural sector. These efforts could be complemented by increasing poor farmers' access to rural markets through infrastructure and extension investments. Housing could be strengthened as a productive asset by creating an enabling environment to help the poor to upgrade their homes so they can be used for small business and other income-generating activities.

A Strong and Stable Demand for Labor. Macroeconomic growth and stability not only provide the Government with resources to support investments in health, education, and services, but also are necessary to create employment opportunities. The poor need employment opportunities to reap the benefits of their education. Labor market deregulation is key to reducing the bias against employment in the higher-paying modern sector.

Financing Social Programs and Targeted Interventions

Reallocating Subsidies Serving the Non-poor. Subsidies for electricity and cooking gas (LPG) together account for about 2 percent of GDP; only 17 percent of the electricity subsidy and only 23 percent of the cooking gas subsidy reach the poor. A simple alternative to the electricity subsidy would be to create a lifeline tariff and charge heavy users the true economic cost of the resource. For cooking gas, there are several options, all of which have advantages and disadvantages. A direct income voucher system is a possibility but should not be based on the Basic Services Indicator used in Ecuador because leakage would be very large. Other options are to restrict the distribution of subsidized containers to low-income areas or to phase out the subsidy while channeling benefits to the poor through improved social programs.

Increasing Tax Revenues. Increasing non-oil tax revenues could also finance poverty reduction programs. Tax revenues could be increased by up to 3 percent of GDP by eliminating exemptions on the value added tax (in the order of 1.4 percent of GDP) and by reducing tax evasion (1.7 percent of GDP). To improve tax collection, the Government could effectively use the established Large Taxpayers Unit.

Improving Education Finance. Education finance has become dramatically imbalanced. Unit costs for higher education are about six times higher than for primary education and double the unit costs for secondary education. While the poor benefit from primary education expenditures, most secondary and especially higher education expenditures directly go to the non-poor. Reallocating expenditures from higher to basic and secondary education not only would have a positive effect on equity, but it is essential for improving the quality of basic education and enable poor children to obtain a secondary school education.

Targeting as a Means To Reduce the Costs of Social Programs. Although targeting of social programs is a cost-effective means of reducing leakage, it is not widely used. Among twenty-five major social programs, only about a third operate with an explicit targeting mechanism; two-thirds are either universal programs intended to reach the entire population or operate without a specific mechanism to identify beneficiaries. In the country's targeted social programs, targeting costs are within reasonable expectations, but the initial emphasis on setting up targeting mechanisms is usually not followed by consistent performance monitoring. Such monitoring is crucial for evaluating and subsequently improving targeting mechanisms.

In addition, not all of the programs need to be financed, let alone carried out, by the public sector. In many areas, for example in housing, stimulating the effective engagement of self-help groups, NGOs, and the private sector would be more cost-effective than large-scale public programs. The scope for an expanded role for NGOs and community organizations is especially large. These and other important "how to" questions of program design and implementation -- including the central issue of decentralization of public service provision -- are not covered in this report but must also be addressed in the near future.

Basic Nutrition and Health Programs

Nutrition. A coordinated effort to expand nutrition programs to reach the most vulnerable groups, young children and pregnant mothers, would bring high returns in the long run. Only well-nourished, healthy children can learn and acquire the skills they need to escape poverty

during their lifetime. But, while chronic malnutrition of children under five years of age is with 45 percent at alarming levels, the many modest nutrition programs only reached a small fraction of the 600.000 poor young children below the age of five in 1994. A close examination of several of these programs reveals that they do attempt to target, and that targeting costs are well invested (i.e., leakage to the non-poor is relatively small). The real problem, however, within financing and implementation constraints, is to reduce the degree of undercoverage. Experience from neighboring Andean countries shows that nutrition programs that piggyback onto health care or day care networks can indeed reach the poor.

Basic Health. Reductions in real per capita expenditure over the last years for the main provider of health services in Ecuador, the Ministry of Health, have plunged the basic health system into a crisis. Many public health posts can no longer provide fundamental services, and the poor have come increasingly to rely on the private sector for health care, which then absorbs 12 to 17 percent of the household budget. But not all the poor can turn to the private sector. About half a million of them cannot afford such expenses and are left without help even when they critically need curative care. Others have turned to non-professional healers and pharmacists. Appropriate funding for basic health care is a necessary condition for helping many of the poor survive.

Strengthening the Assets of the Poor

The Quality of Primary Education and the Importance of Secondary Education for Poor Children. In our view, Ecuador's education policy needs to emphasize two areas: improving the quality of primary school education and enabling poor children to go on the secondary school. While almost all youngsters attend primary school, the repetition and drop-out rates for poor children are quite high, and the quality of the education is not sufficient to help children escape poverty. Attendance in secondary school varies widely, but is clearly much lower for the poor than for the non-poor. Many poor parents do not send their children to secondary school because of the direct private costs of public education and the opportunity costs of the children in school not being able to contribute to family income. However, secondary education can be a way out of poverty, since returns to secondary education are quite high. Financial assistance to the poor, either by reducing the direct costs or by introducing school vouchers, are options for increasing the poor's access to secondary education.

Rural Poverty and the Closeness to the Market.
The more that farmers are integrated into the rural market, the less likely they are to be poor. Demand-driven infrastructure investments ranging from roads to irrigation and from electricity to household water supply can bring the rural poor closer to the market, thereby reducing their reliance on subsistence agriculture and increasing the demand for off-farm activities. A variety of demands exist at the rural community level that need to be taken into account to ensure community participation in development projects. Given the experience to date of World Bank-supported projects such as the Social Investment Fund (FISE) and the Rural Development Project, it is very important to assist isolated communities in expressing their demands for such projects.

The Importance of the Rural Land Market.
Rural poverty is also closely linked to land. In rural areas, the smaller farmers are very often the poorer farmers. But these farmers tend to use their land more intensively and tend to have higher yields for many products than larger farmers. Supporting the existing but informal land market to help increase poor farmers' access to land can therefore increase equity without reducing efficiency. Titling of the many unregistered farms would be an important step toward formal land transactions. Innovative financial schemes such as land grant schemes or Agricultural Banking for the Poor could then be explored to help poor farmers overcome the lack of access to credit.

Women's Participation in the Labor Force.
Participation in the workforce is significantly lower for poor women than for non-poor women. In urban areas, the participation of poor women is constrained by their household duties, especially childcare, and by limited mobility due to increasing violence. Restarting the daycare centers

closed in 1993 could help many women to reenter the workforce, enable the Government to target nutrition programs to young children, and free teenage girls of their duty to attend siblings, allowing them to remain in secondary school. In rural areas, women are more active than their male counterparts in the vibrant off-farm sector. House-based textile production, small rural industries, sales, and services offer for many rural women the opportunity to earn an income. However, their ability to profit from these activities is linked to their closeness to the market; hence the small productive infrastructure projects mentioned above attain an even higher importance.

Housing as a Process for the Urban Poor.
The link between housing and poverty is complex. Housing is a dynamic process, since homes are an asset that can enable poor families to conduct informal sector activities such as repairs, production of textiles, or sale of food and beverage. Renting out a room can supplement family income. Further, in times of need, the house can be used to give shelter to relatives or close friends who would otherwise have to live on the street or in a shanty. Housing is used intensively as an asset in Ecuador, and its use increases with expenditure quintile. Hence, housing can be an important route out of poverty. Ecuador's housing policy should turn away from constructing shelter or providing subsidies, since they never reached the poor. Instead, official recognition, ownership transfer, and titling are the first necessary steps to give inhabitants an incentive to start investing in their dwellings.

A Stable and Strong Demand for Labor

Increasing the demand for labor is related to the elimination of entry barriers and to macroeconomic growth, particularly if growth finances investments in education to prepare workers for the modern workplace.

Reducing Burdensome Regulation in the Labor Market. Ecuador has cumbersome labor legislation. The Government interferes with wagesetting in the private sector through a variety of mechanisms, including different minimum wages by sector and region, side benefits, and mandatory wage adjustments to compensate for increases in the cost of living. These regulations act as an entry barrier to employment in the modern sectors because they tax labor. Estimates show that these interventions are responsible for an eight percent wage differential between the regulated and the unregulated sectors. A fifty percent reduction in the segmentation across sectors and regions would move about 100,000 workers to the modern -- and highest paying -- sector of the economy, significantly improving their living conditions. Deregulation alone, however, cannot overcome poverty in Ecuador. Reform of the labor market must include not only harmonizing the multitude of minimum wages but also restructuring the social security system.

Macroeconomic Growth and Stability. As shown by a model simulating the relationship between investment levels and education, moderately increasing growth rates and investing part of the additional public funds in education could move more than a quarter million workers into the higher paying modern sector of the Ecuadoran economy. There are three reasons for Ecuador's dismal record of past growth: low domestic savings rates, caused largely by short-term macroeconomic instability; lack of technological innovation and low returns to investment, because of long-standing inward-looking economic policies; and vulnerability to external shocks. Continuing macroeconomic stability, increasing the savings rate, and stimulating the development of non-traditional exports would help restore growth to levels that would make possible a serious attack on poverty.

The Poverty Report

The present Poverty Report consists of two parts. Part One summarizes the main results of the analysis. It begins with a background section on the incidence and distribution of poverty and its main correlates, then turning to each of the main components of a poverty reduction strategy for Ecuador. Part Two consists of ten Working Papers, each is a self-contained, in-depth study that addresses a specific poverty issue. The studies range from the determinants of rural poverty to the incidence of fiscal expenditures, and from targeting social programs to the impact of labor market deregulation on employment.

Most of the data and estimates used in the Report stem from the Ecuador Living Standard Measurement Survey (LSMS) and two qualitative studies conducted in urban and rural areas. The LSMS was fielded by the Ecuadoran Training Council SECAP in the summer of 1994. Almost all of the calculations and policy evaluations refer to this time period. This quantitative survey is complemented with findings from two qualitative studies conducted for this Report to learn about the views and preferences of the poor themselves: The first study examines Cisne Dos, a low-income neighborhood in Guayaquil; the second covers seven poor rural communities in the Andean highland, the Costa, and the Amazon jungle.

Introducción y Resumen Ejecutivo

El Ecuador es un país pobre, habida cuenta del número de personas que no puede costearse una canasta basica. Aunque el auge del petróleo de los años setenta condujo a un crecimiento sin precedentes, sigue habiendo pobreza generalizada. La distribución de la riqueza es sumamente asimétrica, y cerca de cuatro millones de ecuatorianos -alrededor del 35% de la población- viven en pobreza. Además, otro 17% de la población corre el riesgo de caer en pobreza. Un millón y medio de habitantes viven en la extrema pobreza y aún gastando todo lo que tienen en la compra de alimentos no logran satisfacer sus necesidades nutricionales. La pobreza es mayor en las zonas rurales, donde viven dos de cada tres personas pobres.

La pobreza presenta características muy diferentes en los sectores rural y urbano. La pobreza rural está vinculada con la falta de educación, acceso a la tierra, la escasa integración en los mercados, y la escasez de empleo en las actividades no agrícolas, las cuales han mostrado ser bastante dinámicas. Además, en las zonas rurales de la Sierra y la Región del Amazónica, la pobreza de los grupos indígenas es mayor que la de la población no indígena. Dichos grupos presentan también niveles alarmantes de malnutrición y mortalidad infantil y sus niveles de educación son muy inferiores a los de la población no indígena. Por otra parte, la pobreza urbana, que afecta a un millón y medio de personas, está vinculada a un grupo de variables diferente a los de la pobreza rural y que además varía según la región. Por ejemplo, si bien en las zonas urbanas de la Sierra los pobres tienen acceso a los servicios básicos, muchos de los que viven en las zonas urbanas de la costa no cuentan con sistemas adecuados de suministro de agua o alcantarillado. No obstante, en varias zonas urbanas los pobres tienen características en común, que consisten en un bajo rendimiento escolar, empleo en el sector informal, vivienda alquilada en lugar de propia, y una tasa baja de participación de la cónyuge la fuerza laboral.

Dada la falta de progreso en la reducción de la pobreza urbana y rural, es evidente que el Ecuador debe reconsiderar cuidadosamente las politicas para abordar este problema. Es de aceptación general que existe la necesidad de una mejor coordinación entre los programas sociales existentes, ya que en muchos de ellos se observa centralización y duplicación de funciones en lugar de complementaridad. Los pobres no tienen acceso a la seguridad social, prácticamente no existe la atención primaria de salud pública y los programas de alimentación sólo abarcan al 6% de los niños pobres menores de cinco años. Las subvenciones que existen, aún en la esfera de la educación, benefician sobre todo a los ricos.

El objetivo de este informe es ayudar al Gobierno y a otros responsables a identificar los aspectos fundamentales de una nueva estrategia para la reducción de la pobreza y a plantear posibles opciones o alternativas de políticas. Más allá de lo que pueda aportar este informe, somos concientes que en la formulación de los programas y proyectos básicos de reforma deberán participar todas las partes interesadas, especialmente los pobres, que son los ultimos afectados.

Componentes de una Estrategia para la Reducción de la Pobreza

En este informe se sostiene que una estrategia eficaz para la reducción de la pobreza puede basarse en los siguientes temas: Programas básicos de nutrición y salud para los pobres; medidas encaminadas a incrementar los activos de los pobres, y, fomento de una demanda firme y estable de mano de obra. En los dos primeros casos, sobre todo, deberán utilizarse recursos públicos. Por lo tanto, la movilización de recursos es un componente esencial de cualquier estrategia para la reducción de la pobreza en el Ecuador.

El crecimiento macroeconómico intensivo en trabajo es la condición más importante para la disminución de la pobreza, pues crea oportunidades de trabajo y más altos salarios para los pobres y adémas proporciona al sector público los recursos para ampliar programas sociales e intervenciones selectivas, sin desplazar a la iniciativa e inversión privadas. Además, la experiencia de varios países ha demostrado que para los pobres es mucho más difícil proteger su ingreso y patrimonio en condiciones de escaso crecimiento económico. Si el país lograra elevar la actual tasa de crecimiento per cápita, que es de alrededor del 1%, al 3% durante cinco años, podría reducirse la pobreza del 35% al 26%. Sin embargo, el crecimiento por si mismo no es suficiente para reducir la pobreza -- especialmente en relación a los aspectos de la pobreza no directamente ligados con el ingreso, particularamente la falta de acceso a los servicions sociales básicos. Además, la reducción de la pobreza para un crecimiento mas acelerado podria verse parcial o totalmente contrarrestada si viniera acompañada por un aumento de la inequidad. Si la participación del 40% más pobre de la población en el consumo total disminuyera del nivel actual de 16% al 10%, la pobreza aumentaría al 40% en cinco años, a pesar de una tasa de crecimiento del 3% per cápita.

Financiamiento de programas sociales e intervenciones dirigidas. El financiamento de programas de pobreza extensivos y mejorados, como se sugiere más adelante, debe llevarse a cabo dentro de un marco macroeconómico sostenible y sólido. Es decir que aún cuando se tiene que tomar decisiones para mantener la disciplina fiscal, no todos los programas descritos pueden ser implementados con la misma velocidad. El Ecuador podría movilizar un considerable volumen de recursos mediante la eliminación o reducción de varios subsidios y exenciones de impuestos y la evasión fiscal, lo que permitiría financiar programas sociales e intervenciones dirigidas manteniendo, al mismo tiempo, el equilibrio del presupuesto. Por ejemplo, una tasa de recuperación de costos del 50% en la educación superior serviría para financiar un incremento del 40% del gasto en educación básica o del 35% en educación secundaria, lo cual beneficiaría a los sectores pobres. Focalizar el subsidio solamente a los hogares que consumen electricidad en menor cantidad (muchos de los cuales son pobres), podría generar recursos equivalentes al total del presupuesto del Ministerio de Salud en 1993.

Además, no todos los programas necesitan ser financiados o llevados a cabo por el sector

público. En muchas areas, por ejemplo el sector de la vivienda, la estimulación de la contratación efectiva de grupos de ayuda-propria, ONGs y el sector privado, podría ser más eficaz que grandes programas publicos. El alcance de un rol más amplio de los ONGs y organizaciones comunitarias es especialmente alto. Estas y otras importantes aspectos en el diseño de programas y su implementación -- incluyendo el problema crítico de la decentralización de la provisión de servicios publicos -- no están cubiertas por este informe pero deben ser tambien enfocadas en el futuro.

Programas básicos de nutrición y salud. Los programas de nutrición para los niños malnutridos y los programas de atención básica de salud para los pobres son condiciones previas para el éxito de cualquier estrategia para la eliminación de la pobreza y el progreso del Ecuador. La inversión en educación o infraestructura sólo generará beneficios importantes si las personas están en buenas condiciones de salud y bien alimentadas para aprovechar esta inversión.

Incrementar los activos de los pobres. Los activos más importantes de los pobres del Ecuador son la mano de obra, la tierra y la vivienda. Para aumentar la productividad y el uso de la mano de obra, es fundamental mejorar la educación primaria y el acceso a la educación secundaria e incrementar la participación de la mujer en la fuerza laboral. Un mayor acceso de los pobres a la tierra no sólo disminuiría la pobreza sino que aumentaría la productividad de la tierra en una gran parte del sector agrícola ecuatoriano. Estas medidas podrían complementarse aumentando el acceso de los agricultores pobres a los mercados rurales a través de la infraestructura y la ampliación de las inversiones. La vivienda podría convertirse en un activo productivo si se creara un medio propicio para ayudar a los pobres a mejorar sus viviendas a fin de que puedan utilizarlas en pequeñas empresas y otras actividades generadoras de ingresos.

Demanda firme y estable de mano de obra. El crecimiento y la estabilidad macro-económicos no sólo proporcionan al Gobierno recursos para inversiones en salud, educación y servicios, sino que también son necesarios para crear oportunidades de empleo. Para aprovechar los beneficios de la educación, los pobres deben contar con oportunidades de empleo. Para reducir el sesgo contra el empleo en los sectores modernos de la economía, donde los sueldos son más altos, es importante desregular el mercado laboral.

Financiamiento de Programas Sociales e Intervenciones Focalizadas a los Pobres

Reasignación de los subsidios que benefician a los que no son pobres. Los subsidios al consumo de electricidad y gas para cocinar representan el 2% del PIB; sólo el 17% y el 23% de los subsidios al consumo de electricidad y gas de cocina, respectivamente, benefician a los pobres. Una alternativa sencilla para la subvención al consumo de electricidad sería establecer una tarifa baja y cobrar el costo económico real del recurso a los consumidores más intensivos. En el caso del gas hay varias alternativas, todas las cuales tienen ventajas y desventajas. Una posibilidad es utilizar un sistema de cupones de ingresos directos, el cual no debería basarse en el Indicador de Servicios Básicos usado en el Ecuador, debido a que gran parte de los benificios caerian en manos de gente no pobre. Otras opciones serían restringir la distribución de envases de gas subvencionados a las zonas de bajos ingresos o eliminar gradualmente la subvención, distribuyendo otros beneficios a los pobres mediante la aplicación de mejores programas sociales.

Aumento de ingresos por impuestos. Con un aumento de los ingresos tributarios no procedentes del petroleo también se podrían financiar programas de reducción de la pobreza. Los ingresos tributarios podrían incrementarse hasta en un 3% del PIB mediante la eliminación de las exenciones del impuesto al valor agregado (que actualmente ascienden a un total del 1,4% del PIB) y la reducción de la evasión tributaria (1,7% del PIB). A fin de aumentar la recaudación impositiva, el Gobierno podría utilizar la oficina ya establecida dirigida a los contribuyentes mas importantes.

Aumento del financiamiento de la educación. El financiamiento de la educación se ha desequilibrado notablemente. Los costos unitarios de la educación superior son alrededor de seis veces más altos que los de la educación primaria y el doble de los de la secundaria. Si bien el gasto en educación primaria y secundaria beneficia más a los pobres, la mayor parte del gasto en educación superior beneficia directamente a los que no son pobres. La reasignación del gasto en educación superior a la educación básica y secundaria no sólo tendría un efecto positivo en la equidad, sino que es fundamental para mejorar la calidad de la educación básica y permitir que los niños pobres tengan acceso a la educación secundaria.

Focalización como método para reducir el costo de los programas sociales. Si bien la focalización de los programas sociales hacia beneficiarios específicos es un método eficaz en función de los costos, su uso no se ha generalizado. De los actuales 25 programas sociales importantes, en sólo aproximadamente un tercio de ellos se contempla expresamente un mecanismo de focalización específica; el resto son programas universales destinados a beneficiar a toda la población o funcionan sin un mecanismo específico para identificar a los beneficiarios. En los programas sociales de enfoque selectivo del país, los costos que ese enfoque entraña son razonables, pero el énfasis inicial puesto en el establecimiento de mecanismos de orientación específica normalmente no se complementa con el seguimiento de los resultados. Esta labor es fundamental para evaluar y mejorar los mecanismos de focalización.

Programas Básicos de Nutrición y Salud

Nutrición. Una labor coordinada para ampliar los programas de nutrición con destino a los grupos más vulnerables, los niños menores de cinco años y las madres embarazadas, rendirá grandes beneficios a largo plazo. Sólo si están bien alimentados y en buenas condiciones de salud, los niños pueden aprender y adquirir los conocimientos prácticos necesarios para salir de la pobreza. Mientras que las tasas de malnutrición crónica alcanzan un nivel alarmante de 45%, en 1994 los programas de nutrición solamente abarcaron a una pequeña parte de los 600.000 niños pobres de menores de cinco años. Al analizar detenidamente varios de estos programas es posible comprobar que se está haciendo un esfuerzo por orientarlos a beneficiarios específicos y que los costos de dicho enfoque selectivo se están invirtiendo adecuadamente (es decir, no hay mucha filtración de los beneficios a personas que no son pobres). No obstante, el verdadero problema es como, dentro de barreras de financiamiento e implementación, se puede reducir el elevado porcentaje de niños que no está comprendido en estos programas. La experiencia de los países andinos vecinos indica que, de hecho, los programas de nutrición vinculados a la atención de salud o las guarderías pueden beneficiar a los pobres.

Atención básica de salud. La reducción en los ultimos años del gasto real per cápita del Ministerio de Salud, el principal encargado de la prestación de servicios de atención de salud en el Ecuador, ha provocado una crisis del sistema de atención básica de salud. Muchos puestos de salud pública no están en condiciones de suministrar servicios básicos, por lo que los pobres han debido recurrir cada vez más a los servicios privados de atención de salud, lo cual absorbe entre el 12% y el 17% del presupuesto de los hogares. Sin embargo, no todos los pobres tienen acceso a servicios de salud privados. Alrededor de medio millón de personas no pueden cubrir ni estos servicios básicos ni medicamentos. Otros han comenzado a recurrir a curadores no profesionales y farmacéuticos. El financiamiento adecuado de la atención básica de salud es una condición necesaria para ayudar a sobrevivir a muchos pobres.

Incremento de los Activos de los Pobres

Calidad de la educación primaria e importancia de la educación secundaria para los niños pobres. Consideramos que la política de educación del Ecuador debe hacer hincapié en dos aspectos: mejorar la calidad de la enseñanza primaria y permitir que los niños pobres asistan a la escuela secundaria. Si bien la mayoría de los niños asiste a la escuela primaria, las tasas de repetición y deserción entre los niños pobres son sumamente altas, y la calidad de la enseñanza no es adecuada para ayudarlos a salir de la pobreza. Los índices de asistencia a la escuela secundaria varían

mucho, pero es indudable que los correspondientes a los pobres son inferiores a aquéllos de quienes no lo son. Muchos padres pobres no envían a sus hijos a la escuela secundaria en gran medida debido al costo directo que significa para ellos la educación pública y los costos de oportunidad, ya que los niños que asisten a la escuela no contribuyen al ingreso familiar. No obstante, la educación secundaria puede ser una forma de salir de la pobreza, pues las tasas de retorno de esta educación son bastante altas. Una forma de mejorar el acceso de los pobres a la educación secundaria es prestándoles asistencia financiera, ya sea mediante una reducción de los costos directos o el uso de cupones para la educación escolar.

Pobreza rural y cercanía a los mercados. Cuanto más integrados están los agricultores en los mercados rurales, tanto más posibilidades tienen de no ser pobres. Las inversiones en infraestructura basadas en la demanda -desde caminos hasta sistemas de riego y desde electricidad hasta el suministro de agua a los hogares- pueden traducirse en una mayor integración de los pobres del sector rural en los mercados, reduciendo así su dependencia de la agricultura de subsistencia y aumentando la demanda de actividades no agrícolas del sector. A fin de lograr la participación de la comunidad en los proyectos de desarrollo, es necesario tomar en cuenta las diversas necesidades de las comunidades rurales. Habida cuenta de los resultados obtenidos hasta ahora a través de algunos proyectos respaldados por el Banco, como el Fondo de Inversión Social de Emergencia (FISE) y el Proyecto de Desarrollo Rural, es muy importante ayudar a las comunidades aisladas a expresar la necesidad que tienen de los proyectos.

Importancia del mercado de tierras del sector rural. La pobreza rural está también estrechamente vinculada a la tierra. En las zonas rurales, los pequeños agricultores suelen ser los más pobres. Sin embargo, estos agricultores tienden a hacer un uso más intensivo de la tierra y, generalmente, obtienen un rendimiento mayor por hectária que los grandes agricultores. Por consiguiente, el respaldo al actual mercado informal de la tierra para ayudar a mejorar el acceso de los agricultores pobres a este recurso puede aumentar la equidad sin reducir la eficiencia.

El otorgamiento de títulos de propiedad respecto de muchas de las granjas no registradas constituiría un paso importante en la creación de un sistema oficial de transacciones inmobiliarias. A continuación podrían examinarse planes novedosos de financiamiento, tales como donación de dinero para que los pobres puedan comprar tierra, o ayudar a los agricultores pobres a superar el problema de la falta de acceso al crédito.

Participación de la mujer en la fuerza laboral. El nivel de participación de las mujeres pobres en la fuerza laboral es inferior al de aquéllas que no lo son. En las zonas urbanas, la participación de las mujeres pobres se ve limitada por sus quehaceres domésticos, especialmente el cuidado de los niños, y por la dificultad de movilizarse debido a la creciente violencia. La reapertura de las guarderías infantiles cerradas en 1993 podría ayudar a muchas mujeres a reintegrarse a la fuerza laboral, posibilitaría al Estado orientar los programas de nutrición específicamente a los niños de corta edad, y liberar a las adolescentes de la obligación de cuidar a sus hermanos menores, permitiéndoles asistir a la escuela secundaria. Las mujeres realizan una labor más activa que los hombres en las dinámicas actividades no agrícolas del sector rural. La producción de textiles en el hogar, las pequeñas industrias rurales, las ventas y los servicios ofrecen a muchas mujeres del sector rural la oportunidad de obtener un ingreso. Sin embargo, su capacidad de obtener beneficios de estas actividades depende de su cercanía a los mercados; por lo tanto, los pequeños proyectos mencionados de infraestructura productiva adquieren mayor importancia.

La vivienda como forma de mejorar la situación de los pobres en las zonas urbanas. El vínculo entre la vivienda y la pobreza es complejo. La vivienda es un factor esencial en permitir que las familias pobres participen en actividades informales, como las reparaciones, la producción de textiles o la venta de alimentos o bebidas. Las familias pueden complementar su ingreso alquilando una habitación. Además, en tiempos difíciles, la casa puede servir de albergue a familiares o amigos que de otra manera tendrían de vivir en la calle o en una vivienda precaria. En el

Ecuador la vivienda se utiliza intensivamente como un activo, y este uso aumenta cuanto mayor es el nivel de gasto per capita del hogar. Por lo tanto, la vivienda puede ser un buen medio para salir de la pobreza. Las políticas de vivienda del Ecuador deben dejar de lado la construcción de albergues y el otorgamiento de subsidios, dado que estas medidas nunca han beneficiado a los pobres. En cambio, a fin de dar a los pobladores un incentivo para comenzar a invertir en sus viviendas, primero es necesario el reconocimiento oficial y la transferencia de la propiedad, así como el otorgamiento de títulos, pues solo con dichos titulos pueden obtener los pobres acceso a servicios basicos y el mercado de credito.

Demanda Estable y Firme de Mano de Obra

Para aumentar la demanda de mano de obra es necesario eliminar los obstáculos al acceso al mercado de trabajo y lograr consolidar crecimiento macroeconómico, especialmente si dicho crecimiento se utiliza para financiar la inversión en educación.

Eliminación de reglamentaciones gravosas del mercado laboral. La legislación laboral ecuatoriana es complicada. El Gobierno interviene en la fijación de salarios del sector privado a través de numerosos mecanismos, incluidos distintos salarios mínimos por sectores y regiones, beneficios adicionales y reajustes salariales obligatorios por variación del costo de vida. Estas normas son un obstáculo para el empleo en los sectores modernos de la economía porque aumentan el costo de la mano de obra. Según las estimaciones, estas intervenciones se traducen en una diferencia salarial del 8% entre los sectores reglamentado y no reglamentado. Una reducción de la segmentación, que reduzca la diferencia salarial a 4%, integraría a unos 100.000 trabajadores en los sectores modernos de la economía, donde los salarios son más altos, mejorando considerablemente sus condiciones de vida. Sin embargo, por sí sola la desregulación no bastará para superar la pobreza en el Ecuador. La reforma del mercado laboral debe comprender no sólo la armonización de los diversos salarios mínimos, sino también la reforma del sistema de seguridad social.

Crecimiento macroeconómico y estabilidad. Se demostró, mediante un modelo que simulaba la relación entre los niveles de inversión y la educación, que un incremento moderado de las tasas de crecimiento económico y la inversión de parte de los fondos públicos adicionales en educación podrían permitir la integración de más de un cuarto de millón de trabajadores en los sectores modernos de la economía, donde los salarios son más altos. Los pésimos resultados obtenidos en materia de crecimiento económico en el pasado se deben a tres causas: bajas tasas de ahorro interno --que en gran parte se deben a la inestabilidad macroeconómica a corto plazo--; la falta de innovación tecnológica y tasas bajas de retorno de inversión --debido a la aplicación persistente de políticas económicas aislacionistas--, y la vulnerabilidad a las conmociones externas. La estabilidad macroeconómica sostenida, un mayor nivel de ahorro y la promoción de las exportaciones de productos no tradicionales contribuirían a restablecer niveles de crecimiento económico que permitirían aplicar medidas eficaces de lucha contra la pobreza.

El Informe sobre la Pobreza

Este *Informe sobre la Pobreza* consta de dos partes. En la primera se resumen los principales resultados de nuestro análisis. En primer lugar se ofrecen antecedentes sobre la incidencia y distribución de la pobreza y los principales factores vinculados con ésta. A continuación se mencionan los principales componentes de una estrategia para la reducción de la pobreza en el Ecuador. La segunda parte del informe consta de 10 estudios individuales e independientes de varios temas de la pobreza. Los estudios cubren una gran variedad de temas desde los determinantes de la pobreza rural hasta la incidencia de gastos fiscales y también desde el objetivo de programas sociales hasta el desempleo con relación al impacto del mercado laboral no reglamentado.

La gran mayoría de nuestros datos y estimaciones provienen de la reciente Encuesta sobre Condiciones de Vida para Ecuador que el Servico Ecuatoriano de Capacitación Profesional (SECAP) condujó en 1994. Casi todas de las calculos y evaluaciones de politicas se refieren a este período de tiempo. Este análisis cuantitativo se complementa con las conclusiones de dos estudios cualitativos realizados para este informe, a fin de conocer los puntos de vista y preferencias de los pobres mismos. El primer estudio se realizó en Cisne Dos, un barrio urbano de bajos ingresos de Guayaquil; el segundo abarca a siete comunidades rurales pobres del altiplano andino, la costa y la selva amazónica.

Part I.

Components of a Poverty Reduction Strategy

1.   Poverty Estimates and Correlates

This section provides an overview of poverty conditions in Ecuador in 1994, and contains three key messages. First, Ecuador is an extremely poor country, measured by the number of people who cannot afford to purchase a basic basket of goods.   Thirty-five percent of its population, close to four million people, lived in poverty in 1994 and an additional seventeen percent were highly vulnerable to poverty.   Second, rural poverty is undoubtedly more severe than urban poverty, in terms of either percentages or absolute numbers. Although more people now live in urban than in rural areas, the outcome of a long process of intersectoral transition, sixty percent of the total poor still reside in rural areas. This picture might change in the coming years if the rapid urban population growth continues.   Third, people who are poor are by no means alike; the relationship between poverty, household characteristics, and social indicators varies considerably across -- and even within -- regions and areas. Nevertheless, a certain set of common characteristics also apply and an understanding of these is important for designing appropriate strategies to help the poor grow out of poverty.

Poverty and Inequality in Ecuador, 1994

Poverty Measurement. This study measures the well-being of individuals by total consumption expenditures, not by total income. This is for a number of reasons, the most important of which being that consumption tends to fluctuate much less during the course of a month or a year than income. Experience has also shown that people tend to provide more accurate information about their consumption behavior than about their income sources. Moreover, if expenditure data can be used for welfare analysis, this has the compelling advantage that the poverty lines can be derived from the data itself and need not be adopted from other surveys. The analyses in this Report are based almost exclusively on the recently completed Living Standard Measurement Survey (LSMS),[1] which is the first nationally representative survey of its kind in Ecuador.

A number of steps were required to arrive at usable consumption figures for households in Ecuador.   First, we converted information on household purchases of food items into a monetary aggregate based on households' reported quantities and prices paid. Second, we calculated the calorie equivalent of the observed food consumption per household.   Third, we evaluated and priced non-food expenditures, paying particular attention to the valuation of water and the 'consumption' of durable goods such as refrigerators, houses, or cars. Finally, we adjusted nominal expenditures of all households for the variation in prices among different areas and regions.[2]

We use three consumption-based poverty lines. The *extreme poverty line* only values a basket of food items which meets the minimum necessary calorie requirements per person. The *full poverty line* includes the same basket of food items but also non-food items. The non-food expenditure component is calculated by looking at those people whose total expenditures are just enough to reach the extreme poverty line and the average fraction of

---

[1]   SECAP (1994).
[2]   See Working Paper 1, Annex 1, for details.

the budget that these households devote to non-food items is used to scale up the extreme poverty line to yield the full poverty line. The philosophy behind this estimate is that the non-food items purchased by this population group are <u>absolutely essential</u> since a direct trade-off between food and non-food items occurs. The *vulnerability line* uses a different reference group to compute the share of non-food items in total expenditures. It chooses the population whose <u>food</u> expenditures exactly finance the minimum basket of goods and records their share of non-food expenditures in total expenditures. The basket of these non-food items is also essential, but somewhat <u>less essential</u> than the one used for the calculation of the full poverty line because no trade-off between food and non-food expenditures is necessary.[3] We can describe the population between the poverty and vulnerability line as being vulnerable to poverty.[4]

Poverty Rates. Table 1 provides estimates of poverty based on two measures. The *incidence* gives the percentage of the population with consumption levels below the vulnerability, full poverty and extreme poverty lines. The *severity* is sensitive to the distribution of the population with per capita expenditures below the lines, attaching greatest weight the further the distance below the applicable poverty line.

Table 1. Poverty in Ecuador 1994:   Summary Measures

		----------- Incidence[a] ----------			------------- Severity[a] ----------		
		Vulnerability Line	Full Poverty Line	Extreme Pov. Line	Vulnerability Line	Full Poverty Line	Extreme Pov. Line
Costa	urban	44	26	9	6	3	1
	rural	69	50	22	13	6	2
Sierra	urban	34	22	11	6	4	1
	rural	64	43	20	12	7	3
Oriente	urban	36	20	7	5	2	1
	rural	80	67	50	25	16	7
National	urban	40	25	10	6	3	1
	rural	<u>67</u>	<u>47</u>	<u>22</u>	<u>13</u>	<u>7</u>	<u>3</u>
Total	national	52	35	15	9	5	2

a Poverty incidence is measured by the headcount ratio; poverty severity is measured by the FGT_2 (see Ravallion 1994).
Source: LSMS, 1994.

In 1994, thirty-five percent of the Ecuadoran population lived in poverty and an additional seventeen percent were vulnerable to poverty. The incidence of poverty varied considerably between urban and rural areas but less between regions. In Table 1, poverty is much higher in rural than in urban areas.[5] Almost every second person lived in poverty in rural Ecuador, while every fourth person was poor in the urban areas (according to the *full poverty line* which we will use as a benchmark in most cases). The predominantly rural bias of poverty is replicated for each of the three distinct regions. The rural Oriente, the scarcely

---

[3]   Compare Ravallion (1994).
[4]   In this Report, unless otherwise states, all references to a poverty line will correspond to *the full poverty line* described above, and all poverty calculations will be with reference to that poverty line.
[5]   The LSMS defines an urban area as a town and city with more than 5,000 inhabitants.

populated jungle area of Ecuador suffers clearly the highest levels of poverty with sixty-seven percent. The most endangered population group in Ecuador is the fifteen percent, or 1.7 million people, unable to finance a basic nutritional basket even if they spend everything they have on food. These are the extremely poor.

Geographical Distribution. The geographical distribution of the poor (i.e., the population below the *full poverty line*) varies widely. As depicted in Graph 1, the rural Sierra, rural Costa, and urban Costa each account for about one million poor. While the incidence of poverty is highest in the rural Oriente, only about 5 percent of the total poor live there. And although 55 percent of the total population, according to the LSMS, lived in urban areas in 1994, we still find sixty percent of the poor, or 2.3 million people, in rural Ecuador.

Ranking. Rural poverty is higher than urban poverty. Graph 2 shows the distribution of expenditures for urban and rural Ecuador: the horizontal axis represents expenditures per capita and the vertical axis shows the percentage of the population with such expenditures or less. No matter which cut-off point, or poverty line, one chooses, it is always true that a much higher proportion of the rural population lives in poverty. In terms of regional distribution, both the urban and rural Costa have a higher *incidence* of poverty than the corresponding Sierra areas. The *severity* of poverty, however, is greater in urban and rural Sierra.

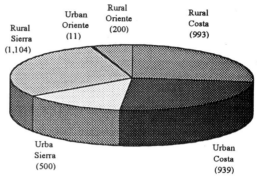

Graph 1. Where Do the Poor Live? (thousands)

Source: LSMS (1994).

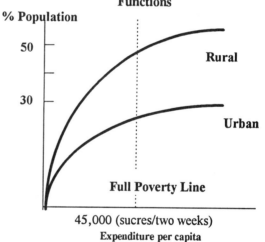

Graph 2. Expenditure Distribution Functions

Source: LSMS (1994).

Consumption Patterns. What does the diet of a 'typical' poor person in Ecuador look like? Per day, the major items in such a diet include about two cups of boiled rice, one potato, half a glass of milk, a slice of bread with a thin spread of margarine or other fat, a small amount of cassava, half an onion, sixty grams of green vegetables, some salt, one banana, and a cup or two of coffee with two spoons of sugar. Eggs, fish, beef and chicken are usually not part of the daily diet and weekly consumption of a poor would not exceed one egg, a piece of chicken and a small portion of meat. Typically, a poor person spends about 55 percent of total expenditures on these (and other minor) food items.

Outlays for health, housing and education are the major non-food budget items for the poor and the non-poor alike. Jointly, they claim about a quarter of all expenditures. Education expenditures have a higher weight in the budget of the non-poor than the poor, largely due to a much higher share of non-poor children attending private instead of public schools. Matriculation fees in private schools are many times the ones in public schools. The share of health expenditures is very high for the

Table 2. Budget Shares, 1994		
	Poor	Non-Poor
Food	54.8	47.6
Health	10.7	7.7
Housing	8.2	9.7
Education	5.2	6.3
Water	0.9	1.0
Electricity	0.9	1.2
Cooking Fuel	1.1	0.6
Other	18.2	25.9

Source: LSMS, 1994.

poor, which, as we will show later on, can be explained by the very high reliance of the poor on the private health sector for medical treatment. Some of the average budget shares shown in the table mask important variations within the group of poor people. For example, the extremely poor users of LPG as a cooking fuel have a budget share of roughly 2.5 percent on this item at the currently highly subsidized prices. This report will largely deal with the major budget items of the poor -- such as health, education, and housing -- but it will also cover several other items. For example, although electricity is a relatively minor budget item for both the poor and the non-poor, about 83 percent of the electricity subsidy is directed to the non-poor, today. Targeting the subsidy to poor consumers only would free scarce financial resources which could help to improve basic social programs and education.

Graph 3. Distribution of Consumption, 1994

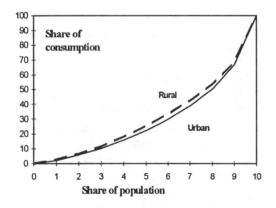

Graph 4. Inequality in Consumption, 1994

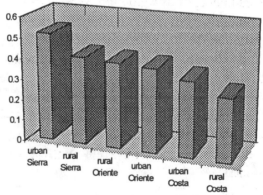

Source: LSMS, 1994. Inequality is measured by the Atkinson Inequality Measure ($E=2$).

Inequality. While the LSMS shows that rural Ecuador is poorer than urban Ecuador by the two poverty indicators, consumption is more equally distributed in the rural areas. Graph 3 depicts the familiar Lorenz curves of consumption distribution in rural and urban Ecuador and Graph 4, based on the Atkinson parameter ($E=2$), shows inequality measures by area and region. Graph 4 shows that consumption in the rural Sierra and Costa is more evenly distributed than in the urban Sierra and Costa, but that both Sierra regions have a higher inequality in consumption than the Oriente and the Costa. On a national basis, the bottom half of the rural population accounted for only slightly more than 25 percent of total rural consumption in 1994, while the top decile realized more than 30 percent. For the urban areas, the share of the bottom half of the population is even smaller, at 22 percent, while the top ten percent accounted for 33 percent.

Living Conditions and Characteristics of the Poor

Although the poor live in marginal circumstances with regard to housing and basic services, living conditions vary strongly across different parts of the country in other respects. These commonalties and differences below present some characteristics of poverty. All distinctions we make here between the 'poor' and the 'non'-poor are based on whether people have per capita expenditures below or above the *full poverty line*.

Household Characteristics. Clear differences between poor and non-poor households emerge with respect to the composition of the household. Poverty is a function of the degree to which the household is extended, that is, how many relatives, such as the elderly or daughters with their own children, are part of the household. About 60 percent of Ecuador's population lives in nuclear households. Extending the households to accommodate one or two more people does not raise the likelihood of the household being poor, but once three or more people are taken in, poverty increases rapidly in households with only one wage earner. Overall, about fifteen percent of the population live in such strongly extended households, of which half are poor, while only about one third of the nuclear and mildly extended households are poor. In the Cisne Dos sample survey on urban poverty in Guayaquil, such expansion of households emerged as one of the main methods of shielding elderly or young relatives with children from falling into extreme poverty.

More of the young and old are poor than the middle-aged. Because poor households tend to contain a higher number of children and tend to provide shelter for extended family members, such as the elderly, the age-poverty profile falls with age and then rises again (Graph 5). While more than forty percent of the population below fourteen live in poverty, less than thirty percent of the population at age thirty to fifty are poor. For the elderly, this ratio again rises above forty percent.

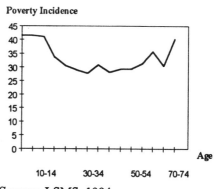

Graph 5. Age distribution of Poverty

Poverty Incidence

Source: LSMS, 1994.

Households headed by certain types of people also have a high risk of poverty. These are not, as one might have expected, females. The LSMS and the survey in Cisne Dos both show that female-headed households do not have a higher poverty incidence than male-headed households.[6] Rather, households headed by middle-aged males living in an 'union libre' with their partner and widow-headed households are both significantly more likely to

---

[6]   This finding can be explained partly by the tendency of very poor female-headed households to move in with their relatives since they simply cannot afford to live alone.

be poorer than all other types of households.[7] This applies to urban and rural areas alike. It appears that widowhood is a key determinant of poverty for many of the rural poor: In the Rural Qualitative Assessment conducted for this Poverty Report, rural people named widows as a particularly poor group because many of them cannot work in the fields and are dependent on outside help.

Housing Materials. Types and quality of housing differ between the poor and non-poor but also between rural and urban areas. Congestion within houses is highest among the poor in urban areas, but the rural poor are considerably more likely to be living in houses with mud or wooden walls and dirt floors. Stone is clearly the preferred housing material in all regions and areas, but few of the poor have access to this material. Further, more poor people rent their houses than the non-poor in urban areas, a fact that we found of high importance in the case study of Cisne Dos. One of the major strategies for households to shield themselves from poverty is to use their house as a shelter or nest for impoverished relatives and for informal sector activities. Often, such use goes hand in hand with small investments made in the house (e.g., addition of another room as a garage or work space), which can only be done to a much lesser extent in rented structures.

Basic Services. The link between poverty and basic services is not uniform but depends on area, region, and type of service. The rural non-poor are worse off than the urban poor in relation to water supply, hygiene facilities, garbage disposal, and electricity connection as depicted in Table 3. However, services can have a different function in urban and rural areas, e.g., the threat from lack of hygiene facilities in rural areas is much lower than in the overcrowded urban centers, especially in the Costa, where the climate helps to breed diseases.

Access to basic services also varies by region. The Sierra is better off in almost all services than the Costa and the Oriente, and this distinction is especially pronounced among the urban poor in these areas. About half the poor in the urban Costa and Oriente dump their trash on the street or burn it, while only one quarter of the poor in the urban Sierra do so; the trash in the Sierra is collected for three quarters of the poor population. Similarly, about half the urban poor in the Costa need to meet their water supply from water trucks, wells, or other private sources because they are not connected to the public water network, implying high prices for water. In Cisne Dos, the low-income community in Guayaquil that we studied in depth, half of all households are solely dependent on water truck vendors. In the Sierra, on the other hand, four out of five poor people obtain their water from the public network and have a flush toilet.

Not all services render themselves useful to distinguish the living conditions of the poor from the non-poor. Electricity in urban Ecuador now reaches nearly every household, independent of its status. In rural areas, however, there is a strong relationship between electricity connection and poverty -- most markedly in the Sierra and the Oriente. Similarly, telephone service is not a distinguishing factor for the rural population but it is for the urban population.

---

[7] Male-headed *union libre* households have a poverty rate of 46 percent; of the total poor, almost one third live in such households. If the heads of households are widows, the poverty rate is 60 percent. However, only about 5 percent of the total poor live in widow-headed households.

Table 3. Some Characteristics of the Poor, 1994

		Urban		Rural		Total	
		Poor	Non-Poor	Poor	Non-Poor	Poor	Non-Poor
Basic Services							
sewerage connection (%)	National	57.3	83.4	12.4	28.2	29.6	63.8
	Costa	43.5	74.4	11.7	17.0	27.3	58.9
	Sierra	78.9	95.6	13.5	35.4	33.5	69.5
	Oriente	62.9	87.9	7.0	31.1	10.8	50.6
electricity supply (%)	National	97.8	99.5	62.0	75.8	75.8	91.1
	Costa	97.9	99.4	55.5	63.3	76.4	89.6
	Sierra	97.7	99.7	69.8	84.3	78.4	93.0
	Oriente	93.6	96.5	36.3	74.4	40.1	81.9
water from public net (%)	National	61.2	78.8	18.3	23.0	34.8	59.3
	Costa	48.9	67.1	6.1	9.1	27.2	51.4
	Sierra	79.9	94.5	27.9	34.0	43.8	68.2
	Oriente	85.3	92.5	12.1	23.2	17.0	47.2
waste collection (%)	National	59.7	76.7	1.1	5.6	23.5	51.5
	Costa	52.2	68.9	1.3	6.8	26.6	52.1
	Sierra	70.5	87.7	0.9	3.9	22.2	51.3
	Oriente	59.9	84.9	1.8	21.5	5.7	43.3
Education							
education of	National	5.2	9.1	3.2	4.7	4.0	7.5
household head (years)	Costa	4.9	8.3	2.8	3.9	3.9	7.1
	Sierra	5.8	10.5	3.4	5.1	4.1	8.0
	Oriente	5.9	8.8	4.5	7.4	4.6	7.8
Health							
diseases treated	National	24.8	14.8	32.7	24.1	29.4	18.0
informally	Costa	27.3	19.0	45.3	33.7	36.4	22.6
	Sierra	19.7	9.6	21.4	19.4	20.8	13.7
	Oriente	26.3	10.7	20.1	14.4	20.4	13.2
Employment							
informal sector	National	54.6	44.1	27.9	35.8	39.2	41.7
	Costa	54.6	44.1	19.6	24.8	37.6	41.6
	Sierra	56.3	41.3	35.1	42.6	42.3	41.9
	Oriente	54.9	40.8	25.7	41.1	27.3	40.9
regulated sector	National	15.5	35.3	3.4	9.9	8.6	26.7
	Costa	11.8	31.1	1.1	3.1	6.6	24.4
	Sierra	22.1	41.3	5.4	12.6	11.1	29.2
	Oriente	8.7	40.0	6.4	26.8	6.5	31.0

Source: LSMS, 1994.

Education. As shown in Table 3, the education level of the head of household is very strongly associated with the level of poverty. The average poor household head in both urban and rural Ecuador has not completed primary school, which lasts 6 years. In rural Ecuador, many of the poor household heads barely complete the basic cycle of primary school (3 years). Not surprisingly, while literacy at the national level now stands at about 90 percent, more than one third of the extremely poor in the rural Sierra cannot read or write. In contrast, the average schooling of the urban non-poor household head is well into secondary school, and even beyond the basic secondary school cycle (9 years) in the Sierra. In the rural areas, even the non-poor heads usually stop schooling before completing primary school, which points to a serious educational deficit in rural Ecuador.

Health. Apart from the fact that the rural population must travel about twice as far as the urban population to reach treatment facilities, the type of treatment varies with a family's material standing. If treatment is necessary, more of the poor than the non-poor treat their ill members with home remedies or seek advice from a pharmacist. As discussed in more detail below, twelve percent of the poor, or about half a million people, cannot obtain curative care in emergencies because they do not have access to public health facilities and cannot afford private services.

Employment. A broad sectoral breakdown of the labor force reveals that informal activities play a different role for the urban and rural poor. The breakdown distinguishes between the informal, modern, public, and a narrowly defined farm sector. As expected, employment shares in the farm sector are negatively correlated, and in the public and modern sectors positively correlated with per capita expenditures, but the more interesting finding relates to the role of the informal sector (Table 3). In the urban areas, the informal sector absorbs a higher share of the poor than the non-poor labor force, especially women. About 65 percent of the occupied poor women work in the informal sector, which is their predominant source of entry into the labor market. In the rural sector, the opposite is the case -- informal sector activity is higher for the non-poor than for the poor.

Rural off-farm employment plays an important role in supplementing agricultural income, and for the poor it has a high potential to become a road out of poverty. Using a broad definition of off-farm employment that includes both primary and secondary occupations, it appears that as many as one in two of the non-poor of working age have some employment in the off-farm sector. In the Rural Qualitative Assessment, many families responded that they have earned income from non-agricultural sources, e.g., as day laborers in nearby townships, through home-based textile production in the Sierra, or with small-scale businesses in the Costa.

The survey also shows a link between household poverty and participation in the labor force of the spouse of the head of household. Poverty in households in which the partner or spouse (mainly women) of the household head does not work is calculated at 32 percent. This is high compared to the 22 percent poverty rate for households in which the spouse or partner of the household head does contribute to income.

The regulation of employment also affects poverty. Regulations that affect workers' benefits, mandatory payroll taxes for social security, and training council contributions drive a wedge between the poor and non-poor as does unionism to a lesser degree. Overall, 21 percent of the Ecuadoran labor force is employed in the regulated sector, largely in urban areas. The share of the urban poor employed in regulated firms is significantly lower (13 percent) than the share of the non-poor in this sector (33 percent). The poor are hurt to the

10

extent that regulations create barriers to entry to better-paying jobs. Unionism, on the other hand, has less effect on the distribution of the poor and non-poor in the urban labor market.

Ethnicity. The 'definition' of the indigenous people is a difficult undertaking because there are no objective characteristics to apply. Indigenous languages (e.g., Quechua, Shuar), traditional clothing, heritage, and observed traditions and beliefs can, but need not be, part of the life of the indigenous people. Ultimately, the classification of who is indigenous depends on self-identification. All statistical estimates of the exact number of indigenous people based on a uni-dimensional indicator are therefore bound to be imprecise and, at best, indicative. Nevertheless, for purposes of this study, language is used as a variable because it is highly correlated with ethnicity and therefore can provide some insight into the living conditions of the indigenous people in Ecuador.

Poverty, living conditions, and language are closely related. The indigenous population, as defined by language, is concentrated in the rural Sierra and the rural Oriente; almost none live in the Costa. Households in which an indigenous language is spoken are more likely to be poor than are Spanish-speaking households.[8] If we use the census from 1990 and distinguish cantons according to a 'strong', 'moderate', or 'low' percentage of the population speaking an indigenous language, the strongly indigenous cantons are worse off with respect to a wide variety of social and service variables, such as education level, illiteracy rate, malnutrition rate, and electricity and water connection. The differences in the education and health indicators are alarming: While the national illiteracy rate was only 9 percent in 1990, more than 40 percent of the population in the strongly indigenous cantons were illiterate (in any language) in 1990, with female illiteracy even higher, impairing the integration of the indigenous female population into national society. A third of the population in these cantons was without any educational instruction. Similarly, in the strongly indigenous cantons, child malnutrition, at 64 percent, was clearly above the national average of 45 percent, and so was infant mortality. Further, in the labor market, workers who speak or even know an indigenous language suffer discrimination. If we control for a wide range of other variables such as experience and education, indigenous language speaking workers earn on average 33 percent less in the agricultural sector than those who do not speak an indigenous language.[9]

The Correlates of Poverty

This section examines the correlates of poverty for each of the variables described above, controlling for the influence of other variables.[10] Estimating a number of different probability functions, in which a household's poverty status is described as a function of many 'exogenous' variables allows us to determine what variables have an association with poverty that is independent of the association between poverty and the other variables in the equation. Such relationships should be interpreted as correlates and not as determinants since causality can run both ways.

---

[8]   See Working Paper 1.
[9]   Compare Working Paper 8.
[10]   See Working Paper 2, Annex 1, for the urban probability analysis and Working Paper 4 for the rural probability analysis.

Impact of Heterogeneity. Most of the variables that describe the living conditions of the poor, such as housing or access to basic services, are not significantly linked to poverty on a cross-regional basis because many of the living conditions vary from place to place. As noted above, the living conditions of the poor vary significantly across regions and areas, with the poor in the urban Sierra often having better access to basic services than the non-poor in other regions and areas. A certain subset of basic service and housing variables is significantly linked to poverty on a regional and area basis, but these variables become insignificant when we try to find cross-regional associations of poverty.

Other factors such as climatic conditions add to this observed heterogeneity between and within regions. In the agricultural sector, we find that different crops are linked to poverty. In the Costa and the Oriente, maize cultivators are less exposed to poverty while maize cultivators in the Sierra are more likely to be poor. The heterogeneity of living conditions and the resource base in rural areas is also one of the key findings from the Rural Qualitative Assessment. Apart from the obvious inter-regional differences, intra-regional and even intra-community heterogeneity can be very great. This pertains to the degree that families have become active in the off-farm sector, to their access to agricultural extension services, and the quality of cultivated land. Even within seemingly homogenous poor communities, stratification based on family conditions and land access is significant.

Common Urban Factors. But there are also a number of common factors or common themes closely linked to poverty that cut across the diversity of regions in Ecuador. The following four factors all raise the probability of a household being poor: (a) low educational achievement of the household heads, (b) the household living in a rented rather than owned home or apartment, (c) the spouse or partner of the household head not being active in the labor force, and (d) the household head being employed in the informal and not the regulated sector of the economy

> **Common factors raising the likelihood of an urban household being poor:**
> * **low educational achievement of the household head;**
> * **house or apartment rented and not owned;**
> * **spouse not working;**
> * **household head employed in the informal and not the regulated sector.**
> *Source*: Working Paper 2.

Common Rural Factors. In the rural areas, we can also identify a set of common factors closely linked to poverty, although the correlates of rural poverty are even more diverse than in urban areas. Indigenous language households are more likely to be poor than non-indigenous language households. In addition, four other factors increase the probability of the household living in poverty: (a) low educational achievement of the household head, (b) low per capita land holdings, (c) household members not being engaged in regular off-farm income earning activities, and (d) little access to the market. The latter requires some explanation since it is not as easily measurable as the other three factors,

> **Common factors that increase the likelihood of a rural household being poor**
> * **household speaking an indigenous language;**
> * **low education achievement of the household head;**
> * **low per capita land holding**
> * **no employment in the informal, off-farm rural sector;**
> * **little access to the market**
> *Source*: Working Paper 4.

although it is a phenomenon observed in all three regions. In the Costa, if a household is engaged mainly in subsistence agriculture (i.e., selling less than 30 percent of output on the market), it is significantly more likely to be poor. While this relationship also holds in the Sierra, it is not as strong, and only becomes significant at the 80 percent level. But another variable attains importance in the Sierra: households having benefited from technical assistance in agriculture (from Ministry of Agriculture extension, NGOs or private sources) show significantly lower poverty levels than rural households that did not receive such assistance. Further, in all areas, access to infrastructure such as electricity, telephones, or gas appear to be important correlates, although to varying degrees in different parts of the country.

The Results in the Context of the Ecuadoran Debate on Poverty

There is intense debate about poverty now going on in Ecuador among NGOs, universities, and many government officials. This debate is largely focused on which regions are poorest and on whether public funds are being targeted correctly (i.e., in accordance with the geographic distribution of the poor).

Two remarks are in order. The first concerns the regional aspect of the debate. Regionalism clouds the much more important distinction between urban and rural poverty, particularly since a regional ranking of poverty very much depends on the poverty measure chosen and the exact location of the poverty line. For example, while the incidence of poverty in the rural Costa was higher than the incidence of poverty in the rural Sierra, the rankings reversed when we compared its severity. In any case, poverty in the rural areas is higher than in urban areas independent of the poverty measures chosen, and the determinants of rural poverty are quite distinct from those of urban poverty.[11]

The second remark concerns the link between basic services and poverty. Several institutions in Ecuador have advocated the use of a Basic Services Indicator (BSI) to identify the poor and to develop poverty maps. But access to basic services such as sewerage, water, and garbage disposal varies considerably across regions and between urban and rural areas. While it is difficult to judge how good the poverty maps based on such a Basic Service Indicator (with fixed weights given to the supply of different services) are, the indicator is definitely not suited to identify individual poor households. On a household basis, we have compared the Basic Service Indicator with a poverty measure based on expenditures and found that, if applied, the Basic Service Indicator would lead to significant undercoverage and leakage -- almost half of the poor would not be identified and targeted resources would reach the non-poor.[12]

---

[11]   In this context, it is important to distinguish between a fair geographical distribution of budget resources and effective targeting. It is entirely possible that resources that are 'optimally' allocated between provinces according, for example, to the amount of poor people, do not reach the poor within the provinces and are thus distributed fairly among regions but targeted badly. Similarly, a program that exhibits no leakage to the non-poor, and as such is targeted optimally, can exhibit a strong regional bias.

[12]   While the provision of basic services to the poor is one of the central roles of government, it is not clear that rural and urban areas *should* obtain similar levels of services, as is sometimes advocated in Ecuador. In urban areas, greater population densities pose greater health risks if sewage, electricity, or organized garbage disposal are not available. Also, the unit cost of networked services will be considerably higher in rural than in urban areas. In deciding whether the current

It remains clear, nevertheless, that the link between infrastructure services and poverty is very strong. Several basic services are a prerequisite for a family to be able to earn income to pay for basic life necessities. Decent hygiene facilities, potable water, and garbage collection are necessary in crowded cities to avoid diseases. And if people are ill they cannot learn or work to their full potential, hence reducing their ability to earn income. Similarly, the many inhabitants of rural Ecuador with no electricity cannot earn non-agricultural incomes through, for example, home-based textile production. Although the lack of basic services at one point in time might not necessarily determine a family as poor or non-poor, it could mean that the family is constrained from growing out of poverty, which access to basic services might enable them to do.

2. The Financing of Social Programs and Targeted Interventions

Before describing areas where the expansion or introduction of social programs would be beneficial to the poor, it is important to look at the financing possibilities for such programs. Although the national budget was under pressure in early 1995, Ecuador has made major progress over the past couple of years in improving the fiscal position of the public sector: While the consolidated budget deficit averaged 5 percent of GDP in the second half of the 1980s, it has since been reduced sharply and actually recorded a small surplus in 1994. Ecuador must maintain this fiscal balance in order to create an environment conducive to growth. Efforts can be made to alleviate poverty without jeopardizing the fiscal balance.

Ecuador can raise substantial resources by improving policies related to subsidies, higher education finance, tax evasion, and tax exemptions. Reducing subsidies on electricity and cooking gas (LPG) alone -- which now benefit mostly the non-poor -- could yield up to 2 percent of GDP. Reducing income tax evasion and eliminating value added tax exemptions could provide as much as 3 percent of GDP in additional revenues. Partial cost recovery for higher education could raise an additional 0.6 percent of GDP. In addition, effective targeting can reduce the costs of poverty alleviation programs.

Financing of social programs and targeted interventions is compatible with maintaining fiscal balance. Even if all of the resources available from subsidy reductions, tax revenue increases, and higher education tuition are not fully realized, Ecuador can still seriously attack poverty. Some simple illustrations reinforce this finding. Achieving a cost recovery rate of one half for higher education finance would finance a 40 percent increase in expenditures on primary or a 35 percent increase on secondary education. Targeting the subsidy on electricity use through a lifeline rate to the light (and often poor) consumers could generate resources equivalent to the entire budget in 1993 of the Ministry of Health. And reducing income tax evasion by 25 percent could triple the budget of all nutritional programs together.

---

distribution of services is acceptable, it is necessary also to ask what alternative arrangements exist (i.e., whether the fact that a rural household has no access to piped water means that it has no access to any potable water).

Reallocating Subsidies Serving the Non-Poor

Over the past several years, the Government of Ecuador has eliminated major direct and indirect subsidies that catered to the rich, including petroleum product subsidies, but several important subsidies remain in place, including those for electricity, cooking gas, water, urban transport, and housing.

From an efficiency and equity perspective, subsidies have to fulfill two conditions to justify their existence. From an efficiency perspective, subsidies should induce only minimal shifts in the society's consumption of goods and resources (unless they are introduced in order to reflect the existence of positive externalities associated with the consumption of the subsidized good). Hence, subsidized goods should display very low substitution and income elasticities. Second, from an equity perspective, the poor should be the main beneficiaries of subsidies, and leakage to higher income groups should be small. Inferior goods will fulfill such a condition.

None of the four subsidies we examined -- electricity, cooking gas, water, and transport -- fulfills such 'classifying' criteria: none caters to the poor and the two largest subsidies, namely electricity and cooking gas, are from an efficiency perspective highly distortive. Studies from other countries have shown that both price and income elasticities for these energy sources can be quite substantial,[13] especially if leakage from residential to commercial users is possible. Since these two subsidies are far larger than the subsidies for water and urban transport and together account for about 2 percent of GDP, they have to be the priority targets for reform.

The Electricity Subsidy. INECEL, the Ecuadoran electricity company, adopted a complicated tariff scheme in June 1993 that subsidizes the residential sector but roughly covers long-run marginal costs in the commercial sector. For residential users, INECEL applies a graduated tariff structure, with most unit prices significantly lower than the long-run marginal cost, which INECEL estimates to be 189 sucres per kWh. Average consumption of a typical household in the richest quintile of the population is 226 kWh and even these consumers are subsidized, although at a lower per-kWh rate than the lower consuming households.

Graph 6. Distribution of the Electricity Subsidy, 1994

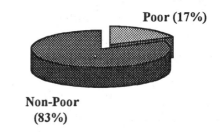

Poor (17%)

Non-Poor (83%)

Source: LSMS, 1994.

The large electricity subsidy does not reach the poor. We estimate the monthly residential electricity subsidy at around US$14 million (US$170 million yearly for 1994), only 17 percent of which went to the poor.[14] The unfavorable distribution is due to two

---

[13]   See Hope and Singh (1995) for references.

[14]   Our estimate of the electricity subsidy, which we derived from individual household expenditure data, is higher than INECEL's official estimate of US$9 million per month. The discrepancy might be due to an overreporting of expenditures of households that are illegally connected, a

factors: First, far fewer poor than rich families -- especially in the rural areas -- are connected to electricity, which restricts their access to the subsidy. Second, while the rich get a lower subsidy rate per hour of electricity use, they consume so much that the total subsidy amount is much higher for them than for the poor.

An Option: Restructuring the Tariff While Protecting the Poor. Restructuring the tariff system to introduce a simple two or three stage tariff schedule protecting low-volume consumers can considerably improve both efficiency and equity while reducing the total subsidy to about US$35 million.[15] Electricity is an income-elastic good which a very large percentage of the non-poor consume beyond a certain level. While we find today that even a fair amount of the poor consume above these levels due to a very low price of electricity, their demand behavior would likely change if a simple lifeline tariff scheme were introduced. Such a tariff scheme would consist of (a) a low fixed-cost rate for consumers of electricity up to about 80 or 90 kWh; (b) a different charge rate once consumers go beyond the lifeline quantity, also retroactively billing the initial 80 or 90 kWh at the charge rate.[16] If desired, this charge rate could be broken up into several progressive rate increases. Such a schedule would be economically efficient since it would signal to the heavy consumers the true economic cost of electricity consumption. While part of the subsidy would continue to flow to the non-poor -- because electricity consumption is only imperfectly correlated with household expenditures -- the poor's share in the total subsidy would significantly increase. With a total subsidy amount of around US$35 million, such a scheme would free considerable resources to finance poverty alleviation programs.

Cooking Gas Subsidy. Cooking gas is heavily subsidized. In 1994, consumers paid only about 25 percent of the import price of cooking gas, which had a strong fiscal impact because most of Ecuador's gas comes largely from foreign sources. The Government planned several times to remove the subsidy and substitute it with targeted income support, but these plans never materialized.

The largest part of the subsidy benefits the residential sector, since only gas in small bottles is subsidized. The Government estimates the total subsidy to have reached US$120 million in 1994, a figure that is almost exactly reproduced when we use the LSMS and derive subsidies per household as three times the household expenditures. However, the past years have shown that gas consumption grows very quickly at the current low price because gas is used not only for cooking but also for heating and car fuel.

Once again, the rich in Ecuador benefit the most from the subsidy, only 23 percent of which goes to the poor. Average household consumption actually varies very little with

---

seasonal bias, or an actually higher energy consumption in the residential sector than was estimated by INECEL.

[15]   The total subsidy and its distribution depends on the price elasticity for electricity for the different consumer groups. If all households in the two lowest expenditure quintiles would consume 80 kWh in order to be eligible for the lifeline rate, the total subsidy would be around US$35 million (without any charge for the lifeline rate).

[16]   Such a tariff scheme introduces a steep kink in the expenditure curve of electricity since for the consumer, the marginal cost of the 81st unit is not only the new charge rate but also the cost of the first eighty kWh times the new charge rate. However, few better-off households would be deterred by this kink since the level of 80 kWh is incompatible with their life style.

expenditure class, although per capita consumption increases due to the smaller household size of richer families. Use is another determining factor of the subsidy distribution. While a simple gas stove does not represent extraordinarily high fixed-costs as an investment, the remoteness of many rural areas combined with the bulkiness of the gas bottles limits access for many of the rural poor.

Options. Complete removal of the gas subsidy, without accompanying compensation measures, would inflict sizable welfare losses on the very poor gas users. The extremely poor households that use gas (85 percent in urban and 50 percent in rural areas) spend up to 2.5 percent[17] of their total budget on gas purchase. Assuming a relatively modest price elasticity for gas (-0.2), a quadrupling of the gas price -- which would be necessary to eliminate the subsidy -- would lead to a welfare loss of 5.3 percent[18] for the very poor. A complete removal without compensating measures would also worsen expenditure distribution in Ecuador, since the poor spend a much higher proportion of their budget on cooking gas than the rich.

Several alternative options can be studied. A phasing out of the gas subsidy while introducing targeted benefits might be the best, and politically most viable, option. Such phasing out could follow predetermined and preannounced steps. The benefits could take the form of the general expansion of programs for nutrition and basic health, or of direct income transfers as previously planned (see Box 1). Another alternative would be an attempt to target the subsidy by only selling the subsidized gas (in special containers) in low-income neighborhoods. Leakage of such a scheme would depend on the degree this self-targeting mechanism works and the non-poor avoid either the transaction costs or the 'social blame' of using marked containers for low-income areas. This self-targeting scheme could be combined with a mechanical device that hooks up the subsidized gas bottles only to certain very simple one- or two-flame stoves, which most of the non-poor will avoid. Finally, and economically most efficient, the subsidy could be redirected entirely from the variable input to the fixed input, the stove. However, with 90 percent of the urban poor and almost 50 percent of the rural poor owning gas stoves today, the extent of shielding the poor from the price increase would be minimal.

---

[17]   This estimate is somewhat lower than in ESMAP (1994), which estimated the budget share of all households in the lowest expenditure quintile to be 3.9 percent. The difference in the measurement of total expenditures is likely responsible for this discrepancy since we have included rent, consumer durables, and other items.

[18]   This calculation measures the welfare loss as the reduction in the consumer surplus, assuming linearity of the Marshallian demand curve in the respective range. See Hope and Singh (1995), p. 29.

Box 1: Direct Income Support to Mitigate the Gas Price Increase

Efforts to compensate poor households for an increase in the gas price through an already developed income targeting scheme based on a Basic Services Indicator would have extremely high leakage.   In conjunction with previous plans to eliminate the gas subsidy, various Government institutions had developed a direct income support scheme based on a Basic Needs Indicator using census data from 1990.   The scheme assigned points to each household based on the type of services, e.g., water, sewerage, or electricity, and was supposed to cover 420,000 households of which 60 percent were to be in urban and 40 percent in rural areas.   Drawing on the Living Standard Measurement

Which households would have benefited from the direct income support (percent of all households in quintile)?	
Household quintile	% of beneficiary households
poorest 20	31.0
20-40	27.4
40-60	23.3
60-80	13.9
richest 20	4.5

Survey, we can calculate how efficient the scheme would have been in reaching the poorest 20 percent of all households, as it was designed to do.   The result is stunning -- 70 percent of resources would not have reached the target group. The reasons are simple: First, and as observed above, the access to services is not a good indicator to determine the welfare level of households, especially if employed in a rigid way which pre-assigns weights to all services.   Second, the political decision to choose 60 percent of benefiting households in the urban areas has to lead to mistargeting, since 62 percent of the poorest household in the first quintile are located in rural areas.

If the Government decides to introduce a direct income support scheme, a regional pre-identification of target areas would have to be complemented with individual assessment mechanisms which identify individual households.   A new geographic poverty map could be developed by applying LSMS results to the census. A model could be derived from the LSMS in which expenditures are 'explained' by a large number of exogenous variables which are all included in the census data as well. This model could then be applied to the census in order to predict total expenditures and the poverty level of geographic areas. There are, however, several caveats associated with a direct income targeting scheme. Such a scheme has to be consistently monitored by municipalities or other local institutions, and it would be difficult to prevent its continuous expansion.   Self-targeting public works programs are an alternative to provide income support to the very poor. With a wage rate set below the market rate, such programs in fact provide a safety net in times of bad recession. Construction of projects under the Social Emergency Fund in part act as such a public works program today.

Improving Education Finance

Changes in both absolute and relative expenditures for the different education levels have brought imbalances in education finance to dramatic levels. According to Ministry of Finance data, per capita real education expenditures stagnated over the past years. Today, unit costs for higher education, at US$518, are about six times higher than for basic education, at US$82,

Table 4. Unit Cost Estimates of Public Education, 1994	
	US$ per Student
Primary	81.9
Secondary	256.7
Higher	518.3
Source: Pfister (1995) and Working Paper 6.	

and twice as high as for secondary education, at US$256.[19] Relative preference in education finance over the past years was given to higher education -- in 1990, unit costs for higher education were 'only' 4.5 times the unit costs of primary education. Today, more than a

---

[19]   See Pfister (1995) and Working Paper 6.

quarter of the budget of the Education Ministry goes to higher education, financing a mere 7 percent of total enrolled students at all educational levels. Only slightly more than one third of total education expenditures is directed to the two million pupils or 68 percent of enrolled students in public primary schools.

Education finance benefits those who are already well-off in Ecuador. Using access to schooling to compute the incidence of public education expenditures in 1994, we discover that the poor benefit mainly from primary school expenditures but much less so from secondary and especially higher education financing. The education expenditure concentration curves in Graph 7 show the benefits that the five population quintiles obtain from the expenditures. For primary education expenditures, the

Graph 7. Incidence of Education Expenditure by Quintile, 1994

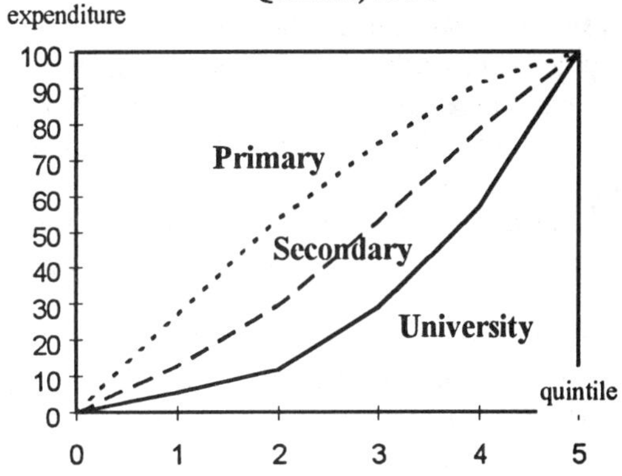

Source: LSMS, 1994.

poorest population quintile obtains 27.2 percent of total expenditures, which can be explained by the very high attendance level in primary school, with richer families sending many of their children to private schools. But the picture changes quickly for the distribution of secondary expenditures: benefits are realized by the upper expenditure classes because secondary school attendance of children in richer households far exceeds that in poorer households. The most unjust distribution is associated with higher education expenditures. The poorest 40 percent of the population only obtain 12 percent of these expenditures.

Reallocating expenditures from higher to primary and secondary education would have a positive effect on equity. Requiring the mostly non-poor students at universities to cover half of their costs would raise revenues of about 0.6 percent of GDP, which, if redirected, would enable the Ministry of Education to increase funding for primary education by 40 percent or for secondary education by 35 percent. Such increases are needed to improve the quality of primary education and enable poor children to obtain a secondary school education.

Increasing Tax Revenues

The Government also needs to expand its non-oil tax revenues to finance poverty alleviation programs. Over the past decades, the Government's non-oil tax effort decreased substantially. While non-oil revenues represented 11.4 percent of GDP in 1971-1973, they only reached 8.7 percent of GDP in 1993. Today, public sector revenues from oil production are almost as important as non-oil taxes but they fluctuate widely with production output and the international price of petroleum. Over the past four years, oil revenues of the public sector decreased from 11.6 percent of GDP in 1990 to 7.2 percent of GDP in 1994. An increase of non-oil tax revenues would not only provide additional resources needed for poverty alleviation but also ease the planning and budgeting of Government programs in general.

Tax revenues could be increased by around 3 percent of GDP by eliminating exemptions to the value added tax and by reducing income tax evasion. Preliminary World Bank calculations show that discontinuing selected *de facto* value added tax exemptions (a tax of 0 percent is applied) could raise 1.4 percent of GDP. A 50 percent reduction of income tax evasion could add another 1.7 percent of GDP to revenues. To improve tax collection, the Government should make more effective use of the established Large Taxpayers Unit.

Targeting as a Means to Reduce the Costs of Social Programs

Targeting of social programs is not widely applied in Ecuador. Of the twenty-five major social programs, only about a third operate with an explicit targeting mechanism; two thirds either are universal programs intended to reach the entire population or operate without a specific mechanism for identifying beneficiaries.[20] Examining seven of such programs, we find that targeting costs are within reasonable expectations but that the initial emphasis on setting up targeting mechanisms is usually not followed by consistent monitoring of performance (Box 2). Such monitoring is crucial to evaluate and subsequently improve the targeting mechanisms. Further, several programs contain obvious flaws in the targeting methodology and almost all of the examined programs use their own targeting map. A new, generalized map should be developed from information in the LSMS and the census.

3.   Basic Nutrition and Health Programs for the Poor

Many of the poor in Ecuador do not have access to basic preventive health care services, and almost half a million are not served by public health care and cannot afford curative care even in cases of emergency. Almost every second child under the age of five is malnourished, but the many small nutrition programs reach only about six percent of poor children. The importance of nutrition programs for malnourished children and of a basic health program for the poor go beyond short-term poverty alleviation objectives; they are a precondition for a successful strategy to help poor people grow out of poverty. Any investments in people in the form of education or infrastructure provision will carry a significant return only if people are able to take advantage of these investments. To do so, they need to be healthy.

Nutrition

Malnutrition of infants and young children carries serious long-term implications. As a consequence of chronically inadequate food consumption or repeated episodes of illness, many children die in infancy. Those who survive are often malnourished, underweight, undersized, suffer more frequent and more severe illness, cannot learn, and end up being less productive as adults. Many who suffer from protein/calorie malnutrition also lack essential

---

[20]   See Working Paper 7.

micronutrients such as iron, iodine, and vitamin A, the lack of which can cause irreversible mental retardation.

Poverty and malnutrition are closely linked. The link can be as direct as a family not having enough money or the knowledge to purchase a basic and balanced basket of food. It can also be indirect through illnesses. Child malnutrition rates in Ecuador are strongly associated with socio-economic variables, primarily with education of the mother and with household living conditions.[21]

Malnutrition Rates of Minors. Malnutrition rates for children below the age of five are extremely high in Ecuador. While the Government has made progress over the last decade in reducing malnutrition, the absolute rates of both chronic and global malnutrition in 1990 were still at alarming levels. Forty-five percent of children below the age of five were chronically malnourished (i.e. their height was low for their age), and 33.9 percent were globally malnourished (i.e., they displayed low weight for their age). This implies that close to 800,000 children below the age of five were malnourished in Ecuador in 1990. The rates increase with age but even in the first five months, when babies are nourished from their mother's milk, fifteen percent of the babies show signs of chronic malnutrition. According to the 1986 national nutrition survey and subsequent sample surveys, about 80 percent of child malnutrition occurs among children under age two. Furthermore, 70 percent of children between ages 1 and 2 have iron deficiency anemia.[22]

There is a pronounced variation in malnutrition rates among regions and areas, with the rural Sierra holding the saddest record: almost seven out of ten children were malnourished in 1990. The Rural Qualitative Assessment (RQA), which examined five indigenous communities in the Sierra, shows that cutting food purchases is often the only possibility for rural families to reduce expenditures in hard times. Additionally, many indigenous families consume a poor and repetitive diet, consisting mainly of barley flour, cinnamon, potatoes, and water.

Table 5. Malnutrition Rates by Region and Area, 1990[a]		Chronic (heigh/age)	Global (weigh/age)
Sierra	urban	45.1	30.5
	rural	67.0	48.5
Costa	urban	34.4	26.4
	rural	45.3	36.5
National		45.3	33.9

[a] Children under the age of five.
Source: Freire and Waters (1994).

---

[21]   See Freire and Waters (1994).
[22]   World Bank (1990). See also World Bank (1994, p. 60).

Box 2. Targeting Social Programs to the Poor in Ecuador

We examined seven targeted programs, among them three child support and nutrition programs (Operation Child Rescue (ORI), School Lunch Program, Child Development Program (INNFA)), the Basic Primary Health Project (FASBASE) which also contains a nutrition component, the Emergency Fund (FISE), and the basic education projects (EB/PRODEC and PROMECEB). All seven rely on geographical targeting based on their own poverty map, and some of the programs also use individual screening methodologies. Several lessons emerge from our analysis (compare Working Paper 7):

The costs of running these programs and identifying potential beneficiaries are within reasonable expectations. These costs are more a function of program design and managerial efficiency than of efforts to reach poor beneficiaries. Strategies such as increasing the scale of pilot programs, controlling unit costs, and improving managerial efficiency could further reduce the overhead spent on delivering program benefits.

Scale of targeting matters tremendously. To reduce leakage and other forms of mistargeting, the scale of the geographical unit selected should be aligned as closely as possible to the scale of potential benefits. For instance, using the canton level for large urban areas is ineffective in allocating resources to poor urban areas due to the heterogeneity of socio-economic conditions within the canton. Employing indicators at the lowest administrative level (*parroquias*) improves the chances of identifying poor areas, although flexibility should be allowed for programs to reach the poor within better-off *parroquias*, which are very large. Clearly, no reliable targeting can be done on a provincial or regional level.

Program design affects outcome independent of targeting mechanism. Focusing exclusively on methodologies for selecting beneficiaries misses important issues in overall program design, which in the end might have more relevance for reaching the poor. Each program should be analyzed to identify elements in design and procedures that would either promote or reduce participation by the poor. For instance, ORI's and INNFA's reliance on existing infrastructure limits flexibility in assigning resources to priority areas. Criteria used by EB/PRODEC and PROMECEB in defining school networks, including the requirement that the hub be a complete school with a minimum number of students, are correct given the overall objectives of these programs. However, they tend to be biased against the poorest, most remote dispersed populations.

The initial emphasis on setting up targeting mechanisms is usually not followed by consistent monitoring of performance. Despite efforts to establish targeting mechanisms, in the end most programs are not able to say to what extent they are reaching the poor. We found a general lack of monitoring of targeting performance by both the individual program administrations and by the central Government. While programs usually keep information on *where* they reach, *who* they reach is not monitored, as could be done through beneficiary assessments. In addition, rarely are adjustments made to methodology or new data incorporated in the targeting effort as they become available.

Geographical targeting appears deceptively simple, but in fact can be methodologically quite complex. Selecting criteria and building operational targeting mechanisms can be difficult. In several instances, the relative weights of criteria and the screening processes were not transparent. In other cases there were flaws in methodology. Further, the types of indicators used to develop a geographical map depend on the objective of the program, and objectives are not clearly stated in many instances. For example, a malnutrition program has to clearly define whether it intends to reach malnourished children, poor children, or poor children who are malnourished. In the first instance, a geographical map based on malnutrition rates alone would be appropriate; in the latter case a generalized poverty map has to identify the poorest areas in the country, which are then crossed with a malnutrition map to identify priority areas.

Although geographical targeting is accepted as a guideline for allocating resources, a new poverty map has to be developed. Each program uses a different set of indicators to define priority areas. The majority have used CONADE's Poverty Map, which is not sufficiently dissaggregated in urban areas. Also, the validity of the map itself is questionable, since it is built from several different indicators that vary widely in the degree of coverage, reliability, and timeliness of the statistics used. A generalized map, which could be developed by applying the determinants of poverty derived from the LSMS to the census, is a needed tool on which individual programs can build (see Working Paper 1, Annex 2). Nevertheless, individuals programs would have to supplement the map with additional indicators and targeting tools to meet their individual objectives. A new map would also reduce the current bias of most programs to spend most of their resources in the Sierra.

In general, coordination among programs should be increased, particularly at the operational level. Most programs operate in the same locations, with limited interaction. Coordination would avoid duplication and help maximize synergies among programs. Some examples include: (a) FISE financing of daycare centers to address the targeting constraint faced by ORI in terms of lack of resources for new infrastructure; (b) nutrition screening of children entering daycare assisted by health programs operating in the area to reduce program costs; and (c) EB/PRODEC and PROMECEB financing main infrastructure and FISE small satellite schools under the network umbrella. Such coordination needs to be carried out effectively at the local level.

Source: Working Paper 7.

<u>Malnutrition Among Women of Reproductive Age</u>. Ecuador is a country with a serious micronutrient problem affecting low-income pregnant and lactating women. About 60 percent of the latter suffer from some degree of anemia due to deficiency of iron -- a life-

sustaining nutrient needed only in small quantities and found in red meat and breastmilk as well as in grains, legumes and vegetables.   Children born of anemic mothers are often stunted and sickly, and iron deficiency in the preschool years reduces their manual dexterity, limits their attention span, and lowers their ability to retain information.   In the 1980s, a national nutrition survey found that 69 percent of infants and 46 percent of children 1 to 2 years old suffered from anemia.   Deficiency in iron among adults also reduces energy and therefore the capacity to work.   Since iron deficiency is prevalent among poor Ecuadoran women and children, anemia control should receive high visibility in maternal and child health programs. Additionally, as shown by the experience of the United States and Sweden, long-term iron fortification of selected and widely consumed foods, such as refined flour used in the production of bread and pasta, can dramatically reduce anemia.

Nutrition Programs and Coverage.
Ecuador has a number of nutritional programs, administered by different ministries and agencies, that try to reach preschool children. The programs include the *Programa de Complementacion Alimentaria Materno-Infantil* directed at pregnant and breastfeeding mothers and their infants (6-23 months), operated by the Ministry of Health through health centers; the nutritional component of the

Table 6. Nutritional Programs in Ecuador: Coverage of children below the age of 5 (percent 1994)		
	1990	1994
Poor	n.a.	5.5
Non-Poor	n.a.	3.4
	----	----
Total	10.8	4.3

Source: Musgrove (1991) and LSMS, 1994.

Operation Rescue the Children (ORI), which offers nutritional supplements in its daycare centers; the feeding component of the National Institute of Children and the Family (INNFA), the nutrition component of the FASBASE primary health project; and the small CARITAS- supported Mothers Club program.   In-depth analyses of many of these programs have concluded that they (a) do not supply children or lactating mothers with nutritional aid over a continuous period of time, which undermines their nutritional impact; (b) are often tiny in scope; and (c) generally operate independently of each other so whatever impact that could be achieved is jeopardized.[23]

The targeting efficiency of the nutrition programs is generally unknown.   Examining two nutrition programs, INNFA and ORI, we found that both have developed targeting frameworks based on a combination of geographical targeting and self-selection mechanisms; additionally, INNFA assesses the nutrition status of individual children who enter the program.   The potential for geographical targeting is limited, however, since both programs depend on existing daycare center infrastructure and can only target priority areas at the margin. Further, INNFA and ORI, like the other targeted social program we studied, need to improve their monitoring and evaluation method in order to assess how many of the poor and malnourished children they reach.

An evaluation of all nutritional programs directed at infants and children below the age of five, including the ones offered by NGOs, shows that they achieve a low coverage rate. While the programs leak somewhat to non-poor children, the errors of excluding poor malnourished children are clearly higher and weigh much more than the errors of including

---

[23]   Compare UNICEF, DyA (1992); World Bank (1990); Feire and Waters (1994); Musgrove (1991).

well-nourished children. Of the one and a half million Ecuadoran children below the age of five, about 600,000 lived in poor households in 1994 and 5.5 percent of these were reached by the various nutrition programs, according to the LSMS. Total coverage of the under-five population stood at 4.3 percent, a clear decrease from the 10.8 percent coverage achieved in 1990. This decrease was largely due to the discontinuation of the *Red Comunitaria*, a community-based childcare network supported by the Ministry of Social Welfare, in 1993. The *Red Comunitaria* was replaced by Operation Child Rescue (ORI), which is achieving lower than programmed coverage rates due to financial restraints. According to information from the Ministry of Social Welfare, coverage rates have improved in 1995 and about 130,000 children below the age of six are being reached by the two largest programs, INNFA and ORI.[24]

<u>Coverage in Neighboring Countries</u>. Compared to other Andean countries, the coverage rate of Ecuador's nutrition programs is extremely low. Its Andean neighbors reach many more infants and the very young, even though the types of programs in these countries do not differ from Ecuadoran programs. On the contrary: of the nine-teen programs run by its Andean neighbors, eight operated through the public health system and six were linked to childcare centers. Several programs were community-supported soup kitchens -- a type of program that does not exist in Ecuador today.

Table 7. Nutrition: Comparison to Andean Countries		
	Global Malnutrition[a]	Coverage[b] (<5)
Bolivia	18	40.2
Colombia	12	29.2
Ecuador	34	4.3
Peru	13	84.5

a Malnutrition rates for Bolivia, Colombia and Peru from World Bank (1993a) for 1990; for Ecuador Freire and Waters (1994) based on 1990 data.
b For Bolivia, Colombia and Peru from Musgrove (1991); for Ecuador LSMS, 1994.

<u>Options for Ecuador</u>. Perhaps the most important, least-cost, and realizable nutrition program over the short-term would concentrate on fortifying staple foods with micronutrients, as currently contemplated under the basic health program, FASBASE. International experience shows that salt or sugar fortification can be achieved at costs ranging from 2 and 12 cents per person per year.[25] The entire Ecuadoran population could be covered by such a fortification program for a total cost of US$ 1 or 2 million.

Nevertheless, concentrating on supplying micronutrients will not solve the widespread caloric/protein malnutrition. Going beyond the fortification of staple foods requires the Government's willingness to commit resources to two networks on which the existing nutrition programs can piggyback: daycare (which is important in helping women to enter the labor force, as we will discuss later) and health centers in both rural and urban areas. Both geographical and self-targeting mechanisms will limit the leakage of these programs. It is important to fund these networks of daycare centers and public health posts adequately so that they can provide a base on which nutrition programs can piggyback.

---

[24] According to the information supplied by the Minister of Social Welfare, the joint coverage of INNFA and ORI amounted to about 75,000 children below the age of six during the period of June to September, 1994. This coverage number is close to the figure we compute from the LSMS for the same months (65,000 for children below the age of five).

[25] See World Bank (1994, p. 15).

Making the networks functional, while ensuring community involvement, is a precondition for the successful implementation of nutrition programs.[26]

Basic Health Care

Importance. The *World Development Report 1993* spelled out the important role of public basic health care: providing cost-effective health services to the poor is an effective and socially acceptable way to reduce poverty; many health-related services provide information that helps control contagious diseases; and Government intervention helps to compensate for problems of economic uncertainty and insurance market failure. The *WDR* also stresses the link between basic health care and malnutrition.

Health Statistics. Ecuador's health statistics compare quite unfavorably with those of most other middle-income Latin countries. A 1992 infant mortality rate of 45 per one thousand births is high compared to, e.g., Colombia (21), El Salvador (40), Costa Rica (14), Panama (21), and Chile (17),[27] and the same holds for the under-five mortality rate of 64 per one thousand births in 1992. Lack of safe water and sanitation, the prevalence of infectious and communicable diseases, and malnutrition are the most common causes of child death in Ecuador. With a maternal mortality rate of 170 per one hundred thousand births (1992), Ecuador lies slightly behind El Salvador (148 in 1988) but is clearly worse off than Costa Rica (18 in 1988), Panama (60 in 1988) and Chile (40 in 1988).[28] The vaccination of minors against tuberculosis, measles, polio, and dyptheria have, on the other hand, been largely successful: the LSMS records coverage rates above 90 percent for all types of vaccinations, independent of area, region, and poverty class.

Sector Institutions. Several institutions comprise Ecuador's public health system. The largest provider is the Provincial Health Directorates of the Ministry of Health which treats 27 percent of the people seeking professional curative care (38 percent of the poor, 23 percent of the non-poor). The second largest provider is the Ecuadoran Social Security Institute (IESS), which has its own network including hospitals and pharmacies. The IESS also provides two formal insurance schemes -- the General Social Security System which covers only the affiliated individuals themselves, and the Peasant Insurance Scheme which also covers the dependents. The IESS is the only provider of formal health insurance, and both of its schemes together serve about 11 percent of all people seeking professional curative care (12 percent of the poor, 10 percent of the non-poor). The Ministry of Defense administers hospitals and other facilities for military personnel and their dependents which provide about 1 percent of curative treatments. Finally, the Charity Board of Guayaquil and several small programs under the responsibility of other small agencies and NGOs (6.6 percent of the population) complete the complex public involvement in the health sector.

---

[26]   The physical distribution of food through these centers could be limited by using the centers only as distribution points for food stamps targeted to children or pregnant/lactating mothers. The food stamps would need to be tailored to specific foods that will really be consumed by those most in danger.

[27]   World Bank (1993a).

[28]   World Bank (1993a).

Real public expenditures of the largest public health entity, the Ministry of Health, decreased continuously over the past years. Between 1990 and 1993 alone, the budget allocated to the health sector as a share of the total central Government budget decreased from 8.2 percent to 5.4 percent, and real per capita spending declined by 37 percent. In terms of 'use', the public expenditures of the Ministry of Health tend to benefit the poor most: about forty percent of the Ministry of Health resources benefit the thirty-five percent of the population that is poor. Conversely, the wealthiest quintile of the Ecuadoran population obtains only about eleven percent of expenditures.[29] Taking into account quality considerations, these rather favorable figures might well change as health posts in remote rural areas (where most of the poor live) are often poorly equipped and staffed. The overall constraint on resources has meant diminishing funds for all types of expenditures. As a result, salaries are low and there are little or no funds for medicines, supplies, and equipment repairs. Even so, there is a substantial bias in expenditures toward the larger, curative care hospitals in the urban centers. About 45 percent of total Ministry of Health resources support 32 large urban hospitals, while only 35 percent is allocated for primary care facilities.[30]

The public health system in Ecuador is problem ridden. As amply demonstrated in a large number of investigations,[31] the main problems are: (a) large gaps in service provision of a basic health care package, especially in rural areas; (b) insufficient quality of health services due to maldistribution of resources and underfunding; (c) duplication of health services supplied by the major public sector agencies due; (d) staffing imbalances heavily favoring urban areas;[32] and (e) emphasis on curative instead of preventive care and health education. For example, about a quarter of demand for family planning education is not met by either private or public facilities.[33]

Type of Health Care. The Living Standard Measurement Survey reports that the type of health treatment varies considerably with the material standing of a family. If medical treatment is necessary, many poor families, especially in the rural areas, choose either to treat their ill members with home remedies or to seek advice from a pharmacist. This pattern is more pronounced in rural than in urban areas. Nationally, almost two-thirds of the non-poor population

Table 8. Health: How are the Sick Treated? Percent 1994		
	Poor	Non-Poor
by doctor/nurse	49	64
by pharmacist	22	13
by home remedy	11	10
no remedy (not nec.)	6	7
no remedy (no money or far away)	12	6
Source: LSMS, 1994.		

seek professional treatment if they are sick from either a nurse or a doctor while only about half of the poor do so; the other half either turns to a pharmacist or to self-curing or is

---

[29]   Compare Working Paper 6.

[30]   Enriquez (1994).

[31]   IDB (1993); ILDIS (1994); Mesa-Lago (1993), UNICEF-DyA (1992), World Bank (1990,1992).

[32]   As an outcome of this biased provision of basic health care, the health status of the population varies widely. For example, the infant mortality rate ranges between 20 per 1000 in certain urban areas to 150 per 1000 in remote rural ones.

[33]   ILDIS (1994).

condemned to do nothing. Twice as many poor (12 percent) than non-poor state that they were not able to afford necessary treatment or medicine. Even 6 percent of the non-poor are caught in this trap (Table 8).

In the seven villages participating in the Rural Qualitative Assessment, poor families said they would spend less on health care (including transport to clinics) if money is short for food. Many households have opted to limit visits to clinics and hospitals to the strictly unavoidable, and instead visit traditional curers and midwives. Similarly, they often use locally available herbs and other remedies instead of antibiotics or other prescription medication.

Public vs. Private Curative Care. The private sector performs a large part of professional curative medical services even for the poorest groups in Ecuador, signaling that basic public health services are in scarce supply. While the non-poor are more likely to turn to the private sector for professional health services, 42.5 percent of the poor also seek private services when they need to see a nurse or a doctor (Table 9). Further, 37 percent of the extremely poor, who are not even able to afford a basic nutritional basket of goods,

Table 9. Professional Health Services: (Of those seeing a doctor or nurse) Percent 1994		
	Poor	Non-Poor
Public	52.5	35.0
- hospital	19.1	15.4
- health center	33.4	19.6
Private	42.5	57.9
Charity Board, NGOs	4.9	7.1
Source: LSMS, 1994.		

also turn to the more costly private sector rather than use the free or very low-cost public health service. As the trade-off between health care and food for these families is so extreme, it is likely that this group does not have access to a functioning public health center; the actual rate is probably much higher.

The situation in Cisne Dos, the poor urban neighborhood in Guayaquil, illustrates the role of the private health sector in urban areas. Analysis of health facilities usage shows that the private sector, providing almost half the health care in that area, is as important as public facilities, which are used more for serious medical problems. Preference for private sector health care relates directly to perceived differences in quality of service (multiple specialties, a medical lab, and minor surgery is available), but also to the availability of credit for their services, short waiting times, and flexible hours. While public hospitals in the area are free, they are characterized by declining resources and infrastructure, long waiting times, and limited night access.

The Poor's Expenditures on Health. Health care is a very big budget item for the poor who turn to the private sector. Poor households seeking curative care predominantly from the private sector spend on average 12 percent of their total budget in urban and 17 percent in rural areas. For the non-poor, curative care averages less than 10 percent of expenditures in both areas. On the other hand, poor families that obtain curative care mainly from public sector health posts or hospitals spend on average 6 percent of the budgets, and the non-poor spend 3 percent.

Results. The poor suffer more than other groups from the weak basic public health network. While other public or semi-public institutions, namely IESS, the military, and the Charity Board are also part of the health system, about 85 percent of the poor do not have access to these institutions and so rely on the network run by the Ministry of Health. While the LSMS shows only the distribution and access to curative care, we have found that many of the poor -- and even the poorest of the poor -- turn to the private sector for emergency help. Such service is very expensive, requiring between 12 percent and 17 percent of their total budget per month per incident. Close to half a million poor people with-out access to public health centers cannot afford private service or the purchase of essential medicine.

While the LSMS says little about a basic package of preventive health care, it is clear from available statistics that the system does not function properly. In 1992, more than 70 percent of births in rural areas (and 20 percent in urban areas) took place without professional help. Professional health consultations during pregnancies reach only half of the determined target rates.[34] The ongoing treatment that are part of a basic health program include prenatal care, child delivery, postnatal controls, basic care for adults, immunizations, health education, nutrition education, surveillance, food supplements, and family planning services.

Options. Detailed reform proposals for the sector have been made by many donor agencies and external consultants.[35] Most of these call for a fundamental, integrative reform to bring the many disparate actors and institutions together while strengthening the role of local and provincial health agencies in providing services. Obviously, this is a long-term aim and must go hand in hand with a restructuring of the Social Security Institute.

But many of the poor cannot wait for the long-term overhaul of the health system. While most are able to bear the costs of basic health care for a period of time by using informal credit arrangements or sacrificing other goods -- often food -- the current situation is unsustainable. About half a million people cannot even afford medicine in cases of severe sickness; this number will increase rapidly if resources of the Ministry of Health are cut in 1996.[36] Further, it is important to note that these cuts also impact on existing infrastructure: many small health posts already have been abandoned because staff could not be paid and there were no basic supplies.

A study of health provision arrangements in other Latin American countries might be useful to help Ecuador identify complementary or supplementary arrangements to reach its poor population. In Costa Rica, for example, free affiliation to a national health insurance program is granted to the medically indigent based on evaluation by a social worker. The program, which covers 12 percent of the population, is designed to reach those who cannot afford the insurance. Other countries increasingly seek cooperation with private non-profit organizations to deliver basic health services in low-income neighborhoods. In Bolivia, for example, private non-profit providers own a quarter of all the health facilities in the three largest cities. The largest provider, ProSalud, is assigned catchment zones in both urban

---

[34]   INEC (1992).

[35]   See, for example, IDB (1993) and World Bank (1990).

[36]   The provision of a basic health care package to the poor need not necessarily imply that only primary health posts are supported or financed. As shown above, many of the peri-urban and rural poor also receive medical care at provincial hospitals.

and rural areas. Unit cost estimates show that ProSalud is providing efficient, low-cost preventive and curative medical service.[37]

4.   Strengthening the Assets of the Poor

This section is concerned with the main assets of the poor -- labor, land, and housing -- and reports on key survey findings about how the poor are able to use these assets compared to the non-poor. These findings concern: (a) the quality of primary education and access to secondary education, (b) the importance of the rural land market, (c) the positive effect of rural market integration, (d) female labor participation, and (e) the role of housing as an asset for the urban poor. The focus of this discussion is on enhancing the assets of the poor in both qualitative and quantitative terms. All of these points are supported by the earlier discussion of common factors linking urban and rural poverty across regions.

Quality of Public Primary Education and the Importance of Secondary Education for Poor Children

The *World Development Report 1990* showed that education and poverty reduction are closely linked. Education increases the productivity of labor, the principal asset of the poor. At the individual level, increased productivity leads to higher incomes; at the macroeconomic level, it leads to higher growth rates, which in turn create employment and lead to higher wages. And this virtuous circle can be observed not only in modern economic sectors but also in the rural and informal sectors.

While current poverty is strongly influenced by what Ecuadoran fathers and mothers learned in their youth, the poverty of the next generation will depend on what the children of the poor learn today. Attendance levels in primary and secondary schools, repetition and failure rates, the degree to which children miss classes due to health problems or work loads, and the quality of education all determine the potential for poor children to escape poverty in the course of their lives.

In our view, Ecuador's education policy needs to emphasize two areas: improving the quality of primary school education and enabling poor children to go on to secondary school. As we will describe in this section, almost all youngsters now attend primary school, although the repetition and drop-out rates for poor children are high. Attendance levels in secondary schools, however, are clearly much lower for the poor than the non-poor. Secondary education needs to be made available to poor children because it can be a way out of poverty; the private returns from secondary education are high.

Education Expenditures and Quality. While real education expenditures declined in the 1980s, enrollment increased which led to a severe decline in the quality of education. Total primary school enrollment increased by 27 percent from 1980 to 1991, while secondary school enrollment jumped by 51 percent. Enrollment in higher education

---

[37]   Grosh (1994, p. 146) and World Bank (1993a, p. 127).

doubled. At the same time, per pupil primary expenditures declined strongly.[38] The result was a severe deterioration in the quality of education. Half of the most wealthy urban families in Ecuador send their children to private schools, which also indicates a gap between the quality of public and private education.

Primary School: Attendance, Repetition, and Drop-out Rates: Primary school attendance in urban and rural Ecuador is almost universal (around 90 percent), and does not vary significantly with poverty group, but early grade repetition is high and drop-out rates of poor children are clearly higher than for non-poor children. While the average primary school repetition rate is 8 percent, which compares quite favorably to other Latin American

Table 10. Repetition and Drop-Out Rates in Primary School Percent 1994		
	Poor	Non-Poor
Repetition		
- first grade	18.4	13.5
- second grade	8.5	5.9
Drop-out primary	**13.3**	**5.0**
Source: LSMS, 1994.		

countries,[39] a closer examination shows that the first grader repetition rate is 18.5 percent for poor children and 13.5 percent for non-poor ones (Table 10). While repetition rates in higher grades decline (partly because the repeaters drop-out of school), the clear link between poverty and repetition remains. The same picture emerges when we look at drop-out rates for primary school: of the 13- to 15-year old children (who had all started primary school but are no longer enrolled), we find that 13.3 percent of poor children and only 5 percent of non-poor children leave school before completing the six-year cycle.

Graph 8. Secondary School Attendance, urban, 1994

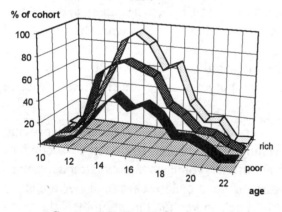

Graph 9. Secondary School Attendance, rural, 1994

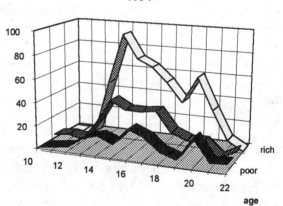

Source: LSMS, 1994.

Secondary School: Attendance, Repetition, and Drop-out Rates. There is a major distinction between poor and non-poor attendance in secondary schools. Graphs 8 and 9 illustrate the attendance rate in secondary schools of children by age. Up to 90 percent of children from families in the highest expenditure quintile attend secondary schools in both urban and rural areas (although the peak is much shorter in rural areas) but only 30 percent of the poor in the urban area and almost none in the rural area attend secondary school. The

---

[38]   Calculations based on data from EB/PRODEC.
[39]   Compare UNICEF (1993).

difference in the attendance record does not stem from the distance to the nearest secondary school, which is only slightly lower for the non-poor children (33 vs. 37 minutes in rural areas and 25 vs. 28 minutes in urban areas).

Repetition and drop-out rates during secondary school again illustrate the difference between the poor and non-poor. Repetition rates in the beginning years of secondary schools are consistently higher for the poor children, at 16 percent in the first year of secondary school and at 14 percent for the second year. Even more pronounced, the drop-out rate during the basic cycle of secondary school is 22.9 percent and during

Table 11. Repetition and Drop-out Rates in Secondary School, 1994		
	Poor	Non-Poor
Repetition		
- **first grade**	16.1	9.0
- **second grade**	14.0	9.6
Drop-Out		
- **basic cycle**	22.9	8.3
- **advanced cycle**	16.3	12.1
Source: LSMS, 1994.		

the advanced three-year cycle another 16.3 percent for poor children (Table 11). Of the few poor children who actually start school, two-fifths drop out before completing the secondary degree.[40]

Private Returns: Private returns to education are significant, as illustrated by the earnings equation which includes a large number of exogenous variables,[41] with dummy variables specified for different levels of schooling. We find that the earnings differential between base and end primary school years is modest, which points to the poor quality of primary education. But private returns increase significantly for secondary education, reaching about 9 percent for women and 11

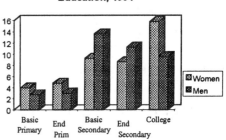

Graph 10. Private Yearly Returns to Education, 1994

Source: LSMS, 1994.

and 13 percent for men (Graph 10). The earnings differential due to college education is extremely high for women, even surpassing that for secondary education, but it declines somewhat for men.

The Private Costs of Public Education. While education definitely pays off in the long run, the private costs of education are high even in public schools. Although families pay only a low registration fee in public schools, there are other significant costs for books, writing materials, uniforms, and transport. For poor families, sending a child to public primary school

Table 12. Private Costs of Public Education Per Child (Average Budget Share1994)		
	Poor	Non-Poor
Primary School	2.0	1.8
Secondary School	4.0	2.9
Source: LSMS, 1994.		

---

40   The drop-out rate for the basic secondary cycle is calculated for the fifteen to seventeen year old population and the drop-out rate for the advanced cycle is calculated for the twenty to twenty-two year old population.

41   Compare Working Paper 8.

costs about 2 percent of their budget (1.8 percent for the non-poor), and sending a child on to public secondary education absorbs 4 percent of their budget (2.9 percent for the non-poor). Asked why their children (aged 14 and 15) do not attend secondary school, half of poor parents surveyed mentioned these direct costs as the primary reason, while only twenty percent of non-poor parents viewed these costs as a major obstacle.

Two aspects of these costs of education require attention. First, the private costs of public education are not fixed. They are discretionary with respect to the type of uniform, number and quality of books, and type of transport the child takes to school. In absolute terms, non-poor families spend 80 percent more on educating their child in a public primary school and 60 percent more on the education in a public secondary school. Second, if poorer households have to finance the education of several children, education can quickly absorb ten or fifteen percent of total household expenditures.

In addition to the private direct costs of public education, the opportunity costs of keeping children in school for a longer time are very high, especially for poor households. While field interviews in Guayaquil and seven rural communities indicate that poor parents make a serious effort to keep their children in primary school, they also highlight the costs of keeping children in school. In rural Ecuador, child labor is particularly important in times of scarce household income, and three out of the seven communities view female and child labor as the most or second most important source of scarce income. In Cisne Dos, 12- to 14-year old boys and girls spend an average of fifteen hours per week assisting in household enterprises. For girls, there are also additional household tasks, especially caring for younger siblings.

Options for Helping the Poor. Raising the quality of primary education and designing targeted programs to financially enable poor families to send their children on to secondary school would most benefit poor families. The quality of primary education depends on proper teacher training and motivation; an appropriate and modern curriculum, and a basic schooling infrastructure including supplies. This would enable poor children to compete much more effectively on the formal labor market. Large primary education projects of the Inter-American Development Bank and the World Bank address primary education quality today but the Ecuadoran Government needs to fund an equal effort.

Targeted programs to encourage poor parents to enroll their children in secondary schools can take various forms, which must be analyzed in detail. There are several ways to lower the direct private and opportunity costs of education for poor children: loosening uniform requirements, supplying basic textbooks through the school, or waiving the matriculation fee. Also, introducing a secondary school voucher system for poor families could reduce or even eliminate the opportunity cost of the child not working and supporting the family while attending classes. In urban areas, the provision of child care alone could have a substantial effect on freeing secondary school-age girls from guarding their younger siblings. These and other options should be evaluated in depth to see which ones might address the most pressing problems in particular communities.

Importance of the Rural Land Market

Poverty in rural Ecuador is closely linked to land. While the rural sector should not be equated with agriculture per se because there is also a large, vibrant non-farm sector, agricultural activities nevertheless employ the greatest number of persons and provide the largest proportion of household incomes in rural areas. There is a strong inverse relationship between per capita land holdings and poverty so that the smaller farmers are generally the poorer farmers. But smaller farmers use their land more intensively and have higher yields for many products than do the larger farmers. Reducing agricultural subsidies to the rich and enabling smaller farmers to use the newly created land market would be important steps toward improving both equity and efficiency in rural Ecuador.

Land and Poverty. Ecuador's several land reforms have not altered the unequal distribution of land over the past four decades. In 1994, 1.6 percent of farms in the Sierra occupied 42.9 percent of the land; in the Costa, 3.9 percent of farms command 55.1 percent of the land. The unequal distribution cannot be ascribed simply to the subdivision of land into small plots, since the total number of farms increased much more slowly between 1974 and 1994 than the total amount of land under cultivation. Calculating the Gini coefficient of distribution of operated land (for 1994), we find it to be very high at 0.80. The distribution of land is similarly

Graph 12. Yields in Ecuador, 1994

Output per hectar (Index)

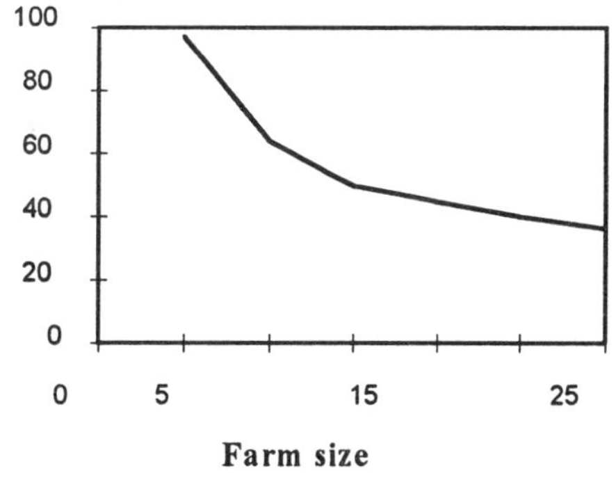

Source: LSMS, 1994.

unequal in the Costa and Sierra but more equal in the Oriente. Average land holdings (in terms of land cultivated or owned) are the lowest in the Sierra.

Regardless of which measure of poverty we use, there is a clear relationship between the degree or extent of poverty and the household's per capita land holdings. This pattern becomes particularly strong if we use distribution-sensitive measures of poverty. Supporting the prominent role land plays in the definition of poverty, the rural population of six of the seven communities participating in the Rural Qualitative Assessment view limited access to land as the most important component of poverty and as the yardstick by which they compare their community to neighboring ones.

Yields, Returns, and Farm Size. One of the most important findings we derive from the LSMS is that yields tend to decline with increasing farm size.[42] This can be observed not only at the level of individual crops such as rice, maize, or fruits -- where one can assume a more homogenous land quality among farms -- but also at an aggregate level looking at the value of total output per hectare. On average, among all cultivators,

---

[42]   In support of the estimations based on the Living Standard Measurement Study, we derive the same negative relationship between farm size and productivity from a different datasource, the rural module of the 1990 Household Survey by the National Employment Institute (INEM 1990).

increasing farm size by 10 percent will lead to an increase in gross output value of only 5.5 percent. This does not change with alternative sub-groupings of crops. Small farmers universally achieve higher yields than large farmers, quite in line with findings from many other countries.[43]

While we can make a statement about yield differences among farms, we are not able to calculate the net financial returns per hectare, although it is likely that our observation result will remain valid. Farming decisions are ultimately guided by net financial returns (or profits) per hectare and not by yields. No information on several inputs, especially the amount of labor used in the production process and the services derived from capital, is recorded in the LSMS. Small

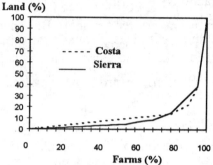

Graph 11. Land Distribution, 1994

Source: LSMS, 1994.

farmers generally apply much more of their own and household labor to the land than larger farmers since their production technology is less capital-intensive and the opportunity cost of labor in poor rural areas is often quite low. However, subtracting expenditures on pesticides, fertilizers, and seed from total output does not change the result that small farmers tend to have higher returns. And if the opportunity cost of labor is indeed quite low in many areas in Ecuador, computations of net financial returns will show the same.

Subsidies in the agricultural sector support the larger and richer farmers, thereby artificially increasing their net financial returns per hectare and hindering land transfers to the smaller and poorer farmers. Public irrigation water is almost free of charge, benefiting the larger farmers. With a cost recovery ratio of 4 percent, subsidies in the sector are very high. Total public irrigation outlays for investments, maintenance, salaries and overhead were around US$200 million in 1993. These expenditures largely benefited larger farmers because the expenditures were directly linked to the size of the landholding.[44] Further, public credit from the Banco Nacional de Fomento (BNF) is limited (covering farmers that own about 12 percent of total land), and -- although designed to do so -- reaches few small farmers. BNF subsidies through the directed credit scheme, estimated at around $80 million[45] in the 1988 to 1991 period, were the result of a low recovery rate and subsidized interest rates on previously made loans.[46] Lastly, the little extension service that exists reaches mainly non-poor farmers -- 4 percent of the non-poor and 1 percent of the poor farmers report having received technical assistance from public or private sources in the LSMS.

---

[43]   See Binswanger, Deininger, and Feder (1993).

[44]   Whitaker (1990, p. 243) estimates that the smallest 60 percent of farms internalized only 13 percent of the implicit irrigation subsidy in 1988.

[45]   Op. cit., Annex 2, p.10.

[46]   The interest rate subsidy is now eliminated but still applies to loans made while the subsidy was in place. While the LSMS records credit obtained from BNF, only about 3 percent (or 29) of all farmers recorded such credits. We feel uncomfortable basing an estimate of the poor/non-poor distinction on so few observations.

The Importance of the Land Market. The land market plays a crucial role in both alleviating poverty and in increasing the efficiency of the agricultural sector. Since smaller and poorer farmers achieve higher returns per hectare than larger farmers, increasing the land under cultivation by the former through sale, lease, or rent would benefit both. These transactions would be eased by the existence of a formal land market with clearly defined transactions. Security of tenure through titling and registration hence becomes a crucial variable for increasing land transactions while at the same time fostering sustainable agriculture practices, providing incentives for land conservation, and increasing the supply of credit, since land can be used as collateral. If large farmers fear that by leasing out their land they will lose title, then they will generally be reluctant to engage in such land transactions.

Currently, the rural land market in Ecuador is informal but significant. About 6 percent of landless households are able to lease land and therefore remain engaged in cultivation, and nearly 47 percent of all rural households report some land leased-in. Share-tenancy is slightly more common among poor households, while cash-renting is slightly more common among the non-poor. These transactions are largely informal because about half of small and

Table 13. Average Percentage of Titled Land Across Farms, 1994	
Farm size	% of Land Titled
0 - 1 ha	54.6
1- 2.5 ha	51.4
2.5 - 5 ha	44.8
3 - 30 ha	60.2
30+ ha	80.4
Ecuador	55.9
Source: LSMS, 1994.	

medium-sized farms (about 50 percent) are not titled (Table 13). What is more, only a fraction of the titled land is properly registered with the Land Registry, and only proper registration gives the owner the right to rent, lease, or sell land. However, since land is registered in Ecuador by name and not geographic area, conflicts can easily arise even if the land is registered. These impediments make short-term transactions without ownership transfers much more likely than longer contracts.

The Option for Helping the Poor: Making the Land Market Work. An effort to properly register land, in combination with a reduction of agricultural subsidies favoring larger farmers, would make the land market more beneficial for the poor. The recently passed Agricultural Law (1994) defines the framework necessary for the land market to function properly. It also increases the flexibility of land sales, defines associated water rights, and limits the expropriation of private land. Over the past thirty years, since the Agricultural Reform of 1963, expropriation has been unsuccessful to achieving a more equitable land distribution, since the political power of the landowners was stronger than the expropriation law. To take advantage of the new Agricultural Law, the newly created National Institute of Agricultural Development (INDA) will have to work closely with the Land Valuation and Cadastre Directorate to foster land delineation, titling, and registry. This procedure must be affordable for poor farmers, especially considering the potential benefits in terms of poverty alleviation and productivity improvements in the sector. Further, removing of subsidies for irrigation and the credit markets will make the difference in returns per hectare even more apparent and provide an additional incentive for larger farmers to sell or lease their land.

Once formal land registration procedures are established, targeting financial help to the poor might be necessary to enable them to purchase land, particularly since they often cannot use their small, poor quality plots as collateral with commercial agricultural banks. As in many other countries, formal credit has not reached the rural poor. A matching grant scheme that forces participants to use some of their own resources, such as labor, to gain access to land could be a viable alternative.[47]

Rural Poverty and Access to the Market

Rural poverty is intimately linked to market access: The less rural households are able to benefit from market transactions, the less they can protect themselves from poverty, for several reasons. First, farmers benefit from exchanging produce with each other. Second, the market is the most important medium of information exchange; in rural areas farmers with market exposure learn from each other about best agricultural techniques, inputs and prices. They can also seek technical assistance from either public or private organizations more easily. Third, the rural market is much more than an exchange place of agricultural produce or labor. It is closely connected to a host of off-farm activities, including services, in-house production of textiles, and other small-scale rural industry.

Market Exchange. Isolated farming households that cannot exchange produce or animals in the local market, tend to be poorer than more integrated farming households. The costs of bringing products to the market are still very high in remote rural areas, where it can take a day or more by foot or mule to reach the nearest local market. While we do not have data to measure the degree of isolation by infrastructure variables such as feeder roads or transport, we can compare the degree to which farmers use the market to sell and buy. The share of output sold on the market tends to be higher for the non-poor than for the poor (Table 14).

Table 14. Output Share Sold on the Market (percent of cultivating households, 1994)		
	Poor	Non-Poor
Costa rural	64	73
Sierra rural	34	42
Oriente rural	37	--
National rural	45	54
Source: LSMS, 1994.		

Agricultural Information. Closeness to the rural market also implies access to information, which helps farmers to use their assets, both land and labor, more productively. Information includes both informal exchanges with other farmers and access to the formal technical assistance services provided by private, non-profit, or public agencies. Of all poor farming households that responded to the LSMS, only one in one hundred reported having received any form of technical assistance (4 in one hundred for the non-poor). While access to technical assistance is a measure of closeness to the market, it is also true that technical assistance is an important instrument for familiarizing the poor with the market. For example, small farmer extension services can provide important inputs and information on the diversification of agricultural production, which can increase a farmer's marketable surplus.

---

[47]   On rural credit markets and the poor, see Binswanger (1995). On the matching grant scheme, see World Bank (1993d).

Off-farm Employment. While agriculture remains the most important economic activity in rural Ecuador, employing the greatest number of persons and providing the largest proportion of household incomes, the large and vibrant off-farm rural sector offers regular and often quite sizable income. The relationship between the off-farm sector and agriculture is also quite close. Off-farm activities can contribute to improved agricultural productivity through, for example, the manufacture of agricultural inputs, and at the same time, rising agricultural incomes can stimulate the expansion of off-farm activities, particularly services and manufacture of basic consumer goods. The off-farm sector in countries such as China and other East Asian economies has been key to determining the pace and direction of change in rural living standards, e.g., nearly one-third of China's GDP is calculated to come from township enterprises, which employ about 100 million people. Ecuador also has rural township enterprises, albeit on a more modest scale.

The rural off-farm market is a possible route out of poverty. The percentage of poor involved in off-farm employment is lower than of the non-poor in all regions of Ecuador, suggesting that it is indeed an important source of income for those able to obtain such employment. In rural Ecuador as a whole, 31 percent of the non-poor and 19 percent of the poor working population are primarily occupied in the off-farm sector, with off-farm activities assuming particularly importance in the Sierra and Oriente. In the Sierra, the most important non-farm activities for both the poor and non-poor are sales, manufacturing, and textiles. However, these occupations are more common among the non-poor than the poor. In the Costa, the most important occupations outside of agriculture are sales (for both poor and non-poor), transportation (for non-poor), and 'other' (which includes a variety of service occupations). In the Oriente, off-farm employment occurs in virtually all categories, with sales being the most important.

Agricultural Policy. The rural poor's ability to benefit from market exchange is also closely linked to the degree farm prices are at competitive levels. Recent estimates show that the producer prices of export products are suppressed, which worsens the agricultural terms of trade and diminishes income for poor farmers producing these exportable products (especially in the Costa). In 1993, effective protection rates were negative for the main export commodities such as bananas (-42 percent), cocoa (-32 percent) and coffee (-50 percent).[48] Non-competitive market structures for bananas, cocoa, and coffee, and an unfavorable export price setting scheme, in which exporters have to liquidate export proceeds at certain reference points, account for this suppression of farm prices. Fostering competition among exporters would raise farm prices for agricultural produce to competitive levels and increase agricultural farm income.

An Option: Increasing the Market Access of the Poor through Community Participation. Ecuador's rural economy is very diverse, which necessitates that communities play a key role in fostering their own market integration, particularly since apparently similar neighboring communities can have distinct income structures and poverty issues, depending on the quality of and access to land and on off-farm employment possibilities. Communities therefore will have varying needs for raising the productivity of their land and labor. The seven communities included in the Rural Qualitative Assessment, for example,

---

[48]   Valdes and Schaeffer (1995).

overwhelmingly named small infrastructure projects (48 percent of all suggestions), credit, and training as most needed interventions. Infrastructure projects ranged from small roads, a bridge, irrigation, and a meeting hall to an electricity connection. Similarly, communities asked for training classes ranging from agriculture to land conservation to forestry, and to weaving in the off-farm sector.

Women's Labor Force Participation

As noted in Section One, a household is significantly more likely to be poor if the spouse or partner of the head of household does not work. With more than 80 percent of households in Ecuador being headed by males, this points to the importance of women's participation in the labor force. There is a major difference between poor and non-poor households relating to women's participation in the labor force. Apart from educational differences, obstacles to labor force participation by the poor women in urban areas are primarily household and childcare duties and street violence. In rural areas, remoteness and lack of market integration preclude many women from entering the non-farm rural economy.

Female Labor Force Participation. Participation in the labor force is considerably lower for poor than for non-poor women. This difference becomes very pronounced if we add an age dimension (Graph 13). Only at the very end of the working life cycle (age 60-64) do participation rates for the three female groups become similar.

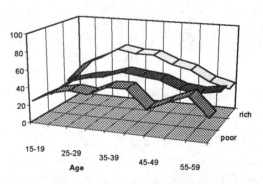

Graph 13. Female Labor Force Participation, 1994

Source: LSMS, 1994.

Female Labor Force Participation as a Household Adjustment Strategy. Despite these differences, female labor force participation is one of the most important possibilities for the poor. When incomes decline and households become poorer, the most important response, mainly by women spouses, is to try to involve themselves in income-generating activities, either in the market or in their homes. Labor market participation in urban Cisne Dos has expanded, with the number of working women increasing from 32 percent in 1978 to 46 percent in 1992.[49] Similarly, the RQA

Table 15. Urban Area: Female Labor Force Participation, 1994 (percent)[a]		
	poor	non-poor
participation	50.9	62.7
no participation	49.1	37.3
-- household/children	38.2	27.4
-- student	2.1	2.5
-- other	8.8	7.4
a Female population aged 21 to 64 only.		
Source: LSMS, 1994.		

---

[49]   At the national level, female labor force participation rose form 34 percent in 1988 to 46 percent in 1993. Compare Working Paper 9.

records that in the seven rural communities, female (and child) work is the most important strategy for households to earn additional income.

Obstacles. But poor women face key obstacles to working, which (besides their education level and demand side constraints for their labor) are quite different in urban and rural areas. In urban areas, household and childcare duties are the major reason why women do not participate in the workforce, and these are more pressing the poorer they are. Thirty-eight percent of all poor urban women aged 21 to 64 do not participate in the labor force because of their household and childcare duties (Table 15). The figure for non-poor women is considerably lower at 27.4 percent, but within that group we observe a very strong variation by total household expenditures. Many of the worse-off among the non-poor women cannot afford domestic servants or private kindergartens which would enable them to go work.

The importance of childcare centers for women's ability to work is exemplified by the effect of the closure of the *Red Comunitaria*, a community-based childcare program, in 1993. Although initially expected to reopen under the newly created Operation Child Rescue, many of the childcare centers have not reopened. In Cisne Dos, for example, the childcare center has remained closed. A small survey of thirty women who had been sending their children to the local *Hogar Comunitaria* revealed that fifteen had to give up their jobs because they did not have a place to leave their children. Others changed jobs to work nearer to home, or at home, or if they were domestic servants in two houses, gave up one of their jobs.

Another issue that is becoming increasingly important in Ecuador's poor urban neighborhoods today is violence, which limits women's physical mobility to work far from or even outside the home. While national data on the extent of street violence is not available, indications from Cisne Dos mark this as a particular problem: over a six-month period (February-July 1992), 50 percent of respondents witnessed a bus robbery, one-third were victims of street and household theft, and more than half of all family members were robbed. About half of the respondents identified the *pantillas* (gangs of young unemployed males) as a major cause of crime. This has resulted in a drop in the use of public transport, particularly at night, and an increase in the use of small trucks by people working late shifts, especially women.

Options. Helping today's poor women and tomorrow's mothers enter the workforce is key to enabling them to overcome poverty. With secondary education carrying a high private return and raising the probability of participation in the labor market, it is crucial that teenage girls are able to continue school. Similarly, reopening the childcare network in urban areas would enable many women to work and teenage daughters to remain in school (in addition to reaching malnourished poor children, as discussed above). Measures to increase the physical safety of women in certain neighborhoods would increase their ability to work away from home. Functioning street lightening and guarded public buses in the evening could be simple but effective measures. In rural areas, many of the small investment and training proposals suggested by the communities entail possibilities for women to enter the informal off-farm sector.

Housing as a Process for the Urban Poor

As discussed above, urban families that rent their house, apartment, or shanty are more likely to be poor than those that own their dwelling. Field analysis suggests that ownership is closely linked to families using their house as an asset. One of the major variables we analyze below, therefore, relates to the degree to which urban families use their house as their workplace.

The Importance of Housing as an Asset. In urban Ecuador, housing variables and poverty are closely linked. Many of the urban poor live in smaller, more crowded houses with less access to basic services than the non-poor, and their houses are built with inferior materials such as bamboo in the Costa or clay in the Sierra.

However, the link between housing and urban poverty is more complex than that the non-poor are able to afford superior housing materials and more spacious dwellings and live in areas with better basic services. Housing is a dynamic process; it is an asset that can help the poor to grow out of poverty or shield them against slipping deeper into poverty. Housing often enables families to start informal sector activities, such as repairs, production of textiles or food and beverage sales. Renting out a room can supplement family income. Further, in times of need, the house can give shelter to relatives or close friends who would otherwise have to live on the street or in a shanty.

The importance of housing as 'dynamic' is exemplified by Cisne Dos, the low-income neighborhood in Guayaquil. In 1992, one in three households earned additional income from home-based enterprises, while about 20 percent received cash income from remittances, rent, or other non-wage sources. It is homeowners with electricity connections who are more likely to run enterprises dependent on electricity such as stores with refrigerators and textile making sewing machines. The main types of enterprises run out of homes are retail operations (57 percent), followed by workshops and small industries (35 percent), and some personal services (8 percent). They are run largely by women, and cushion households against extreme poverty.

At the national level, the relationship between urban poverty and the productive use of the dwelling supports the characterization of housing as an asset (Graph 14). Distinguishing between population quintiles (rather than between the poor and non-poor) to present a more differentiated picture, we find that only 8.3 percent of the poorest working population use their dwellings for home-based enterprises. This ratio climbs steadily until it declines slightly for the richest population quintile. Hence, the use of housing as a productive asset can be an important route out of poverty for the urban poor.

Housing as a Process. In accordance with this view, housing is a process of developing and then consolidating the housing unit to become and asset for its inhabitants. A key to supporting this process becomes the appropriate institutional and legal framework. A very important step is to make it possible for families to obtain title to the house, which is generally a precondition to get water connections and other services from the municipality.

Research has shown that the security of ownership through registered titles gives inhabitants an incentive to invest in their dwellings.[50] Once they obtain title, they begin the process of incremental upgrading and consolidation. The combination of lack of title and the widespread perception, both within and outside the neighborhood, that one's settlement is not officially recognized (illegal, pirated, invaded) contributes to residents spending their income on consumer durables rather than investing in the house. Once ownership is secured, however, residents place high priority on water, electricity, transport, schools, health centers, sewerage, and solid waste disposal. Finally, once service delivery is secured, many residents tend to seek credit to upgrade their dwelling.

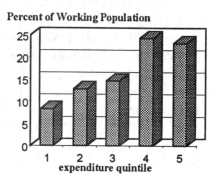

Graph 14. Home-Based Urban Employment, 1994

Percent of Working Population

Source: LSMS, 1994.

Such a consolidation process was observed in Cisne Dos, which is a typical squatter settlement. The settlement process, which started in the early 1970s, involved the creation of solid land (through infilling) and the construction of squatter housing. During the 1970s, Cisne Dos was characterized by low population density, little access to services, and small, incrementally built bamboo and timber houses standing on poles over polluted water. A complex system of interconnected catwalks linked the houses within this area, as well as with the nearest solid land. Over the next decade, upgraded brick and cement housing replaced less durable houses, population densities increased, and services were provided. Most importantly, home ownership was legalized with the rate of households holding title to their land increasing from 8.8 percent in 1978 to 24 percent in 1988 and to 52 percent in 1992. Without the threat of eviction, home ownership in Cisne Dos has provided a strong incentive for families to mobilize economic resources to improve their housing, as shown by the significant improvements in the quality and size of the housing stock since 1978.

An Option: A New Direction for Ecuador's Housing Policy. Ecuador's housing policy has traditionally, and unsuccessfully, focused on providing housing structures for the poor rather than enabling them to build and upgrade their own dwellings. Ecuador's housing policy, especially through the *Banco Ecuatoriana de Vivienda* (BEV*)*, has emphasized closing the housing gap, estimated at 1.3 million dwellings which are either needed to shelter the homeless (317,000 houses in 1991) or exist but are qualitatively insufficient (900,000 houses in 1991). BEV provides housing financing but physical output is very low.[51] Furthermore, BEV does not reach the poor with their operation. BEV's long-standing policy has been to require a minimum household income as a precondition for loan approval, with the loan being a function of the *salario minimo* and the loan size. The lowest monthly income to qualify a family for a loan is estimated at US$335 per month. A comparison of average monthly household expenditures for the households in the lowest

---

50   Persaud (1992).
51   Persaud (1992, p. 23).

quintile (US$121) or the second quintile (US$185) reveals that few poor families in Ecuador have qualified for such BEV loans and have hence also not been the beneficiaries of the subsidies.[52]

An important priority for Ecuadoran housing policy is to legalize the many dwellings now without proper title and to record them in a modern cadastre (compare Table 16). With home investment so crucially dependent on secure tenureship, the legalization of these dwelling is the first and most important step to helping the poor.   Service provision, most importantly water and sewerage connection in the urban Costa, would then further enable the

Table 16. Unauthorized Housing in Latin American Countries (percent), 1990	
Brazil	27%
Chile	20%
Colombia	8%
Ecuador	54%
Mexico	16%
Venezuela	54%
Source: Persaud (1992).	

poor to use their homes as productive investments.   In terms of direct intervention, the housing policy should limit itself to providing direct grants to those extremely poor (the old, widows, the ill) who are not able to upgrade their own homes.

5.   A Stable and Growing Demand for Labor

Finally, we turn away from asset-supply considerations to focus on the demand for labor.   The efficient allocation of workers in the Ecuadoran economy is hampered by regulations and lack of technological innovation in the formal sector.   Consequently, the rapid increase in labor supply stemming from both demographic and behavioral changes over the past years has not been matched by an equal increase in the demand for labor in the formal sector.   This has resulted in an increase in the informal sector and a decline in average productivity of labor for the economy as a whole.   Ensuring a stable and growing demand for labor will involve two sets of actions: first, reducing the direct and indirect tax on labor related to existing regulations; and second, pursuing economic policies conducive to long-term economic growth.

Reducing Burdensome Regulation in the Labor Market

Labor Market Regulation and Inequality.   Ecuador has cumbersome labor legislation.   The Government interferes with wage setting in the private sector through specific mechanisms, including nationwide minimum wages, specific minimum wages by sector and occupation, minimum mandatory wage adjustments, and an array of mandated benefits, each determined according to a specific rule and paid at a different point in time. Some of these benefits are proportional to the base wage of the worker, while others are set as a lump sum; some are paid monthly, while others are due once or several times a year. Both the employee and the employer have to make contributions to the social security

---

[52]   Compare Working Paper 6. The implicit housing subsidy incorporated in the operation of BEV stems from a longtime subsidy of mortgage interest rates and a low collection effort. In a cross-country study, Persaud (1992, p. 49) finds that only 6 percent of housing subsidies in Ecuador reached the population below the median income.

system, which represents a tax on labor rather than a delayed payment, because benefits are not linked to payments. Finally, firms willing to downsize or restructure might end up paying a severance equal to many years' salary to the displaced workers. In addition to these observable costs of labor market legislation, employers also incur transaction and management costs that we cannot directly observe.

In addition to causing efficiency problems, the resulting labor market segmentation has a direct link to equality and poverty. In terms of efficiency, by precluding labor from being allocated optimally across different sectors of the economy, segmentation undermines international competitiveness. But such regulation can be a source of increasing inequality in society as well. Regulations create benefits that protect only a few while putting a heavy toll on informal sector workers: not only is their wage rate artificially reduced, but they are hindered from entering the regulated sector making it much more difficult for the poor to grow out of poverty by using their own labor.

Degree of Labor Market Segmentation. We employ data on individual earnings from the LSMS to estimate the effect of labor market regulations, controlling for the characteristics of the workers. If the labor market were efficient, individuals with the same characteristics (such as schooling and experience) would earn similar wages across different sectors and activities. If, on the other hand, excessive regulation created labor market segmentation, then the earnings in a particular sector would differ depending on whether or not the employer abides by the law.

We estimate that labor market regulations raise labor costs. Using the LSMS, we find that individuals who earn the benefits mandated by law enjoy higher take-home pay than their identical counterparts. Total labor costs, including social security contributions and payroll taxes, are about 8 percent higher for an employer who complies with labor regulations. As mentioned above, however, this calculation of the degree of labor market segmentation is based on the direct cost impact of the regulation. Additional factors such as administrative or transaction costs might add to labor costs and thereby to segmentation.

Quantifying the Impact of Deregulation. Would reducing regulations have a significant impact on labor demand and thereby benefit the poor? To answer this question, we use a simple General Equilibrium Model to simulate the effects of reducing labor market regulation.[53] The model starts from a detailed description of the labor market, distinguishing among a modern (regulated) urban sector, an informal urban sector, a commercial agricultural sector, and a subsistence agricultural sector. Labor is a production factor in all four sectors and capital is a production factor only in commercial agriculture and the modern sector. The educational level of workers employed in the informal sector, commercial agriculture, and the modern sector is a crucial variable determining the equilibrium wage rates between the different sectors. In fact, wage differentials among sectors are due to either the difference in educational levels or to the segmentation of labor markets. For our purpose of identifying the importance of labor market deregulation, we can identify the modern sector as a non-poor sector because the average worker earns about 50 percent more than in the informal and commercial agricultural sectors and about 100

---

[53]   Compare Working Paper 10.

percent more than in the subsistence agriculture sector. Workers moving into the modern sector hence significantly improve their welfare position.

The General Equilibrium Model shows that reduction in labor market segmentation through deregulation from eight to four percent would lead to a shift of about 100,000 workers from the (poor) informal and agricultural sectors to the (non-poor) modern sector. These workers would realize a real income gain of 37 percent. However, the increase in the modern sector labor force would reduce the real wage in this sector slightly, by about 6.5 percent, contributing to an improved distribution of labor income. The labor reallocation would increase the modern sector work force from 22.8 percent to 26.2 percent of the total working population in Ecuador. Hence, we determine that deregulation would indeed have a desired impact on the labor force distribution. But while it can be an important component of a pro-poor policy because it raises labor demand in the modern sector and increases overall efficiency in the economy, thereby contributing to higher growth, it emerges that labor market deregulation alone cannot be relied on to improve the living conditions of the poor.

Important Steps Towards Labor Market Deregulation. There are three priority areas for reform to reduce the observed segmentation of the labor market and lower the additional transaction and information costs that reduce labor demand. First, a rationalization of the basic wage policy is very important. The degree of intervention can be reduced by (a) unifying the various components of the minimum wage, and (b) adjusting the minimum wage to one level for the entire country. CONADES, the Wage Setting Council, can begin to adjust sectoral wages in inverse proportion to a newly defined 'general minimum wage'. After some time, all basic salaries would converge to a single minimum wage.

Second, the Ecuadoran labor law needs to unambiguously determine the obligations of employees and employers towards the Social Security Institute IESS. Currently, the system is unsustainable because contributions (20.5 percent of the basic salary) come from a tax that is not correlated to future benefits. The contribution makes affiliates eligible for public sector health care benefits, a pension and worker's compensation in case of accidents on the job. The accidence insurance is structured in a way that cross-subsidizes unsafe jobs. In the case of pensions, an actuarial balance between required contributions and guaranteed benefits needs to be established. Since pensions are paid in the future, for an unknown period of time, an actuarial balance can be attained by combining a life insurance policy and a savings account. In its current form, the poor in Ecuador benefit very little from the social security system because their coverage is low and the benefits reaching them -- mainly in the form of health care -- are minimal.[54]

Third, a reform of Article 189 of the labor law, regulating dismissals and voluntary separations, is essential to encourage the establishment of a better working environment within firms. The current law leaves much to be desired in terms of acceptance or enforceability. It creates an environment that makes employers reluctant to hire new workers. The severance payment also creates perverse incentives for both employers and

---

[54]   Compare detailed discussion in Working Paper 1.

employees.   Returning to the maximum of 12 months, employment before workers are eligible for severance, as had been the law until 1991, can be a start.   A more substantive reform, however, might be a more effective approach, i.e. introducing some notion of 'economic cause' for separation and transforming the severance formula into a contribution-defined benefit.

Macroeconomic Growth and Stability

Importance of Growth for Poverty Reduction.   The *World Development Report 1990* established the importance of sustained growth for reducing poverty. While, theoretically, poverty can also be alleviated in a low growth environment through improved targeting of Government expenditures and improved distribution of available resources, it is without doubt much easier to alleviate poverty in a growing economy.   One reason is that a growing economy increases the demand for labor.   The translation of growth into higher labor demand will be more pronounced the less capital is explicitly or implicitly subsidized. A second reason is that the public sector is more able to raise resources needed for poverty alleviation without crowding out private initiative and investment.   Third, international experience has shown that it is much more difficult for the poor to protect their income and assets in a low-growth economy.[55]

Growth, Inequality, and Poverty in Urban Ecuador 1989-1993. We can see the link between poverty and growth between 1989 and 1993 by the fact that during this period, urban poverty increased in a low growth environment.   GNP per capita grew only by 1 percent on average, with urban growth even lower since agriculture in the Costa was the source of most growth during those years.   Between 1990 and 1993, the share of the urban informal sector in total employment increased from 45 to 48 percent.   With poverty closely linked to informal sector employment

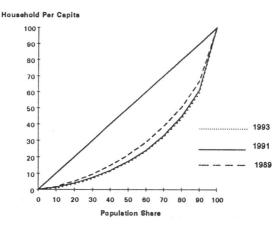

Graph 15. Income Distribution Urban Ecuador Lorenz Curve, 1989-93

Source: Working Paper 3 based on INEM (1989, 1991, 1993).

and with wage rates in the informal sector significantly lower than in the formal sector -- at the end of 1993 the difference between average wages in these sectors was about 50 percent -- the income distribution worsened (Graph 15) and poverty increased at the national urban level and in the urban Costa and Sierra.[56]

---

[55]   World Bank (1993b).
[56]   See Working Paper 2.

45

Growth and Poverty Reduction. A per capita growth rate of three percent over a five year period could reduce poverty from 35 to 26 percent, provided it were not offset by a deterioration in income distribution. In fact, the impact on poverty reduction could be completely offset if inequality increases: If the share of the bottom 40 percent of the population in total consumption were to fall from the current 16 to 10 percent, poverty would increase to 40 percent despite high growth (Table 17). Conversely, inequality could be reduced by increasing the share of

Table 17. Poverty Rates with a Per Capita Growth Rate of 3 Percent Over Five Years (change from current level)	
no change in inequality	26 (-9)
increasing inequality[a]	40 (+5)
inequality declines[b]	16 (-19)

Source: LSMS, 1994
a Share of bottom 40 percent in consumption drops from 15.7 to 10 percent.
b Share of bottom 40% in total consumption increases from 15.7 to 20 percent.

the bottom two quintiles to 20 percent, poverty could be reduced to 16 percent. A growth rate of three percent per capita is not without reach. In 1994, the economy rebounded strongly, real growth was four percent, and per capita increase of GDP almost two percent.

Improving Ecuador's Growth Record. What are the underlying causes of Ecuador's poor growth record, not only over the past five but over the last fifteen years? The discovery of oil at the beginning of the 1970s created a boom period during which per capita growth averaged 6.4 percent between 1972 and 1981. But then per capita growth slowed considerably between 1982 and 1992 and was only tenths of a point above zero. Three major reasons underlay this malaise: (a) low and stagnant domestic savings were insufficient to finance a net resource transfer abroad to repay debt without affecting investment; (b) low growth in productivity meant that technological change could not be relied on to supplement reduced investment; and (c) a reduced availability of foreign exchange signified the economy's vulnerability to imported goods and capital used intensively in production.

The primary reason for the slowdown since the early 1980s has been the decline in investment, stemming from low savings (Table 18). Investment rates declined sharply from 25 percent of GDP in the 1974-78 period to 20 percent of GDP since. Close to half of the decline in the rate of investments was due to reduced domestic savings, while the rest was due to an increase of net factor payments which domestic savings had to finance. Net foreign savings, on the

Table 18. Sources of Investment Decline, 1974 to 1982 and 1983 to 1992	
	Percent of GDP
domestic savings	-2.5
net factor payments	-2.4
foreign savings	-0.4
Investment	-5.3

Source: Central Bank of Ecuador.

other hand, did not decline as much due to the accumulation of arrears. It followed that the decline in the investment rates during the 1980s lowered the rate of growth of the capital stock and thereby the productive capacity of the economy.

The second major factor responsible for the disappointing growth in Ecuador has been an extremely slow growth in productivity due to the lack of technological change. While badly needed during times of declining investments, technological progress was extremely low during the 1980s, estimated at 0.2 percent and 1.5 percent;[57] much lower than the comparable rate for the developing countries as a whole.[58] The poor technological performance was largely due to an inward-looking development strategy during the 1970s, which fostered investments in capital-intensive, import-substituting and non-tradable industries.

The third reason for the slowdown is that Ecuador was vulnerable to external shocks at the beginning of the 1980s. Its exports were highly undiversified and the country was dependent on imports of capital and intermediate goods, which were used intensively in domestic production. Evidence suggests that substitution elasticities between imported and domestic factors of production were limited, due at least in part to the capital-intensive production technology fostered by the industrialization strategy.[59] Although the economy is still vulnerable to imports, it is less so than ten years ago, mainly because significant trade and exchange rate liberalization, and a redesign of industrial policy has taken place. Since 1990, non-traditional exports grew on average by 35 percent per annum, now accounting for almost 20 percent of total export receipts. A continuation of this trend towards export diversification would make the country even less vulnerable to swings in the international price of petroleum.

Increasing the Savings Rate. Several conditions would promote higher savings, including most importantly continued progress toward macroeconomic stability. A more stable environment would reduce uncertainty and the threat of unexpected policy changes, both of which discourage saving and investment. Greater stability will increase the confidence of the private sector that future governments will not rely on periodic ad-hoc stabilization policies. Further, while the current Government has taken important steps to reform financial and capital markets, the necessary reform of the social security system has not been tackled. This would allow for the creation of a parallel private sector pension system, thereby deepening the financial markets.

Promoting Technical Innovation. New theories of growth stress the importance of technological progress for economic development. In Ecuador, the reduction of trade barriers has already discouraged investments in uncompetitive domestic industries and stimulated the development of non-traditional exports, which are an important transmitter of technological innovation and thus have positive externalities. Creating a framework, e.g. , a trade information center cofinanced with the private sector, to help entrepreneurs explore non-traditional export markets might help this process along. Foreign direct investments can be not only a major source of technology and know-how transfer, but also of special importance in opening marketing channels. Foreign investors look for a regulatory framework that is not biased against foreign investments, and for macroeconomic stability and reform.

Reducing Vulnerability to External Shocks by Diversifying Exports. While the trade liberalization of 1991-1992 and the recent reversal of the real exchange rate appreciation of

---

[57]   These estimates are for the period 1970 to 1991. They vary with the specification of the production function. Compare World Bank (1996).
[58]   Renelt (1991).
[59]   Hentschel (1994) and World Bank (1996).

47

the 1980s have greatly helped non-oil export development, several barriers still exist. The export regulatory and institutional framework is highly fragmented. The depth of the financial market in Ecuador is still too shallow to cater to exporters' needs, and no reliable export guarantee or insurance scheme exists. Also, non-traditional export development rests with small- to medium-sized enterprises and it is difficult for these firms to internalize the substantial investments into information about the export process and foreign markets.

Growth cum Education: The High Payoff. The importance of growth for reducing poverty in Ecuador can be seen by a simulation exercise using the Computable General Equilibrium model. The simulation consists a strong increase in investment of 2.5 percent of GDP per year over a five-year period. We choose such an increase in investment because it corresponds to the observed drop in the domestic savings rate (between 1982 and 1992), and hence would be compatible with restoring the savings rate to levels observed before the debt

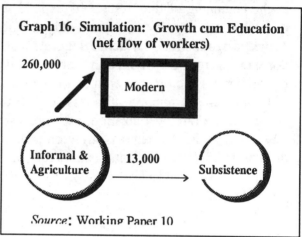

Graph 16. Simulation: Growth cum Education (net flow of workers)

Source: Working Paper 10

crisis. In order to show that the effects of growth will not only translate directly into higher labor demand but also enable the public sector to raise a higher (absolute) amount of resources, we combine the physical investment scenario with human capital investment. Specifically, we assume that the mean educational level of workers is increased by half a year.

This growth-cum-education scenario, shows the strong effects of reallocating labor in favor of the modern, non-poor sector of the economy. A strong growth performance is the result of both higher physical and higher human capital stocks. Further, more than a quarter million workers would be drawn into the modern, non-poor economic sector, improving their real income by 40 percent (compare Graph 16). As already observed in the case of deregulation, this movement of workers will cause the real wage in the modern sector to decline by 4 percent which shows an important trade-off of which policymakers should be aware: while a growth and education strategy promises to help create better lives for the poor over the medium to long term, the movement of labor between sectors can impact on the real wages of the non-poor today. The stronger the growth environment, however, the smaller this adjustment will be.

References

Berg, A. (1981), <u>Malnourished People: A Policy View</u>, World Bank, Washington D.C..Binswanger, H. (1995), "Best Practice in Rural Finance", mimeo, World Bank, Washington D.C.

Binswanger, H., K. Deininger and G. Feder (1993), <u>Power, Distortions, Revolt, and Reform in Agricultural Land Relations</u>, World Bank Working Paper Series 1164, World Bank.

Cabrera, Y., J. Martinez and R. Morales (1993), <u>Medición de la Pobreza en el Ecuador</u>, Quito.

Enriquez, F. (1994), "La reforma del ministrio de salud: algunos elementos", draft, Quito.

ESMAP (1994), "Energy Pricing, Poverty and Social Mitigation", Report No. 12831-EC, Energy Sector Management Assistance Program, Washington D.C..

Freire, W. and W. Waters (1994), "Pobreza y Malnutricion en el Ecuador", Background Paper for Ecuador Poverty Report, Quito.

Grosh, M. (1994), <u>Administering Targeted Social Programs in Latin America</u>, World Bank Regional and Sectoral Studies, Washington.

Hentschel, J. (1994), Trade and growth in Ecuador: A Pertial Equilibrium View, World Bank Working Paper xx, Washington, D.C.

Hope, E. and B. Singh (1995), <u>Energy Price Increases in Developing Countries</u>, Policy Research Working Paper 1442, World Bank.

IDB (1993), <u>Ecuador: Informe Socio-Economico</u>, Washington D.C.

ILDIS (1994), <u>Informe Social 1994</u>, Quito.

INEC (1992), <u>Estatisticas Vitales</u>, Quito.

INEM (1989, 1990, 1991, 1993), <u>Encuesta Permanente de Hogares</u>, Quito.

Mesa-Lago, C. (1993), <u>The Ecuadoran Social Security Institute: Economic Evaluation and Options for Reform</u>, INCAE, Washington D.C.

Musgrove, P. (1991), <u>Feeding Latin America's Children</u>, Latin America and the Caribbean Technical Paper No.11, Washington D.C.

Persaud, T. (1992), <u>Housing Delivery Systems and the Urban Poor: A Comparison Among Six Latin Countries</u>, Latin America and the Caribbean Technical Department, Regional Studies Program 23, Washington D.C..

Pfister, E. (1995), "El Presupuesto de Educacion", mimeo, EB/PRODEC, Quito.

Ravallion, M. (1994), <u>Poverty Comparisons</u>, Harwood Press, Chur.

Renelt, D. (1991), <u>Economic Growth - A Review of the Theoretical and Empirical Literature</u>, Policy Research Working Papers 678, 1991.

SECAP (1994), "Encuesta Sobre Condiciones de Vida", Quito.

UNICEF (1993), <u>World Education Report</u>, New York.

UNICEF, DyA (1992), <u>Bienestar de los Ninos en el Ecuador</u>, Quito.

Valdes, A. and B. Schaeffer (1995), "Handbook on Surveillance of Agricultural Price and Trade, Ecuador", draft mimeo, World Bank.

Whitaker, M.D. (1990), <u>El Rol de la Agricultura en el Desarrollo Economico del Ecuador</u>, IDEA, Quito.

World Bank (1990), <u>A Social Sector Strategy for the 1990s</u>, Washington D.C.

World Bank (1992), "Staff Appraisal Report, Second Social Sector Development Project", Washington, D.C.

World Bank (1993a), <u>World Development Report: Investing in Health</u>, Washington.

World Bank (1993b), <u>Implementing the Bank's Poverty Reduction Strategy: Progress and Challenges</u>, Washington D.C.

World Bank (1993c), "Ecuador: Agricultural Sector Review", Report No. 11398-EC, Washington D.C..

World Bank (1993d), "Options for Land Reform and Rural Restructuring in South Africa", draft, Washington D.C..

World Bank (1994), <u>Enriching Lives</u>, Washington D.C..

World Bank (1996),"Ecuador: Macroeconomic Assessment", forthcoming, Washington D.C.

Part II.

Working Papers

Working Paper 1: Poverty Profile
Jesko Hentschel and Peter Lanjouw

In this paper, we want to provide the reader with the statistical background on which many of the following Working Papers build: the measurement, distribution and severity of poverty as well a description of the living conditions of the poor.

The paper is structured as follows. The first section comments briefly on the data source underlying the study, the Living Standard Measurement Survey, and presents the most important statistics on poverty and inequality in Ecuador. The second section investigates how another poverty measure, a Basic Needs Indicator -- which is not based on a consumption basket -- compares to our estimates and whether it can be used as a means to identify the poor. We describe the living conditions of the poor in the Ecuadoran society in Section Three, looking at many variables ranging from service access to education and from transport to health. We defer most of the technical discussions to Annex 1. It deals with the derivation of the different poverty lines for which we employ a consumption-based welfare measure, paying particular attention to the pricing of housing, durable consumer goods and water. Annex 1 goes on to study how robust the estimates of poverty are when we alter some basic assumptions underlying the derivation of the poverty line. Annex 2 describes a methodology how to operationalize the Living Standard Measurement Survey to derive a geographic poverty map for Ecuador. Annex 3, finally, contains a reference table for the interested reader in which we present cross tabulations between expenditure classes and other variables.

We can describe the picture that emerges from this profile as follows: Ecuador is an extremely poor country measured by the number of people that cannot afford to purchase a basic basket of goods. Thirty-five percent of its population -- or more than three and a half million people -- lived in poverty in 1994 and an additional one a half million were vulnerable to being poor. Although more people now live in urban areas than in rural areas, the outcome of a long process of intersectoral transition, sixty percent of the total poor still reside in rural areas today. Because of the great heterogeneity across regions and sectors in the relationship between poverty and social indicators, efforts to measure poverty on an individual level using basic needs, or related indicators, are difficult to employ.

1.   A Snapshot of Poverty

The Data: From Income to a Consumption Based Measure of Poverty in Ecuador

Throughout the largest part of this Poverty Assessment, we measure the well-being of individuals by their total consumption and not income for a number of reasons. First, consumption of a household tends to fluctuate much less during the course of a month or even a year than income. The income of the poor is often quite volatile: in the urban centers, the poor frequently depend on jobs as day laborers in the informal sector. In the rural sector, income from agriculture fluctuates with prices and harvest conditions. While income of a household may thus vary during the course of a year, consumption patterns are much more stable. Savings during periods of high income and borrowings, in periods of income shortfalls, help smooth the consumption of food and other goods. Hence, poverty analysis based on consumption as the welfare variable is more likely to accurately represent the well-being of a population than one based on an income measure.

Second, experience shows that consumption data is easier and more accurately collectable. Asking people about their consumption during a fixed recall period is more reliable than asking them about all kinds of earnings and incomes. This is particularly true for agricultural and informal sector activities. Third, one of the attractions of a survey which contains consumption data is that it allows the specification of a poverty line from the same data source and the researcher avoids many of the problems of comparability which one encounters when one has to impose a poverty line derived elsewhere.

Box 1. The Ecuador Living Standard Measurement Survey

The Ecuador *Encuesta de Condiciones de Vida,* or Living Standard Measurement Survey (LSMS), is a nationally representative household survey, comparable to Living Standard Measurement Surveys conducted in many other countries. Conducted by the Servicio Ecuatoriana de Capacitacion (SECAP) with financial support of the World Bank under the EB/PRODEC basic education loan, the LSMS questioned around 4,500 households in urban and rural Ecuador with over 20,000 individuals. Sampling design achieves representability for the two major cities in the country, Guayaquil and Quito, as well as for all urban and rural areas at the regional (Costa, Sierra, Oriente) level. However, the LSMS does not allow for poverty comparisons at the provincial level. SECAP conducted the LSMS in a short time period between end-June and beginning of September 1994 in order to maximize the comparability of the welfare between households in a (modestly) inflationary environment.

The 1994 round of the LSMS marks the start of two more surveys to follow in 1995 and 1996. Lessons learned from the evaluation of the 1994 data can be taken into account in the next rounds. One of the most important lessons is the undersampling of rural areas which took place during the first round. Of the 4500 households in the sample, only 1374 households were located in rural Ecuador which limits the applicability of an analysis at a disaggregated level, for example by quintile and region. The Instituto Ecuatoriano de Estadisticas y Census (INEC), which is the executing agency for the next two rounds of the LSMS, plans to resurvey a number of the households already included in the first round. This would create a unique panel data set which could serve policy impact analysis in the near future.

This Poverty Report draws intensively on the recently completed Living Standard Measurement Survey (*Encuesta de Condiciones de Vida*) which is preferable to other existing data sources in Ecuador in several respects. The LSMS is modeled after similar surveys developed and promoted by the World Bank in many countries (compare Box 1). Most importantly, it is the first nationally representative household survey containing expenditure data.   While the Instituto Nacional de Empleo (INEM) conducted one representative national employment survey in 1990,[1] it cannot be used for welfare analysis as it only reports gross instead of net agricultural income and does not include off-farm employment income in a consistent way. Further, household income data derived from the survey is imprecise in the urban areas as well because the main focus of the survey was to measure employment, underemployment and wages but not necessarily total household income. Measuring household income correctly would, among others, include income from transfers, borrowings and income from secondary sources. This is only insufficiently incorporated in the survey. Last but not least, the LSMS includes a large range of variables tailored for welfare analysis which are generally not included in employment surveys. For example, the survey places specific emphasis on measuring food and non-food expenditures, education and health.

---

[1]   INEM (1990).

Base Results: Poverty and Inequality

<u>Poverty Estimates</u>. We turn to the three most frequently used poverty indicators. First, the incidence or headcount ratio which describes a percentage of the population as being poor. Second, the depth of poverty (or poverty gap) which measures the amount of income required to bring all impoverished individuals to the poverty line expressed as a proportion of the poverty line itself. Third, the severity of poverty is a derivation of the depth of poverty but takes into account the distribution of expenditures among the poor themselves. It attaches higher importance to the poorest within the poor group of poor.[2]

We calculate statistics for three consumption-based welfare lines, the derivation of which are detailed in Annex 1. The *extreme poverty line* only values a basket of food items which meets the minimum necessary calorie requirements per person. The *poverty line* includes the same basket of food items but also non-food items. The share of total expenditures spent on non-food items is calculated by looking at those people whose <u>total</u> expenditures are just enough to reach the extreme poverty line. The philosophy behind this estimate is that the non-food items purchased by this population group are <u>absolutely essential</u> since a direct trade-off between food and non-food items occurs. The *vulnerability line* (and the one conventionally applied in most poverty analyses) uses a different reference group to compute the share of non-food items in total expenditures. It chooses the population whose <u>food</u> expenditures exactly finance the minimum basket of goods and records their share of non-food expenditures in total expenditures. The basket of these non-food items is also essential, but somewhat <u>less essential</u> than the one used for the calculation of the vulnerability line because no trade-off between food and non-food expenditures is necessary. According to Ravallion (1994), the 'true' poverty line is somewhere between the poverty and vulnerability line.

In 1994, thirty-five percent of the Ecuadoran population lived in poverty -- measured by the poverty line -- and an additional 17 percent was vulnerable to be poor. The incidence of poverty varied considerably between urban and rural areas. Between regions, comparisons are less obvious. As shown in Table 1, the incidence of rural poverty is much higher than in urban areas: Using the poverty line, almost every second person lived in poverty in rural Ecuador while every fourth person was poor in the urban areas. The predominantly rural nature of poverty in Ecuador is replicated for each of the three very distinct regions. Rural poverty is highest in the Oriente, the scarcely populated jungle area of Ecuador, where it reaches sixty-seven percent. Although 55 percent of the total population in Ecuador, according to the LSMS, lived in urban areas in 1994, we still locate around sixty percent of the poor in rural areas.

---

[2]   The distance between a poor's expenditure and the poverty line is squared so that the poorer among the poor obtain a higher weight in the summary statistic. This is the Foster-Geer-Thorbeck measure with a weight of two. See Ravallion (1994).

Table 1. Poverty in Ecuador 1994: Summary Measures for Vulnerability and Poverty Line

		Incidence[a]		Depth[a]		Severity[a]		Distribution ('000)	
		Vulner.	Poverty	Vulner.	Poverty	Vulner.	Poverty	Vulner.	Poverty
Costa	urban	44	26	14	7	6	3	1,589	939
	rural	69	50	26	15	13	6	1,370	993
Sierra	urban	34	22	13	8	6	4	773	500
	rural	64	43	24	14	12	7	1,643	1,104
Oriente	urban	36	20	11	5	5	2	20	11
	rural	80	67	41	30	25	16	240	200
National	urban	40	25	13	7	6	3	2,320	1,450
	rural	67	47	26	15	13	7	3,274	2,297
Total		52	35	19	11	9	11	5,594	3,747

a Poverty incidence is measured by the headcount ratio; poverty depth is measured by the FGT measure with a parameter of 1; poverty severity is measured by the FGT measure with a parameter value of 2 (see Ravallion, 1994). The poverty line corresponds to 45,446 Sucres per person per fortnight, the vulnerability line to 60,371. Expenditures across regions and sectors were adjusted with a Laspeyres price index based on the differential cost of a food basket yielding 2237 kcals per person per day (for selection of this cut-off point see Cabrera et al. 1993).
Source: LSMS, 1994.

The ranking of poverty between different regions and areas based on this 'snapshot' is not stable across poverty measures. While the observed pronounced difference between rural and urban areas holds for all three poverty measures, regional comparisons are sensitive to the poverty measure chosen. For the poverty line, the Costa region has a higher incidence of poverty both in the urban and rural areas than the Sierra. However, the severity of poverty is higher for both areas in the latter. The rural Oriente is the poorest region independently of the poverty measure and line chosen.

The most seriously endangered population group in Ecuador in 1994 were the 1.7 million people unable to finance a basic nutritional basket even if they spent everything they had on food. Table 2 shows the same poverty statistics as above for this extreme poverty line. Two third of the extremely poor live in rural areas, relatively equally distributed between the Sierra and the Costa. Again, the rural Oriente is by far the poorest area in the country irrespective of the poverty measure chosen but in population numbers both the rural Sierra and Costa are home to the largest groups of the extremely poor.

Table 2. Poverty in Ecuador 1994: Summary Measures for Extreme Poverty Line

		Incidence[a]	Depth[a]	Severity[a]	Distribution of Poor ('000)
Costa	urban	9	2	1	325
	rural	22	5	2	436
Sierra	urban	11	3	1	249
	rural	20	6	3	513
Oriente	urban	7	2	1	4
	rural	50	16	7	149
National	urban	10	3	1	578
	rural	22	6	3	1,098
Total		15	4	2	1,676

a   Poverty incidence is measured by the headcount ratio; poverty depth is measured by the FGT measure with a parameter of 1; poverty severity is measured by the FGT measure with a parameter value of 2 (see Ravallion, 1994). The extreme poverty line corresponds to 30,733 Sucres per person per fortnight. Expenditures across regions and sectors were adjusted with a Laspeyres price index based on the differential cost of a food basket yielding 2237 kcals per person per day (for selection of this cut-off point see Cabrera et al.,1993).

Source: LSMS, 1994.

How do these results compare to other studies of poverty in Ecuador? Comparing the results for our vulnerability line (as this is the methodology applied by other studies), the estimates obtained here are comparable but somewhat lower than reported in other studies of recent years (compare Table 3). All other studies base their estimates on an income measure of welfare and most of them use the Employment Survey of INEM (now conducted by INEC). As explained above -- and also particularly stressed in Working Paper 4 on rural poverty -- this survey is not ideal for the welfare measurement of households because it is likely to underestimate total household income. To counterbalance this underreporting of income, most studies adjust the mean average income of the surveys to GDP per capita. Two problems arise. First, it is quite unclear whether GDP per capita is indeed a good reference in an economy in which the informal sector plays such a predominant role. Second, all studies that followed such an adjustment procedure have made an implicit judgment about the distribution of urban versus rural GDP which is not available.

While we are 'confident' about our estimates as they were derived from a household survey specifically designed to measure the welfare of households, we would like to stress one specific point. Poverty estimates are always a 'snapshot' as they are based on one particular poverty line at one particular point in time. Much more important for the policy maker and actors in the social sector is what characteristics the poorest segments of society have. We will turn to this question later in this Working Paper. And to answer this question it is quite irrelevant whether nine out of ten people are poor in a country or whether 'only' every second person is poor.

Ranking and Robustness. Robustness tests show that rural poverty is indeed higher than urban poverty but that we can say little about poverty rankings if we add the Sierra-Costa-Oriente regional dimension. Varying the poverty line over an extremely wide range, we always find that rural poverty is higher than urban poverty, even independent of the different poverty measures shown in Table 1.[3] But we can make no judgment about poverty rankings when we integrate a regional dimension. Partly, this can be already gauged from looking at the 'snapshot' in Table 1: For the poverty line, the Costa region has a higher incidence of poverty both in the urban and rural areas than the Sierra. However, the severity of poverty -- which gives particular weight to the poorest of the poor -- is higher for both areas in the latter.

Table 3. Poverty Estimates For Ecuador

Study Incidence of	Year	Area	Poverty measure, survey	Poverty
Larrea (1990)	1988	urban national	vulnerability line: income vulnerability line: Employment Survey	60.7
Urbana Consult (1991)	1988	urban national	vulnerability line: income vulnerability line: Employment Survey	57.0
Aguingaga (1993)	1991	urban national	vulnerability line: income vulnerability line: Expenditure Survey	48.9
Cabrera et al. (1993)	1990	urban national rural national	income, Employment Survey income, Employment Survey	47.7 85.0
this study (1995)	1994	urban national rural national	vulnerability line, expenditure, LSMS vulnerability line, expenditure, LSMS	40.0 67.0
	1994	urban national rural national	poverty line, expenditure, LSMS poverty line, expenditure, LSMS	25.0 47.0

This list only includes several of the large amount of studies measuring poverty in Ecuador.

Inequality of Consumption. Graph 1 below presents the familiar Lorenz curve of the distribution of consumption for urban and rural areas. We calculate the national Gini coefficient of expenditure distribution as .43, with the coefficient for urban consumption distribution at .43 and for rural at .37. While we observed that rural Ecuador is poorer judging from all three poverty indicators, consumption is more equally distributed in rural areas. Nevertheless, the bottom half of the population only accounted for slightly more than 25 percent of total rural consumption while the top decile realized more than 30 percent of expenditures. For the urban areas, the share of the bottom half of the population is even smaller at 22 percent while the top ten percent accounted for 34 percent in 1994.

A regional examination of a different inequality measure in expenditure distribution shows that pronounced differences exist. Graph 2 presents calculations of the Atkinson

---

[3]   We measure the robustness of the poverty estimates with statistical dominance tests. The results are included in Annex 1. The reader can intuitively follow the above-made argument by looking at Figure 1 in Working Paper 4 which plots the expenditure distribution functions for urban and rural Ecuador: no matter which cut-off point, or poverty line, we choose, it is always true that a higher proportion of the rural population live in poverty than of the urban population.

measure (E=2.0).[4] We find that inequality in the urban Sierra is clearly higher than inequality in the other regions and areas in Ecuador. Further, both Sierra regions show higher inequality than the Oriente regions. While inequality in the urban Costa is again higher than in the rural Costa, both areas show the most equal distribution of consumption in Ecuador.

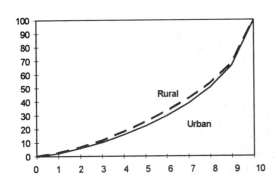

Graph 1. Distribution of Consumption, 1994   **Graph 2. Inequality in Consumption, 1994**

Source: LSMS, 1994.

2.   The Basic Services Indicator and Poverty

In recent years, the statistical institute of Ecuador (INEC) has produced a number of maps based on a Basic Services Indicator (BSI) which have been used as general poverty maps. Generally, INEC promotes these maps to identify geographic pockets of poverty (at the cantonal and parroquial level) and does not advocate to use the BSI to identify whether *individual* households are poor or not poor. The BSI is a weighted composite of seven services which include electricity, water, garbage disposal, telephone service, sewerage, and hygiene and shower facilities. Each service is assigned a certain number of points according to its availability and type of supply.[5] INEC applied the measurement to the Census of 1990 and developed separate urban and rural poverty maps.[6]

INEC chose to develop these maps based on the BSI indicator instead of an expenditure or income measure of poverty mainly because the Census did not include such variables. But the skepticism towards using welfare based poverty measures was also very high due to the difficulty to price services, especially water, at a common price for all

---

[4]   The Atkinson inequality parameter E reflects the degree of inequality aversion. The higher is E, the more sensitive is the measure to inequality among the poor. As E goes to infinity we become solely concurred with the level of the lowest income in the distribution. An $E=2$ is generally considered as quite inequality averse.

[5]   The following weighting is used: water supply: public net 250, water truck 50, well 25, other 0; sewerage: public net 150, septic tank 50, other tank 25, none 0; electricity: available 100, not available 0; telephone service: yes 200, no 0; garbage disposal: collected 75, other 0; hygiene facility: exclusive use 150, joint use 50, latrine 25, none 0; shower: yes 75, no 0.

[6]   INEC (1993a) and INEC (1993b).

households. As outlined in Annex 1, we have tried to adjust for these differences in prices by imputing water and housing expenditures.

It is difficult to judge how good the geographic ranking contained in INEC's poverty maps is. The LSMS is a household survey and it is hence not possible to derive a desegregate geographic ranking which could be compared to INEC's maps. Two observations are important, however. First, while it is commendable that geographic poverty maps are developed and used in Ecuador, the Basic Service Indicator is only an ad-hoc measure which can probably be improved considerably if it contained relationships between basic services (and other variables), on the one hand, and household expenditures, on the other. Annex 2 reports on some early results we have obtained in using the LSMS to derive such models which can then be applied to the Census.

Second, we would like to warn against using the BSI (or a related indicator) to identify *individual* poor households instead of identifying larger geographic areas. A simple experiment illustrates why we make this point: We first calculate the BSI index for all households contained in the LSMS. We then choose the population with the 25 percent lowest BSI in urban areas and the lowest 47 percent in rural areas according to the poverty rates for the poverty line as presented above. If the BSI is a good indicator of poverty, the identified population with a low basic service indicator should coincide with the poor population. In Graphs 3 and 4 we picture the overlap of the two indicators by expenditure quintile. A bar to the left of the axis shows the percentage of the quintile population which is poor but not identified so by the Basic Services Indicator. A bar to the right of the axis, on the other hand, shows the percentage of the quintile population which is not poor but identified as such by the BSI. As can be observed, a serious mismatch between the BSI and poverty exists in both urban and rural areas. Hence, using such indicators for individual targeting should not be contemplated.

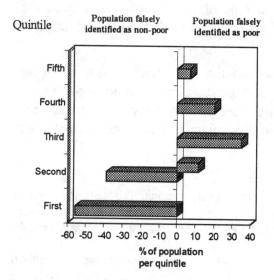

Graph 3. Urban Ecuador: Poverty and BSI

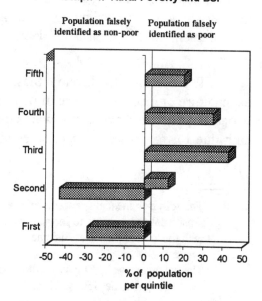

Graph 4. Rural Poverty and BSI

Source: LSMS, 1994.

3.   A Profile of the Poor

What are the characteristics of the poor? How do they live and work? How do their access to services, health and education compare to the rich's access? We will examine these and other related questions in this section. Most of the analysis is presented by expenditure quintiles which gives us an insight into the relationship between expenditures and socio-economic variables. If we refer to the 'poor' and the 'non-poor', we stick to the poverty line estimate (35 percent) -- and not the vulnerability line -- for the purpose of this Working Paper.

As a reference for the reader we include a table containing cross-tabulations variables in Annex 3 of this Working Paper to ion refer. The quintiles presented in Annex 3 are nce cover the same expenditure ranges in both the first urban and rural quintile make the 20 they do not represent 20 percent of the rural and

hips between variables such as household size id poverty, on the other, are not as clear as World Bank and elsewhere has shown that the larger households. This is generally explained in l single mothers with kids, tend to live with their to secure assistance in old age. Lacking birth ther reason, aggravating their already strained tween household size and poverty builds on the ole and non-durable consumption goods in the differently, it is assumed that no economies of If this assumption is relaxed, the relationship be reevaluated.[7]

en access to services and poverty can indicate etter able to afford service connection, such as for a telephone, or they can move into areas which have a good coverage with basic services and are therefore more expensive. On the other hand, causality can also run the other way. Several basic services are a prerequisite for a family to be able to earn income which will pay for basic life necessities. Decent hygiene facilities, potable water supply and garbage collection are necessary in crowded cities to avoid diseases. And if people are ill they cannot learn or work at their full strength hence reducing their income earning capabilities. Similarly, many inhabitants of rural Ecuador have no electricity. Opportunities for these rural households to earn their living from non-agricultural incomes through, e.g. home-based textile production, are hampered. Although lacking services at one point in time might not determine a family as poor or not poor, this might well be the

---

[7]   See Lanjouw and Ravallion (1994).

case if we think more about the role of basic services as *enabling* people to grow out of poverty.

Household Characteristics. Clear differences between poor and non-poor households emerge with respect to the composition of the household. Poverty is a function of the degree to which the household is extended, that is, how many relatives, such as the elderly or daughters with their own children, are part of the household. About 60 percent of Ecuador's population lives in nuclear households. Extending the households to accommodate one or two more people does not raise the likelihood of the household being poor, but once three or more people are taken in, poverty increases rapidly in households with only one wage earner. Overall, about fifteen percent of the population live in such strongly extended households, of which half are poor, while only about one third of the nuclear and mildly extended households are poor. In the Cisne Dos sample survey on urban poverty in Guayaquil, such expansion of households emerged as one of the main methods of shielding elderly or young relatives with children from falling into extreme poverty.

From this observation, it follows that more of the young and old are poor than the middle-aged (Graph 5).   Since poor households tend to contain a higher number of children and to provide shelter for extended family members, such as the elderly, the age-poverty profile falls with age and then rises again. While more than forty percent of the population below fourteen live in poverty, less than thirty percent of the population at age thirty to fifty are poor. For the elderly, this ratio again rises above forty percent.

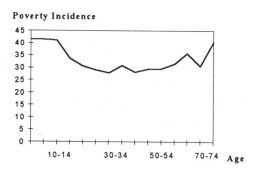

Graph 5. Age distribution of Poverty

Poverty Incidence

Households headed by certain types of people also have a high risk of poverty. These are not, as one might have expected, women. The LSMS and the survey in Cisne Dos both show that female-headed households do not have a higher poverty incidence than male-headed households.[8] Rather, households headed by middle-aged men living in an *'union libre'* with their partner and elderly female-headed households are both significantly more likely to be poorer than all other types of households.[9] This applies to urban and rural areas alike. It appears that widowhood is a key determinant of poverty for many of the rural poor: In the Rural Qualitative Assessment conducted for this Poverty Report, rural people named widows as a particularly poor group because many of them cannot work in the fields and are dependent on outside help.

---

[8]   This finding can be explained partly by the tendency of very poor female-headed households to move in with their relatives since they simply cannot afford to live alone. Compare Working Paper 3 for the Cisne Dos qualitative=five study.

[9]   Male-headed *union libre* households have a poverty rate of 46 percent; of the total poor, almost one third live in such households. If the heads of households are widows, the poverty rate is 60 percent. However, only about 5 percent of the total poor live in widow-headed households.

Housing Materials. Types and quality of housing differ between the poor and non-poor but also between rural and urban areas. Congestion within houses is highest among the poor in urban areas, but the rural poor are considerably more likely to be living in houses with mud or wooden walls and dirt floors. Stone is clearly the preferred housing material in all regions and areas, but few of the poor have access to this material. Further, more poor than non-poor people rent their houses in urban areas, a fact that we found of high importance in the case study of Cisne Dos (Working Paper 3). One of the major strategies for households to shield themselves from poverty is to use their house as a shelter or nest for impoverished relatives and for informal sector activities. Often, such use goes hand in hand with small investments made in the house (e.g., addition of another room as a garage or work space), which can be done to a much lesser extent in rented structures.

Basic Services. The link between poverty and basic services is not uniform but depends on area, region, and type of service. The rural non-poor are worse off than the urban poor in relation to water supply, hygiene facilities, garbage disposal, and electricity connection. However, services can have a different function in urban and rural areas, e.g., the threat from lack of hygiene facilities in rural areas is much lower than in the overcrowded urban centers, especially in the Costa, where the climate helps to breed diseases.

Access to basic services also varies by region. The Sierra is better off in almost all services than the Costa and the Oriente, and this distinction is especially pronounced among the urban poor in these areas. About half the poor in the urban Costa and Oriente dump their trash on the street or burn it, while only one quarter of the poor in the urban Sierra do so; the trash in the Sierra is collected for three quarters of the poor population. Similarly, about half the urban poor in the Costa need to meet their water supply from water trucks, wells, or other private sources because they are not connected to the public water network, implying high prices for water. In Cisne Dos, the low-income community in Guayaquil that we studied in depth (Working Paper 3), half of all households are solely dependent on water truck vendors. In the Sierra, on the other hand, four out of five poor people obtain their water from the public network and have a flush toilet. Not all services render themselves useful to distinguish the living conditions of the poor from the non-poor. Electricity in urban Ecuador now reaches nearly every household, independent of its status. In rural areas, however, there is a strong relationship between electricity connection and poverty -- most markedly in the Sierra and the Oriente. Similarly, telephone service is not a distinguishing factor for the rural population but it is for the urban population.

Education

The *World Development Report 1990* showed that education and poverty reduction are closely linked. Education increases the productivity of labor, the principal asset of the poor. At the individual level, increased productivity leads to higher incomes; at the macroeconomic level, it leads to higher growth rates, which in turn create employment and lead to higher wages. And this virtuous circle can be observed not only in modern economic sectors but also in the rural and informal sectors.

Educational Achievement and Poverty Today. The educational snapshot we take for Ecuador tells a very similar story. Linking education of the household head to expenditure levels, we find a very strong correlation especially in urban areas. More than

80 percent of first quintile household heads hold only a primary school degree or even less in urban Ecuador. In contrast, more than 70 percent of the heads of households in the richest quintile have at least a secondary school degree. In rural areas, this relationship between education and poverty is also observable but much less pronounced. The same holds true for literacy rates: illiteracy in Ecuador is low today, affecting about 10 percent of the poor in urban and somewhat more than 20 percent of the poor in rural areas. Almost 30 percent of the first quintile population in the rural Sierra are illiterate and the rate decreases rapidly with expenditure quintile.

While current poverty is strongly influenced by what Ecuadoran fathers and mothers learned in their youth, the poverty of the next generation will depend on what the children of the poor learn today. Attendance levels in primary and secondary schools, repetition and failure rates, the degree to which children miss classes due to health problems or work loads, and the quality of education all determine the potential for poor children to escape poverty in the course of their lives.

Primary School: Attendance, Repetition, and Drop-out Rates: Primary school attendance in urban and rural Ecuador is almost universal[10] (around 90 percent), and does not vary significantly with poverty group, but early grade repetition is high and drop-out rates of poor children are clearly higher than for non-poor children. While the average primary school repetition rate is 8 percent, which compares quite favorably to other Latin American countries,[11] a

Table 4. Repetition and Drop-Out Rates in Primary School, 1994		
	Poor	Non-Poor
Repetition		
- first grade	18.4	13.5
- second grade	8.5	5.9
Drop-out primary	**13.3**	**5.0**
Source: LSMS, 1994.		

closer examination shows that the first grader repetition rate is 18.5 percent for poor children and 13.5 percent for non-poor ones. While repetition rates in higher grades decline (partly because the repeaters drop-out of school), the clear link between poverty and repetition remains. The same picture emerges when we look at drop-out rates for primary school: of the 13- to 15-year old children (who had all started primary school but are no longer enrolled in primary school, we find that 13.3 percent of poor children and only 5 percent of non-poor children leave school before completing the six-year cycle.

Secondary School: Attendance, Repetition, and Drop-out Rates. There is a major distinction between poor and non-poor attendance in secondary schools. Graphs 6 and 7 illustrate the attendance rate in secondary schools of children by age. Up to 90 percent of children from families in the highest expenditure quintile attend secondary schools in both urban and rural areas but only 30 percent of the poor in the urban area and almost none in the rural area attend secondary school. The difference in the attendance record does not stem from

---

[10]   Parents have protected the primary education of their children in the past years. In the two qualitative surveys which we conducted in urban and rural areas (Working Papers 3 and 5), parents have explicitly stated that they did not take their children out of primary school during economically hard times. Nevertheless, the children often had to balance the attendance of primary school with increased work demands in the household.

[11]   According to the UNICEF (1993), repetition rates for primary school in other LAC countries are Brazil 19 percent, Costa Rica 11 percent, Columbia 11 percent, El Salvador 8 percent, Mexico 9 percent, Paraguay 9 percent, Uruguay 9 percent and Venezuela 11 percent.

the distance to the nearest secondary school, which is only slightly lower for the non-poor children (33 vs. 37 minutes in rural areas and 25 vs. 28 minutes in urban areas).

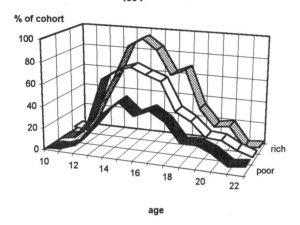

Graph 6. Urban Secondary School Attendance, 1994

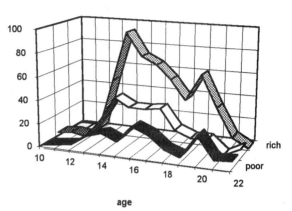

Graph 7. Rural Secondary School Attendance, 1994

Source: LSMS, 1994.

Repetition and drop-out rates during secondary school again illustrate the difference between the poor and non-poor. Repetition rates in the beginning years of secondary schools are consistently higher for the poor children, at 16 percent in the first year of secondary school and at 14 percent in the second year. Even more pronounced, the drop-out rate during the basic cycle of secondary

Table 5. Repetition and Drop-out Rates in Secondary School, 1994		
	Poor	**Non-Poor**
Repetition		
- first grade	16.1	9.0
- second grade	14.0	9.6
Drop-Out		
- basic cycle	22.9	8.3
- advanced cycle	16.3	12.1
Source: LSMS, 1994.		

school is 22.9 percent and during the advanced three-year cycle another 16.3 percent for poor children. Of the few poor children who actually start school, about two-fifths drop out before completing the secondary degree.[12]

Private Returns: Private returns to education are significant, as illustrated by the earnings equation which includes a large number of exogenous variables,[13] with dummy variables specified for different levels of schooling. We find that the earnings differential between base and end primary school years is modest, which points to the poor quality of primary education. But private returns increase significantly for secondary

Graph 8. Private Yearly Returns to Education

Source: LSMS, 1994.

---

[12]   The drop-out rate for the basic secondary cycle is calculated for the fifteen to seventeen year old population and the drop-out rate for the advanced cycle is calculated for the twenty to twenty-two year old population.

[13]   Compare Working Paper 8.

education, reaching about 9 percent for women and 11 and 13 percent for men. The earnings differential due to college education is extremely high for women, even surpassing that for secondary education, but it declines somewhat for men.

The Private Costs of Public Education.
While education definitely pays off in the long run, the private costs of education are high even in public schools. Although families pay only a low registration fee in public schools, there are other significant costs for books, writing materials, uniforms, and transport. For poor families, sending a child to primary school costs

Table 6. Private Costs of Public Education Per Child (Average Budget Share)		
	Poor	Non-Poor
Primary School	2.0	1.8
Secondary School	4.0	2.9

Source: LSMS, 1994.

about 2 percent of their budget (1.8 percent for the non-poor), and sending a child on to public secondary education absorbs 4 percent their budget (2.9 percent for the non-poor). Asked why their children (aged 14 and 15) do not attend secondary school, half of poor parents surveyed mentioned these direct costs as the primary reason, while only twenty percent of non-poor parents viewed these costs as a major obstacle.

Two aspects of these costs of education require attention. First, the private costs of public education are not fixed. They are discretionary with respect to the type of uniform, number and quality of books, and type of transport the child takes to school. In absolute terms, non-poor families spend 80 percent more on educating their child in a public primary school and 60 percent more on the education in a public secondary school. Second, poor households tend to have more young dependents than non-poor households. Education can therefore quickly absorb ten or fifteen percent of total household expenditures.[14]

In addition to the private direct costs of public education, the opportunity costs of keeping children in school for a longer time are very high, especially for poor households. While field interviews in Guayaquil and seven rural communities indicate that poor parents make a serious effort to keep their children in primary school, they also highlight the costs of keeping children in primary and secondary school. In rural Ecuador, child labor is particularly important in times of scarce household income, and three out of the seven communities view female and child labor as the most or second most important source of scarce income. In Cisne Dos, 12- to 14-year old boys and girls spend an average of fifteen hours per week assisting in household enterprises. For girls, there are also additional household tasks, especially caring for younger siblings.

Social Security

The Ecuadoran social security system is in a deep crisis. Numerous studies have concluded that, if the current operation of the Ecuadoran Social Security Institute (IESS) continues, the system will collapse financially in the near future.[15] The real value of IESS

---

14   The importance of the private costs of education are also reflected in the Cisne Dos survey (Working Paper 3). In this low-income community, education expenditures comprise the single largest non-consumption expenditure, significantly lower at the primary than at the secondary or tertiary level. Nearly a third of overall education expenditure is on books, a quarter on uniforms, and almost 14 per cent on transportation.

15   Mesa-Lago (1993).

assets fell by over 25 percent between 1978 and 1991, owing largely to highly subsidized personal and mortgage loans which represented up to 90 percent of invested assets in the mid-1980s. These loans are not subsidized any more but financial problems continue because projected expenditures for pensions, the main benefit extended under the IESS, will far exceed projected income from contributions. Two of the main contributors to the social security system, the central government and employers, are far behind with their payments.

The two-part social security system extends benefits far beyond old-age pensions. The social security system is composed of the General Security System and the Peasant Insurance. Coverage of the General System is quite low by Latin American standards -- about a third of the work force -- but the insured enjoy more benefits and entitlements than in most countries in the region.[16] Those insured under the General System are protected against most social risks, comprising: old age, disability and survivor pensions; medical, hospital and dental care; medicines; paid leave in the case of illness; maternity and occupational accidents and diseases; severance payments, unemployment pensions and funeral aid. The maternal health program extends additional health benefits. All these benefits from the General System are, however, open only for the actual affiliates with the IESS and not their dependents. The second tier of the IESS is the Peasant Insurance. Created in 1968 specifically to extend social benefits also to the poor rural population, the Peasant Insurance scheme is comprised of old age and disability pensions, funeral aid and health services. Contrary to General Security System, also dependents of the affiliate are enrolled in the scheme and can use, e.g., the health facilities.

Social security benefits are unevenly distributed. Pensions for military personnel are much higher than for public or private employees. While IESS health expenditures per capita are about five times as high than comparable expenditures of the Ministry of Health, they are very unevenly distributed. The ratio of hospital beds per 1,000 insured among provinces ranges from four to one, heavily biased in favor of urban areas. The best hospitals are concentrated in Quito and Guayaquil, many provinces have no IESS hospitals at all. In 1990, the ratio of physicians per 10,000 insured was sixteen for the General System and only one for the Peasant Insurance.[17]

In its current form the poor in Ecuador benefit little from the social security system because the poor's coverage is low and benefits reaching them are minimal. Using household data from the LSMS, we calculate that General Social Security System coverage of the urban population in the highest expenditure quintile as 27 percent while it is only around 7 percent for the poor. The General System mainly includes workers in the formal and regulated sector of the economy which explains that the poor's access to the system is much more limited than for wealthier groups in society. Only 2 percent of the poor elderly (above sixty) receive pension payments from IESS (1994) while 15 percent of the non-poor elderly receive these pensions. Health service is the largest potential current benefit but due to the quality of the service under the General System, 22 percent of the poor who are entitled to the service choose to attend private clinics instead of any public health centers or hospitals. The Peasant Insurance covers a higher percentage of the poor

---

[16]   Mesa-Lago (1993).
[17]   Mesa-Lago (1993).

in rural areas (19 percent in the lowest and 12 percent in the second quintile). We find that about 27 percent of the rural population in the first two quintiles do not attend the rural health posts (or any other public health facilities) set up by the Peasant Insurance although they are entitled to it. They seek medical attention in private clinics instead because posts are ill-equipped and often lack essential medicine.[18]

Health Care

Importance. The *World Development Report 1993* spelled out the important role of public basic health care: providing cost-effective health services to the poor is an effective and socially acceptable way to reduce poverty; many health-related services provide information that helps control contagious diseases; and Government intervention helps to compensate for problems of economic uncertainty and insurance market failure. The *WDR* also stresses the link between basic health care and malnutrition.

Health Statistics. Ecuador's health statistics compare quite unfavorably with those of most other middle-income Latin countries. A 1992 infant mortality rate of 45 per one thousand births is high compared to, e.g., Colombia (21), El Salvador (40), Costa Rica (14), Panama (21), and Chile (17),[19] and the same holds for the under-five mortality rate of 64 per one thousand births in 1992. Lack of safe water and sanitation, the prevalence of infectious and communicable diseases, and malnutrition are the most common causes of child death in Ecuador. With a maternal mortality rate of 170 per one hundred thousand births (1992), Ecuador lies slightly behind El Salvador (148 in 1988) but is clearly worse off than Costa Rica (18 in 1988), Panama (60 in 1988) and Chile (40 in 1988).[20] The vaccination of minors against tuberculosis, measles, polio, and dyptheria have, on the other hand, been largely successful: the LSMS records coverage rates above 90 percent for all types of vaccinations, independent of area, region, and poverty class (see Annex 3).

Sector Institutions. Numerous institutions comprise Ecuador's public health system. The largest provider is the Provincial Health Directorates of the Ministry of Health which treats 27 percent of the people seeking professional curative care (38 percent of the poor, 23 percent of the non-poor). The second largest provider is the Ecuadoran Social Security Institute (IESS), which has its own network including hospitals and pharmacies. The IESS also provides two formal insurance schemes -- the General Social Security System which covers only the affiliated individuals themselves, and the Peasant Insurance Scheme which also covers the dependents. As discussed above, the IESS is the only provider of formal health insurance, and both of its schemes together serve about 11 percent of all people seeking professional curative care (12 percent of the poor, 10 percent of the non-poor). The Ministry of Defense administers hospitals and other facilities for military personnel and their dependents which provide about 1 percent of curative treatments. Finally, the Charity Board of Guayaquil and several small programs under the responsibility of other small agencies and NGOs (6.6 percent of the population) complete the complex public involvement in the health sector.

Real public expenditures of the largest public health entity, the Ministry of Health, decreased continuously over the past years. Between 1990 and 1993 alone, the budget

---

[18]   See ILDIS (1994).
[19]   World Bank (1993).
[20]   World Bank (1993).

allocated to the health sector as a share of the total central Government budget decreased from 8.2 percent to 5.4 percent, and real per capita spending declined by 37 percent. The public expenditures of Ministry of Health tend to benefit the poor most: about forty percent of the Ministry of Health resources benefit the thirty-five percent of the population that is poor. Conversely, the wealthiest quintile of the Ecuadoran population obtains only about eleven percent of expenditures.[21] The overall constraint on resources has meant diminishing funds for all types of expenditures. As a result, salaries are low and there are little or no funds for medicines, supplies, and equipment repairs. In many hospitals, particularly in rural areas, it is common for nurses to give patients a list of items to be purchased in the private sector, which they must bring with them to the hospital. Even so, there is a substantial bias in expenditures toward the larger, curative care hospitals in the urban centers. About 45 percent of total Ministry of Health resources support 32 large urban hospitals, while only 35 percent is allocated for primary care facilities.[22]

The public health system in Ecuador is problem ridden. As amply demonstrated in a large number of investigations,[23] the main problems are: (a) large gaps in service provision of a basic health care package, especially in rural areas; and (b) insufficient quality of health services due to maldistribution of resources and underfunding. This affects both rural centers, due to lack of medical staff and drugs, and urban hospitals. The World Bank estimated in 1992 that up to half of all public hospital beds are unusable due to leaking roofs and the lack of drugs.[24] Still, many public hospitals run by the Ministry of Health are found to be underutilized.[25] Other problems are (c) duplication of health services supplied by the major public sector agencies due to lack of coordination, leading to a waste of scarce resources; (d) staffing imbalances heavily favoring urban areas (as an outcome of this biased provision of basic health care, the health status of the population varies widely. For example, the infant mortality rate ranges between 20 per 1000 in certain urban areas to 150 per 1000 in remote rural ones); and (e) emphasis on curative instead of preventive care and health education (health education, theoretically also a responsibility of the Ministry of Health) is only given a low priority. For example, about a quarter of demand for family planning education is not met by either private or public facilities.[26]

Type of Health Care. The Living Standard Measurement Survey reports that the type of health treatment varies considerably with the material standing of a family. If medical treatment is necessary, many poor families, especially in the rural areas, choose either to treat their ill members with home remedies or to seek advice from a pharmacist. This pattern is more pronounced in rural than

Table 7. Health: How are the Sick Treated?		
	Poor	Non-Poor
by doctor/nurse	49	64
by pharmacist	22	13
by home remedy	11	10
no remedy (not nec.)	6	7
no remedy (no money or far away)	12	6
Source: LSMS, 1994.		

---

[21]   Compare Working Paper 6.

[22]   Enriquez (1994).

[23]   IDB (1993); ILDIS (1994); Mesa-Lago (1993), UNICEF-DyA (1992), World Bank (1992), World Bank (1990)

[24]   World Bank (1992).

[25]   World Bank (1990).

[26]   ILDIS (1994).

in urban areas. Nationally, almost two-thirds of the non-poor population seek professional treatment (if they are sick) from either a nurse or a doctor while only about half of the poor do so; the other half either turns to a pharmacist, to self-curing or is condemned to do nothing. Twice as many poor (12 percent) than non-poor state that they were not able to afford necessary treatment or medicine. Even 6 percent of the non-poor are caught in this trap.

In the seven villages participating in the Rural Qualitative Assessment (Working Paper 5), poor families said they would spend less on health care (including transport to clinics) if money is short for food. Many households have opted to limit visits to clinics and hospitals to the strictly unavoidable, and instead visit traditional curers and midwives. Similarly, they often use locally available herbs and other remedies instead of antibiotics or other prescription medication.

Public vs. Private Curative Care. The private sector performs a large part of professional curative medical services even for the poorest groups in Ecuador, signaling that basic public health services are in scarce supply. While the non-poor are more likely to turn to the private sector for professional health services, 42.5 percent of the poor also seek private services when they need to see a nurse or a doctor. Further, 37 percent of the extremely poor, who are not even able to afford a basic nutritional

Table 8. Professional Health Services: (Of those seeing a doctor or nurse)		
	Poor	Non-Poor
Public	52.5	35.0
- hospital	19.1	15.4
- health center	33.4	19.6
Private	42.5	57.9
Charity Board	4.9	7.1
NGOs	4.9	7.1
Source: LSMS, 1994.		

basket of goods, also turn to the more costly private sector rather than use the free or very low-cost public health service. As the trade-off between health care and food for these families is so extreme, it is likely that this group does not have access to a functioning public health center; the actual rate is probably much higher.[27]

The situation in Cisne Dos, the poor urban neighborhood in Guayaquil, illustrates the role of the private health sector in urban areas. Analysis of health facilities usage shows that the private sector, providing almost half the health care in that area, is as important as public facilities, which are used more for serious medical problems. Preference for private sector health care relates directly to perceived differences in quality of service. The long-term sustainability of private practices is related not only to diversification in the services offered, such as the combination of multiple specialties, a medical lab, and minor surgery, but also to the availability of credit for their services, short waiting times, and flexible hours. While public hospitals in the area are free, they are characterized by declining resources and infrastructure, long waiting times, and limited night access.

The Poor's Expenditures on Health. Health care is a very big budget item for the poor who turn to the private sector. Poor households seeking curative care predominantly from the private sector spend on average 12 percent of their total budget in urban and 17 percent in rural areas. For the non-poor, curative care averages less than 10 percent of expenditures in both areas. On the other hand, poor families that obtain curative care mainly from public sector

---

[27]   The poor report slightly longer travel and waiting times than the non-poor, both in urban and rural areas, but the difference is not very pronounced. The average travel time alone in rural areas to either public or private facilities is more than one hour. Private clinics serve their patients considerably faster (within twenty to thirty minutes of waiting) than public ones (seventy five minutes).

health posts or hospitals spend on average 6 percent of the budgets, and the non-poor spend 3 percent.

Summary. The poor suffer more than other groups from the weak basic public health network. While other public or semi-public institutions, namely IESS, the military, and the Charity Board are also part of the health system, about 85 percent of the poor do not have access to these institutions and so rely on the network run by the Ministry of Health. While the LSMS shows only the distribution and access to curative care, we have found that many of the poor -- and even the poorest of the poor -- turn to the private sector for emergency help. Such service is very expensive, requiring between 12 percent and 17 percent of their total budget per month. Close to half a million poor people without access to public health centers cannot afford private service or the purchase of essential medicine.

While the LSMS says little about a basic package of preventive health care, it is clear from available statistics that the system does not function properly. In 1992, more than 70 percent of births in rural areas (and 20 percent in urban areas) took place without professional help. Professional health consultations during pregnancies reach only half of the determined target rates: On average, pregnant mothers receive only two and half professional consultations (which mostly take place in the last three months of the pregnancy) before giving birth and one and a half after giving birth.[28] The ongoing treatment that are part of a basic health program include prenatal care, child delivery, postnatal controls, basic care for adults, immunizations, health education, nutrition education, surveillance, food supplements, and family planning services.

Nutrition

Malnutrition of infants and young children carries serious long-term implications. As a consequence of chronically inadequate food consumption or repeated episodes of illness, many children die in infancy. Those who survive are often malnourished, underweight, undersized, suffer more frequent and more severe illness, cannot learn, and end up being less productive as adults. Many who suffer from protein/calorie malnutrition also lack essential micronutrients such as iron, iodine, and vitamin A, the lack of which can cause irreversible mental retardation.[29]

Malnutrition Rates of Minors. Malnutrition rates for children below the age of five are extremely high in Ecuador. While the Government has made progress over the last decade in reducing malnutrition, the absolute rates of both chronic and global malnutrition in 1990 were still at alarming levels. Forty-five percent of children below the age of five were chronically malnourished (i.e. their height was low for their age), and 33.9 percent were globally malnourished (i.e., they displayed low weight for their age). This implies that close to 800,000 children below the age of five were malnourished in Ecuador in 1990. The rates increase with age but even in the first five months, when babies are nourished from their mother's milk, fifteen percent of the babies show signs of chronic malnutrition. According to the 1986 national nutrition survey and subsequent sample surveys, about 80 percent of child malnutrition

---

[28]   INEC (1992).
[29]   Musgrove (1991).

occurs among children under age two. Furthermore, 70 percent of children between ages 1 and 2 have iron deficiency anemia.[30]

There is a pronounced variation in malnutrition rates among regions and areas, with the rural Sierra holding the saddest record: almost seven out of ten children were malnourished in 1990 (Table 9). The Rural Qualitative Assessment (RQA), which examined five indigenous communities in the Sierra (Working Paper 5), shows that saving on food purchases is often the only possibility for rural families to reduce expenditures in hard times. Additionally, many indigenous families consume a poor and repetitive diet, consisting mainly of barley flour, cinnamon, potatoes, and water.[31]

Malnutrition rates are strongly associated with socio-economic variables.[32] Maternal education of the mother and household living conditions are important determinants of child malnutrition: more educated mothers can compose a more balanced diet for their children and at the same time their higher education helps them to earn an income sufficient to buy elemental foodstuff. Similarly, better household living conditions, such as non-dirt floors, water supply and decent hygiene facilities, will reduce illnesses affecting the children. Better living conditions are themselves an indication of a more wealthy household which can afford a better nutrition.

Table 9. Malnutrition Rates by Region and Area, 1982, 1986, 1990[a]

		Chronic Malnutrition				Global Malnutrition			
		1982	1986	1990	d(82-90)	1982	1986	1990	d(82-90)
Sierra	urban	50.2	44.2	45.1	-5.1	35.1	31.9	30.5	-4.6
	rural	69.8	66.6	67.0	-2.8	51.9	47.4	48.5	-3.4
Costa	urban	41.8	37.3	34.4	-7.4	31.7	30.2	26.4	-5.3
	rural	47.1	47.3	43.3	-3.8	41.1	40.9	36.5	-4.6
National		51.0	49.4	45.3	-5.7	39.1	37.5	33.9	-5.2

a Children under the age of five.
Source: Freire and Waters (1994). Estimates based on Freire et al. (1992).

Malnutrition Among Women of Reproductive Age. Ecuador is a country with a serious micronutrient problem affecting low-income pregnant and lactating women. About 60 percent of the latter suffer from some degree of anemia due to deficiency of iron -- a life-sustaining nutrient needed only in small quantities and found in red meat and breastmilk as well as in grains, legumes and vegetables. High fertility and poor health exacerbate this problem, which is associated with the observed high maternal mortality and child malnutrition rates discussed above. Children born of anemic mothers are often stunted and sickly, and iron deficiency in the preschool years reduces their manual dexterity, limits their attention span, and lowers their ability to retain information. In the 1980s, a national nutrition survey found that 69

---

[30]   World Bank (1990). See also World Bank (1994, p. 60).

[31]   Weissmantel (1988).

[32]   A logit model explaining malnutrition rates by maternal education and household and social living conditions achieves a high explanatory power. See Freire and Waters (1994).

percent of infants and 46 percent of children 1 to 2 years old suffered from anemia in Ecuador. Deficiency in iron among adults also reduces energy and therefore the capacity to work. Since iron deficiency is prevalent among poor Ecuadoran women and children, anemia control should receive high visibility in maternal and child health programs. Additionally, as shown by the experience of the United States and Sweden, long-term iron fortification of selected and widely consumed foods, such as refined flour used in the production of bread and pasta, can dramatically reduce anemia.

Nutrition Programs and Coverage. Ecuador has a number of nutritional programs, administered by different ministries and agencies, that try to reach preschool children.[33] The programs, many of them financed by the World Food Program, include the *Programa de Complementacion Alimentaria Materno-Infantil* directed at pregnant and breastfeeding mothers and their

Table 10. Nutritional Programs in Ecuador: Coverage of children below the age of 5 (percent)		
	1990	1994
Poor	n.a.	5.5
Non-Poor	n.a.	3.4
	—	—
Total	10.8	4.3

Source: Musgrove (1991) and LSMS, 1994.

infants (6-23 months), operated by the Ministry of Health through health centers; the nutritional component of the Operation Rescue the Children (ORI), which offers nutritional supplements in its daycare centers; the feeding component of the National Institute of Children and the Family (INNFA), which works through children's centers; and the small CARITAS-supported Mothers Club program.[34] There are also a number of nutrition programs aimed at the primary school population, but they are not targeted at the most vulnerable malnourished group, namely children below the age of five and pregnant mothers. In-depth analyses of many of these programs have concluded that they (a) do not supply children or lactating mothers with nutritional aid over a continuous period of time, which undermines their nutritional impact; (b) are tiny in scope; and (c) operate independently of each other so whatever impact that could be achieved is jeopardized.[35]

The targeting efficiency of the nutrition programs is generally unknown. Examining two nutrition programs, INNFA and ORI, we found that both have developed targeting frameworks based on a combination of geographical targeting and self-selection mechanisms; additionally, INNFA assesses the nutrition status of individual children who enter the program. The potential for geographical targeting is limited, however, since both programs depend on existing daycare center infrastructure and can only target priority areas at the margin. Further, INNFA and ORI, like the other targeted social program we studied, need to improve their monitoring and evaluation method in order to assess how many the poor and malnourished children they reach.

An evaluation of all nutritional programs directed at infants and children below the age of five, including the ones offered by NGOs, shows that they achieve an extremely low

---

[33]   The programs listed here do not include the school feeding programs.

[34]   Additionally, the nutrition component under the World Bank-supported primary health project, FASBASE, provides nutritional supplements as an integral part of the basic primary health care package to be provided in health facilities. The component included nutritional education and promotion, growth monitoring and the provision of food supplements and micronutrients. The project will finance US$6 million for this nutritional component until 1999.

[35]   Compare UNICEF, DyA (1992); World Bank (1990); Feire and Waters (1994); Musgrove (1991).

coverage rate. While the programs leak somewhat to non-poor children, the errors of excluding poor malnourished children are clearly higher and weigh much more than the errors of including well-nourished children. Of the one and a half million Ecuadoran children below the age of five, about 600,000 lived in poor households in 1994 and only 5.5 percent of these were reached by the various nutrition programs. Total coverage of the under-five population stood at 4.3 percent, a clear decrease from the 10.8 percent coverage achieved in 1990. This decrease was largely due to the discontinuation of the *Red Comunitaria*, a community-based childcare network supported by the Ministry of Social Welfare, in 1993. The *Red Comunitaria* was replaced by Operation Child Rescue (ORI), which is achieving lower than programmed coverage rates due to financial restraints.

Labor Market Characteristics

In this section, we look at some of the labor market characteristics of the different population quintiles in Ecuador. We examine broad characteristics such as the rate of labor force participation and reasons why working-age adults do not actively participate in the labor market. We describe the distribution of the labor force among broad sectors, economic activities, regulation characteristics and unionization. Further, we analyze whether poorer workers hold their job permanently or temporarily, whether they change their jobs frequently and whether they are eligible for pensions as are wealthier workers (see also data in Annex 3). This section does not describe general features of the Ecuadoran labor market which the reader can study in depth in Working Papers 8 and 9.

Labor Force Participation. While male labor force participation is high in all areas and regions and varies relatively little with expenditure class, we observe differences in the degree of female labor force participation between regions and a marked increase of female participation for higher expenditure classes. As observed in Annex 3, male labor force participation fluctuates around 80 percent in both urban and rural areas, independent of the region we look at. The fluctuation is somewhat higher in the rural areas, especially in the Costa where the participation rate is about 70 percent for the first and fifth quintile but jumps to 90 percent for the third quintile. On the other hand, participation in the labor force is lower for the poorest women in Ecuador than for wealthier ones. At the national level we find a clear trend that poorer women are less probable to be integrated in the labor force than richer ones.

The difference in the pattern of labor force participation between men and women becomes more accentuated if we add an age dimension. Graphs 9 and 10 compare the participation rates of men and women in five year intervals between 15 and 64 -- the generally assumed 'working age' -- for the different expenditure quintiles. To ease the graphical interpretation, we aggregate the lowest two and the following two population quintiles. While poorer men start to work earlier in their life cycle (largely because they tend not to be in school that long), the participation rates between the different groups is not significantly different. For females, however, we observe a markedly lower participation rate for the poorer group -- only at the very end of the working life cycle (age 60-64) does the difference between the participation rates for the three groups become insignificant.

Graph 9. Male Labor Force Participation, 1994

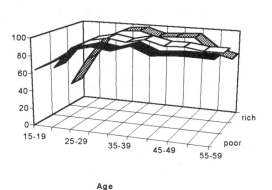

Age

Graph 10. Female Labor Force Participation, 1994

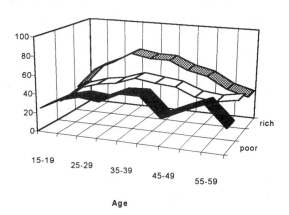

Age

Source: LSMS, 1994.

Another observation relating to spouse work supports the argument that female labor participation is an important determinant of the ability of families to shed themselves from poverty. Given our above finding about the correlation between female labor participation and expenditure quintiles, we are not surprised to find that of the male-headed households fewer fall into the lowest two quintiles if their spouses work.

Household and child care duties are the major reason why women do not participate in the workforce and this is the more pressing the poorer the women are which holds especially in urban areas. The LSMS records that 63 percent of the women belonging to the lowest expenditure quintile cannot work because their work in the household does not allow them to do so. This ratio steadily decreases with higher expenditure groups and the same reason is an obstacle for 46 percent of the women in the highest quintile. While this is still a high number, the trend signifies that wealthier women are better able to hand over household and childcare tasks to domestic servants or childcare centers.

<u>Labor Force Distribution.</u> We examine the distribution of the labor force in Ecuador using four categories. The first one looks at broad functional sectors: the public, informal, farm, and modern sectors. While the public sector is self-explanatory, we define the informal sector along standard ILO definitions as made up of those non-professional labor force participants which work in establishments with less than five employees. The farm sector is narrowly defined as only including agricultural day laborers and small farmers, the modern sector is composed of professionals, employers and workers in establishments with more than five employees. The second category relates to economic sector. We distinguish the agricultural sector from mining, manufacturing, service, construction and transport. The third categorization distinguishes between 'regulated' and 'unregulated' parts of the economy where we define a 'regulated' environment as one where the employee is entitled to the famous Ecuadoran teen-payments: Apart from the direct salary, the employee receives a thirteenth, fourteenth, fifteen, and even sixteenth

salary at varying times during the year. Naturally, only the sector of the economy which is somehow reached by legislation will award such payments. Finally, the LSMS also provides us with the opportunity to distinguish between union and non-unionized participants in the labor force which comprises our fourth categorization.

As expected, employment in the farm sector varies negatively, and in the public and modern sectors positively with per capita expenditures, but the more interesting finding relates to the role of the informal sector (compare Annex 3). First, in the urban areas, informal sector activities decrease with expenditure class. Poor women predominantly work in the informal sector (72 percent in the first quintile and 62 percent in the second) which appears to be their major option for entry into the labor market. The ratio of women working in the informal sector decreases much stronger with expenditure class than the ratio for men. Second, in the rural sector, we observe the opposite -- informal sector activity increases with expenditure class. Poorer male workers are less likely to be employed in the informal sector than better-off workers. The ratio of rural women to be working in the informal sector is again very high but not decreasing with the expenditure class and rather showing a slight increase, too. Both of these findings relating to the rural sector point to the immense importance off-farm employment plays today and its potential role in employment creation and income diversification.

Employment by economic activity shows a very different pattern by area and gender. In rural Ecuador, the agricultural sector is predominant, especially for the poor. The share of the work force in manufacturing (such as in small textile or ag processing plants) is a venue for women workers and service activities (such as trade) for men as their absorption increases with expenditure quintile. In urban areas, we find that around 80 percent of working women are employed in service activities, independent of the expenditure quintile. The same sector is important for men employed in urban Ecuador but here we trace a positive association with the expenditure class. Finally, we note that the construction sector is an entry to the urban labor market for 17 percent of the poorest men. Many migrants from the rural sector start out to work as day laborers on construction sites.[36]

Regulation appears to be a stronger correlate with poverty than unionism. Overall, 21 percent of the Ecuadoran labor force are employed in the regulated sector as defined above but it becomes clear from the presented data (Annex 3) that these are almost exclusively the non-poor in the urban areas. Half of the urban labor force in the highest expenditure quintile, both women and men, work in the regulated sector. The share of organized urban workers in the labor force does rise with higher expenditure quintiles but unionism is low. Nationally, only 9.7 percent of the labor force belong to a union, almost all of them are part of the urban labor force.

Other Work Characteristics. The poor change their jobs more frequently than the non-poor, they are less likely to be eligible for company or social security pensions and they are also less probable to engage into a secondary occupation apart from their main one. These differences hold across region and gender.

---

[36]   Waters (1991).

Gender

Poverty is a phenomenon which affects households independent of the gender of the household head. Based on the LSMS, we determine that women-headed households are not more likely to be poor than are men-headed households. Although it is widely assumed that a large proportion of the female-headed households are poor, we find that their share is almost constant across expenditure classes, being about 10 percent in rural areas and 16 percent to 17 percent in urban ones. This finding is supported by examining the expenditure survey by INEC from 1991.[37]

However, several observations which distinguish poor women's from poor men's lives are important and we can only name a few here. First, with reference to the labor market, female labor force participation is lower than the male one and varies with expenditure quintile. We have also noted that the informal sector plays a different role for women than for men, being a 'point of entry' into the urban labor force for poor women while being something like a 'road out of poverty' in rural areas. As pointed out in Working Paper 8, discrimination in the labor market is present as women earn 30 percent less income than men even though they show exactly the same characteristics relating to education and experience.

Second, the educational gap between women and men is narrowing but still present. Looking at the educational achievement by gender of headship, women are still less educated than men. In urban areas, for example, 95 percent of women as household heads achieved only a primary degree or less in the poorest expenditure quintile while the corresponding figure for male-headed households is 80 percent. This difference can be encountered in all quintiles, areas and regions (Annex 3). On the other hand, female enrollment in schools increased substantially over the past fifteen years. At the university level, for example, female enrollment as a percentage of total enrollment increased from 29 percent in 1970 to 47 percent in 1988.

Third, we pointed out above that a basic health program does not reach many of the poor in Ecuador and this affects women as the prime users. With 40 percent of all births in Ecuador unattended professionally, it does not come as a surprise that toxemia during pregnancy is responsible for 30 percent of maternal mortality. These and other maternal mortality deaths can be avoided with proper prenatal control. Little information is available on the enforcement of the Ecuadoran Labor Code which determines that women should not work two weeks prior and 10 weeks after giving births. But these and other provisions only reach few poor women as most of them work in the informal or farm sectors of the economy.

Fourth, domestic and street violence is a big problem for women. Surveys show that the rate of domestic violence is alarmingly high in Ecuador. Vega and Gomez (1994) find that the domestic violence rate in Quito is 58 percent and in Guayaquil 80 percent. While national data on the extent of street violence is not available, indications from Cisne Dos (Working Paper 3) mark this as a particular problem: over a 6-months period (Feb-July 1992), 50 percent of respondents witnessed a bus robbery, one third were victims of

---

[37]   CEPLAES (1994).

street and house theft, and more than half of family members were robbed. About half of the respondents identified the pantillas (gangs of young unemployed males) as a major cause of crime. This has resulted in a drop in the use of public transport, particularly at night, and increased use of safer small trucks by women working late shifts. In the case of night school this has resulted in lower attendance, again affecting women more than men, unwilling to travel on public transport at night.

Fifth, female representation in Ecuadoran politics is far from achieved but increasing steadily. Of all provincial and national delegates from 1979 to 1992, only 3.5 percent were women. Close to 10 percent of all judges in the judicial administration are women today. However, if we extrapolate from the candidacies for elections, a steady increase in female participation becomes visible. Also, the decade of the 1980s has witnessed an increasing importance female leaders have in community and farmers organizations and unions.[38]

Ethnicity

The 'definition' of the indigenous people is a difficult undertaking because there are no objective characteristics to apply. Indigenous languages (e.g., quechua, shuari), traditional clothing, heritage, and observed traditions and believes can, but need not be, part of the life of the indigenous people. Ultimately, the classification of who is indigenous depends on self-identification. All statistical estimates of the exact number of the indigenous people based on a uni-dimensional indicator are hence bound to be imprecise and, at best, indicative.

Nevertheless, for the purpose of this study, we use language as a variable which we think is going to be highly correlated with ethnicity and which can provide us some insight into poverty and living conditions of the indigenous people in Ecuador. Noting the above-mentioned difficulty in identifying the indigenous population, we do not employ the language variable as a means to estimate how many indigenous people live in Ecuador. Rather, its function is merely to identify a population group whose living circumstances we can examine.

Poverty, living conditions, and language are closely linked. The indigenous language speaking population in Ecuador is concentrated in the rural Sierra and the Oriente; almost none live in the Costa. Almost a quarter of the poorest expenditure quintile in the rural Sierra speak an indigenous language and this ratio rapidly declines with expenditure quintile, reaching only 1.4 percent for the fifth quintile in the rural Sierra. We observe the same pattern in the urban Oriente and, albeit at much higher levels, in the rural Oriente (Annex 3).

Based on the Census of 1990, the disadvantaged living conditions of the indigenous people in Ecuador become more visible. Again using indigenous languages as the key variable, we compare three different types of Cantons in Ecuador with respect to a variety of basic service and social variables. If more than 50 percent of the inhabitants in the Cantons speak Quechua or Shuari, we term the Canton to be 'strongly indigenous'; between 20 percent and 50 percent of indigenous language speakers define it to be

---

[38]   CEPLEAS (1994), p.87.

'moderately indigenous'; and the Cantons with less than 20 percent of indigenous language speakers are labeled 'mildly indigenous'.

The strongly indigenous Cantons are worse off with respect to any of the recorded social and service variables, both when compared to other Cantons in the rural and those in the urban areas (Table 11). Alarming are the differences in the education and health indicators: While the national illiteracy rate was only 10 percent, more than 40 percent of the population in the strongly indigenous Cantons were illiterate in 1990, with female illiteracy even higher, impairing the integration of the indigenous female population into the national society. A third of the population in these Cantons was without any educational instruction. Sanchez Parga (1994) reports that repetition and drop out rates are very high for indigenous children and have grown at an average 2 percent in the Sierra and Oriente rural indigenous areas. The housing and living conditions do not encourage children to study at home or continue their education. The indigenous dwelling usually consists of one room that serves as a kitchen and bed-room for the whole family. Few households have sewerage, natural gas or electricity for lighting, necessary for studying and reading in the early dark of the Ecuadoran Andes. The clay construction, apart from being ill-suited for connection to public services, cannot be used as collateral for bank or public credit.

Table 11. Ethnicity and Poverty in Ecuador, 1990

| | Rural | | | Urban | |
	strongly indigenous[a]	moderately indigenous[a]	mildly indigenous[a]	mildly indigenous[a]	National Average
Illiteracy rate	41	22	12	4	10
Education					
no instruction	33	30	25	5	9
primary	45	52	62	42	51
secondary	3	9	7	36	26
Cooking Fuel					
gas	4	20	29	87	67
wood/other	96	80	71	13	33
Public sewerage	6	7	14	62	38
Electricity supply	35	51	67	95	78
Chronic child malnut[b].	64	59	56	41	45
Infant Mortality[c]	63	58	54	na	51

a   'Strongly indigenous' refers to Cantons in which more than half of the population speak a native language; 'modestly indigenous' are Cantons in the 20 percent to 50 percent bracket and 'mildly' are those with less than 20 percent of the population.
b   Census data adjusted to Freire and Waters (1994).
c   Data refers to 1992 and is based on INEC (1992), Estatisticas Vitales.

Source: Sanchez-Parga (1994).

Child malnutrition, as well as infant mortality rates, were clearly above the rural and national averages and two factors contribute to this high incidence according to Sanchez Parga (1994): First, due to productive and ecological constraints, the indigenous people cultivate only few basic crops which do not provide for a balanced diet. Second, indigenous people often consume only two meals per day, a result of impoverishment and the lack of cooking fuel (organic materials).[39] Also, women increasingly help in the field or some other income earning activity which reduces the time they can spend on preparing food for the family.[40]

As a direct consequence of poverty and living conditions of the indigenous people, migration out of indigenous areas is very high. In the Sierra, the large majority of the indigenous population lives in five provinces (Canar, Cotopaxi, Bolivar, Chimborazo, Imbabura). These five provinces have a migration rate of 26 percent in 1992 while the national rate was only 19 percent.

Political integration of the indigenous population in the Ecuadoran society is slim. While the provinces with a high share of indigenous people have historically had voter turn-outs above the country average, the number of void or null votes has also been very high. This cannot be attributed to the high level of illiteracy in these areas because the share of void and null votes has increased from 1979 to 1992. Rather, this is an expression of the lacking representation of the indigenous people in mainstream Ecuadoran parties and politics. Supporting such an interpretation is the finding that in 1988, 46.1 percent of interviewed indigenous voters mentioned that they did not feel represented by any party in the elections.[41]

---

[39] Families participating in the Rural Qualitative Assessment (Working Paper 5) mentioned that the reduction of meals to two per day was an important means how to reduce expenditures in difficult times.

[40] We also find in the labor market analysis (Working Paper 8) that indigenous language speakers are discriminated against. Other things being equal, like education or experience, they earn less income than non-native speakers.

[41] Chiriboga and Rivera (1989).

References

Aguinaga, C. (1993), Determinacion de los Niveles de Pobreza: Area Urbana de Ecuador, INEC, Quito.

Atkinson, A. (1989), Poverty and Social Security, Hempstead: Harvester Wheatsheaf.

Cabrera, Y., J. Martinez, and R. Morales (1993), Medición de la Pobreza en las Areas Urbana y Rural del Ecuador, Quito.

CEPLAES (1994), Mujer y Pobreza en el Ecuador, Background Study for the Ecuador Poverty Report, Quito.

CEPAL (1991), Magnitud de la Pobreza en America Latina en los Ochenta, Estudios e Informes de la CEPAL, Santiago de Chile.

Chiriboga, M. and Rivera, F. (1989), Eleciones de Enero de 1988 y Participación Indigena, ECUADOR-DEBATE, no. 17.

Enriquez, F. (1994), La Reforma del Ministerio de Salud: Algunos Elementos, draft, Quito.

Freire, W. and J. Bacallao (1992), Primer Censo Nacional de Talla de Los Niñoa Ecuatorianos de Primer grado: Resultados, CONADE/UNICEF/OPS, Quito.

Freire, W. and W. Waters (1994), Pobreza y Desnutrición en Ecuador, Background Study for the Ecuador Poverty Report, Quito.

Hentschel, J. and P. Lanjouw (1996), Poverty Analysis and Pricing of Services, forthcoming.

Howes, S. (1994), Income Distribution: Measurement, Transition and Analysis of Urban China, 1981-1990, Ph.D. dissertation, London School of Economics, University of London.

IDB (1993), Ecuador: Informe Socio-Economico, Washington.

ILDIS (1994), Informe Social, Quito.

INEC (1992), Estatisticas Vitales, Quito.

INEC (1993a), Informe Sobre los Servicios en el Campo, Quito.

INEC (1993b), Servicios Basicos en las Ciudades, Quito.

INEM (1990), Encuesta Permanente de Hogares, Empleo-Salud-Vivienda, Quito.

Lanjouw, P. and M. Ravallion (1994), Poverty and Household Size, World Bank Working Paper 1332, Washington.

Larrea, C. (1990), Pobreza, Necesidades Basicas y Desempleo: Area Urbana del Ecuador, Instituto Nacional del Empleo, Quito.

Mesa-Lago, C. (1993), The Ecuadoran Social Security Institute: Economic Evaluation and Options for Reform, INCAE.

Musgrove, P. (1991), Feeding Latin America's Children: An Analytical Survey of Food Programs, LAC Technical Department Discussion Papers 21, Washington.

Psacharopoulos, G. (1993), Returns to Investment in Education, World Bank Working Papers 1067, Washington.

Ravallion, M. (1994), Poverty Comparisons, Chur: Harwood.

Sanchez-Parga, J. (1994), Pobreza y Población Indigena en el Ecuador, Background Study for the Ecuador Poverty Report.

UNICEF, Dya (1992), Bienestar de los Niños en el Ecuador, Quito.

UNICEF (1993), World Education Report, Paris.

Urbana Consultores (1991), Pobreza Urbana y Crecimiento Economico en el Ecuador, USAID Ecuador, Quito.

Vega, S. and R. Gomez (1994), La Violencia Contra la Mujer en la Relación Doméstica de Pareja, in: Las Mujeres y los Derechos Humanos en America Latina, Red Entre Mujeres, Lima.

Waters, W. (1991), Rural Bases of the Informal Urban Economy in Ecuador, USFQ No. 4, Universidad San Francisco de Quito, Quito.

Weissmantel, M. (1988), Food, Gender and Poverty in the Ecuadorian Andes, Philadelphia: University of Pennsylvania Press.

World Bank (1990), Ecuador: A Social Sector Strategy for the Nineties, No. 8935-EC, Washington.

World Bank (1992), Staff Appraisal Report Ecuador Second Social Development Project, Health and Nutrition, No. 10486 EC.

World Bank (1993), World Development Report: Investing in Health, Washington.

World Bank (1994), Enriching Lives, Washington D.C.

Annex 1

This Annex spells out how we derived the poverty line and how robust our estimates of poverty are with respect to several key underlying assumptions. The first section, concerned with the poverty line, pays particular attention to our methodology to value housing, consumer durables and water consumption. In the second section, we examine the robustness of our estimates with respect to adult equivalency scales and the chosen imputation methodology for housing and water. Further, we present the results of statistical dominance tests, important when comparing regional poverty independent of the poverty line chosen.

Derivation of a Poverty Line

We needed a fair number of steps to arrive at a consumption-based poverty line for Ecuador. Several of these steps were also required for the general process of constructing consumption aggregates from the item-by-item entries in the dataset. First, we converted information on household purchases of food items into a monetary aggregate. Second, we calculated the calorie equivalent of the observed food consumption per household and derived the extreme poverty line. Third, we evaluated and priced non-food expenditures. Fourth, we derived the poverty and vulnerability lines. Finally, we adjusted nominal expenditures of all households for the variation in prices between different areas and regions. We briefly describe each of these steps below.

Conversion of Household Purchases of Food Items into a Monetary Aggregate. The LSMS contains detailed information on the quantity of up to 73 food items although the respective data were not always complete for all households; e.g. in some cases the entry for quantity, expenditure, price, the quantity unit (gram, pound, 'basket', 'bunch', etc.), or the frequency of purchase, was not reported or was incomplete. In such cases we corrected for these omissions by judiciously imputing responses at the level of ciudades or regions.

Calorie Conversion and Food Poverty Line Derivation. Using a standard conversion table, we derived calorie equivalents from the observed consumption pattern. The food poverty line indicates what expenditure is needed to acquire a minimum caloric intake per person (2237 kcal per capita[42]) associated with the consumption pattern of those in the second and third quintiles of the expenditure distribution.

The food poverty line was calculated in a series of steps. First, the average consumption bundle consumed by households in the 2nd and 3rd quintile of the national consumption expenditure distribution (in raw terms, without any previous adjustment to expenditures) was calculated. Using a calorie conversion table we estimated the kilocalorie content of this consumption bundle by first converting the quantity consumed of each item in the bundle into a calorie figure and then summing up these calorie figures across all food items in the consumption bundle. The figure obtained was then compared against the calorie cut-off level of 2237 kcal per person taken from Cabrera et al. (1993). All quantities in the consumption bundle were then uniformly scaled by the ratio of 2237

---

[42]   This kcal intake is taken from the study by Cabrera et al., 1993.

to the total calorie figure obtained, so as to ensure that the consumption bundle, based on the consumption pattern of the 2nd and 3rd quintile of the national population, yielded exactly 2237 kcals.

The vector of quantities in the consumption bundle was then valued by multiplying each good in the basket by the ciudad-specific modal price of that good. Summing across all values in the basket thus yielded a 'food poverty line' for each ciudad in the data set. A national-level food poverty line was then obtained by taking a population-weighted average of all ciudad level food poverty lines. The line obtained corresponds to 30,733 sucres per person per fortnight (equivalent roughly to US$ 1.00 per person per day in 1994).

Box A1.1. Evaluation of Consumer Durables and Housing

As we are concerned with the most accurate definition of welfare for the purpose of poverty analysis, we included both the consumption of durable consumer goods and housing in the household expenditure indicator. Households which possess goods such as cars or washing machines derive a value from the consumption of these goods which increases their welfare. Our welfare measure should take account of these goods.

We calculated the consumption of consumer durables applying a standard age profile to consumer durables reported in the LSMS. Section 1 (housing) of the LSMS reports the type, amount, age and replacement value for seventeen consumer durables ranging from refrigerators to sewing machines and from kitchens to cars. We assumed that the *average* replacement value of a particular durable (of the sample) would be a good proxy for those observations which did not give a replacement value. Further, we estimated the lifetime of each durable as twice its average age found in the survey. This computation is based on the premise that the purchase of consumer durables did not vary significantly over the past ten years in Ecuador which would result in a flat distribution of the age of durables over time. In this setting, the lifetime of a durable is twice its average age. Finally, we defined consumption (or depreciation) of a consumer durable as the sum of all replacement values divided by the average lifetime of this type of durable.

Regarding housing, we imputed the housing rent for a relatively small fraction of households which had not reported this variable. The LSMS contains two variables related to rent: one which records rent actually paid and one which inhabitants think they would have paid had they rented their apartment or building. We spliced both of these answers together assuming that inhabitants have a rational idea about the rental market. After excluding several obvious outliers (or misrecordings), about 5 percent of the observations in the dataset were missing. We imputed the rent variable separately for all areas and regions in the country using the predictive power of simple regression analysis. Exogenous variables were largely housing variables (wall material, number of rooms, number of bathrooms, availability of kitchen) but also other wealth indicators such as the consumption of durable consumer goods.

<u>Evaluation and Pricing of Non-Food Expenditures</u>. We have included a large number of non-food expenditures in the welfare measurement of households: electricity, water, transport, durable consumer goods, clothing, miscellaneous purchases, education and services, including also expenditures on prepared foods purchased outside the home. For some of these such as clothing and transportation this was quite easy as the data included both a category of monthly and yearly expenses which we could adjust to a bi-weekly period. For others, such as housing or consumer durables, we applied a relatively straight forward imputation or evaluation method (see Box A.1).

For water, the task was more complex. Theoretically, if our aim is to measure the welfare level of a household, we would want to ensure that we include all consumed goods during a certain reference period. We implicitly assume that welfare arises from the consumption of goods. Hence, in order to enable us to make welfare comparisons between households, we have to control both for the price and the quality of the item looked at. In the case of water, households report only their total water expenditures and not the actual quantity of water consumed.

Prices of water vary widely in Ecuador, depending largely on the form of access: Consumers of water with access to the public water network tend to be heavily subsidized -- almost two thirds of the sampled households connected to the public water network actually reported that they do not pay for their consumed water at all. On the other hand, especially households with little access to river water or wells pay dearly for this life necessity. The population in urban areas without connection, often the poor, are forced to buy their water from street vendors. Simply aggregating nominal expenditures without adjusting the data in some way, would induce a bias in our welfare measurement: we would either overstate the welfare of the not connected households or understate the welfare of the connected ones.

As we could not deduce the actual quantity of water consumed for consumers connected to the public water network, we imputed total water expenditures for all households not purchasing water from private vendors. Most public network water consumers specified that they did not pay for the service they received so that the actual price for them was zero, rendering the calculation of actual quantities consumed impossible. Under a number of restrictive assumptions, we therefore imputed both price and quantity of water consumed jointly (see Box A.2).

If the quality of a consumed good varies and we cannot observe its price for a specific household or at least region, an imputation method to make welfare levels comparable between households becomes impossible. We were only able to impute water expenditures because we assumed that the water quality between the piped water and the one street vendors sell does not vary significantly. Health expenditures are an example where we cannot control for such quality. The coverage of health care, especially in rural areas, is dismal in Ecuador, forcing many of the rural poor to seek help in private clinics or from traveling doctors. We have no yardstick to compare the health services rendered by these private clinics to public health centers. If everybody had access to public health care we could assume that the population which does seek help at private facilities expects a better service than the one provided in the public health posts.[43] But since this access is not universal, simply including health expenditures in our welfare measure would not be correct. The point is that by excluding health expenditures altogether, we have a better chance of preserving the 'true' welfare rankings than by either including expenditures without adjustment or some type of imputed health expenditures.

---

[43] Along this line of argumentation, we have included nominal education expenditures in our aggregate poverty measure. Access to both primary and secondary public education is given in Ecuador although at times it involves a lengthy commute in rural areas. With access to public education given, we can interpret the choice of households for private education as a choice for a different, and better, quality of the education.

Box A1.2. Imputation of Water Expenditures

We paid particular attention to the adjustments of water expenditures because access to this service is widely discussed in Ecuador. In the debate, water is generally used as the most important example of the unequal access to many basic services which tend to be biased in favor of the urban Sierra region. Further, access to water is used as an example in the debate why expenditures (or income) cannot be used to measure poverty. While a large part of the households connected to the public network receive their water for free, others have to pay high prices to purchase water from street vendors.

We imputed water expenditures by evaluating household consumption of water at its marginal value. As a starting point for the adjustment procedure, we only looked at the private market for water represented by water vendors which we find to operate almost exclusively in urban areas. We are only able to observe the marginal value of water for these households: in rural areas, no price is attached to water consumption although the opportunity cost can be significant; and in the public water network, the marginal value of water consumption and the actual price differ because of supply constraints and hence demand rationing. We imputed water expenditures using a number of wealth and living standard variables. Using a stepwise regression procedure to estimate a log-model, we determined variables such as household size, expenditures on cooking fuel, consumption of durable consumer goods and an array of housing variables to be significantly correlated to water expenditures.

Such an imputation is a valid method to adjust water expenditures if a number of assumptions hold. First, water of different sources and in different areas must have approximately the same quality. Second, water supply in the public water network must be restricted so that the marginal value of water differs from the actual price paid to the water companies. Third, a ranking of expenditures must reflect a ranking of quantities actually consumed which implies that the demand for water has to be very inelastic in a certain range. Fourth, the vendors water market has to be competitive with few barriers to entry and exit. Finally, (marginal) transportation costs of water need to be relatively small. See Hentschel and Lanjouw (1995) for a detailed analysis of the imputation methodology and its underlying assumptions.

Poverty Line and Vulnerability Line Derivation. We then obtained the *poverty line* by determining the average proportion of total consumption which was spent on non-food items by those members of the population who were in principle just able to meet their calorie needs, if they were to devote their total expenditure to the purchase of food items. The poverty line was then calculated by scaling up the national-level food poverty line by that empirically estimated proportion (for further details consult Ravallion 1994). In order to derive the *vulnerability line*, we determined the average proportion of total consumption which was spent on non-food items by those members of the population who recorded food expenditures equal to the food poverty line. Again, we then computed the vulnerability line by scaling up the food poverty line by this proportion.

Price adjustments. Finally, rather than operating with a large amount of poverty lines, we adjusted total household expenditures for price variations in the different regions and areas in Ecuador. Price variations are very pronounced in Ecuador due to its geographic and climate diversity. Having calculated food poverty lines at the ciudad-level we adjusted nominal expenditures of households with a cost-of-living index obtained by taking the ratio of the ciudad-level food poverty line to a population weighted average, and dividing the expenditure figure in the sample by this ratio. Note that imputed water expenditures were not adjusted in this way but were added to 'real' expenditures after adjustment.

Robustness of the Poverty Estimates

In this section, we are concerned with how robust the above presented estimates of poverty in Ecuador are. We start with examining how sensitive the calculated poverty rates are to the choice of the poverty line. The above described derivation of the poverty line depends on a large number of assumptions ranging from the implicit application of an adult calorie equivalency scale to the economic rationale under which we imputed water and housing expenditures, the exact poverty line chosen, or the specific poverty measure employed. By changing these assumptions, we will discover how important they are for our overall poverty estimates. The second part of this section then turns to regional poverty rankings. We examine regional poverty indicators for a wide range of possible poverty lines to find out whether we can make statements about the relative regional rankings of poverty without referring to a specific poverty line.

Sensitivity Analysis

We conduct two sensitivity analyses of our poverty estimates. First, we apply an explicit adult equivalency scale. The equivalency scale adjustment is based on the assumption that adults and children have different kcal requirements so that, consequently, the poverty line for each different household is a function of the composition of the household itself. In the base case, the 2237 cut-off point of Cabrera et al. (1993, p.174) reflects the nutritional requirements of an 'average' household in terms of size with an 'average' composition. Hence, the base case takes an equivalency scale implicitly into account by arriving at the kcal average but it does not explicitly endogenize the poverty line for each individual household. Second, we conduct a sensitivity analysis regarding our above referenced imputation of water and housing values. Instead of using the imputed values, we include the nominal expenditures recorded in the LSMS in the sensitivity analysis.

Poverty rate estimates of the two alternative calculations vary somewhat from the base case. We conduct the analysis for the extreme poverty line (only food expenditures), applying an adult equivalency scale of .5 for infants and .7 for children to an adult calorie requirement of 2700 kcal, the amount suggested by CEPAL (1991). Poverty rate calculations vary only marginally from our base case with the national estimate of extreme poverty increasing slightly from 15 to 16 percent. Even reducing the adult equivalency units of children to .5 and infants to .3 leaves us with an extreme poverty rate of 13 percent. Turning to the sensitivity of our estimates with respect to imputations of water, rent and our evaluation of consumer durables, the poverty rate increases from 15 percent (base case) to 18 percent if we include the nominal instead of the imputed values for water and housing and exclude the user value of consumer durables. The direction of this shift could be expected as we adjust recorded expenditures in the LSMS upward in the base case scenario. It is interesting to observe that the (absolute) influence of the imputation exercise is higher than the adult equivalency scale application.

Table A1.1. Poverty in Ecuador 1994: Sensitivity Analysis of Extreme Poverty Rates

		Base Case Extreme Adult Poverty Line	Alternative Equivalency Scale[a]	Alternative Water, Rent and	
				Adult Equivalency Scal[b]	Consumer Durables[c]
Costa	urban	9	9	6	10
	rural	22	24	19	25
Sierra	urban	11	12	10	13
	rural	20	19	16	22
Oriente	urban	7	7	3	8
	rural	50	46	38	53
National	urban	10	10	8	12
	rural	22	23	19	25
Total		15	16	13	18

a   Equivalency scale of children as .7 adult equivalents and infants as .5 starting from an adult calorie requirement of 2700 kcal.

b   Equivalency scale of children as .5 adult equivalents and infants as .3 starting from an adult calorie requirement of 2700 kcal.

c   Uses nominal expenditures for water and housing instead of imputed values, and excludes consumer durables consumption.

Rankings of Poverty

How confident can we be about our finding that rural poverty is higher than urban poverty? Further, can we make a judgment about poverty rankings between regions which do not depend on the exact poverty line chosen? In order to answer these two questions, we conducted tests of stochastic dominance.

Stochastic Dominance Tests. Advances in the measurement of poverty have in recent years yielded very simple to apply techniques for comparing poverty while retaining a firm focus on the robustness of the comparison.[44] We begin with a straightforward plot of the distribution functions between the populations being compared. The location of the distribution functions is of immense importance for making judgments about poverty rankings: From the theory underlying these techniques, it can be shown that if the curves do not intersect at any point in the graph, poverty in the population represented by the curve lying everywhere above the other is greater. And this is true not only for the incidence of poverty but is also true for any other poverty measure in common use.

Urban - Rural Comparison. Examining the distribution function for urban and rural poverty first, we find unequivocally that rural poverty is higher than urban poverty independently of the poverty line chosen (compare Figure 1 in Working Paper 4). The rural distribution function of consumption lies above the urban distribution function over

---

[44]   The literature on poverty measurement using stochastic dominance techniques has been growing rapidly. Good overviews can be found in Atkinson (1989), Howes (1994) and Ravallion (1994).

the whole range of per capita expenditures. Hence, for whatever poverty line we choose, rural poverty indicators like the headcount index or the depth and severity of poverty are above those for the urban areas.

The expenditure distribution function also helps us to calculate how the poverty rate varies with the poverty line. The poverty line of Sucres 45,000 per person per fortnight cuts the rural distribution function in a relatively steep and the urban distribution function in a somewhat flatter part. This indicates that relatively minor adjustments to the poverty line will have a pronounced impact on the measured incidence of poverty. The vulnerability line, for example, is around Sucres 60,000 (an increase of about US$0.5 to US$2.0 per person per day) which increases the incidence of poverty in rural areas from 47 percent to 67 percent (a rate much closer to what other studies have found) while the urban rate rises from 25 percent to 40 percent.

Regional Rankings.   Turning from the aggregate urban and rural areas to examining stochastic dominance between regions, we find that we can draw only few conclusions. The results of both first and second order tests of stochastic dominance are presented in Table A1.2.[45] Varying the poverty line over a very wide range (from sucres 10,000 to 60,000), we can only say that both the rural Oriente and the rural Sierra are poorer than the urban Oriente and urban Costa, irrespective of the location of the poverty line and the type of poverty measure used. And even this result has to be interpreted with care, however, as it does not take the contribution towards poverty into account. Thus, for example, poverty rates in the rural Oriente are always higher than in the urban Costa but the number of poor is always greater in the latter has the urban Costa has a large population.

---

[45]   While first order stochastic dominance tests compared the distribution functions, second order stochastic dominance tests examine the location of the deficit curves.

Table A1.2. Regional Rankings of Poverty: Statistical Dominance Tests

	Urban Costa	Urban Sierra	Rural Costa	Rural Sierra	Rural Oriente
Urban Oriente	Second-Order[a]	X[c]	Second-Order[b]	First-Order[a]	First-Order[a]
Urban Costa		X[c]	X[c]	First-Order[a]	First-Order[a]
Urban Sierra			X[c]	X[c]	X[c]
Rural Costa				X[c]	X[c]
Rural Sierra					X[c]

a   First-Order indicates that with 95 percent confidence, poverty in the population corresponding to the row entry is lower than in the population corresponding to the column entry over all poverty lines between sucres 10,000 and 60,000 per fortnight and over all poverty measures, including the head county ratio (see Atkinson, 1989, and Ravallion, 1994. On statistical testing of stochastic dominance see Howes, 1994).

b   'Second-Order' indicates that with 95 percent confidence, poverty in the population corresponding to the row entry is lower than in the population corresponding to the column entry over all poverty lines between sucres 10,000 and 60,000 per person per fortnight and over all poverty measures which are strictly decreasing and at least weakly convex, i.e. excluding the head count ratio but including the poverty gap and poverty severity measurers.

c   Where an 'X' is entered these is no unambiguous ranking of the two regions over all poverty measures and all poverty lines (in the range between sucres 10,000 and 60,000 per person per fortnight).

Annex 2: Using the Living Standard Measurement Survey to Derive a General Geographic Poverty Map for Ecuador

This Annex describes findings from an attempt to extend results from the Ecuador LSMS to the development of a general geographic poverty map for Ecuador. The LSMS is a household survey and is representative only at the regional and area level (i.e., for both rural and urban areas for the Costa, Sierra, and the Oriente). It alone can not be used to derive a geographic poverty map capable of reaching the cantonal, or even more ideally the *parroquial* level. The data source which contains sufficient information to reach such a level of disaggregation is the national Census from 1990. However, the Census does not contain an income or expenditure variable which -- as we have already described -- is our preferred variable to measure poverty.

The LSMS will serve us to derive a variety of different 'poverty models' which we can then apply to the Census, thereby introducing an expenditure variable to the Census data. If we are able to 'explain' household expenditures using a number of exogenous variables, this relationship can then be used to 'predict' expenditures at the household level using the Census information. Obviously, one important limitation exists: the variables used to explain household expenditures in the Living Standard Measurement Survey have to be contained in the Census as well. However, as we will describe in more detail below, a number of very restrictive assumptions have to be made in order to apply the described methodology. Analysts following this approach should be aware of these assumptions. The following steps are necessary:

Step 1: Explaining Household Expenditures Using the LSMS. The first, and probably most important step is to achieve the best possible explanation of household expenditures with a host of exogenous variables. As mentioned above, the pool of these exogenous variables is determined by those variables contained in both the LSMS and the Census. Experimenting with a large number of different models, we find that a simple log-linear model achieves the best fit. We run the models at the most disaggreagte level possible with the LSMS, namely by region and area. As the imputation of household expenditures later on depends on the accuracy of these models, it is very important that analysts try to 'optimize' the explanatory power of the different models

The implicit assumption behind these explanatory models is that the heterogeneity *within* each region and area is modest. Heterogeneity does not mean that poverty levels within an area do not differ but rather that the relationship between the exogenous variables (such as services, education level, occupation, housing characteristics) and the endogenous variables (household expenditures) is relatively stable. Only under this premise is the here described methodology applicable.

Another important simplification we have to make is to assume that the structural relationship between household expenditures and exogenous variables is relatively constant *over time*. The LSMS, on which basis we conduct the model estimations, is from 1994 while the Census data stems from 1990. If the relationship between household expenditures and exogenous housing and household characteristics changes rapidly, our approach is -- again -- invalid.

Step 2: Imputing Expenditures From Census Data. We use the estimated models to impute household expenditures for all Ecuadoran households contained in the Census of 1990. A problems arises here as we discover that the political definition of geographic areas is different between the Census and the LSMS so that we can only approximate the areas where we have to apply each one of our six models. Analysts should pay great attention to this fact and try to harmonize as much as possible the geographic definitions between the two data sources.

Step 3: Some Simple Checks. Before using the imputed household expenditures, we conduct a number of checks to gain some confidence in our results. Specifically, we calculate the poverty rate for two different poverty lines and measures to compare them to the results obtained from the LSMS (see Table A3.1). We cannot expect that we are exactly 'on target' with the calculated poverty indicators from the imputed expenditures for a number of reasons. First, our models 'only' had an explanatory power of (at most) 70 percent; second, the data sources differ in their political definition of regions and areas; third, we apply 1994 models to the Census of 1990. As can be observed Table A2.1, poverty estimates using the imposed consumption variable are very close to the original estimates from the LSMS.

Table A2.1. Comparison between LSMS and Preliminary Census Model Results

		LSMS incidence	rank	Census incidence	rank	LSMS severity	rank	Census severity	rank
Costa	urban	25	6	26	4	.030	7	.03	4
	rural	50	2	49	2	.063	3	.07	2
Sierra	urban	19	8	17	8	.030	6	.02	7
	rural	43	3	49	3	.067	2	.06	3
Oriente	urban	20	7	20	7	.030	8	.02	5
	rural	67	1	65	1	.160	1	.18	1
Guayaquil		29	4	23	5	.030	5	.01	8
Quito		25	5	21	6	.040	4	.02	6

a   Poverty incidence is measured by the headcount ratio; poverty severity is measured by the FGT measure with a parameter value of 2 (see Ravallion, 1994). The poverty line corresponds to 45,446 Sucres per person per fortnight. Imputed household expenditures were used to derive the statistics applying to the Census.

Source: LSMS, 1994; Census, 1990.

Annex 3

		Rural Area					Urban Area				
		1	2	3	4	5	1	2	3	4	5

Housing material (percent)

Costa	stone	15	24.8	32.7	24.4	44.2	59.9	71.6	71.8	83.9	90.5
	cley	0	0	0	0	0	0	1.1	0	0.4	0.44
	wood	9.5	6.2	6.2	3.2	6.3	5.6	3.3	4.7	2.6	2.2
	bamboo	73.7	69	61.1	71.5	49.4	34.4	24	23.5	12.7	6.4
	other	1.8	0	0	0.9	0.1	0.1	0	0	0.4	0.46
		100	100	100	100	100	100	100	100	100	100
Sierra	stone	38.6	52.4	55.9	52.2	78.8	76.5	69.5	81.7	83	88.5
	adoba	28.3	19.5	19.2	22.3	10.4	21.3	28.8	16.9	14.9	11
	wood	21.9	18.1	17.3	19	4.1	2.1	1.7	0.6	2	0.2
	rohr	10.4	9.9	7.5	6.4	3.5	0	0	0.7	0	0.2
	other	0.8	0.1	0.1	0.1	3.2	0.1	0	0.1	0.1	0.1
		100	100	100	100	100	100	100	100	100	100
Oriente	stone	na	na	na	na	na	30	29.8	42.4	68.8	65.2
	adoba	na	na	na	na	na	0	3.6	0	1.3	0
	wood	na	na	na	na	na	64.2	64.3	50.7	27.8	31.2
	rohr	na	na	na	na	na	5.8	0	4.3	0	0.7
	other	na	na	na	na	na	0	2.3	2.6	2.1	2.9
							100	100	100	100	100

Water source (percent)

Costa	public net	2.5	10.7	10.9	1	19.8	44.5	52.7	52.7	65.4	78.7
	private net	4.7	18	13.4	7.9	12.5	4.7	4.9	3.4	3.4	0.7
	rain/river	54.5	41.6	51.5	61.1	36.9	2.6	1	0.4	0.8	0
	well	36.6	26.5	23.1	28.8	28.8	10.2	8.2	9.1	9.1	6.8
	truck	0.7	1.2	0.9	0.9	1.6	22.7	22.5	25.5	16.6	10.9
	other	1	2	0.2	0.3	0.4	15.3	10.7	8.9	4.7	2.9
		100	100	100	100	100	100	100	100	100	100
Sierra	public net	22.1	34.7	34.7	30.8	35.6	83.5	77.1	87	93.7	97.7
	private net	29.4	19.7	31.9	32.2	22.4	4.3	8.7	4.8	2.1	1.1
	rain/river	37.3	26.9	19.1	23	18.2	0	1.1	0	0	0
	well	10.5	17.2	13.9	12.5	23.8	5.9	3.8	1.6	1.8	0.8
	truck	0	0	0.3	0.2	0	3.7	4.8	3.1	1.5	0.4
	other	0.7	1.5	0.1	1.3	0	2.6	4.5	3.5	0.9	0
		100	100	100	100	100	100	100	100	100	100
Oriente	public net	na	na	na	na	na	79.6	92.4	78	93.2	96.7
	private net	na	na	na	na	na	9.2	3.4	10.9	2.7	0
	rain/river	na	na	na	na	na	5.4	4.2	11	1.6	3.3
	well	na	na	na	na	na	5.8	0	0	0	0
	truck	na	na	na	na	na	0	0	0	0	0
	other	na	na	na	na	na	0	0	0.1	2.5	0
							100	100	100	100	100

		Rural Area					Urban Area				
		1	2	3	4	5	1	2	3	4	5

Hygiene Facility (percent)

Costa	flush	4.7	18.3	18.9	10.1	29.7	37.9	48.9	59.5	72.4	87.7
	letrine	38.9	49.1	32.1	47	29.8	51.5	39.7	32.3	22.3	9.7
	none	56.4	32.6	49	42.9	40.5	10.6	11.4	8.2	5.3	2.6
		100	100	100	100	100	100	100	100	100	100
Sierra	flush	11.4	17.5	27.6	41.6	44	80.2	81.4	88.6	94.8	98.4
	letrine	31.2	39.9	35	31.5	44.3	9	7.7	6.3	3.2	1.1
	none	57.4	42.6	37.4	26.9	11.7	10.8	10.9	5.1	2	0.5
		100	100	100	100	100	100	100	100	100	100
Oriente	flush	na	na	na	na	na	48.2	78.8	75.5	90.8	90.1
	letrine	na	na	na	na	na	9.2	15.5	10.4	6.7	5.9
	none	na	na	na	na	na	42.6	5.7	14.1	2.5	4
							100	100	100	100	100

Electricity Supply (percent)

Costa	public	56.9	54.2	63.4	56.3	79.1	96.6	98.9	99.6	98.9	99.8
	private	0	0.1	1.8	2.4	4.1	0	0.5	0.3	0.4	0.2
	none	43.1	45.7	34.8	41.3	16.8	3.4	0.6	0.1	0.7	0
		100	100	100	100	100	100	100	100	100	100
Sierra	public	59.3	80.8	78.8	86.7	90.8	97.1	99.1	99.3	99.6	99.8
	private	0	0.9	0.8	2	1.7	0	0	0	0.3	0.2
	none	40.7	18.3	20.4	11.3	7.5	2.9	0.9	0.7	0.1	0
		100	100	100	100	100	100	100	100	100	100
Oriente	public	na	na	na	na	na	89.2	97.9	92.8	98.8	96.2
	private	na	na	na	na	na	0	0	0	0	0
	none	na	na	na	na	na	10.8	2.1	7.2	1.2	3.8
							100	100	100	100	100

telephone service (percent)

Costa	with phone	0	0	0	0	0.1	1.6	2.4	6.3	17	37.9
Sierra	with phone	0	1.1	4	4.1	12.8	11.5	12.1	15.4	31.6	60.4
Oriente	with phone	na	na	na	na	na	0	2.1	10	18.5	40.6

		Rural Area					Urban Area				
		1	2	3	4	5	1	2	3	4	5
garbage disposal (percent)											
Costa	collected	0	4.4	8.7	0.2	14	51.7	56.9	56.4	67.1	77.8
	thrown or burned	100	95.6	91.3	99.8	86	48.3	43.1	43.6	32.9	22.2
Sierra	collected	0	2	2.9	3.4	6.7	69.5	75.2	77.4	88.2	91.2
	thrown/burned	100	98	97.1	96.6	93.3	30.5	24.8	22.6	11.8	8.8
Oriente	collected	na	na	na	na	na	41.7	75.4	70.9	87.3	88.5
	thrown/burned	na	na	na	na	na	58.3	24.6	29.1	12.7	11.5
cooking fuel (percent)											
Costa	gas	58.8	72.6	68.9	70	72.1	81.5	91.7	94.5	94.7	89.7
	wood/coal	41	27.1	28.7	29.9	16.8	14.5	3.1	3.4	1.4	0.6
	other	0.2	0.3	2.4	0.1	11.1	4	5.2	2.1	3.9	9.7
		100	100	100	100	100	100	100	100	100	100
Sierra	gas	32.8	60.4	72.2	68.8	73.9	89.7	95.6	95.6	96.8	96.3
	wood/coal	62.7	39.3	27.6	27.6	18.7	9.7	4.4	3.7	2	0.5
	other	4.5	0.3	0.2	3.6	7.4	0.6	0	0.7	1.2	3.2
		100	100	100	100	100	100	100	100	100	100
Oriente	gas	na	na	na	na	na	90.2	97.9	95.7	96.6	92.6
	wood/coal	na	na	na	na	na	4.6	2.1	4.3	3.4	1.4
	other	na	na	na	na	na	5.2	0	0	0	6
							100	100	100	100	100
crowding index (persons per room)											
National	crowding index	2.2	1.8	1.8	1.3	0.8	2.4	2.1	1.7	1.3	0.8
literacy rate* (percent)											
Costa	(pop over 14)	76.7	78.7	78.5	76.3	67.7	83.1	89.5	93.8	95.3	97.9
Sierra	(pop over 14)	71.5	85.6	84.4	87.6	93.1	89.9	93.6	95.2	96.6	98.5
Oriente	(pop over 14)	80.9	93.1	91.5	92.4	95.7	88.3	90.3	92.9	97.8	95.8

			Rural Area					Urban Area				
			1	2	3	4	5	1	2	3	4	5
repition rates rates in school (% of children in quintile)												
National	primary school											
		Grade 1	17	20.9	29.5	16.7	7.7	17.8	16.6	12.6	7.1	3.5
		Grade 2	3.6	10.9	13.7	6.5	7.5	13.2	6.9	0.5	5.9	2.1
		Grade 3	na	na	na	na	na	13	11.5	2.7	6.2	0.5
		OVERALL	7.1	10.4	12.9	6.2	7.5	11.6	11	3.9	6.4	2.7
	secondary school											
		Grade 1	na	na	na	na	na	28	12.9	12.1	13.5	4.6
		Grade 2	na	na	na	na	na	12.9	18	17.3	16.8	1.1
		Grade 3	na	na	na	na	na	11.8	7.9	3.5	7.6	3.9
		OVERALL	9.8	4.3	7	5.1	13.4	14.6	11.2	8.5	9.7	4.6
School type (percent)												
National	primary	public	91.6	89.8	86.1	88.2	80.2	93.6	85.3	82.2	66.3	38.2
		private	8.4	10.2	13.9	11.8	19.8	6.4	14.7	17.8	33.7	61.8
			100	100	100	100	100	100	100	100	100	100
	secondary	public	92.1	81.1	78.7	68.6	85.2	89.9	83.7	85.8	76.3	47.5
		private	7.9	18.9	21.3	31.4	14.8	10.1	16.3	14.2	23.7	52.5
			100	100	100	100	100	100	100	100	100	100
	superior	public	na	na	na	na	na	97	100	90.1	74.1	56.2
		private	na	na	na	na	na	3	0	9.9	25.9	43.8
								100	100	100	100	100
Education level of household head (percent)												
National	primary&less	total	96.5	94	88.3	88.6	65.1	82.9	71.2	62	50.4	25.6
	secondary		3.5	5.8	9.3	10.3	22.2	13.5	24.9	29.7	33.2	32.7
	superior		0	0.2	2.4	1.1	12.7	3.6	3.9	8.3	16.4	41.6
			100	100	100	100	100	100	100	100	100	99.9
	primary&less	female	99.4	98	97.7	83.8	67.4	95.3	82.2	65.9	52.1	39.5
	secondary		0.6	1.9	2.3	16.2	31.8	3.1	17.8	26.1	28.6	33.9
	superior		0	0	0	0	0.8	1.6	0	7.9	19.3	26.6
			100	99.9	100	100	100	100	100	99.9	100	100
	primary&less	male	96.1	93.6	87.6	89.2	64.9	80.4	68.8	61.4	49.6	22.6
	secondary		3.9	6.3	10.1	9.5	21.2	15.8	26.4	30.3	34.5	32.5
	superior		0	0.1	2.3	1.2	14	3.82	4.8	8.3	15.9	44.9
			100	100	100	99.9	100	100	100	100	100	100

	Rural Area					Urban Area				
	1	2	3	4	5	1	2	3	4	5

Distance from school (in minutes)

National	primary	25	22	19	22	19	16	16	15	15	19
	secondary	39	34	31	37	30	26	29	25	23	26
	superior	na	na	na	na	na	45	32	35	33	32

Students Missing Classes during past month (% of children in quintile, by area)

National	primary	36.4	32.3	31.8	32	42.2	38.1	32.2	32.9	29.9	33
	secondary	45.8	35.8	29.8	20.7	51.1	30.1	30.3	30.2	37.2	33.3

Working Students

National	primary	35.9	41.6	44.8	33.7	24.2	14.6	9.3	21.9	14.7	15.3
	secondary	75.1	36.7	56.7	54.8	65.6	24	28.5	27.4	26.7	24.6

Reasons why children not enrolled in secondary school

National	costs	44.7	27.6	24.7	30.1	25.9	25.2	34.2	34.6	16.9	5
	work	23.3	39.9	20.7	38.9	14.3	34.8	33.2	42.9	46.6	54.3
	other	32	32.5	54.6	31	59.8	40	32.6	22.5	36.5	40.7
		100	100	100	100	100	100	100	100	100	100

Gender of Household Head

National	women	11.1	8.9	8.1	10.8	10.2	17.2	17.2	14	16.4	18.3
	male	88.9	91.1	91.9	89.2	89.8	82.8	82.8	86	83.6	81.7
		100	100	100	100	100	100	100	100	100	100

Migration Flows (% of population living in different area 10 years ago)

Costa	came from urban	5.3	5.4	4.1	7.8	12.1	11.8	8.8	12.4	8.7	9.6
	came from rural	7.9	8.7	2.7	5.7	3.8	8.7	7.9	2.1	5.2	1.1
	TOTAL inmigration rate	13.2	14.1	6.8	13.5	15.9	20.5	16.7	14.5	13.9	10.7
Sierra	came from urban	8.4	7.2	13.6	14	21.6	19.5	8.9	18.2	9.2	14.5
	came from rural	8.9	2.5	2.7	2.1	3.8	8.7	7.9	2.1	5.2	1.1
	TOTAL inmigration rate	17.3	9.7	16.3	16.1	25.4	28.2	16.8	20.3	14.4	15.6
Oriente	came from urban	6.4	14.5	26.4	15.3	30.8	24.6	12	14.4	25.7	31.2
	came from rural	8.8	11.6	5.3	24.5	8.1	32.6	22.8	14	13.2	8.4
	TOTAL inmigration rate	15.2	26.1	31.7	39.8	38.9	57.2	34.8	28.4	38.9	39.6

		Rural Area					Urban Area				
		1	2	3	4	5	1	2	3	4	5
health insurance (percent)											
National	IESS -- general	1.2	2.1	2.9	5.4	9.3	6.1	8.2	11.5	16.6	26.7
	IESS -- campensino	19.2	12.8	21.6	13.3	13.8	0.4	0.4	0.4	0.3	0.8
	private	0	0	0.1	0.3	1.7	0.3	0.5	0.3	1.3	5.4
	none	79.2	84.6	75.3	80.5	74.1	92.9	90.3	86.9	80.5	62.9
	other	0.4	0.5	0.1	0.5	1.1	0.3	0.6	0.9	1.3	4.2
		100	100	100	100	100	100	100	100	100	100
Type of Last Attendance											
Costa	family	4.6	1.5	6.3	4.6	4.7	2.8	1.3	2.1	1.7	1
	pharmacist	35.9	44.7	28	28.3	10.2	27.2	21.7	19	17.5	13.1
	nurse/doctor	58.6	52.2	60.8	66.5	80.6	69.1	75.3	78.8	80.3	84.8
	other	0.86	1.6	4.9	0.6	4.5	0.9	1.7	0.1	0.5	1.1
		100	100	100	100	100	100	100	100	100	100
Sierra	family	15.6	7.4	8.4	9	3.3	6.7	1.6	4	3.3	2.1
	pharma	1.7	10.9	16.1	14.9	4.4	11.1	16.7	12.8	6.9	2.7
	nurse/doctor	80	79.6	73.2	73.7	92	81.9	78.7	81	88.2	94.6
	other	2.7	2.1	2.3	2.4	0.3	0.3	3	2.2	1.6	0.6
		100	100	100	100	100	100	100	100	100	100
Oriente	family	0.4	0	4.2	1.4	2.3	0	4.6	0	0	0
	pharmacist	17.1	11.1	15.4	6.9	17.9	18.7	18.6	10.9	6.8	8.9
	nures/doctor	70.5	88.3	80.3	91.3	79.7	72.5	72.9	88.9	90.9	89.5
	other	12	0.6	0.1	0.4	0.1	na	3.9	0.2	2.3	1.6
		100	100	100	100	100	na	100	100	100	100
Location of Last Attendance											
Costa	public hospital	5	5.3	1.8	0.2	9.7	11.1	19.3	12.5	17	10.9
	public center**	24.9	8.6	26.3	16.8	1.4	29.1	25.1	24.1	13.4	11.2
	private clinic or doctor	26.5	36.8	37.7	50.5	64.5	21.2	29.9	39.6	45	54.9
	house and other	43.6	49.3	34.2	32.5	24.4	38.6	25.7	23.8	24.6	23
		100	100	100	100	100	100	100	100	100	100
Sierra	public hospital	4.6	9.7	10	12.1	11.6	24.1	12.9	17.7	20.7	12.4
	public center	30.3	20.6	23	20.4	9.9	25.8	28.4	17.3	16.1	8.7
	private clinic or doctor	40.4	45.6	40.1	42.1	64.9	28.2	27.8	39	42.6	63.5
	house and other	24.7	24.1	26.9	25.4	13.6	21.9	30.9	26	20.6	15.4
		100	100	100	100	100	100	100	100	100	100

		Rural Area					Urban Area				
		1	2	3	4	5	1	2	3	4	5
Oriente	public hospital	19.2	28.6	24.3	25.3	23.7	31.8	27.7	32.1	30.4	30.8
	public center	40.3	25	36.4	26.7	14.8	10.7	16.1	14.7	21.3	14.3
	private clinic or doctor	14.3	21.6	19	27.6	34	30.3	27.8	34.8	33.7	37.4
	other	26.2	24.8	20.3	20.4	27.5	27.2	28.4	18.4	14.6	17.5
		100	100	100	100	100	100	100	100	100	100
Vacination	TBC	90.1	93.5	97.9	93.3	97.2	95	98.9	95.1	92.3	97.9
	diarrea	96.2	89.9	94.8	84.3	94.1	91.7	96.2	93.9	94.6	96.7
	polio	85.1	88.1	94.8	81.9	94.0	89.9	95.9	93.3	93.6	95.2
	measles	73.9	69.9	84.8	81.9	94.0	80.1	84.1	82.5	74.6	71.2

Recipients of Child Nutritional Aid

		Rural Area					Urban Area				
National	coverage rate	5.7	6.2	7.1	0.9	0	5.2	5.5	4.5	1.6	0.6

Distance to Public Health Center

	Rural Area					Urban Area				
distance (in hours)	1.1	0.95	0.96	0.76	0.72	0.41	0.5	0.46	0.52	0.49

Labor Force Participation (age 15 to 64)

		Rural Area					Urban Area				
Costa	female	16.5	15.1	14.5	14.2	20.7	40.7	39.1	40.3	42.4	53.3
	male	81.6	89.4	82.3	93.9	92.1	84.9	81.7	84.8	85.1	80.9
Sierra	female	38.5	47.2	36.4	49.2	40.3	49.3	43.4	48.7	48.3	56.7
	male	70.3	88.5	91.3	79.0	72.1	78.9	87.4	83.0	79.9	72.4
Oriente	female	21.9	41.5	37.4	54.4	69.1	43.7	43.2	45.3	40.0	56.6
	male	72.1	79.7	74.8	80.9	87.7	na	na	na	na	na
National	female	25.9	33.7	27.3	35.3	37.1	44.4	40.3	43.2	44.5	55.0
	male	76.3	88.5	86.7	85.6	78.4	82.5	83.0	84.2	83.2	76.7

Working Spouses

	Rural Area					Urban Area				
National	22.9	23.8	25.7	23.4	34.5	36.8	36.2	40.2	42.6	52.3

Reasons for Out of Labor Force

			Rural Area					Urban Area				
National	female	household/kids	76.4	72.3	69.6	68.2	77	63.5	63.1	57.3	57.7	46.7
		student	4.6	14.3	8.1	15	20.5	16.7	19.6	24	27	34.8
		other	19	13.4	22.3	16.8	2.5	19.8	17.3	18.7	15.3	18.5
			100	100	100	100	100	100	100	100	100	100

			Rural Area					Urban Area				
			1	2	3	4	5	1	2	3	4	5

Labor Force Distribution

by functional sector

			1	2	3	4	5	1	2	3	4	5
National	female	public	0	8.1	5.7	5.4	16.8	2.1	3.7	6.8	15.7	21.5
		modern	6.7	14.4	15.9	20.9	14.6	21.3	32.3	30.3	26.2	34.4
		farm	37.9	28.9	23	36.5	5.5	5	1.9	2	0.9	0.2
		informal	55.4	48.6	55.5	37.1	63.1	71.6	62	60.8	56.9	43.8
			100	100	100.1	99.9	100	100	99.9	99.9	99.7	99.9
	male	public	1.1	0.5	0.8	5.7	9	4.9	6.2	9.3	14.9	17.7
		modern	8.9	16	21.4	19	25.5	37.8	38.4	40.3	40	45.7
		farm	77.7	55.3	45	47.3	25.9	9.4	8.5	4.6	2.7	1.3
		informal	12.1	28.2	32.6	28	39.6	47.7	47	45.8	42.2	35
			99.8	100	99.8	100	100	99.8	100	100	99.8	99.7

by economic sector

			1	2	3	4	5	1	2	3	4	5
National	female	agriculture	77.9	56.6	55.2	56.8	49.4	7.4	6.5	5.9	4.4	3.2
		mining	0.3	0.3	0.1	0	0	0	0	0	0.4	0.2
		manufacturing	5.5	4.5	11.7	11.7	15.9	12.4	22.3	15.4	15.2	8.8
		service	15.9	38.3	33	30.4	34.7	78.7	70.5	76.7	78.3	85.2
		construction	0.4	0	0	1.1	0	1	0.4	1.2	1	0.9
		transport	0	0.3	0	0	0	0.5	0.3	0.8	0.7	1.7
			100	100	100	100	100	100	100	100	100	100
	male	agriculture	87	69.8	68.1	70.6	53.5	15.5	14.9	10.1	8	7.7
		mining	0.2	0.1	0.2	0.9	0	1.8	0.8	0.2	0.6	0.8
		manufacturing	3.9	10.3	11.6	5.2	8.6	22.1	20.5	19	17.7	13.1
		service	3.9	9.5	11.8	15.3	25.8	40.3	41.9	42.7	57.6	64.1
		construction	4.2	8.3	5.7	5.1	2.7	17.1	12.7	18.9	7.6	5.8
		transport	0.8	2.1	2.6	2.9	9.4	3.2	9.1	8.9	8.5	8.6
			100	100	100	100	100	100	99.9	99.8	100	100

by regulation

			1	2	3	4	5	1	2	3	4	5
National	female	regulated	0.8	2.9	7.7	15.6	13.2	9.1	18.5	24.6	28.9	46
		unregulated	99.2	97.1	92.3	84.4	86.8	90.9	81.5	75.4	71.1	54
			100	100	100	100	100	100	100	100	100	100
	male	regulated	2.7	4.5	5.2	14.5	14.9	16.2	20.8	25.3	33.3	42.9
		unregulated	97.3	95.5	94.8	85.5	85.1	83.8	79.2	74.7	66.7	57.1
			100	100	100	100	100	100	100	100	100	100

			Rural Area					Urban Area				
			1	2	3	4	5	1	2	3	4	5

by unionization

			1	2	3	4	5	1	2	3	4	5
National	female	unionized	0	1.2	2.3	2.4	9.8	3.3	10.1	8.6	15.9	21.3
		non-unionized	100	98.8	97.7	97.6	90.2	96.7	89.9	91.4	84.1	78.7
			100	100	100	100	100	100	100	100	100	100
	male	unionized	1.4	1.3	1.7	4.2	9.2	8.4	10.9	9.5	14.3	21.5
		non-unionized	98.6	98.7	98.3	95.8	90.8	91.6	89.1	90.5	85.7	78.5
			100	100	100	100	100	100	100	100	100	100

Secondary Work (percentage of working population)

			1	2	3	4	5	1	2	3	4	5
National	female		23.2	31.3	24.2	26	36.8	4.5	7.9	8.1	10.4	12.2
	male		23.2	19.7	31.6	25.4	26.7	8.5	8.3	7.6	15.2	18.7

Pension elegibility under work arrangement (percentage of working population)

			1	2	3	4	5	1	2	3	4	5
National	female		0.3	2.9	7.2	10	8.3	8.9	14.9	17.1	23.9	38.9
	male		1.8	2.9	4.4	11.5	12.9	13.5	18.3	20.5	27.8	37.5

Different Occupation today than one year ago (percentage of working population)

			1	2	3	4	5	1	2	3	4	5
National	female		20.3	14.9	18.8	14.5	16.6	12	12.8	7.6	7.5	6.8
	male		31.9	30.8	30.7	24.5	21.1	20.4	16.7	15.8	10.3	9.5

Permance of Job Held

			1	2	3	4	5	1	2	3	4	5
National	female	permanent	79.5	84.8	88.7	94.6	92.8	74.6	81.7	78.7	84.3	87.7
		temporary	20.5	15.2	11.3	5.4	7.2	25.4	18.3	21.3	15.7	12.3
			100	100	100	100	100	100	100	100	100	100
	male	permanent	90.4	90.4	89	95.7	8.3	71.2	79.9	81.7	85.1	91
		temporary	9.6	9.6	11	4.3	91.7	28.8	20.1	18.3	14.9	9
			100	100	100	100	100	100	100	100	100	100

indigenous language (percent of population)

	1	2	3	4	5	1	2	3	4	5
Costa	0.0	0.0	0.2	0.0	0.0	0.8	0.0	0.0	0.0	0.5
Sierra	23.4	4.8	5.2	6.3	1.4	5.1	4.2	1.7	0.8	0.3
Oriente	88.4	59.7	61.6	45.1	54.6	19.2	24.1	3.7	4.5	5

Source: **LSMS (1994)**

Working Paper 2.: Poverty and Inequality Developments in Urban Ecuador, 1989 to 1993
Donna MacIsaac and Jesko Hentschel

1.   Introduction

A very lively Ecuadoran debate about living conditions suggests that poverty has increased over the past years but few studies have tested the allegation. The extent, distribution and development of poverty are the focus of numerous articles in newspapers and journals, as well as in private and government publications. A number of variables are used to support an alleged increase in poverty, especially in the urban areas: slow macroeconomic growth, a shift of employment towards the urban informal sector, and the decrease of wage income (mostly generated in urban areas) as a percentage in overall GDP. But little or no attempts have been made to rigorously test whether poverty increased or decreased in urban Ecuador. This Working Paper tries to fill this gap as we examine developments of income distribution and poverty in urban Ecuador between 1989 and 1993.

The measurement of poverty developments is controversial by nature which largely depends on the very definition of poverty in the first place. As outlined in Working Paper 1, researchers and analysts generally rely on income or expenditure to determine whether a household can afford to buy a minimum basket of goods.[1] A poverty line is chosen and several poverty measures are calculated. However, the choice of the poverty line itself is highly arbitrary as a certain calorie requirement and its composition is determined, often adjusted for age and sex. And when comparing poverty across time, the choice of the poverty line can be of crucial importance -- the number of poor people might increase for one poverty line but not for a marginally different one.

How can we measure poverty developments without being vulnerable to arguments that our selected poverty line is wrong? This Working Paper demonstrates poverty developments in Ecuador using stochastic dominance tests which examine poverty developments for all possible poverty lines. The tests allow us to compare different poverty indicators in urban Ecuador in 1989, 1991 and 1993.

Two key messages emerge from these tests:
*   the income distribution in urban Ecuador worsened from 1989 to 1993 both at the national as well as at the regional level;
*   the severity of poverty -- but not necessarily the percentage of the urban population living in poverty -- also increased unequivocally between 1989 and 1993. Again, this result holds for the national urban area as well as for both the urban Costa and the urban Sierra.

This paper is structured as follows. In Section 2, we describe the data source. We point out strength and limitations of the survey and shortly discuss how we have gone about

---

[1]   Another widely applied measure of poverty in Ecuador is the Basic Needs Indicator. A number of basic services (such as potable water or electricity access) and social indicators (such as level of education) are used and weighted so that an individual is assigned a number of total points describing her or his supply with basic needs. This weighting is generally conducted in an arbitrary fashion. Individuals below a "cut-off line" are then considered as poor.

defining important variables. Section 3 then examines income inequality developments in urban Ecuador, both at the national and regional level. We study whether poverty has decreased or increased in Section 4 and conclude this Working Paper with a short summery of the obtained results. The Annex to this Working Paper also deals with urban poverty but with a different subject. Using the 1994 Living Standard Measurement Study, the Annex reports on probit estimations of the likelihood of an urban household to be poor.

2.   Data Sources and Manipulation

The only available household survey which allows us to analyze inequality and poverty in urban Ecuador over time is the Employment Household Survey by the Instituto Nacional de Empleo (INEM). It is conducted on an annual basis, quite contrary to the Living Standard Measurement Survey, used in the large body of this study, which the Government conducted for the first time in 1994.[2]

We encountered several difficulties with the Employment Survey, the most severe one being a very crude definition of income. The employment survey was primarily geared towards measuring unemployment, underemployment and the sectoral distribution of the labor force. The measurement of income from employment sources was imprecise. For example, INEM adjusted incomes for extra benefits (like the teen salaries) by using a fixed multiplication factor across the board. This method is questionable because (a) not all benefits are actually calculated as a proportion to the base salary but are lump sum payments independent of the level of the monthly base salary, and (b) income earners in the informal sector (e.g. domestic employees) are not assured such an augmentation. Further, the Catholic University of Guayaquil examined the accuracy of the income survey and found that around 15% of reported household incomes were significantly false. These problems added to our initial hesitation to derive judgments about poverty developments using a pre-defined poverty line.

While we were skeptical of the absolute income figures reported in the survey, we still felt comfortable to make judgments about the developments of urban income distribution and urban poverty over time. We hence made the assumption that problems with the surveys (such as the correct definition of income or measurement errors) would impact on the *absolute* income figures within one survey but not on *relative* ones when comparing the different surveys. In other words, we assumed that the distribution of income is independent of the measurement errors.

Income definitions. Based on the Employment Surveys, we used per capita household income to measure welfare.[3] It is created by dividing the aggregate of all household income equally among all household members. Thus, our understanding of poverty developments began with an understanding of the components of income within each of the surveys. We

---

[2]   We cannot compare poverty rates or other results obtained from the Living Standard Measurement Survey with the INEM Household Employment Surveys. As Scott (1994) shows, using different types of household surveys to compare welfare measures is almost impossible as the way in which data is obtained and variables are defined is almost never identical. The employment survey by INEM primarily aims to define wage income while the LSMS is much broader in scope.

[3]   When using household income per capita, the analyst makes two strong assumptions: first, that income is equally distributed/required among all household members and second, that no economies of scale in consumption exist. If these assumptions are wrong, the resulting poverty analysis will include a bias.

tried to harmonize income definitions as much as possible between the different surveys.[4] INEM had changed the survey design and employment income specification in particular, which affected the measurement of income and required adjustments from year to year. Using our understanding of the Ecuadoran labor market we harmonized these income definitions as much as possible between the different surveys, to create an income definition which is consistent throughout the years and yet best reflect actual incomes within the years. Thus we adjusted the wages of public employees and private sector workers for extra-benefits by a factor of 29% in 1989 and 35% in both 1990 and 1991.[5]

Price adjustments. We made incomes in different years comparable by adjusting for intertemporal and inter-regional price variation. Following Aguinaga (1994), we first chose the national food consumption basket of the second quintile population from the 1991 INEC expenditure survey and valued this consumption basket at Sierra and Costa prices for consecutive years from 1989 to 1993. Then we deflated the income in each region by the regional price of the food basket relative to the national price for the different years using the 1993 prices as the base year.[6] This gave us coherent, regionally adjusted real incomes in 1993 prices. Table 1 presents the resulting average household income per capita, weighted by the factor expansion factors given in the surveys.

Table 1. Average Household Income in Urban Ecuador, 1989 -1993
(1993 prices)

1989	113,103
1990	103,678
1991	117,389
1992	93,852
1993	119,278

Source: INEM, Encuesta Permanente de Hogares, 1989-1993.

Degree of Underreporting. One of the greatest problems of comparing surveys across time is the varying degree of underreporting. As observed in Table 1, average real income as recorded by the household surveys, fluctuates tremendously between the different years which is at least partially due to the differing degrees of underreporting income because aggregate income (GDP) of the economy does not show such large variations. As we are not interested in presenting absolute poverty figures but rather in looking at poverty changes over time, we are much more concerned with the *varying* degree of underreporting than with the fact that underreporting itself occurred.[7]

---

[4]   We excluded those households for which one member had a missing observation for one of the income data entries while it was obvious that this household member had an income.

[5]   We adjusted both formal and informal sector income from wage earners in all years. INEM had switched in 1990 to adjusting every wage income for benefits while INEC had only adjusted the formal sector wage income in 1989. We did not have to adjust the 1992 and 1993 surveys as this had already been processed by INEM.

[6]   We applied the Costa prices to the Oriente region given the lack of price information in that region.

[7]   Even if we wanted to adjust for the degree of underreporting in the surveys, this would be very complicated. In general, adjustments for underreporting in household surveys are made by using

We assessed the similarity of the different datasets by comparing mean average per capita income in each urban employment survey to GDP per capita. Results are presented in Table 2:

Table 2. Ratio of mean household income to GDP per capita (per cent)

1989	88.7
1990	78.0
1991	85.4
1992	67.3
1993	81.6

Source: INEM, Encuesta Permanente de Hogares, 1989-1993.

Based on these results we decided to look at changes in poverty indicators only for the years 1989, 1991 and 1993 as the ratios were rather similar. If the degree of underreporting is the same in different years, the observed moderate decline of our indicator between the three years is due to an increasing share of national GDP being generated in the rural sector -- something which is supported by national income data as the fastest growing sector over the past years was the agricultural sector in the Costa.

3.   Inequality Developments

Income distributions in both the Costa and the Sierra unequivocally worsened in the period from 1989 to 1993. Graphs 1 and 2 show the familiar Lorenz curves, which plot population share by the accumulated household per capita income. As can be seen, income distribution both in the Ecuadoran Sierra and Costa worsened continuously so that the poor segments of society captured less of national income while the rich increased their share. In 1993, the richest 10% of the Sierra population held 42% of total Sierra incomes while the poorest 50% only hold 18%. In the Costa, the richest 10% gained 40% of total Costa income and the poorest 50% captured 18%. Nationally, the proportion of income accruing to each of the nine lowest deciles successively decreased from 1989 to 1993 -- all at the expense of an increasing income share in the highest decile.[8]

---

overall Gross National Product as a reference mark so that GNP per capita is equal to the average household income reported in the survey. However, since we only have urban household survey data we would only need *urban* GNP which is not available.

[8] In the Sierra, the top decile share in 1993 had increased by 23% over its 1989 share of 30% while the lowest quintile income share of 5.2% fell by 36%. The income share of the lowest quintile in the Costa was not as severely reduced and the greater increase, 28%, in the uppermost decile share came at the expense of those close to the top. Comparing the proportions of income in 1989 to the respective proportions of income in 1993, we found that for all points up to the 70th percentile the reduction was greater in the Sierra than in the Costa.

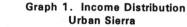

Graph 1. Income Distribution
Urban Sierra

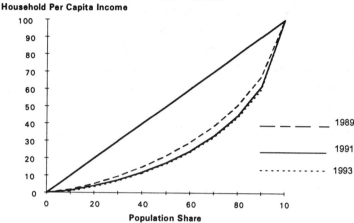

Graph 2. Income Distribution
Urban Costa

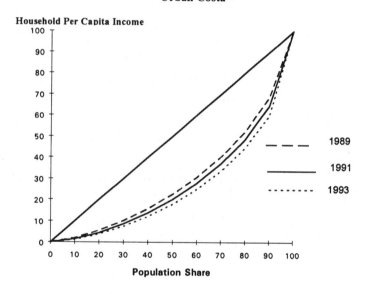

4. Poverty Developments

Tests of Statistical Dominance: The Methodology. We used two similar tests to examine the development of poverty over time. These tests, referred to as stochastic dominance tests, have the advantage that they can asses the development of poverty for various poverty measures without committing to a specific poverty line (Atkinson 1989). This is accomplished by testing, or more specifically plotting, the development of poverty over classes of poverty measures. This allows us to determine whether standard poverty measures such the headcount index, the poverty gap or severity measures have increased or decreased over all income levels. The two tests, which we also apply to the Living Standard Measurement Survey in Working Papers 1 and 4, are shortly described below:

First Order Dominance Test. First order statistical dominance involves comparing the cumulative income distribution functions for each of the survey years. One distribution dominates another if the income distribution functions for that year lies above that of another year at all levels of income. If, however, the distributions do not exhibit a clear dominance relationship and the functions cross, it is possible to derive a partial ordering over a range of incomes. If we find that first order dominance holds between two different years, this implies that the whole range of poverty measures in one year is higher than in the other, i.e. the headcount index, the poverty gap and any measure of the severity of poverty.

Second Order Dominance Test. The second methodology we used is a natural development from the first. This test of second order dominance can determine whether poverty has improved/worsened over time for all poverty measures apart from the headcount index. For example, we can determine if the amount of money we would have had to give to all poor people to raise their income to the poverty line (the poverty gap) increased over time. Second order dominance testing involves the analysis of 'deficit' curves or the integral of the cumulative income distribution functions.

Poverty Developments in Urban Ecuador, 1989 to 1993. Using tests of statistical dominance, we find that the severity of poverty increased in the national urban areas and the urban Sierra and urban Costa separately. To demonstrate the interpretation of the curves, we plot the first and second order dominance tests for the urban areas in Graphs 3 and 4.

Graph 3 presents the cumulative distribution functions for our chosen survey years. Had distribution for one year been consistently above/below that of another year we could state not only that the proportion of the urban population in poverty (headcount index) increased or decreased between years, regardless of the poverty line chosen, but also that the depth (poverty gap) and severity of poverty had a similar relationship (compare Working Paper 1). However, we can observe that the two distribution functions cross at various points so that we can reach no conclusions regarding the evolution of poverty at the national urban level.

Graph 3. First Order Dominance:
National Distribution Functions for Income, 1989, 1991, 1993

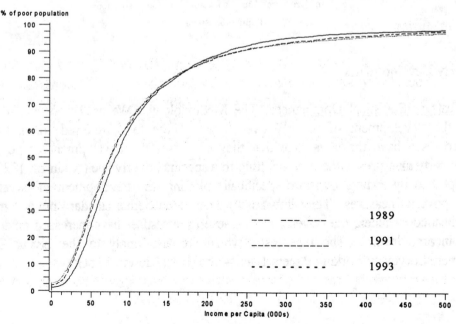

Since we cannot make a clear statement whether poverty increased or decreased using the test of first order statistical dominance, we proceed to conduct the test for second order dominance and we obtain a different result. Graph 4 plots the deficit curves for the national urban area (which are the integrals of the cumulative income distribution functions). As can be observed, the 1993 curve clearly dominates the 1991 curve and the latter the 1989 one. Therefore, we can unequivocally state that the depth and severity of poverty has increased from 1989 to 1991 and, although to a lesser extent, from 1991 to 1993.

Graph 4. National Deficit Curves for Income 1989, 1991, 1993

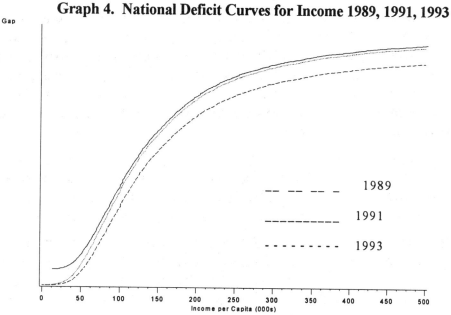

Dominance tests for the two sub-regions separately show the exact same result: the severity of urban poverty has increased from 1989 to 1991 and from 1991 to 1993 in the urban Costa and urban Sierra.

5.   Conclusion

Modest economic growth in the period between 1989 and 1993 (0.5% in per capita terms) did not benefit the weak segments of the Ecuadoran society. In accordance with GNP growth rates, we found that real per capita income of the urban population increased slightly between 1989, 1991 and 1993. However, the income distribution worsened significantly with the lower deciles of the society capturing less and less of total disposable income.

This Working Paper showed that the depth and severity of poverty and income distribution in urban areas worsened from 1989 to 1993. We used income surveys which are comparable in their degree of underreporting and derived real per household income by adjusting employment income between the different years. We employed tests of statistical dominance to measure poverty developments over time. While we were not able to say anything about poverty developments over time using the headcount index for different poverty lines, we found that poverty unequivocally increased judged by its depth and severity. This holds for the national urban as well as for the regional areas.

References

Aguinaga, Consuelo (1993)   Determinacion de los Niveles de Pobreza: Area Urbana de Ecuador, INEC, Quito.

Atkinson, A.B. (1989)   Poverty and Social Security, Menpel Hempstead: Harvester Wheatsheaf.

Scott, Kinnon (1994)   Venezuela: Poverty Measurement with Multiple Data Sets, mimeo, World Bank.

Annex: Probit Estimations of Urban Poverty

In order to complement our discussion of the correlates of poverty which we started in Working Paper 1, Table 1 presents the results of performing a PROBIT estimation for the likelihood of an urban household to be poor in Ecuador. We perform the estimation with the Living Standard Measurement Study of 1994.

We include two broad variables in the estimation: first, infrastructure variables such as electricity or water connection, telephone or sewerage. As pointed out various times in this Poverty Report, causality between basic services and poverty can, and probably does, run both ways: a wealthier household is better able to afford a water connection or move to an area which is better serviced. But these services can, on the other hand, also be important for the poor to grow out of poverty as they increase the possibility of the poor household to use its land and housing as an asset to earn additional incomes. Further, as clean water is necessary for good health, a family without good water access is more likely to be ill which in turn will impact on their ability to earn a sufficient income to meet the basic consumption needs of the family. Second, another set of variables relates to the household: its size, headship, education level of the household head, spouse working arrangements and employment activity.

The results reported in Table 1 support many of the characteristics of the poor we pointed out in Working Paper 1. Some, but not all basic service variables are significantly linked to poverty which reflects the diverse living conditions of the urban poor. We find headship not to be significant but many of the other household level variables are: the likelihood of an urban household being poor is increased if the household head has little education, if the household is large, the spouse is not working, and if the household head works in the informal sector.

Table A.1. Probit Estimates for Urban Poverty in Ecuador, 1994	
Variable	National Urban Ecuador
Intercept	-0.55
	(0.05)
Number of People in Household	0.18
	(0.0001)
Connection to Public Water Net	-0.05
	(0.50)
House or Apartment Rented	0.34
	(0.0001)
Sewerage Connection	-0.49
	(0.0001)
Household Head Having More than Primary Education	-0.44
	(0.0001)
Electricity Connection	-0.54
	(0.05)
Telephone Connection	-0.70
	(0.001)
Male Household Head	-0.05
	(0.48)
Household Head Working in the Informal Sector	0.10
	(0.09)
Spouse of Household Head Working	-0.13
	(0.04)
Asymptotic Probability Values in Parentheses	
Log Likelihood	-1153.86
Total Observations	3013
Observations at 0	2457
Observations at 1	556

Working Paper 3: Urban Poverty: How Do Households Adjust?
Caroline Moser

1.   Introduction

Against the background of urban poverty increasing between 1989 and 1993, this Working Paper uses a detailed case study from Guayaquil to highlight how living conditions of poor families changed and, more importantly, what kind of strategies urban poor households adopted to reduce vulnerability and prevent increased impoverishment during macroeconomic recession and reform. The paper also identifies the constraints that limit the poor's capacity to respond to opportunities created by policy change.

The findings from the community of Cisne Dos comes from a four city comparative research project on *"Urban Poverty and Social Policy in the Context of Adjustment"* undertaken by the Urban Development Division of the World Bank (TWURD) between 1991-1994.[1] We specifically selected Cisne Dos as a case study because it provided characteristics of a poor, but upwardly mobile community useful to study during a period of macroeconomic stagnation, adjustment, and reform. First, it was a consolidated low-income community established in the 1970s by young upwardly mobile families. These were 'pioneer settlers' who had moved from inner-city rental accommodation to the periphery of the city to acquire a 10 by 30 meter plot as *de facto* home owners. The first households arrived in 1970, with the highest in-migration period between 1975 and 1979.

Second, at that time the residents, far from being societies casualties, were an aspiring community, struggling through hard work and initiative to improve their standard of living, and, through better health and education the employment prospects for their children, if not themselves. As such it was a stable increasingly urban born community with little outward mobility. In 1992, more than half of the residents had lived there an average of 12 years, suggesting settlement stability. With less than half of the population rural born, this is essentially an urban rather than a 'migrant' community.

Third, the community had been incrementally upgraded. On arrival houses were built on wooden stilts with split bamboo walls, wooden catwalks were roads and households relied on irregularly delivered water tanks and pirated electricity. During the later 1970s and early 1980s the residents mobilized and petitioned local politicians and government to provide road infill, drinking water and electricity for their community. At the same time families slowly transformed their houses into permanent structures with brick walls and cement floors (see Moser 1981; 1982; 1987; 1992b).

---

[1]   This is a comparative research project using longitudinal data of poor urban community, household and intra-household coping strategies during the past decade, and their implication for urban social policy. It comprises four sub-city level case studies in Commonwealth, Metro Manila, (Philippines); Angyalföld, Budapest (Hungary); and Chawama, Lusaka (Zambia); as well as Cisne Dos, Guayaquil (Ecuador). Fieldwork was undertaken by local women's NGO/research organizations, working collaboratively with the research team in Washington D.C. In the case of Guayaquil fieldwork was undertaken by Caroline Moser, with Peter Sollis and Alicia Herbert (consultants), together with the interview team of local community women. Financial support for the project comes from the Netherlands Ministry of Development Cooperation, UNICEF, SIDA, the UNDP-financed, UNCHS/World Bank Urban Management Program and the World Bank.

As mentioned above, this Working Paper aims to provide an insight into the type of adjustments used by poor urban households in times of economic hardship. It also hopes to identify some of the main obstacles faced by these households which hinder them from successfully overcoming crisis situations. The Working Paper is structured as follows. Section 2 provides the reader with a description of poverty and changes in living conditions in the community of Cisne Dos, including an evaluation where Cisne Dos fits in the more general urban poverty picture. Section 3 turns to the adjustment strategies of households in Cisne Dos in times of economic hardship and change. We distinguish four different levels when analyzing these household coping strategies: the individual, the intra-, inter-, and community level. This paper concludes with a short analysis of the obstacles poor urban families in Cisne Dos face to overcome poverty.

2.   Poverty in Cisne Dos

Where Does Cisne Dos Fit in the National Urban Picture?

Although the case study cannot, from a statistical perspective, be 'representative' of the larger urban area because it sampled only a small geographic area, it can nevertheless be indicative of larger trends. The weight attached to policy recommendations derived from the case study depends on this comparison. The methodology of the Cisne Dos study is a community panel data study, providing sample-survey longitudinal trend data that explores changes over a fourteen year period (1978-92). The first survey of 244 households was undertaken in 1978, the second of 141 households in 1988, and the third in 1992, with 263 households surveyed. The Cisne Dos settlement must be compared to other urban areas in the Costa and the national level to provide a context for the analysis of urban poverty in Cisne Dos.

Reported income (and hence absolute poverty figures) is an imperfect variable with which to compare the Cisne Dos data and other surveys for a number of reasons. First, surveys frequently apply different concepts to measure household income, relating, for example, to the treatment of in-kind income, government bonuses not disbursed on a monthly basis, social security contributions, and transfers. Further, the accuracy of income measurement depends strongly on the thoroughness with which questions are asked and the role of the respondent in the household. Second, even if average income or levels of poverty can be compared between surveys, this produces a one-dimensional view of living conditions. Hence, while poverty rates between Cisne Dos and the whole urban Costa region might be comparable, the community may differ considerably from the 'average' urban picture with respect to water supply, levels of education or other variables. Further, no other household survey which would render itself operationable was conducted in the same year than the Cisne Dos community survey of 1992 which limits the uni-dimensional reliance on income comparisons.

We choose eight indicators to compare Cisne Dos to the urban Costa and national urban areas. These variables reflect both household and community characteristics: education and gender of the household head, household size, average number of rooms per household, water source, hygiene facilities, garbage disposal method, and cooking fuel. Urban Costa and national areas are defined in terms of the five different income quintiles derived from the 1990

Urban Employment Survey (INEM).[2] The values of the eight variables for Cisne Dos are matched to the respective values for *each* income quintile of the urban population, in order to identify *in which urban segment* the settlement best fits. Closeness is then defined as the smallest variation between the Cisne Dos values and the larger urban area values *per indicator* because most indicators themselves contain different values.[3] The eight indicators are then aggregated by assigning rank values according to the sum of variances for each individual indicator.

Evaluating the closeness of similarity between all eight variables together, Cisne Dos is closest to the poorest income quintiles of the urban Costa and national urban area. As expected, the Costa community is closer to the poor segments of the Costa urban area than for the national urban area. For example, the high incidence of households that rely on private water vendors in Cisne Dos (44 percent) is symptomatic of the poor's limited access to public water in the urban Costa region and their use of private water vendors as suppliers. This contrasts with the considerably better access to water by the urban Sierra population, where four out of five households in the lowest quintile are connected to the public net.

But Cisne Dos has some specific characteristics which distinguish it from an 'average' poor urban area. First, educational achievements of household-heads in Cisne Dos are better than in the lowest quintile. As shown in Table 1 below, the educational pattern fits closest the second income quintile and is actually closer to the third and fourth quintile than to the first one. Second, households' use of gas as a cooking fuel is very high in Cisne Dos, reported at 93 percent. This gas use corresponds more to the pattern of the upper end of the income spectrum of the urban Costa and urban national areas -- although at the national urban level over 85 percent of households in the lowest quintile use gas. Third, and not truly reflected in the table shown below, hygiene facilities are in a very bad shape in Cisne Dos. Only 3.8 percent of households in Cisne Dos are connected to sewerage and have their own flush toilet system while 40 percent of the poorest quintile in the Costa and 46 percent on the national urban level have this service.

To sum up, characteristics of Cisne Dos fit best the lowest income quintile of larger urban areas. Nevertheless, in those socio-economic respects where it differs from an 'average' lower income urban community, policy conclusions from the case study should be made carefully.

Characteristics of Poverty in Cisne Dos

As we have seen, Cisne Dos is without doubt a poor neighborhood when measured against the larger urban area. Applying a 1992 poverty line estimate to the survey in 1992,[4] we find that the most important characteristics of poor households are its structure, the dependency burden and the levels of education of the household head. The 1992 data shows that in Cisne Dos, the majority of poor households have the following characteristics:

---

[2] We chose the INEM employment survey over the LSMS to analyze the fit of Cisne Dos because the former has a higher number of observations for urban areas.

[3] The education variable, for example, contains the share of the population having attended primary school, secondary school and a higher education institution.

[4] We apply a poverty line estimate of 84,243 sucres per capita per month to the income data from the random sample survey to distinguish different households within Cisne Dos.

Table 1. Cisne Dos: Closeness to Costa and National Urban Area, Rank Results[a]

	Income quintile, urban				
	First	Second	Third	Fourth	Fifth
Costa comparison					
Education of household head	4	1	2	3	5
Gender of household head	1	3	2	4	5
Household size	2	1	2	4	5
Number of rooms	1	2	3	4	5
Water source	1	2	3	4	5
Toilet facilities	1	2	3	4	5
Garbage disposal	1	2	3	4	5
Cooking fuel	5	4	3	1	2
Rank result	1 16	2 17	3 21	4 28	5 27
National comparison					
Education of household head	3	1	2	4	5
Gender of household head	1	2	3	4	5
Household size	1	1	3	4	5
Number of rooms	1	2	3	4	5
Water source	1	2	3	4	5
Toilet facilities	1	2	4	4	5
Garbage disposal	1	2	3	4	5
Cooking fuel	5	4	3	2	1
Rank result	1 14	2 16	3 24	4 30	5 36

a   Each entry presents the closeness of fit for each variable between Cisne Dos and the larger urban area. The closeness of fit is measured by the minimum variance for each indicator separately, e.g., for the water source as the percentage of households connected to the public net, buying water from vendors, obtaining it from wells or other sources.

Source: INEM, Encuesta Permanente de Hogares, 1990, and Cisne Dos Random Sample Survey.

- They have large families with more children. Adult members are less likely to be working, translating into a higher dependency burden (i.e., the number of non-working household members to working household members). The mean household size of very poor households is 6.1 as against an average of 3.4 for non-poor households with a dependency ratio of 2.6 as against 2.1 for non-poor households.

- In terms of household structure, the highest incidence of poverty is found among the following three household types; first, nuclear households with younger male heads (with a mean age of 38 years, as against an average of 42 years); second,

Graph 1

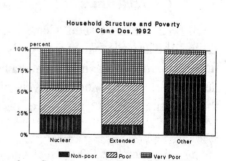

Source: Random Sample Survey, 1992

male headed couple-extended households; and third, extended households with single female-heads, usually an elderly widow or divorcee.

- Heads of poor households are more likely to have lower levels of education than those of non-poor households. About 90 percent of heads with incomplete primary education are from poor households while 63 percent of heads with completed secondary education are non-poor.

Expenditure Patterns and Basic Service Access. Overall, households in Cisne Dos spend almost a quarter of their income on services such as water, electricity, fuel, transportation and education -- with food, rent, healthcare and clothing expenditure still to be accounted for. As Graph 2 shows, poor households spend nearly a third of their income on basic services while non-poor households spend just over a tenth of their income.

Poverty levels are also correlated with both access and quality of service provisions. Poor households have significantly lower access to piped water

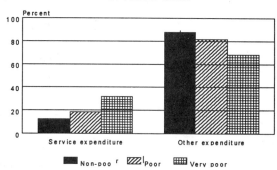

Graph 2

Share of Services and Other Expenditures
By Poverty Group

Source: Random Sample Survey, 1992

than non-poor households, imposing constraints in terms of time and cost. Similarly, non-poor households have more legal connections to electricity, with poor households more likely to pirate it. Analysis of differential costs in private and public healthcare include both direct costs of consultation itself, as well as indirect costs including transportation and lost wages in time queuing, making the private sector increasingly attractive. There is a direct correlation between poverty level and usage -- very poor households use public health care providers more heavily than the poor and non-poor.

Within households, women are particularly affected by deficiencies in public services. Inefficient water and energy sources impose additional constraints on cooking, laundry and most other household reproductive tasks. Missing street lighting affects women's personal safety considerably more than men's, while unsafe transport limits women's mobility. Male students attend evening school significantly more than female students.

Educational levels of household heads were strongly linked

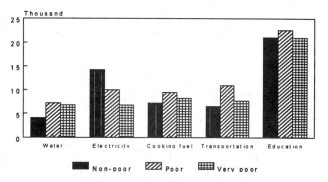

Graph 3

Average Montly Services Expenditures
By Poverty Group

Source: Random Sample Survey, 1992

to poverty levels according to the 1992 data; families of illiterate household heads were all poor. In direct contrast, two-thirds of heads with completed secondary education headed non-poor households. Education expenditures comprise the single largest non-food expenditure, significantly lower at primary than at secondary or tertiary level. Nearly a third of overall education expenditure is on books, a quarter on uniforms, and almost 14 percent on transportation. Education expenditures are a much heavier burden on very poor households than poor or non-poor due to their having significantly more dependents (1.03 students/household for the non-poor compared to 1.86 and 2.42 for the poor and very poor respectively). Poor households compensate by paying less per student. Table 2 summarizes the above described poverty characteristics of Cisne Dos.

Table 2. Summary of characteristics of urban poverty characteristics in Cisne Dos at different levels

	Household Characteristics of urban poverty
Headship	• Headship is not a primary determinant of poverty. The incidence of poverty is comparable for male-headed households and female-headed households.
Household type	• There is a significant correlation between poverty status and household structure. Almost half of nuclear households, mostly with young male heads, as well as nine out of ten couple-extended households, are either poor or very poor. • Female-headed households are more likely to be extended in structure. • *De jure* female heads are worse-off than *de facto* female heads. • Poor households tend to have lower education levels than non-poor households.
Intra-household	• The poorest are the very young, sick, disabled and the elderly
Dependency ratio	• Poor households have high dependency ratios.
Education	• Female heads have lower education levels than male heads.

Changes at the micro-level in Cisne Dos

Longitudinal panel data from Cisne Dos, as well as participatory anthropological fieldwork, provides a detailed picture of the changes affecting individuals, households and the community over a period of time. As we will see in this section, living conditions of the population in Cisne Dos improved significantly between 1978 and 1988 but deteriorated somewhat between 1988 and 1992.

Informalization of Employment. Between 1978 and 1992, the share of working men employed in industry and transport declined from 50 percent to 43 percent. Disaggregation within these sectors shows a decline in the construction sector, and an increase in transport and laboring activities. The service and sales sectors continue to be the major employers of women. Domestic work, mainly private household work, and sales activity consistently employed approximately 70 percent of economically active women over the period 1978 to 1992. In terms of job stability, 1992 data shows men with an average of 7.4 years in their current job, with 4.6 years for women.

Box 1. Casualization of a construction worker's life

Juan has always worked as an *albanil*, a construction worker, since arriving in Guayaquil in 1968. In the 1970s he started as a daily laborer, or *official*, queuing up outside building sites for casual work as available. By the mid-1970s he was working on regular contracts, ranging from three to six months for a *maestro* sub-contractor, building the large city-center banks that sprung up during the oil boom years. Although the rainy season was always slack, during the rest of the year he was on a regular weekly salary paying pension contributions. Following the arrival of in-fill in Cisne Dos in 1978, the local building boom allowed him simultaneously to become a weekend *maestro* builder in the community. In construction gangs with two or three fellow builders he built both wooden/split-cane houses used by newly arriving settlers, as well as cement and block houses by consolidating home owners. The bottom dropped out of the city center building boom by the mid-1980s, and Juan, despite his age and considerable skill had to become once again a daily laborer. Lack of resources within Cisne Dos has reduced considerably the demand for local building activity, and, with younger men now competing, Juan's income earning capacity is very limited. Any spare cash is spent drinking while his wife inadequately supports the family through laundry work.

Source: Interviews in Cisne Dos, 1992.

Going hand in hand with this change in employment structure was the most important change we witness between 1988 and 1992: a reduction in formal sector employment in the urban area itself, resulting in an informalization of work arrangements. Partly, workers outmigrated to seek formal sector employment in the newly developing agro-export shrimp industry, with their families remaining in their urban homes. However, with only 5.5 percent of workers in this sector it had a major impact in Cisne Dos. A small increase in female clerical positions as secretaries in formal sector jobs did also not offset the major trend of an informalization of work (see also Working Papers 8 and 9). Using the ILO definition for informal sector occupation (i.e., employed in enterprises with less than 5 employees, excluding all professional occupations), the informal sector in Cisne Dos in 1992 comprised 54% of the workforce.

Wage employment trends show the degree of informalization of employment in Cisne Dos between 1988 and 1992. Between 1988 and 1992 wage employment dropped by 30 percent. Temporary and casual work, on the other hand increased by 25 percent. Self-employment of women continued to decline (as in the 1978 to 1988 period) but the rate of decline slowed markedly due to the low supply of wage work.

> **Box 2. From shop girls to secretaries: Women's work opportunities**
>
> Angela, aged 30 has lived with her older sister Maria, since she was a young child. In 1980 as a seventeen year old schoolgirl, she had a causal affair with a married man, and, misinformed about contraception, had a son, Pedro. After the initial shock the family welcomed Pedro as another son. Determined to be both successful and financially independent, Angela coordinated childcare and cooking on a shift system with both Maria, and her niece, Nelly in order to complete her high school certificate. Her first job, after a long struggle was as a shop assistant in a large city center supermarket. With rolling three month contracts, low pay and no social security, after two years Angela moved on to become a sales agent for an office supplies company, earning on commission. In 1989, leaving Pedro with her sister, Angela moved to another city, Riobamba, to live with Franco. He didn't want her to work so Angela studied accounting at night school. By 1991, domestic violence had forced her to return to her sister's house, bringing with her a second son. She now lives independently with her two children in a room at the back of the plot. With both children in school and dovetailed childcare support from Maria and Nelly, Angela now works as a secretary in a legal company, leaving early each morning with her briefcase and not home before 7.30 at night, to earn a salary double that of a shop girl.
>
> *Source*: Interviews in Cisne Dos, 1992.

The informal sector is especially important for female employment. Almost three quarters of all working women in Cisne Dos (74 percent) are employed in the informal sector, predominantly in sales and private household work. This compares to 46 percent of male workers who are mainly employed in sales, artisanary, and transport activity. The informal sector provides residual work for women. For the majority trading and domestic service provide the backbone of their lives, with significant differences between the two. Domestic service, quintessential 'women's work' in Cisne Dos, is itself a highly complex sector with different income earning capacity associated with both skill level and mobility. At one end of the spectrum is laundering, a low-paid piece work job. It is undertaken both locally for neighbors and more lucratively in middle class households which means that women travel across town for collection and delivery, often leaving their young children locked up at home. At the other end of the mobility spectrum are domestic servants who leave home at 6.a.m. and return after 6 p.m. (or only at weekends in the case of housekeepers).

For men, mobility within the informal sector is the most important requisite for economic survival. Traditionally, tailors in Cisne Dos have always been men, working as both as artisan producers locally, as well as out-workers with city center workshops. In 1978, this was a respected if arduous craft in which 5 percent of men worked, declining to 3.8 percent in 1988 and 1.2 percent in 1992. This decline was largely due to imports of cheap factory produced garments from Colombia and more competition from local factory production. At the same time new opportunities opened up in repair work for electrical items such as refrigerators, radio, TVs and cassette recorders. Similarly, transport sector mechanical repairs increasingly attract younger men. Not everyone has fared equally well, as Box 3 shows.

Finally, in the informal sales sector increasingly men and women compete, with men earning on average twice as much as females -- reflecting different gender constraints and opportunities. These relate to access to capital, mobility and market saturation. Cisne Dos, as with many low-income urban areas, has a glut of small home-based female enterprises, competing with each other selling soft drinks, ice and other items. Forced to work from home because of reproductive responsibilities, these women earn less than do the more mobile street sellers. Overall, the data shows that in 1992 the informal sector is mainly involutionary, particularly in the sales sector, where it absorbs large numbers into highly competitive under-productive enterprises.

Box 3. Informal sector mobility and diversification: The story of two tailors

Two brothers, Pancho and Julian, both tailors, have had very different experiences over the past fifteen years. In 1978 elder brother Julian was well-established with a diversity of clients locally as well as a standing outwork contract with a city center workshop. With his wife Margarita assisting him, they were putting three children through primary schooling. His younger brother Pancho, aged twenty two, recently starting out on his own having been apprenticed to his brother, had acquired a plot next door, bought a sewing machine on credit, and was doing subcontracting work in the center.

By 1992 both brothers were still tailors, both had suffered from a drastic decline in real income which could not be rectified by working even longer hours - both households were below the poverty line. Julian's household, however, had survived extreme poverty by diversifying, Margarita ran a small home based enterprise set up with family saving, while Julian's eldest son, who had trained as a refrigerator repair mechanic while undertaking military service, was now the primary income earner. Without such a cushion, Pancho's family had fallen into extreme poverty. Despite both his wife and he working seven days a week on piece rate work, with three younger teenage and pre-teen children to support, they were in a desperate situation. The house lacked side and back walls and part of the roof, the children received free meals three days a week from the Evangelical church feeding program, as well as a assistance with matriculation fees from the Plan International Program.

Source: Interviews in Cisne Dos, 1992.

Land, Housing and Plot Ownership. Cisne Dos, is a typical squatter settlement, developed as a result of the unmet housing needs of the urban poor in Guayaquil which resulted from the rapid urban population growth in the 1970s. Led by the petroleum-boom and inner-city office development, this population growth reduced affordable tenement rental accommodations. Invasions of private and municipal swampland on the peripheral areas of the city (*suburbios*) absorbed most of the growth of the city: in 1950 they accommodated 12 percent of the population, which increased to 60 percent by 1975.

The settlement of Cisne Dos, as in many of the poor areas of Guayaquil involved the creation of solid land (through infilling), and the construction of squatter housing. As it consolidated, its characteristics in terms of housing structures, type of tenancy, density of the population, and access to services evolved. During the 1970s, Cisne Dos was characterized by higher incidence of "ownership", low population densities, little access to services, and a housing stock constituted mainly of small, incrementally built bamboo and timber houses standing on poles over polluted water. A complex system of interconnected catwalks linked the houses within this area, as well as with the nearest solid land.

As the settlement evolved over more than a decade, upgraded brick and cement housing replaced less durable ones, population densities increased, and services were provided (Moser, 1982;1987) (see Annex 1). While some settlements were the consequence of large-scale, politically motivated invasions, Cisne Dos was settled primarily through incremental plot squatting and *de facto* ownership of 10 by 30 meter plots. Most consolidation occurred between 1970-80. By 1992, although there was still a considerable proportion of the original settlers, new acquisition was entirely by purchase. The percentage of tenants has remained very low during the entire period.

The average plot size decreased significantly between 1978 and 1988, and remained unchanged during the 1988-92 period. Plot size changes reflect an unregulated land market which has allowed households to use their land as a flexible asset. The average number of years that households have lived in Cisne Dos has steadily increased since 1978. While homeowners tend to be older, more established and with larger families, tenants tend to be the newcomers, more educated, with fewer children, and with a larger *per capita* income.

Without the threat of eviction, home ownership has provided a strong incentive for households to mobilize economic resources to improve housing, as shown by the significant improvements in the housing stock since 1978 in terms of both quality and size. The average house size increased steadily during the 1978-92 period. Lack of stringent building regulations allowed households to expand units according to resources and needs. Housing density decreased significantly between the 1978-88 period, reflecting primarily the increase in the size of houses, which has offset the increase in household size during the same period.

Housing quality deteriorated from 1988-92 as the households had less income to allocate to upgrading. Toilet facilities had improved significantly since 1978 when almost non existed. Over the years, latrines and W.C. replaced the traditional 'holes' located inside or outside the houses. However, housing quality still varies greatly with income. Non-poor households are less crowded than poor households and have better housing in terms of toilet facilities and maintenance. Houses of poor households are in greater need of repair. In 1992, more than four fifths of households maintained urgent repairs were needed, three quarters of whom cited lack of sufficient resources as the reason preventing this from occurring.

Trends in Infrastructure Provision. When the original settlers invaded Cisne Dos in the early 1970s it was a mangrove swamp without land, roads, or any basic services. Provision of urban services was obtained through intense community mobilization and collective bargaining with different actors -- local and national level politicians for land titles, infill, water mains and roads; the private sector for electricity and bus routes; international and local NGOs (such as UNICEF and Plan International) for community services and schooling. As illustrated in Annex 2 during the overall 1978-92 period, two very different trends can be identified.

- 1978-88: A steady improvement in access and quality of services, particularly water mains, electricity, infill, and roads.

- 1988-92: A significant decline in the quality of services, particularly water, together with an increase in the cost of some services, especially education.

The *electricity* lines first reached the Cisne Dos area at the same time as the main roads were infilled in 1976. By 1978, 72 percent of households had illegal connections. Legal household level electricity connections were obtained in 1979 and by 1988, 95 percent of households had access. By 1992 this had reached 100 percent, but of those only 65.8 percent were legal and 34 percent were illegal -- a considerable resurgence of pirated electricity by those households that were disconnected by the electric company for non-payment of their electricity bills.

Access to *water* improved since 1978, when all the water was provided by a private transport cooperative of 44 tankers. Piped water was introduced in 1983-84 and by 1988 the majority of households had access, with only a third of households still dependent on street vendors. Between 1988 and 1992, the percentage of households with access to piped water remained unchanged, with a third still relying completely on street vendors, but households had to compensate for a dramatic reduction in quality of the service. Some households returned to purchasing drinking water from street vendors in 1992 as this water is often perceived as being purer in quality. A second type of 'private' investment to ameliorate water system deficiencies was the purchasing of water pumps to cope with discontinuous supply.

Access to other services varies considerably in the community. Sewerage services are still almost non-existent. In 1992, the main cooking fuel used was gas, which is most efficient in terms of time, both cooking and fetching it, as well as cost. A few households used carbon (charcoal wood) which was considerably more expensive, while some used kerosene, which was almost as cheap in 1992 as gas but considerably more risky and time consuming. Garbage collection first began in 1992 as a result of a crisis in the garbage collection system and cholera outbreak. The main road from the central business district to Cisne Dos and most of the main streets within the community were paved during the middle to late 1980s, while most minor streets were still unpaved in 1992. However, the lack of coordination between the agencies responsible for road maintenance resulted in a serious and continuous deterioration of roads within the community. Street lighting on the main roads was installed beginning in 1976. However, lighting in certain areas was still deficient or absent in 1992.

The number of *educational facilities* in Cisne Dos has increased dramatically since 1978. In 1992, a total of 39 preschool, primary, and secondary schools were utilized by the community, the majority located within its boundaries, but with a number of state primary and private secondary schools located outside. These differed in terms of ownership, fees, number of shifts, average class sizes and availability of services and programs. While many of the community preschools were introduced through the UNICEF Urban Basic Services program of the late 1970s and early 1980s, improvements and diversification of both state primary and secondary schools had been undertaken during the mid and late 1980s, largely with financial assistance from Plan International.

In 1992, the following educational facilities in Cisne Dos existed: preschool -- 5 community, 2 private; primary -- 10 state, 6 private; secondary -- 5 state, 6 private. While preschool and primary schools generally operate with one shift per day, secondary schools have up to 3 shifts, with multi-grade teaching prevalent especially in the state primary. By 1992, one out of five students attended a private institution. By 1992, therefore, access to education in Cisne Dos was not a problem. However, children often did not receive a good education. With class sizes very large and textbooks scarce, drop-out and repetition rates were very high.

The increase in private *health facilities* over the past years has been dramatic. Three out of the four public sector facilities servicing the area had been established before 1980 -- the Hospital de Guayaquil, the Mariana de Jesus Maternity Hospital and the Atahualpa Policlinic -- while the forth, the SAFIC primary health care center, established in 1989, was a targeted initiative of the Borja government, responding to public sector health cut-backs during the

1980s. During the same 1978-92 period the growth in private-for-profit services in Cisne Dos accompanied both settlement consolidation and increased demand. Small pharmacies came first, then doctors and finally dentists. In 1992, the private health sector in Cisne Dos consisted of six doctors, three dentists, one medical laboratory, nine pharmacies, and two trained nurses.

Overall, the population of Cisne Dos had access to health care in 1992. Individuals sought professional health treatment in over 95% of all sickness cases. The private sector provided about half of these health care interventions with public help being sought more in cases of serious medical problems. Preference for private sector health care related directly to the perceived differences in service quality. The long term sustainability of private practices was related not only to diversification in services offered, such as the combination of multiple specialties, a medical lab, minor surgery, but also to the availability of credit for their services, short waiting times, and flexible hours. While public hospitals were free, they were characterized by declining resources and infrastructure, long waiting times, and limited night access.

Table 3. Summary of changes increasing household vulnerability, Cisne Dos, 1988-1992

Issue	Empirical evidence from Cisne Dos
• Decline in formal sector employment and wage income	Between 1988-1992 permanent wage employment dropped from 44 to 30 percent, accompanied by an increase in casual work from 7 percent to 25 percent over the same period. 28 percent of respondents maintained household income had decreased from 1991 to 1992; 80% of income came from earned sources in 1992.
• Decline in plot ownership	Between 1978-1992, plot ownership decreased from 88 percent to 75 percent, with the number of 'nesters' -- households living on plots owned by relatives -- increasing from 10 to 19 percent
• Decline in quality of urban services • Increase in service prices	Water -- In 1988 access to piped water 64 percent, with tanker-bought water accounting for 36 percent. In 1992, access remained unchanged but decline in water quality and running time meant 14 percent of households had to increasingly rely on water vendors. Education -- In 1992, private costs of education reached 8 percent of household income; declining quality meant a quarter of households had children attending private schools. Health -- Lacking public coverage provision has resulted in an increased demand and supply of private medical services. Private doctors treat about half of the population in case of sickness.
• Decline in personal safety • Increase in community violence	Subsample data show an escalating level of violence in Cisne Dos. Over a 6-month period (Feb-July 1992), 50 percent of respondents witnessed a bus robbery, one-third were victims of street and house theft, and more than half other family members robbed. 45 percent identified the "pantillas" (gangs of young unemployed males) as a major cause of crime.

Finally, a decline in public safety in the period between 1988 and 1992 reduced physical mobility. This resulted in a drop in the use of public transport, particularly at night, and increased use of safer small trucks by workers working late shifts, especially women. Reduced physical mobility also lowered the attendance rates of night school, again affecting women more than men as they were unwilling to travel on public transport at night.

Summary. Table 3 provides a brief summary of the most important factors identified as increasing household vulnerability in Cisne Dos in the period between 1988 and 1992. These relate to changes in income and employment, as well as housing and infrastructure, with brief conclusions relating to each of these summarized below. As described above, living conditions of the population in Cisne Dos improved significantly between 1978 and 1988, for example with respect to income earning possibilities, housing quality, service access, and the available education and health infrastructure. However, due to a number of exogenous influences such as the decline in formal sector wage employment and the deterioration of public services, vulnerability of the population increased between 1988 and 1992.

3.   Household Responses: Strategies to Reduce Vulnerability

The urban poor in Cisne Dos are not passive in the face of economic change. Longitudinal random sample and sub-sample data highlight responses in terms of household income-earning activities, consumption behavior and satisfaction of basic needs. The following text provides a brief summary elaboration of strategies at four different levels: the individual, intra-, inter- and community level. With the classification of strategies according to these different levels somewhat arbitrary, our emphasis is more to provide the reader with the spectrum of different strategies than to classify the latter.

Individual strategies

Increase in Female and Child Labor Force Participation. When 'traditional' incomes decline, the most important response of poor families is that women spouses try to increase their role in income generating activities, either in or outside their homes. In Cisne Dos, female labor market participation has expanded, with the numbers of working women spouses increasing from 32 percent in 1978 to 46 percent in 1992.[5] The 1992 data shows that the poorer the household, the more important is a woman's earnings for total family income. The 1978-92 data shows that the number of income earners per household increased from 1.7 to 2.1. Fewer households depended in 1992 on the income of one earner alone. Other household members also raise additional income by assisting in home-based enterprises, especially children. 1992 data show that 12-14 year old boys and girls spent an average of fifteen hours assisting in household enterprises.

Private Investment in Education. Since educational attainment equips household members to adapt better to changing economic circumstances, a second long-term strategy has been the investment in education. Between 1978-92 the average level of education of

[5]   This data corroborates National Census data which show that the female labor force participation in Ecuador increased from 23.9 percent in 1982 to 30.6 percent in 1990. Married women show the most significant increase, from 20.8 percent in 1982 to 29.5 percent in 1992. Urban female participation rates are much higher, with INEC data showing an increase from 34 percent in 1988 to 46 percent in 1993 (INEC, 1993).

household heads and spouses increased -- with illiteracy rates declining from 9.0 percent in 1978 to 3.5 percent in 1992. By 1992, those household heads only with primary level education (or less) decreased from 77 percent to 57.5 percent, with a comparable increase in the share of household heads with secondary education. Similarly, the gender gap in levels of education narrowed. Between 1978-1992 the proportion of spouses with incomplete primary education declined by more than one-half, such that nearly a quarter of heads and spouses had primary level schooling in 1992. In 1992, male and female educational attainment among the total working population was remarkably similar. Equally amongst male and female workers, less than a quarter had failed to complete primary education, while half had progressed beyond primary level.

Intra-household Strategies

Changes in Household Structure. The most important strategy at the intra-household level was to increase informal family support networks through changes in household structure. Although the percentage of women-headed households rose strongly between 1978 (13 percent) and 1992 (20 percent), headship in itself did not constitute a determinant of poverty. In contrast, household structure emerged as a significant correlate of poverty. The decline in nuclear households -- from 67 percent in 1978 to 62 percent in 1992 -- and associated increase in extended households -- from 33 percent to 38 percent -- was a strategy to shield vulnerable family members from falling into poverty.[6]

---

[6]   In 1992, the poorest households were couple-extended households (93 percent), both male and female headed. Disaggregation within female headed households shows that the 86 percent *de jure* female headed comprised the economically poorest group. Although mean household size declined slightly, the dependency ratio per se was not a determinant of poverty but rather the relationship between the dependency ratio and earning capacity of working members. In terms of average earnings per working member, nuclear units were better-off than couple-extended households. Despite a slightly higher dependency ratio, earnings were 20 percent higher for nuclear compared to couple-extended households. Further, there was a strong correlation between the household head's educational level and household structure: While the heads of couple-extended households were more likely to command only a primary level education, heads of nuclear households tended to have at least some secondary education. Of the few with tertiary level education the majority were again found among nuclear households.

Household vulnerability analysis of the Cisne Dos sub-sample data over a ten year period reveals that households are highly dynamic and undergo changes generally of a semi-permanent, rather than short-term nature. The vast majority of households have altered their composition (83 percent) with external reasons slightly more influential than those internal to the household (56 percent and 44 percent). Accessing adequate shelter is the single most important external reason, while marital conflict is more important than life cycle factors such as birth or death.

Box 4. Reducing vulnerability: Older women as female heads of extended households

In 1983, 42 year-old Maria was abandoned by her husband, Carlos. While he set-up home with another woman, Maria was left with their seven children to support. Despite some financial help from Carlos, Maria was forced to work as a washerwoman. However, these combined income sources were barely enough to ensure the basic survival of the family. Faced with such economic hardship, Maria accepted Carlos' pleas to return home 5 years later. While initially resisting because he was a "mujeriego" (womanizer), she finally agreed on financial grounds as he had since found a relatively well-paid job as a van driver. The household was under even greater economic pressure, with the birth of a grandchild to Maria's eldest daughter, Gardenia. Although by 1992, they were still living in poverty with a per capita income of 52,000 sucres, the household was coping better - with Carlos the main breadwinner again, Gardenia working as a laundry woman, and one of Maria's sons and a recently-moved in son-in-law all working. Over a 10 year period, Maria's household changed five times; involving two shifts in headship and three extensions. While Maria's abandonment and the birth of her grandchildren made the household more vulnerable, the other shifts were made to mobilize resources for household survival.

In 1986, Consuela's husband, Mario, died. Although she tried to live alone with her 4 children for a few months, the economic pressure soon became too much for her, as she could not find a job. As a result, she was forced first to sell her main economic asset, her house, and second, to move in with her parents. After a year, Consuela managed to get a job as a ticket collector in the local bus terminal. However, still needing childcare, she remained living with her parents, taking over full responsibility for the household in 1991 after the death of her father. Although Consuela still lived in poverty with a per capita income of 37,714 sucres, widowhood forced her to mobilize scarce resources, and adopt various coping strategies through a series of balancing mechanisms in order to survive.

Source: Interviews in Cisne Dos, 1992.

In conditions of poverty households act as safety nets. This can mean different things at different points in time. For individuals facing economic difficulties the family is a 'shock absorber', with restructuring a reactive response. In the short-term this increases vulnerability as dependents move in to deal with temporary difficulty, such as lack of shelter or employment. Over time, kin absorption often acts to the long-term advantage of the host household, if additional members contribute income or childcare. In Cisne Dos, gender, age and asset ownership mediate coping strategies in different ways, two in particular being of greatest importance: older women utilizing the extended household to reduce vulnerability and younger female heads avoiding poverty by 'hiding' in extended households.

Older women utilize the extended household to reduce vulnerability. While headship in itself is not necessarily a determinant of poverty, many women avoid heading a household. Older women, widowed, divorced or separated and left as lone parents often restructure forming extended households. In 1992, 42 percent of female-headed households were either separated or divorced, with an average age of 46 years of the woman head. A further 34 percent were widows with a mean average age of 57 years. They absorb younger extended kin and pool economic contributions to avoid extreme poverty. Thus female headed households are more likely to be extended than nuclear -- two-generational families with their own children and respective families, or in wider extended family arrangements, incorporating relatives such as siblings or nephews and nieces. In both cases, these additional members contribute economically or with childcare or elderly support. Such strategies are not full-proof, especially when elderly women are unable to mobilize second generation kin support, or when the extension primarily benefits absorbed kin members themselves. At times, through economic necessity, women may even be forced to take back errant husbands.

Box 5. Avoiding poverty: Young women as 'hidden' female heads

In 1982, Bella's 'comprometido', Jorge, moved in with her, her widowed mother and 2 brothers. He had no job and so they could not afford to live independently. By 1986 Bella had two children, yet Jorge had still not found work. When her youngest child was only 8 months old, Bella threw Jorge out of the house as "vago" (lazy, good-for-nothing). Having supported the entire family since 1982 selling children's clothes from home, she finally grew tired of Jorge's financial dependence on her. Although the household was still very poor in 1992, living below the poverty line, Bella still lived with her mother mainly due to the emotional and childcare support and had no intention of looking for another partner. "I am afraid that a new husband will harm me or my children."

23 year-old Maritza lives with her aged mother and father, along with her 9 month-old daughter, Isabel. As an only daughter, Maritza' parents had just enough money to send her to secondary school and then to college. However, in 1991, she got pregnant by a *companero* with whom she lived until the baby was born. One month after the birth, he deserted her for another women, and Maritza returned to her parent's home. By this time, Maritza had given-up college, yet she could not find a job. With her mother working 18 hours a day as an ambulant fruit seller there was no-one else to look after Isabel. Her father received a small retirement pension, Maritza's mother was the primary breadwinner with earnings which barely covered the household expenses (the family lived below the poverty line with per capita income of 32,000 sucres). Maritza feels very trapped by the situation, unable to depend on her parent's economic support, nor to find a job herself.

Source: Interviews in Cisne Dos, 1992.

Younger female heads avoiding poverty 'hidden' in extended households. When young couples split up, younger women incorporate themselves within their parent's or other relatives homes, as 'hidden' female heads. Although largely unrecognized, random sample survey data shows 50 percent of extended households incorporate lone mothers with their children. Such sub-units take two forms; first, young women, who have been living independently, return home on the spouses' departure; second, women already residing as a conjugal unit with their children within extended households, separate from partners who leave.

Restructuring is primarily undertaken by younger women for financial reasons. Within extended households, single women delegate childcare, participate in resource pooling, and are more likely of finding employment. The need for emotional security also influences their decision. they receive support to raise their children and they are shielded from the stigma associated with single parenthood.   However, hidden headship, undertaken in extreme economic circumstances, generally mitigates but need not necessarily prevent poverty.

Box 6. Balancing productive, reproductive work and spatial mobility:

The story of two domestic servants

Marta's husband Miguel, a daily laborer, has always been financially unreliable - sometimes he disappears for days at a time - and so she has worked as a washerwoman since the first of her six children was born. Initially she worked locally, securing piece work from neighbors, but later locked the children up and went across town for better paid work in middle class households. Marta, aged 38, is pregnant again -- Miguel would not allow her to use birth control. Unwell and unable to travel, she is once again reduced to working locally and cannot make ends meet. So far, two women neighbors and a comadre have lent money, Padre Francisco from the Jospice Internacional paid recent medical bills, while an emergency matriculation fee grants from Plan Internacional ensured two daughters entered secondary school this year. Friends are concerned about her well-being. As one commented "You need guts to survive. Women with hopeless husbands are no better than women without husbands".

For more than a decade, fifty year old Josefina brought up her nine children within a woman-headed household - her husband deserted her after the birth of their sixth child, but continued to claim visiting rights, making very occasional, unreliable financial contributions. Throughout she worked in domestic service. Until 1983 she worked locally as a washerwoman. Then when eldest daughter Anna became pregnant, Josefina found better paid laundry work in the city center, leaving her youngest children with their aunt. By 1992, Anna, a 'hidden household head' had five children of her own and Josefina was a full-time domestic servant, coming home three nights a week - preferring the tranquillity of her live-in job. With three of her daughters now married, the eleven member extended household is now managed by Anna assisted by a younger sister. Although Josefina provides financial support to this three generational household, they are still very poor - two of Anna's children get lunch provided by the Evangelical church feeding program, while another child attended the *Hogar Comunitario* until it was closed down.

Source: Interviews in Cisne Dos, 1992.

Change in the Intra-household time allocation. Intra-household time allocation and job distribution changes when households strive for additional income. 1992 random sample data shows that while men average 47 hours a week in productive activities, women average 39 hours. However with reproductive and domestic tasks designated as 'women's work', they also spend an additional average of 16 hours per week on domestic reproductive activities excluding childcare, as well as 3-5 hours per

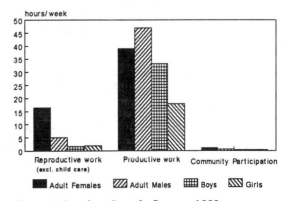

Graph 4
Intra-household Time Allocation
Cisne Dos, 1992

Source: Random Sample Survey, 1992.

week on community participation. Coping strategies that rely on women's income --
particularly important in poor households -- therefore put pressure on women in their triple role
of reproductive, productive and community managing work. Not only must they balance
different tasks, but there are also severe constraints associated with the labor intensity of time
use.

Child labor. Economic pressures and women's entry into paid work in turn affects
children. Women forced out to work with only very young children have no alternative than to
lock them up while away. In this case it is young children themselves that carry the burden of
inadequate attention, often suffering additional nutritional problems when not fed by their
mothers. Eldest daughters very rapidly assume responsibility for their siblings. Households
with two or more daughters use the half-day school shift system by sending daughters to
different shifts, thus freeing up women for full-time work. 1992 data shows that two out of
three daughters in school are involved in child care on a daily basis, with some mothers
effectively handing over the entire reproductive role to daughters. Sons are more likely to be
involved in child labor. More than two thirds of working boys age 14 and below manage to
continue their schooling, however.

Use of Housing as a Productive Asset. Intra-household strategies to diversify income
include the use of housing as a productive asset. One in three households earns additional
income from a home-based enterprise, while about 20 percent of households receive other cash
income from remittances, rent or other non-wage sources. It is homeowners, with legal
electricity connections, who are more likely to run enterprises dependent on electricity such as
refrigerators and sewing machines. The main types are retail operations (57 percent), followed
by workshops and small industries (35 percent), and some personal services (8 percent). They
are run largely by women, and 'cushion' households against extreme poverty. In particular,
they allow housebound women with children to generate income.

Expenditure Reduction. It is women who control intra-household decision-making
expenditure-minimizing strategies relating to food consumption. A threefold strategy consists
of cutbacks in overall consumption levels (decline in consumption of meat, milk and fish),
changes in dietary habits and types of food consumed, and reductions in the purchase of non-
essential goods with education prioritized over health care needs and housing repairs (80
percent deferring major house repairs).

Substitution of Private for Public Goods. At the intra-household level, another strategy
concerns the substitution of private for public goods as a response either to declining quality or
to rising costs. Although the majority of households have piped water, low pressure means that
water must be lifted out of a pit outside the house. 40 percent of women, men and children
fetch water daily, averaging 45 minutes on this task. More than a quarter of economically
active individuals either work at home or use non-motorized transport -- in both cases saving
on transport fares. To access NGO provided welfare assistance (such as free medicine,
children's cooked lunches), household improvements (such as septic tanks) and income
generating opportunities (such as training courses), a third of women participate in community
level organizations spending 3-5 hours weekly on this activity. Lack of quality education and
healthcare increasingly resulted in households purchasing both education and healthcare. In
1992, one in five students attended private schooling, proportionately higher at secondary than
primary level. In the health sector, almost as many sick people attended private healthcare

facilities as those provided by the state -- due to the quality of service provided, credit availability, short waiting time and flexible hours.

Box 7. Balancing Reproductive Work and Education: Teenage life

In a household of six children, Isabel, aged sixteen and Maria, aged thirteen, are the two daughters. With their father Moises' income as a carpenter declining, in 1990 their mother Vera was finally forced to go back to work as a domestic servant -- to pay for the costs of three children in secondary school. Vera leaves for work at 6.30 each morning, while the daughters cope with all the domestic work by selecting school shifts in alteration -- Isabel in the morning and Maria in the afternoon. Juan, aged fifteen often assists his father in the afternoons. The daughters complain that their homework time suffers as they cook and clean for their parents and four brothers. It is not ideal but the family is committed to getting the children through high school.

In the Lopez household, Marlene, Lucy and Olga the three eldest of five daughters, have complete responsibility for all household tasks including the attendance of community meetings on Saturday. Their father, an informal sector fruit juice seller, has virtually abandoned the family and the mother as the only income earner is forced to work a six-day week washing clothes in three city center households. The girls have had so many conflicts over divisions of labor that a year ago they started a rotation system. Each girl now stays home one week in three, missing school. Marlene, the eldest says she is always behind at school, but there is no alternative if the family wants to eat.

Armando and Juan, aged fifteen and thirteen, are the two elder sons in a household of seven children. Their father Santiago is a skilled construction worker (*maestro*). A declining market for fixed contract construction work has reduced him to be a casual daily worker, with an irregular income. With five younger children their mother Teresa cannot get out to work. In 1991 the boys were forced to leave day school to assist keeping their younger siblings in school. They both work as shoe-shine boys in the city's bus terminal, together providing half the family's income. Although they registered for 7-9 pm night shift at the local school, they are often too tired to go.

Source: Interviews in Cisne Dos, 1992.

Inter-Household Strategies

Asset Sharing between Households. In Cisne Dos, land and housing are assets that clearly reduce vulnerability. Not only does it mean households save on rental expenditure, but younger households can, through plot densification, also avoid rent or up-start costs of their own land acquisition. The most important inter-household asset sharing strategy is 'nesting' -- the dramatic increase in unregistered land sub-divisions and sharing of space between different households. Indeed plot ownership acts as a magnet for extended relatives. In Cisne Dos, with its informal land markets and lack of strict building regulations, one in four households now have '*nesters*' living on their plot -- the phenomenon whereby adult children live independently with their own households on their parent's plot. Nesting is significantly more common as a strategy among poor and very-poor young households (28 percent and 35 percent respectively) than among non-poor ones (14 percent).

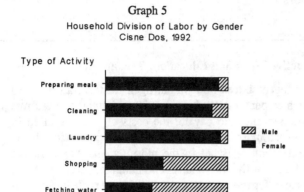

Graph 5
Household Division of Labor by Gender
Cisne Dos, 1992

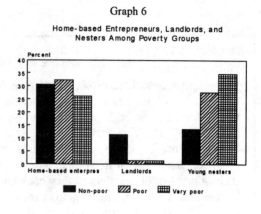

Graph 6
Home-based Entrepreneurs, Landlords, and
Nesters Among Poverty Groups

For each parent household, there is an average of two children's families nesting with them. Sometimes they even share the same living space while running their household independently, cooking and eating separately. More frequently, however, they live in separate space, either building a second floor onto the existing house or a separate structure at the back of the plot. It is a multiple purpose strategy, providing access to land for young households without assets of their own, while allowing parents and nesters to benefit from time efficiencies in terms of shared reproductive tasks such as child care and cooking. Finally, it allows children to care for elderly parents while living independently, thereby reducing the cost of other assistance.

Informal Credit Arrangements. When short-term crisis occur, credit can rapidly be raised not only from the immediate family but also from neighbors, emergency funds from the international NGO's crisis fund, and -- least likely -- concerned employers. In Cisne Dos nearly half (45 percent) of households borrowed money in 1992, a third from neighbors, a quarter from family and the rest from other sources such as work contacts and employers. In addition, more formal credit was provided by private doctors, used by nearly half of households. More than one-third of households borrowed money to pay for urgent house repairs.

Informal support networks for childcare, space and cooking. Informal support networks are an increasingly important coping strategy, particularly for women within Cisne Dos. Childcare is very common, not only within extended households, as described above, but also between households, with complex informal arrangements between relatives or neighbors. The objective is to release women to undertake critical income earning activities. Equally critical is the sharing of space, particularly in nesting households. Overcrowding results in complex arrangements whereby houses and even rooms are shared between households. Along with sharing of space goes sharing of cooking, food, and water, all of which involve reciprocal arrangements designed to achieve efficiency of time use.

Community-Level Strategies

Increased Participation in -- and Reliance on -- Formal Support Networks. Poor households not only increase their informal bondages between each other in periods of economic hardship but they also rely to an increasing extent on formal support networks as we have seen in Cisne Dos. A number of social programs exist in Cisne Dos today, being offered both from Non-Governmental Organizations and the municipal, state and federal governments. Social programs existing in Cisne Dos today include Plan Internacional's Small Scale Loans Project, the Emergency Social Fund, and a large number of training courses being offered by both the Ecuadoran Training Council and a host of NGOs. Annex 4 gives an overview of the most important social programs in Cisne Dos.

Box 8. The Inter-generational Housing Strategies of the Gonzalez family

Carlos and Brigita Gonzalez moved from city center rental accommodation to Cisne Dos in 1978. Proud owners of a 10 by 30 meter plot they brought up their six children and incrementally infilled their plot -- turning swamp into land -- and upgrading their bamboo walled house. Together they earned their income from the family *ceviche* enterprise in which Brigita cooked, and Carlos sold on street corners, the marinated cooked fish.

First to leave home in 1980 was eldest son Emilio, buying his own solar nearby, followed by their daughter, Anna who moved into her mother-in-law's rented home when getting married in 1984. By 1985 Anna was back home -- unable to afford the rent after her mother-in-law died -- building her own house at the back of the family plot where she still lives with her husband and two children. Saving money they have managed to complete a two floor structure.

In 1984, son Victor brought his bride, Nelly, to live in his parents house, 'sleeping apart' but helping with household cooking and childcare. With two children by an earlier relationship, over the next two years Nelly gradually brought them into the household so they could study in the city. Next to join the household in 1986 was Santiago, husband of Sylvia. While he and Victor went into business together as retail crab sellers, Sylvia was able to continue working as a shop seller after the birth of her first child -- the household needed the money and Brigita was prepared to look after her grandchild.

In 1989 Victor and Nelly became 'independiente', constructing their own home upstairs, to reduce the conflicts Nelly had been having with Brigita, her mother-in-law. By 1992 with two children of their own, and the arrival of two of Nelly's sisters from the countryside -- for education and work -- the extended household upstairs comprised eight members. Nelly would really like a *solar* (plot) apart if they could afford it, but husband Victor is clear, 'I have never left my mother and I never will do'.

The whole family was devastated by the death of Carlos in 1991. Brigita, now widowed, still lives downstairs in the original house with the remaining two children, son-in-law Santiago, two grandchildren and daughter Sylvia, who says 'we will not move: mother must not be left on her own'. In 1978, the Gonzalez were a nuclear household of eight members living on an invaded plot: in 1992 the same plot contained two extended and one nuclear households, two of which were in nesting arrangements, with a total of nineteen people. In the Gonzalez family, economic factors clearly determined inter-generational nesting strategies -- but so too did other types of reciprocity widely prevalent within families in Cisne Dos, including employment, childcare and cooking.

Source: Interviews in Cisne Dos, 1992.

The importance of formal support networks for poor families becomes visible if we assess the impact of the sudden closure of the Red Comunitaria. The Red Comunitaria de Desarrollo Infantile had been introduced by the 1988 national government of Rodrigo Borja. It provided three *hogares communitarias* (home-based day-care centers) for 45 pre-school children as well as two larger Centros de Cuidado Diario (CCDs) with 200 children in their care, and jobs for thirty-eight local women. Under Red Comunitaria, a free feeding program and the SAFIC primary health program (targeted specifically at pre-school children) achieved a coverage of 90 percent of pre-school children in Cisne Dos in 1992. The withdrawal of government support for the program in 1993, at one month's notice, had a particularly adverse affect not only on the children, but also on household income -- about half of mothers which had children in the Red before lost their job -- as well as community morale, as described in detail in Box 9.

**Box 9. Community-level Impact of Withdrawal of Government
Support of Red Communitaria Program in Cisne Dos, 1993**

In mid-1993, the national government withdrew its financial support from the Red Communitaria (Community Network) set up by the previous government. Amongst the programs which were forced to close were community childcare centers (each providing education, nutrition and child-care for up to 120 pre-school children aged 2-5) and small-scale *hogares comuniarias* (providing nutrition and day long child-care for up to 15 children from birth to school age). In Cisne Dos these had been operating since 1978, originally under a UNICEF/UBS program, subsequently incorporated into the Ministerio de Bienestar Social, and then into the Red Communitaria.

A micro-level survey in May 1994, 14 months later, conducted with thirty women who had previously used three hogares communitarias in Cisne Dos, revealed that all but two were deeply dissatisfied with the closure. It had directly affected their employment. 40 percent were forced to give up their jobs, rising to 50 percent a year later. Others had changed jobs to work nearer to, or at home, or in cases where they were domestic servants in two houses, reduce the number of jobs from two to one. Women employed in the hogares communitarias also lost their jobs. The loss of earnings resulting from these employment changes had important implications for household income and poverty.

For those women who continued to work, payments made to child minders also increased economic pressures. Most, however, could not afford the additional costs and were forced to delegate childcare to other family members, 86 percent either to grandmothers or to elder daughters, creating own problems. For grandmothers their frail state caused difficulties, while for elder daughters it increased problems of balancing schoolwork and child care - with a number shifting to night school.

The survey also revealed a number of problems for the children themselves. As one mother said, "the child cries a lot asking for his friends and toys". Others reported children waiting expectantly every morning to go to the center. A number of women noted that their children had become thinner now that they no longer received lunch at the center. Others complained that their children were more sickly as they spent more time in the streets, with an increasing number being 'callajeros' (street children).

At a wider community women's meeting, particularly those involved in the barrio committed resented the withdrawal of childcare services, but also the fact that government mismanagement of funds had undermined trust between the popular sectors and the state. For them this is proof of the rupturing of the social contract between the community and government, carefully negotiated over the years.

Source: Cisne Dos Participatory Community Evaluation, May 1994.

Summary of Coping Strategies

Table 4 below summarizes the coping strategies adopted at the individual, intra-household, inter-household and community level, which shows the innovativeness of the poor to respond to changing circumstances.

Table 4. Coping strategies at Individual, Household, Inter-household, and Community level, 1992

Level	Specific coping strategy
Individual	• *Increased female and child labor force participation, mainly in the informal sector* · increased numbers of women spouses working, from 32% in 1978 to 46% in 1992; · boys and girls (12-14 years) average 15 hours a week's work in home-based enterprises. • *Increased private investment in education*
Intra-household	• *Changed household structure* · change in household type, with decline in nuclear and increase in extended households growing from 33% to 38%, between 1988 and 1992, particularly households headed by older divorced or widowed women. · increase of shielding single mothers in extended households. • *Changed intra-household time allocation* · women's work hours increase with more time devoted to productive labor. Both reproductive and community tasks exist at the same time; · about 50% of children balance schooling and reproductive childcare tasks on a daily basis. • *Reduced household expenditure and changed composition* · changes in food consumption with modified dietary patterns (decline in consumption of meat, milk and fish) and reduced quality of food consumed; · changes in non-food consumption with education prioritized over medical/health care needs, and housing repairs (80% of household deferred major house repairs). • *Diversified income using housing as a productive asset* · one in three households earns additional income from home-based enterprises. Homeowners, with legal electricity connections, are more likely to run enterprises dependent on refrigerators and sewing machines. • *Substituted private goods for declining quality (and increasing cost) of public services* · more than 40% of women, men and children fetch water daily, averaging 45 minutes; installation of pumps to reduce water collection time; installation of illegal electricity connections; · more than 30% of women participate in community projects to access welfare and income generating activities; · more than a quarter of economically active individuals either work at home or use non-motorized transport; · purchase of education, healthcare, and water due to decline in quality.
Inter-household	• *Increased use of asset sharing arrangements between households* · one in four households has kin 'nesters' living on plots, enabling parents to live independently with childcare support, cooking and other reciprocities • *Increased use of inter-household credit arrangements* · 42% of households go to private doctors, many use credit arrangements offered · more than one-third of households borrowed money to pay for urgent house repairs; · 45% borrowed cash for food from neighbors and relatives • *Increased use of informal inter-household support networks* · increase in women's kin and neighbor networks sharing childcare and space. 25% of households with children below 10 years depend on neighbors for child care.
Community	• *Increased community level participation in -- and reliance on -- formal support networks* · increased community participation in NGO projects which provide urban services such as school repairs, latrines, pre-school equipment.

4. Obstacles to Poverty Reduction: The Challenge Ahead

Trend data illustrates the resourcefulness with which households respond to changes both in their internal and external environment. Table 4 highlights the complexity of coping strategies -- at the individual, intra-, inter-household, and community level -- to reduce their vulnerability and prevent increased impoverishment. These provide insights into the capacity of households to respond to opportunities created by policy reform.

At the same time a number of important obstacles exist which constrain the poor from increasing their income as portrayed in Table 5. The correct identification of such obstacles is critical if the most appropriate and effective entry-points for poverty reduction strategies are to be recognized. For example, women in Cisne Dos are critically important secondary-income earners. However, their ability to earn adequate levels of income is hindered by a host of supply-side constraints relating to their low levels of skills, lack of physical access to markets, credit and information and time constraints as a consequence of balancing their reproductive and community tasks. Women in poor urban households do not only have to balance their triple role, they also try to juggle their household budgets to feed, educate and provide adequate shelter for their children.

Table 5. Obstacles to poverty reduction in Cisne Dos, 1992

Obstacle to poverty alleviation	Potential Solutions/Interventions
• general level of economic activity/demand for goods and services	• macro policy solutions.
• inadequate physical labor	• provide adequate access to health care; • target food subsidies to ensure adequate diets for most vulnerable malnourished groups (children and lactating mothers).
• inadequate specialization and skill-level of labor: people are unskilled or not qualified for certain types of jobs that are available	• provide appropriate skill training and retraining programs at the community level especially for young men and women
• inadequate access to credit for raw materials and production inputs	• develop of NGO credit schemes for specific target groups in the community (e.g. women in home-based enterprises); • ensure households access to energy to help them establish home-based enterprises.
• underutilization of housing as a productive asset: non-owner households are unable to use their houses to earn income	• facilitate occupants to obtain legal title for their plot, support community-based technical assistance projects for upgrading.
• inadequate time for women to engage in productive work resulting from balancing domestic and productive roles (especially for those with unmet child care needs)	• support local community-based and community-supported child care.
• unsafe physical environment affect physical mobility: women cannot go out to work due to threat of crime and violence	• increase safety in public transport; • support community organization-based crime solutions; • maintain and repair street lighting; • enhance capacity of policing; • provide community facilities for youths, especially boys, to reduce crime.
• decline in quality of education, increase in private costs of public education	• prioritize educational resources and facilities allocated to local primary and secondary schools (teachers, textbooks and classrooms); • target financial support to low-income families that cannot afford the private costs of public education (matriculation, transport, materials etc.).

On the demand side, rigidity of the labor market in terms of regulations and market segmentation (i.e. gender-specificity of jobs) contributes to the urban poor's problem of earning an income to pay for their basic needs. With labor the most important asset of the poor, the access and quality of urban services has an important role in maximizing returns to these asset. In Cisne Dos as in the rest of Ecuador, considerable social improvements occurred during the early 1980s. Recent trends, however, indicate a deterioration both in access and quality of physical and social infrastructure. This has obvious implications for the physical quality of labor, decline in educational achievement (i.e. grade repetition and drop-outs). A final newly observed phenomenon is the decline in public safety due to increasing levels of crime and violence.

The challenge for the Ecuadorian government relates to the introduction of measures that remove the obstacles that currently affect poor men, women and children -- not only in cushioning them from the short-term economic shocks of adjustment, but also, more importantly from allowing them to benefit from the long-term effects of macro reform.

References

Garcia, M. and Herbert, A. (1993)   "Ecuador in the 1980s: A Historical Review of Social Policy and Urban Level Interventions." *TWURD Working Paper No.6*. Washington, DC: The World Bank.

Instituto Nacional de Estadistica y Censos (1993)*"Empleo, Desempleo y Subempleo en el Sector Urbano a julio 1993."* Quito: INEC.

Moser, C. (1981)   "Surviving in the Suburbios", *Institute of Development Studies Bulletin*, vol. 12, no. 3.

Moser, C. (1987)   "Mobilization is Women's Work: Struggles for Infrastructure in Guayaquil, Ecuador", in Moser, C. and Peake, L. (eds.) *Women, Human Settlements and Housing*. London: Tavistock

Moser, C. (1992a) "Adjustment From Below: Low-Income Women, Time and the Triple Role in Guayaquil, Ecuador" in Afshar, H. and Dennis, C. (eds.) *Women and Adjustment Policies in the Third World*. Basingstoke: Macmillan.

Moser, C. (1992b) "A Home of One's Own: Squatter Housing Strategies in Guayaquil, Ecuador" in Gilbert, A. (ed.) *Urbanization in Contemporary Latin America*. London: John Wiley.

Sollis, P. (1993)   "Demand for Health Care in Ecuador: Household Perspectives from a Low-income Community in Guayaquil" (mimeo). Washington, D.C.

Annex 1:

Trends in access to land and housing (Cisne Dos, 1978, 1988, 1992).

Land Acquisition	In 1978 the majority of households had acquired land through invasion (52 percent); by 1992 most households had acquired it by purchase (69 percent).
Plot Ownership	From 1978-92 Plot ownership decreased from 88 percent to 75 percent, with nesting -- those living on plots owned by relatives -- increasing from 10 percent to 19 percent. The rental market has remained small, increasing from 2 percent to 5 percent.
Documentation	From 1978-92 households with legal documentation for land increased substantially (from 9 percent to 56 percent) but was still far short of universal.
Residential Mobility	The community is becoming more stable, with households' average stay increasing from 3 years in 1978 to 12 years in 1992.
Plot Size	Plot size decreased from 218 m^2 to 191 m^2 during the 1988-92 period.
Housing Size	On average, housing area increased from 38 m^2 in 1978 to 67 m^2 in 1992.
Housing Density	From 1978-92, housing density decreased from 3.6 persons/room to 3 persons/room
Housing Durability[a]	The housing stock has become more durable. Units made of permanent materials, which were non-existent in 1978, accounted for 62 percent of the 1992 housing stock.
Toilet Facilities	Pit latrines and WCs, absent in 1978, accounted for 65 percent of toilet facilities in 1992.

a Based on a quality index accounting for roof, wall and floor materials.

Annex 2
Trends on access to urban services (Cisne Dos, 1978, 1988, 1992).

Lighting Source	Between the 1978-88 access to electricity increased from 0 to 95 percent period. Between 1988-1992 the number of illegal connections grew to 34 percent
Water Supply	Between 1978-88 access to piped water increased from 0 percent to 64 percent, with tanker bought water declining accordingly from 100 percent to 36 percent. In 1992 access remained unchanged, but decline in quality and supply meant 14 percent of households supplemented piped water with tank bought water.
Sewerage	In 1992 sewerage services were still almost non-existent, except for a few unconnected tubes laid prior to the 1992 elections.
Cooking Fuel	Since 1978 charcoal and kerosene have been replaced by gas cylinders, used by 92 percent of households in 1992
Garbage Disposal	In 1992 municipal garbage collection started as a result of a cholera outbreak. Most households still dump or burn it due to limited and unreliable service.
Roads	The main roads within the community were paved during the 1980s, but by 1992 many had fallen into serious disrepair.
Street lighting	Street lighting on the main streets of Cisne Dos began in 1976. Lack of repairs, resulting in deficient street lighting by 1992 contributed to personal safety problems.
Educational facilities	Since 1978 both public and private educational facilities have increased; by 1992, although access was not a problem, costs accounted for 8 percent of household income, were a heavier burden for the very poor; quality of education meant almost half the students in non-poor households attended private schools, particularly at secondary level.
Health facilities	Since 1978 the private health sector has grown dramatically, with private doctors in 1992 providing as much of healthcare as public facilities, particularly for the non-poor.

Annex 3

Share of annual individual education expenditures relative to overall education expenditures per student by poverty status (Cisne Dos, 1992)

Expenditure item	Non-poor		Poor		Very poor		All	
	Sucres	%	Sucres	%	Sucres	%	Sucres	%
Annual fee	12,078	4.3	12,609	10.9	6,703	8.6	9,387	9.3
Term fee	51,098	16.3	19,682	10.1	10,845	8.0	18,766	9.7
Other fees	33,713	8.5	19,350	8.7	16,019	8.6	19,311	8.6
Uniform	33,032	18.4	23,682	21.5	21,429	29.4	23,611	25.3
Books	43,098	24.3	39,985	32.5	26,650	33.1	33,231	31.8
Transportation	50,061	20.3	25,299	14.0	20,218	12.2	25,586	13.8
Total	234,620	100.0	143,944	100.0	101,866	100.0	131,726	100.0

Annex 4: Social Programs in Cisne Dos

Given that Cisne Dos is a well-established community most of the existing physical and social infrastructure has been provided under earlier government programs or through the *comites bariales* (community groups), Indio Guayas and Defensores del Suburbio, working collaboratively with international and local NGOs.[7] However, the high proportion of population still living below the poverty line in 1992 meant that the area continued to receive a diversity of targeted poverty alleviation programs.

Of the programs provided, two were of particular prominence because of their unusually long-term sustainability. First, and as already mentioned above, the Red Comunitaria supplied home-based day-care centers. Introduced in 1988 by the national government of Rodrigo Borja, the Red expanded and extended the existing community services originally introduced as a UNICEF Urban Basic Services program in 1978. Subsequently, it was integrated into the Ministerio de Bienestar Social in the early 1980s. Second, an important community program is Plan Internacional, an internationally funded NGO working in Cisne Dos for some twenty years. Starting in the 1970s as a traditional welfarist agency, 'adopting a child' to make modest cash payments directly to poorest households, over the years it experimented with different support strategies and finally evolved into a developmental NGO. From the mid 1980s onwards it worked directly with the different community committees in the area, negotiating with them to identify their needs, providing 50 percent of funding (to promote sustainability), and requiring the community itself to organize, implement and administer projects. Despite its modest scale, over the decade it has had a remarkable impact in terms of community priorities such as infill, the upgrading of both primary and secondary schools, household priorities such as the provision of septic tanks and latrines, and individual needs such as child and maternal health, small enterprise support and vocational training. Recognizing the interrelationship between external and life-cycle factors it continues to provide short term grant aid safety net emergency funds for health crises, school matriculation and funerals while promoting more sustainable physical and social infrastructure projects, as described in Box A4.1.

Box A4.1. Plan Internacional's 1992 program in Cisne Dos

During a nine month period in 1992, Plan funded eleven projects in the community ranging from a housing program providing 126 loans for individual families, an educational improvement program constructing classroom facilities for one of the local secondary schools, to the provision of septic tanks and latrines, as well as health projects for the community as a whole, and one for pregnant mothers. Overall more than 250 households benefited from these projects. An example of the equity aspect of the program is provided by data showing that in the provision of septic tanks and latrines very poor households were as likely to receive facilities as the non-poor, suggesting that the types of patronage which often pervades such projects was not influential here in terms of access (UPA Community Survey, 1992) .

---

[7]   For a detailed descriptive review of Social Policy and Urban Level Interventions in Ecuador during the 1980s see Garcia and Herbert (1993).

Finally, mention must be made of an uncoordinated group of adult education and vocational courses targeted at unemployed and under-employed men and women. In 1992, of a total of 19 projects, seven were run by government agencies (three by SECAP/Servicio Ecuatoriano de Capacitacion Professional), one by the Ministerio de Educacion, one by the Ministerio de Bienestar Social and two by CECIM -- a woman's NGO), with the remainder (12) provided by the NGO Plan International (see UPA Community Survey, 1992) (see Table A4.1.). Despite this apparent proliferation of training courses, community members identified a number of problems. Among courses identified as useful, such as the electricity and literacy courses, people complained that the short duration (usually only 3 months) was not sufficient to gain any real proficiency. Courses run specifically for women, such as dressmaking and crafts, were identified as inappropriate since they rarely resulted in the generation of income.

Table A4.1. Adult education and vocational courses in Cisne Dos, Guayaquil during 1992.

Type of educational/vocational program	No.	Source of funding
Dressmaking	5	4 Plan; 1 SECAP
Beautician	2	1 Plan; 1 SECAP
Literacy	1	1 Ministerio de Educacion
Electrician	2	1 SECAP; 1 Plan
Accounting	1	1 CECIM
Crafts	4	3 Plan; 1 Ministerio de Bienestar Social
Domestic science	2	1 CECIM, 1 Plan
Other	2	2 Plan
Total	19	12 Plan; 3 SECAP; 1 Ministerio de Educacion; 1 Ministerio de Bienestar Social; 2 CECIM

Source: UPA Community Survey Guayaquil, 1992.

Indeed, the community has seen an increased level of activity in NGO projects, with the increased provision of urban services such as school repairs, latrines, pre-school equipment obtained through community participation in local and international NGO projects.

Working Paper 4: Poverty in Rural Ecuador
Peter Lanjouw

1.   Introduction

There is a rich tradition of poverty analysis in Ecuador. This tradition has been alert to the numerous dimensions of poverty and has resulted in the acquisition of a reasonable body of knowledge regarding living standards of Ecuadoreans and their evolution, in terms of not only incomes but also access to basic services, education levels, nutritional status and health. Yet, with some notable exceptions, rural Ecuador has not featured highly in this direction of inquiry. One of the main impediments to broadening the debate about poverty in Ecuador to include rural areas has been the paucity of reliable data at the household-level.

The purpose of this Working Paper is to provide some further detail to our understanding of the rural economy and rural poverty. To this end, the analysis will draw on the recently completed *Encuesta Sobre Las Condiciones de Vida*, a multi-purpose household survey modeled closely on the format of the Living Standards Measurement Survey (LSMS) developed in recent years at the World Bank. While the evidence and analysis presented here will be mainly descriptive, where the data permits, we will also comment on the causal underpinnings of rural poverty and will point to possible policy imperatives.

This Working Paper is organized as follows. In the next section we will briefly review some salient features of the dataset used in the analysis, contrasting the type of information available from this survey with that which is found in previous surveys. We then turn to examines rural poverty in the context of poverty in Ecuador as a whole. We examine as well how living standards are distributed and where rural inequality fits into the national picture. The fourth section revisits some of the broad correlates of poverty described in the poverty profile of this report and asks what it means to be poor in rural Ecuador. The fifth section follows on from this to look more closely at agriculture in Ecuador. We ask how the distribution of land is linked to rural poverty as well as the influence of land distribution on the efficiency of cultivation; whether the poor differ markedly from the non-poor in terms of cropping patterns; whether cultivation intensity varies across cultivators of different socio-economic status; whether agricultural laborers form a class of the rural population particularly at risk of poverty; and what importance ownership of livestock and domestic animals might have. We turn from agriculture to the non-agricultural rural economy in the following section. The question here is whether the rural poor are participating in the non-farm sector and what importance the off-farm sector can have as a route out of poverty. Before offering some final comments, the seventh section turns to an econometric exercise in which we simultaneously associate a series of correlates with poverty, measured in several different ways. The purpose of this effort is to identify those indicators whose association with poverty remains strong even when other variables are examined concurrently.

The organization of this Working Paper, notably the choice of issues to be examined, has been significantly motivated by the analysis contained in Working Paper 5 entitled 'Rural Qualitative Assessment' (RQA). That study reports on a survey of seven villages in rural Ecuador, using qualitative survey techniques, with the aim of obtaining a perspective of how the poor themselves view their living conditions. The RQA does not pretend to extend its findings to rural Ecuador as a whole. The scale of the study, as well as the sampling and interview techniques which are utilized, impede such broad statements. However, that is not its purpose either. The Rural Qualitative Assessment is particularly useful as a *complement* to the present, more systematic, type of analysis. While one cannot infer from the experience of a relatively small number of villagers to the country as a whole, one is entitled to ask whether the circumstances and the processes which have been found in a Qualitative Survey appear to be significant more broadly. The RQA is useful as a guide in thinking about poverty in rural Ecuador, raising potentially important questions and providing pointers to possible explanations.

2.   Ecuador's Living Standard Measurement Survey

The analysis of poverty based on the 1994 Ecuador LSMS-style survey uses as central indicator of well-being a measure of household consumption. This is a major departure from previous efforts to measure rural poverty in Ecuador, based on household income. The relative merits of different measures, including consumption and income, in identifying the poor have been explored in Chaudhuri and Ravallion (1993) and discussed further in Ravallion (1994). Essentially it is argued that consumption measures are not as prone to vary with seasonal variation or year-to-year harvest fluctuations (so that a 'snap-shot' survey does provide a reasonable indication of longer-term living standards), and it is argued that consumption information is more readily collected - and therefore less likely to suffer from major omissions. An additional attraction of a survey which includes detailed consumption information is that it permits the calculation, from the data, of a calorie-based absolute poverty line. This, in fact, has been undertaken for the present poverty assessment.

The critical importance of reliable and complete data on living standards, when undertaking an analysis of poverty based on household surveys, cannot be overstated. This remark can be explained by elaborating on some specific issues which arise with an alternative household survey available for 1990. Prior to completion of the Ecuador LSMS survey, the only nationally representative and relatively recent source of information on rural-living standards was the *Encuesta Permanente de Hogares: Estacionalidad del Empleo Rural 1990* (INEM). This survey covers 4000 households interviewed during 1990. The dataset contains information on incomes, occupations, landholdings and other aspects of rural livelihoods. While of great use for many purposes, the data suffer from important limitations when applied to the analysis of poverty. Two major problems arise, the consequence probably of the fact that the survey was originally designed to measure occupational status and earnings, and not necessarily living standards more broadly. First, the dataset collects information on gross agricultural output of farming families but there is no information on any costs of cultivation incurred. Using unit values one can express agricultural output in value terms and thereby obtain a measure of gross agricultural income. However, it is misleading to use gross agricultural income as a proxy for relative living standards as costs of cultivation may vary markedly between farmers. Deflating the gross income to net income is impossible since we do not have farm budgets for different farm sizes or income classes and it is clearly unacceptable to impose the assumption that inputs are applied uniformly by all farming households.

The second problem with the INEM data is that the survey failed to collect information on incomes for a large fraction of the rural population which was neither engaged in agriculture, nor explicitly participating in the labor market. Incomes for some 1600 individuals in the dataset (out of a total of roughly 6000 reporting some form of gainful economic activity) were therefore omitted. These individuals were active as own-account merchants, businessmen, tailors, carpenters, construction workers, fishermen, etc. It is likely that many of these individuals would be counted as among the poor (to the extent that poverty is linked to small-scale informal activity), but it is also clear that these types of occupations may well be those that offer people a route to escape poverty.

The two problems highlighted above could have offsetting implications regarding measured poverty. Overstating agricultural income would tend to reduce the incidence of poverty in rural areas, while omitting an important component of household income (for at least some households) would result in an overstatement of actual poverty. It is not known what the relative importance of these two types of error might be but it is clear that any estimate of rural poverty based on a flawed indicator of living standards will remain unreliable. Note that in urban areas the failure to calculate properly agricultural income would presumably be fairly innocuous, but failure to capture certain components of income (such as income from informal sources) could still result in an overstatement of urban poverty.

The methodology adopted in converting LSMS information on household purchases of a whole range of consumption goods into a household aggregate consumption variable is described elsewhere (Working Paper 1, Annex 1). The consumption figures include not only consumption of food items, but also the consumption of services from consumer durables and housing, as well as expenditures on schooling and basic services such as water and electricity. The poverty line which serves as the basic tool for distinguishing between the poor and non-poor is calculated on the basis of the same consumption data. They indicate what expenditure is needed to acquire a minimum caloric intake per person (2237 kcals per capita, a figure taken from the study by Cabrera et al.,1993[1]) associated with the consumption pattern by those in the second and third quintiles of the expenditure distribution. Recognizing that even those just able to purchase their minimal nutritional requirements typically devote some portion of their budget to non-food items, this extreme poverty line is scaled up by the average expenditure on non-food items of those just able to meet their food requirements (yielding the poverty line). Separately -- but not used in this Working Paper -- we have computed a vulnerability line which employs a different concept to determine the non-food expenditure share. Rather than looking at the population which is just even able to a basic food basket with their *total* expenditures, it looks at the population whose *food* expenditures are just enough to buy the basic basket of goods. Obviously, the non-food expenditure share is higher for this latter group. Further details on the methodology applied in calculating the

---

[1]   In Working Paper 1, Annex 1, we report on the impact of taking into account the different needs of adults versus children.

poverty line are described in Working Paper 1 (see also Ravallion, 1994, and Ravallion and Bidani 1994). It merits mention here that the consumption figures used in this Paper, as in the entire Poverty Report, have been adjusted to take into account cost-of-living variation. The geographic and agro-climatic heterogeneity of Ecuador results in similar goods being priced quite differently in different parts of the country. As a result, it is important to adjust household expenditures spatially so as to achieve comparability of living standards. For our purpose attention is devoted specifically on the 1374 households (out of a total of 4391) residing in rural areas.

Our discussion will at times be emphasizing the distinction between the 'poor' and the 'non-poor', as though this were the best, or only, way of comparing across households or individuals. In fact, however, this practice has really been adopted only for presentational purposes in the interest of clarity. It has the potential disadvantage of obscuring the important fact that poverty is not really an either/or condition. There is a whole spectrum of destitution, with those located just under the poverty line considerably better off than those far below it. The attention of policy makers should not necessarily be directed solely at numbers of the 'poor'; in a situation where limited public expenditures are intended to achieve a maximum poverty impact, such a stance would justify a focus on those located just below the poverty line, who require the least in transfers in order to become 'non-poor'. Hence, while it can be useful to emphasize the contrast between the poor and non-poor in order to illustrate a point, it should be kept in mind that this remains a somewhat crude device.

3.   Rural Poverty in the Overall Poverty Picture

The extent of poverty in Ecuador, by region and between urban and rural sectors, is presented in Table 1. The poverty calculations are obtained on the basis of two welfare lines, the 'extreme poverty line' and the 'poverty line' described above. Three different poverty measures are applied; the poverty incidence (corresponding to a 'count' of the poor below the respective poverty lines), poverty depth (which takes into account the distance from the poverty line), and poverty severity (which attaches greater weight the greater the distance below the poverty line). Calculated from the poverty line, the incidence of poverty in Ecuador is 35 percent. At this poverty line, the incidence of rural poverty is measured at 47 percent while in urban areas the incidence of poverty is roughly half that, 25 percent. Comparing across the three main regions of Ecuador, the incidence of rural poverty is highest in the Oriente, followed by the Costa and then the Sierra. In all cases, the incidence of rural poverty is considerably higher than urban poverty. Scrutinizing rural poverty when measures other than the head-count index are used reveals that the regional rankings are not everywhere equally pronounced. In fact, when the poverty severity measure is considered, for example, poverty in the Sierra is found to be more severe than in the Costa - overturning the ranking obtained using the poverty incidence measure.

How does our measure of rural poverty compare with previous work? An incidence of poverty in rural Ecuador of 47 percent is significantly lower than that which has been calculated from alternative data sources, usually income-based analyses (Table 2). There are a number of explanations for this discrepancy. The most important one is that the scaling factor we have used to derive the poverty line corresponds to that fraction of the budget spent on non-food items by those who could in principal have their minimum food requirements had they devoted their entire budget to food. Most other studies conducted in Ecuador employ a different scaling factor, namely the one we used to derive the vulnerability line. The 67 percent poverty we calculate when choosing the vulnerability line as our cut-off point is much closer to other estimates of rural poverty in Ecuador.

Further, we have already described another possibility for the discrepancy in estimates, namely that the income data sources used in the other analyses are problematic (as in the INEM (1990) survey on which the Cabrera et al. estimate is based). These data sources may omit potentially important income components and thus understate the true standard of living of at least certain households in rural areas.

There are three observations which follow from the above remarks. First, it is sometimes useful to step back and ask what the purpose of a poverty profile is. The idea is to help identify sub-groups of the population which are the *most* vulnerable and who face the *greatest* hardship. In this context it is much more important to know the living conditions and causes of poverty of specifically these most vulnerable groups. A poverty figure of 80 percent -- basically the whole population -- does not help us to obtain such a picture and is hence almost meaningless to help design targeted anti-poverty programs.

The second point is that while much of the discussion of poverty seems to center around specific numbers for the incidence of poverty, this is arguably of secondary importance. Usually it is much more critical, given the objective of prioritizing interventions and policies, to be able to make comparisons - across sectors for example, or between regions. Actual cardinal levels of poverty are not essential when the interest is really in making comparisons across groups.

This raises the third point, namely that where poverty comparisons are made, it is important to establish how robust these comparisons are. One is interested to know whether, for example, the rural Costa can be regarded as poorer than the rural Sierra, regardless of what poverty measure one might wish to employ, or the precise location of the poverty line. When a comparison of poverty is found to be robust, it provides a much more compelling case for prioritizing efforts at the region, or sector, which is found to be more poor. Conversely, when comparisons are fragile it becomes less attractive to give preference to one ahead of the other.

Advances in the measurement of poverty have in recent years yielded very simple to apply techniques for comparing poverty while retaining a firm focus on the robustness of the comparison[2]. One begins with a straightforward plot of the distribution functions between the populations being compared. In Figure 1 the distribution function for rural Ecuador is compared with that for urban Ecuador. From the theory underlying these techniques, it can be shown that as these two curves do not intersect at any point in the graph, poverty in the population represented by the curve lying everywhere above the

---

[2]   The literature on poverty measurement using stochastic dominance techniques has been growing rapidly. Good overviews can be found in Atkinson (1989), Howes (1993) and Ravallion (1994).

other is greater. *This is true not only for the incidence of poverty but is also true for any other poverty measure in common use.* Moreover, one could draw a vertical line representing a poverty line anywhere along the horizontal axis and find the conclusion to hold - the conclusion is robust over all possible poverty lines. Hence, from this figure it can be asserted that rural poverty is unambiguously greater than urban poverty.

From Figure 1 we can note that the poverty line which we have employed in Table 1 (corresponding to S. 45,500 per person per fortnight) cuts the rural distribution function at the part where it is particularly steep. This indicates that relatively minor adjustments in the precise location of the line will have a pronounced impact on the measured incidence of poverty corresponding to that poverty line. For example, if one applies the vulnerability line at 60,000 sucres (an increase of about US$0.50 to $2.00 per person per day), the incidence of poverty in rural areas would rise from 47 percent to 67 percent - much closer to the figures obtained in previous studies.[3]

In Figure 2 a similar exercise is performed to compare the rural populations of the three main regions of Ecuador. Here it can be seen that all of the curves do intersect at some point. While the rural Costa would appear less poor (based on poverty incidence) than rural Sierra at the poverty lines employed in Table 1, at a poverty line of around S. 30,000 per capita per week this conclusion would no longer hold, and at lines below that a re-ranking occurs. Similarly, at extremely low poverty lines even the rural Oriente would appear less poor than the rural Sierra. Because of the intersecting distribution functions, at any particular poverty line, one can not assert that the ranking which obtains on the basis of the poverty incidence also obtains with alternative poverty measures. Hence, a ranking of rural regions, robust over all poverty lines and all possible poverty measures cannot be obtained. This cautions against strong statements to the effect that one region is worse off than another in terms of poverty.

If one were prepared to exclude the poverty incidence measure as one upon which one wanted to base poverty comparisons (and indeed, the poverty incidence measure has been said by some to have 'little but its simplicity to recommend it', Watts, 1968) then it is possible to employ a further graphical technique to compare poverty. Drawing 'deficit' curves for the different populations - which represent simply the area under the distribution functions at each consumption level - one then compares curves in an entirely analogous manner as in Figures 1 and 2. In Figure 3 it can be seen that the curves for the Costa and Sierra still intersect at a certain point, but that the curve for rural Oriente now lies above that for the two other curves at all points. This indicates that even if one were to eschew the poverty incidence measure and employ only measures of poverty which were sensitive to levels of consumption below the poverty line, comparisons between rural

---

[3]   Note, we have followed the convention here of adjusting expenditures for spatial cost of living variation. This allows us to compare all expenditures to one poverty line. An alternative, but equivalent, approach would have been to compare nominal expenditures against poverty lines which took different values in different parts of the country. The procedure followed in adjusting expenditures was to deflate nominal expenditures within each sample cluster by the ratio of the cluster specific extreme poverty line to a population weighted average of all extreme poverty lines.

Costa and Sierra would remain inconclusive, while rural Oriente emerges as noticeably poorer than the other two regions.

From the application of these 'stochastic dominance' techniques we have found that comparisons of rural poverty versus urban poverty are highly robust, and point unambiguously towards more pronounced poverty in rural Ecuador than in urban areas. This finding is of interest in the broader Latin American context, given the apparently widespread perception that poverty in Latin America is increasingly becoming an urban problem. This view appears to be based on the notion that while rural poverty in Latin America may be high, the urban population in Latin America is growing far more rapidly than the rural population so that the numbers of urban poor are rising rapidly.[4] It is clear from the above analysis, however, that counting the poor is only one way to measure poverty, and if the wedge between rural and urban areas in Latin America as a whole is comparable to that observed in Ecuador, it is unlikely that the prevailing view is robust to even a very mild relaxation of the implicit judgment that distance below the poverty line carries no weight. To the extent that the current perception is significantly influencing the development of policies and interventions, caution is warranted.

Before concluding this section we comment briefly on the degree of inequality in consumption in Ecuador. It has been argued in the Rural Qualitative Assessment (Working Paper 5) that the notion of a homogeneous rural population, in terms of living standards, is hard to justify. Not only can villages within the same region differ markedly from one another in terms of average consumption levels, but within villages there may be considerable variation in the circumstances of different households and individuals. This viewpoint receives support from an examination of summary inequality measures in Table 3. In rural Ecuador as a whole the gini coefficient of consumption is 0.38. This indicates a fairly high dispersion of consumption expenditures. It is also quite likely lower than the extent of *income* inequality in rural areas.

Comparing rural and urban areas, there is noticeably greater inequality in urban areas than in rural areas. This is true for the country as a whole, and for both Costa and Sierra, regardless of inequality measure.[5] However, in the Oriente, rural inequality is consistently greater than in urban areas. In this region, heterogeneity of living standards is particularly pronounced in the country-side. Inequality can be compared graphically, in an analogous manner to poverty comparisons. A common method of comparing inequality is to draw Lorenz Curves for different populations. This is equivalent to drawing deficit curves (as with poverty measurement) when the horizontal axis now represents expenditures normalized by average expenditure (thereby abstracting away from

---

[4]   While this process has also been taking place in Ecuador, it remains that more than 60% of the country's poor still live in rural areas (see Table 1).

[5]   Note that different inequality measures, like different poverty measures, attach different weights to expenditures located along the income distribution. Poverty measures give zero weight to expenditures above the poverty line and positive weights to expenditures below the line (varying depending on the poverty measure). The gini coefficient can be shown to attach greatest weight to expenditures around the middle of the expenditure distribution, while Atkinson measures with higher values of e attach increasing weight to expenditures at the bottom end of the distribution (Atkinson, 1970).

differences in average expenditure between the populations).[6] From Figure 4 it can be seen that over the population as a whole, inequality in urban Ecuador is uniformly higher than in rural areas.

4.   The Meaning of Poverty in Rural Areas

What does it mean to have consumption expenditures below the poverty line? Our acceptance of consumption expenditure as a meaningful indicator of living standards will be strengthened if we find that on the basis of other indicators, which we intuitively associate with well-being, similar patterns between the poor and the non-poor are observed as with consumption (even if we are unable to offer a precise description of *how* these indicators improve the quality of life). Additionally, the identification of correlates of poverty (with poverty defined in terms of consumption expenditure) provides proxies of poverty in situations when consumption figures might not be available.

For this reason we revisit, in Table 4, some of the salient correlates of poverty presented in Working Paper 1. We can compare not only how well these variables map across the poor and non-poor in rural areas, but we can also examine further the degree of divergence between rural and urban areas in terms of these indicators.

Ownership of consumer durables maps closely with a consumption-based ranking of households. The poor consistently possess fewer durables than the non-poor. The split between rural and urban areas is marked. 37 percent of non-poor rural persons have access to a refrigerator relative to 70 percent of the non-poor in urban areas. Similarly, 26 percent of the rural non-poor own a color television, while 62 percent of the urban non-poor do. Black and white televisions are remarkably widely owned in Ecuador. In urban areas, the poor are relatively more likely to own such durables than the non-poor (who are much more likely to own a color television) while in rural areas, it remains that the rural poor are less likely to own such devices. Car ownership is sharply different between the poor and non-poor, with one in four of the urban non-poor having access to a vehicle while one in a hundred of the rural poor do.

In Ecuador, the urban non-poor tend to live in larger houses than the non-poor in rural areas. On average, the poor in both urban and rural areas live in similarly sized houses. Congestion within houses is highest among the poor in urban areas. There is a sharp distinction between the poor in rural and urban areas in terms of housing quality and the materials with which houses have been built. The poor in rural areas are considerably more likely to be living in houses with mud or wooden walls, and with dirt floors. Even the non-poor in rural areas are rather more likely to inhabit such inferior houses than urban households.

Electricity connections are quite widespread in Ecuador, even in rural areas. More than 60 percent of the rural poor are connected to an electricity network. Of course, this says nothing about the delivery of services, notably the reliability of the power supply. Similar remarks apply to household water connections. Rural households are far less likely to be connected to a water connection than urban households. Unsurprisingly,

---

[6]   See Atkinson (1970) and also Howes (1994).

formal waste disposal arrangements are rare in rural areas although the rural non-poor are much more likely to acquire this service than the poor. Sewage connections are also far more prevalent in urban areas than rural areas, with even the non-poor in rural areas benefiting less from these services than the poor in urban areas. It is perhaps worth mentioning in this context that it is not clear that rural and urban areas *should* obtain similar levels of services such as sewage and water connections. In urban areas, greater population densities are such that greater health risks are imposed in the event that such services are not available. It is also true that the unit-cost of networked services will be considerably higher in rural areas than in urban ones. In deciding whether the current distribution of services is acceptable it is necessary to ask also what alternative arrangements exist, i.e. whether the fact that a rural household has no access to piped water means that it has no access to any potable water.

Education levels in rural areas remain remarkably low. 94 percent of household heads among the rural poor have not advanced beyond primary education. Even among the non-poor this percentage is over 80 percent. In urban areas, 75 percent of poor household heads have received similarly little education, compared with 42 percent of the urban non-poor.

In rural Ecuador those households which receive treatment for illness must travel about twice as long as urban households prior to treatment. These statistics do not reflect the fact that in rural areas it is likely that far more illnesses remain untreated. Among poor households, particularly in rural areas, illnesses which do receive treatment are often treated by health practitioners who are not qualified doctors or nurses. Treatments are sought from healers, pharmacists, midwives, and so on.

Nearly one in ten of the rural poor speak an indigenous language, with the vast majority also speaking Spanish. In urban areas indigenous languages are spoken hardly at all.

Consumption of hard alcohol is considerably more common in rural Ecuador than in urban areas, with the daily amount consumed per household per day more than three times as high as in urban areas.[7] In both rural and urban areas the non-poor tend to consume much more than the poor, but the rural poor, in turn, consume much more than the urban poor. The association of alcohol consumption with poverty, particularly in rural areas, has been noted elsewhere in Latin America. A participatory poverty assessment for Guatemala drew attention to the problem of alcohol consumption in that country and stressed the destructive social effects of such practices.

Calories consumed per person per day, unsurprisingly, are higher among the non-poor than the poor. It is interesting to note that in rural areas calorie consumption is higher than in urban areas. The rural poor consume on average 1621 kcals per person per day, while the urban poor consume 1568 kcals. Similarly the rural non-poor consume more calories than the urban non-poor. This relates, presumably, to the fact that physical activity levels in rural areas are greater than in urban areas. The higher food intakes

---

[7]   Note, 73 mls per household per day translates roughly into 27 litres of liquor per household per year. Assuming that roughly two persons drink within a household and that a standard bottle contains 750 mls, this corresponds to about 1.5 bottles per drinking person per month.

among rural households are reflected also in the fact that the share of total budget devoted to food in rural areas is considerably higher than in urban areas on average. The food share is particularly high among the rural poor. However, if food share were taken as a basis for making comparisons of living standards, it would appear that on average even the non-poor in rural areas are considerably worse-off than the poor in urban areas.

5.   Rural Poverty and Agriculture

Rural poverty is closely linked to the economic opportunities and constraints prevailing in rural areas. Agriculture remains the most important economic activity in rural Ecuador employing the greatest number of persons and providing the largest fraction of household incomes in rural areas. In fact, it is common to encounter the viewpoint that, to all intents and purposes, agriculture *is* the rural economy. This perception is not justified in the rural Ecuador context; a non-agricultural rural economy does exist and is important in offering routes out of poverty. Accordingly we will inquire, in Section 6, into the importance of such non-farm employment to poverty in rural Ecuador. However, the starting point for examining the determinants of rural poverty is agriculture and we will consider six aspects of this sector, namely the distribution of land and land tenure arrangements, cropping patterns and marketed surpluses, farm size and productivity, cultivation intensity, agricultural labor, and ownership of livestock and domestic animals.

Land Distribution and Land Tenancy

The distribution of land in Ecuador, as in most of Latin America, has long been a focus of attention. It has been argued that inequality in the distribution of land is an important explanation for the persistence of rural poverty. In Ecuador land reforms were originally introduced in the early 1960s and became institutionalized through the establishment of IERAC, the government land adjudication office. As there has not been an agricultural census since 1974 it has been difficult to establish precisely how the distribution of land in Ecuador has evolved to the present. In Table 5 we present a breakdown of the distribution of land in the Costa and Sierra regions based on census figures for 1954 and 1974, and derived from the Ecuador LSMS for 1994. Keeping in mind the very different structure and size of the 1994 survey from that of agricultural censuses, the evidence does suggest that the impact of the land reform process has been modest.

In the Sierra, between 1954 and 1974, the number of farms in the smallest two landholding classes declined as a proportion of all farms from 90.4 percent to 87.9 percent, only to rise again to 89.1 percent by 1994. The farms in the largest two land-holding classes never represented more than 1.6 percent during the entire period. In terms of land area, however, in the Sierra some modest improvement does appear to have occurred. The smallest farms increased their share of total land area from 16 percent to 21.4 percent between 1954 and 1974, and then further increase their share, but only very slightly, to 22.2 percent in the subsequent two decades. The biggest reduction in the share of the largest two landholding classes also occurred between 1954 and 1974, with a decline from 42.7 percent to 40.5 percent between 1974 and 1994. In the Costa, the period from 1954 to 1974 saw a decline in the number of farms in the smallest two landholding classes as well as in the largest two land-holding classes. This process of an increasing proportion of medium sized farms continued on to 1994. In terms of land area however, the process was less clear cut; between 1974 and 1994 large farms reversed the previous trend by increasing their share of total land area at the expense of both small and medium sized farms. The over-riding impression obtained from Table 5 is that the broad distribution of land in 1994 is remarkably similar to that which prevailed at the time of the previous two censuses, even though the numbers of farms increased significantly and the total land area also rose.

Measures of the inequality of land in Ecuador, confirm our impression of a sharply skewed distribution of land (Table 6). Two measures of land are used here; land operated and land owned. Land operated allows for the fact that some cultivated holdings include land leased-in and are net of land leased-out. Measuring the distribution of land over all households in rural areas, the gini coefficient for land operated in rural Ecuador as a whole is very high as 0.86 (and 0.89 in terms of land owned). This declines to 0.80 for land operated, if non-cultivating households are excluded, 0.82 when landless households are excluded from the land ownership distribution. The distribution of land is similarly unequal in the Costa and Sierra but more equal in the Oriente. Average land-holdings (in terms of land cultivated or owned) are the lowest in the Sierra.

Are the poor among those with the least land in rural areas? This contention underlies much of the discussion of rural poverty in Ecuador. Table 7 examines the relationship between poverty and per-capita land holdings in rural Ecuador. Regardless of which measure of poverty is used, there is a clear relationship between the degree or extent of poverty and the household's per capita land holdings. This pattern becomes particularly strong if we use distribution-sensitive measures of poverty. It is not entirely obvious that this pattern was to be expected, even though land is clearly a critically important asset in rural areas. This is because land can vary markedly in terms of quality. In terms of topography and agro-climate, Ecuador is a highly heterogeneous country. Even within a certain topographical and agro-climatic zone such as the Sierra, land *quality* and conditions for cultivation in the valleys is much better than on steep hill sides and in the Andean *paramos*.[8] It is plausible that a small plot of land in the valley represents considerably greater economic value than a large landholding on the hillsides or in the paramos. The finding of an inverse relationship between land holdings and poverty suggests that while land quality does vary, the poor do not make up for their poor land quality by owning large plots of land.

This serves to remind us that what should really be focused on is access to land *services*. These services depend on factors such as soil quality, slope, water availability, and so on. In Table 5 we saw that land area in Ecuador has been expanding over time in the Costa and Sierra. To the extent that such land is of progressively inferior quality, as ever higher hill-sides are cleared and cultivated, providing access to the poor of such land cannot be expected to yield sharp improvements in their living standards.

---

[8]   In fact, it has been argued that agricultural pressure on the hillsides in the Andes increased after the 1964 land reform (Whittaker and Coyler, 1990).

The availability, to households, of land for cultivation is not necessarily restricted only to those plots of land owned by the household. In Table 8 we see that there appears to be reasonably widespread land-renting, and that varying contractual arrangements are in use. In rural Ecuador as a whole, around 6 percent of landless households are able to lease-in land and therefore remain engaged in cultivation, and nearly 47 percent of all rural households report some land leased-in. The incidence of renting is not more significant among poor farming households than among the non-poor.

Contractual arrangements for most land rentals frequently remain unspecified in the dataset, but we can assert that both share-tenancy and cash rental arrangements are common. Share-tenancy is more common among poor households while cash-renting occurs relatively more often among the non-poor, but the differences are slight. For both poor and non-poor households these two contractual arrangements represent nearly 30 percent of all contractual arrangements. Across regions, share tenancy appears most common in the Sierra while cash renting is more common in the Costa. However, among the poor in the Costa share-cropping also becomes more important than cash renting. Theories of share-cropping emphasize the advantages to renters of such contracts from the perspective of risk-sharing across agents, so that the relatively higher incidence of share-tenancy among the poor is not surprising.

Cropping Patterns, Marketed Surplus and the Landsize-Productivity Relationship

Cropping patterns in Ecuador vary along with the topography and agro-climate of the country. Crops which are cultivated in the Costa tend not to be cultivated in the Sierra, although crops grown in the Costa do reoccur in the Oriente (Table 9). In the Costa, the most commonly cultivated crops are rice, cocoa, coffee and bananas. The crop which is grown by most Costa farmers is rice. The average share of total output value coming from rice is 49 percent for poor farming households compared with 51 percent for the non-poor. Cropping patterns between poor and non-poor farming households in the Costa do not vary by much although maize cultivation is relatively more common among the non-poor.

In the Sierra, a far greater variety of crops is grown. No single crop approaches the importance that rice takes on in the Costa. The closest in the Sierra to rice is fruit cultivation, representing on average 16-17 percent of farmers' total value of output. Coffee cultivation in the Sierra tends to be more important to the non-poor than the poor. This is strongly the case with tree-tomato (tomate de arbol) and sweet-corn cultivation. In contrast, the poor are considerably more likely to cultivate barley and alfalfa than the non-poor. Crops which are important to both poor and non-poor in the Sierra are maize, potato, and beans.

In the Oriente the three most important crops are fruit, cassava, and plantains. Cassava, fruit, coffee, cacao are relatively more important to the poor, while maize tends to be cultivated by the non-poor.

The extent to which farmers participate in the market economy varies markedly across the regions of Ecuador, and is also linked to poverty (Table 10). In the Costa, on average, 70 percent of output is sold on the market, compared with 39 percent and 36 percent in the Sierra and Oriente, respectively. Within the Costa however, poor farmers tend to retain a larger share of production for home consumption. In the Sierra and Oriente this pattern is also observed.[9]

Farm Size and Productivity

A long-standing question regarding land access and cultivation is whether small farmers are more efficient cultivators than large farmers. Where there is convincing evidence that this pattern does hold, an efficiency-based argument for land redistribution can be added to the equity-based argument discussed above. Redistributing land from large landholdings to small farms can be expected to result in an increase in output. It is typically difficult to establish the relative efficiency of small farmers vis-à-vis large farmers for the same reason as was discussed above in terms of the relationship between poverty and landholding. If small farmers' land tends to be of higher quality, then an observed inverse size-productivity relationship could be mistakenly attributed to differences in efficiency.

In Table 11 the relationship is examined at the level of all cultivators as well as at the level of rice, fruit and maize, for cultivators who report cultivating only that crop. Among all cultivators, increasing farm size by 10% will lead to an increase in gross output value of 5.5%. There is evidence of strongly declining yields with increasing farm size. Looking only at those farmers who derive the bulk of agricultural output from rice (which assuming that land used for rice cultivation has to be of uniform quality, allows us to control for land quality), yields appear to decline even more sharply with farm size. Although the sample size becomes smaller when focusing on maize cultivators, the same patterns occurs. Focusing on fruit cultivators, there is still evidence of higher yields among smaller farmers, but the relationship is weaker than with the other crops. Experimenting with alternative groupings of crops (to increase the number of observations but still trying to control for land quality) does not provide a different picture. Small farmers universally achieve higher yields than large farmers.

Why should small farms be more successfully cultivated, in terms of output per hectare, than large farms? A commonly proposed hypothesis is that small farmers apply labor more intensively than large farmers because they are able to draw on household labor for this purpose. The plausibility of this argument depends on the extent to which alternative sources of employment are available to household members. If some household members are not able to find employment elsewhere, then the opportunity cost

---

[9]   One of the observations in the RQA relates to the participation of households in the cash-economy, namely that larger (not necessarily poorer) farmers are better able to grow the necessary surplus above home-consumption requirements than smaller farmers. This notion receives moderate support when one examines the relationship between average marketed surplus and per capita land-holding class, at the level of Ecuador as a whole. However, across regions the relationship varies. In the Costa, there is, if anything, a suggestion that larger farmers sell a smaller fraction of total output on the market. In the Sierra, in contrast, the smallest farmers tend to retain the bulk of their production at home, while the largest farmers are almost entirely oriented towards the market. In the Oriente a similar pattern to the Sierra is observed.

of their working on the farm is very low and labor can be applied to a point where its marginal product is quite low. Another question arises as to why large farmers do not lease out their land to small farmers if the latter are able to achieve much higher productivity. Here issues of security of tenure become quite important. If large farmers fear that by leasing out their land they will loose title to that land then they will generally be reluctant to engage in such land transactions.

Access to Complementary Inputs

Poor farmers in rural Ecuador devote significantly fewer expenditures on seeds, fertilizers and pesticides than the non-poor (Table 12). These patterns are most sharply evident in the Costa and Sierra. In the Oriente, average expenditure per household on seeds, fertilizers or pesticides are considerably more modest.

On average, households in rural Ecuador report outstanding debts of nearly 900,000 sucres per household (Table 13). This average is driven up largely by the fact that the non-poor in the rural Costa report borrowings of more than 2.5 million sucres per household. On average, poor households in rural Ecuador as a whole report borrowings of roughly one fifth that amount. Of the poor who do report borrowings, the bulk are in the Costa; credit market transactions in the rural Sierra appear to be particularly infrequent, although it is noteworthy that the poor tend to borrow more than the non-poor in this region.

In the Costa, the large debt holdings of the non-poor appear to be a combination of both larger loans taken out as well as more households borrowing than the poor. This is less evident in the Sierra and Oriente. Households in the Costa borrow from various sources, including a significant amount from local money-lenders. In the Sierra and Oriente, the main sources of lending are formal institutions such as the Banco National de Fomento, but few households report borrowings from such institutions at all. As suggested in the RQA, communities in the Sierra are possibly far more close-knit than in the Costa. Arrangements of mutual assistance are not uncommon. It is likely that the respondents to questions on credit market transactions do not perceive such reciprocal arrangements as credit transactions, although they can, of course, be viewed in that way. What does seem clear, however, is that if such arrangements are wide-spread and represent the most important type of credit transaction in Sierra communities, they will suffer from the relatively undiversified nature of the communities' economies. If a village-wide calamity such as a drought occurs, members of the community will have difficulties in turning to each other for assistance as all will have been affected simultaneously.

A common response in the RQA to questions of what the poor felt would be helpful in improving their situation was technical assistance. Indeed, from the LSMS in Ecuador, it appears that very few households report having received any form of technical assistance in the previous year (Table 14). At the all-Ecuador level as well as in each region in turn, the non-poor were more likely to have received technical assistance than the poor. These figures do not provide any indication of quality of assistance received by farmers and it is clear that at heart it will be access to appropriate, relevant, technical assistance which will have a bearing on the productivity of agriculture.

Ownership of productive assets in rural Ecuador is fairly thin, with fewer than 20 percent of households reporting ownership of any of the assets included in Table 15. There appears to be a basis for distinguishing between the poor and the non-poor in the rural Costa in terms of irrigation equipment. The poor in the rural Costa are far more likely to own a water-pump than the non-poor, but the non-poor are more likely to own other types of irrigation equipment. This supports the findings in the RQA for the Costa communities, that water availability is an important concern for farmers.

Agricultural Labor

Among the poor in rural areas, it is often possible to distinguish between two groups of persons or households. One group consists of marginal farmers who are engaged in relatively backward subsistence cultivation. The other group consists of agricultural laborers; persons who rely on wage labor on the farms of large land holders and plantations. In rural Ecuador, wage labor is quite widespread. As many as 40 percent of poor households have at least one family member who supplements household income with wage labor as his or her principal economic activity (Table 16). This proportion rises to 55 percent when one includes households which have at least one family member devoting some of his or her time on wage labor. Between regions, however, the relative importance of wage labor varies markedly. In the Costa, up to 79 percent of poor households have some involvement in wage labor, while in the Sierra the corresponding percentage is 40 percent and in the Oriente it is 39 percent. In all regions, agricultural wage labor is more closely associated with the poor than the non-poor.

Agricultural laboring without also some involvement in home cultivation is uncommon in the Sierra and Oriente, but less so in the Costa. 28 percent of poor households in the Costa have a family member employed in paid agricultural labor while the household does not cultivate for itself. Such households are often singled out as particularly vulnerable, relative to farmers, because during period of harvest failure, they are exposed in two ways - facing reduced employment opportunities in agriculture and at the same time having to purchase their food at rising prices.

Ownership of Livestock and Domestic Animals

In the RQA, ownership of animals is described as a secondary source of income, alongside cultivation, which is important to the poor. Animal ownership can also provide an attractive store if alternative savings institutions are not available. From Table 17 it is clear that ownership of cows is considerably more prevalent among the non-poor in the Costa than anywhere else in the country. Chicken are also much more frequently owned in the Costa than in other regions, although there is not much difference between the poor and non-poor in terms of the average number owned. In the Sierra, ownership of guinea-pigs and rabbits is far more common than in the other two regions, which accords with the more common practice among Andean communities of owning these animals. On the whole, however, the salient observation emerging from Table 17 is that, except for cows and chicken, ownership of animals does not appear to vary markedly with the poverty status of a household. In addition, and possibly as an explanation, ownership of animals is not on average very large, with the exception once again, of chickens and cows particularly in the rural Costa.

6.   Rural Non-Farm Employment

The rural non-farm economy is a relatively poorly understood sector in most countries. This is not surprising given that it is defined, essentially, in a negative way: all economic activity which occurs in rural areas and which is *not* agriculture. As a result the sector is typically highly heterogeneous and it is difficult to obtain anything but partial information on the significance of off-farm activities. From the perspective of poverty analysis, off-farm employment can be an indicator of extreme destitution or a sign of upward mobility. For individuals who are, for one reason or other, excluded from participation in agriculture (perhaps due to old age, illness, or disability) off-farm activities would represent last-resort options. Such individuals might, for example, busy themselves collecting scraps around the village or at the local market for resale elsewhere. At the other end of the spectrum, off-farm employment can offer the opportunity to escape poverty through acquisition of a high, and regular, source of income. The relationship between the off-farm sector and agriculture is quite close. Off-farm activities can contribute to improved agricultural productivity through the manufacture of agricultural inputs, for example, and at the same time rising agricultural incomes can stimulate the expansion of off-farm activities - particularly services and manufacture of basic consumer goods. The off-farm sector in countries such as China and other East Asian economies has been central in determining the pace and direction of change in rural living standards - nearly one-third of China's GDP is calculated to come from township enterprises, employing about 100 million people. In Ecuador, such 'rural township enterprises' also exist, albeit at a more modest scale (see Box).

Table 18 provides a breakdown of non-farm activities by *primary* occupation. To the extent that some people are employed in the off-farm sector on a more casual basis, the Table understates the extent to which the rural population in Ecuador is involved in the off-farm sector. Nonetheless, in rural Ecuador as a whole, 31 percent of the non-poor working population is primarily occupied in the off-farm sector. The corresponding figure for the poor is 19 percent.

Across regions, off-farm activities are particularly important in the Sierra and Oriente, while in the Costa only 10 - 15 percent of the working population are employed outside of agriculture. In the Sierra nearly 40 percent of the non-poor are employed outside of agriculture while nearly 30 percent of the poor are. The percentage of poor involved in off-farm employment is lower than of the non-poor in all regions of Ecuador, suggesting that indeed this is an important route out of poverty for those who are able to obtain such employment. An important consideration is how much worse off the poor with an outside job would have been if they had not had such a source of income.

Box 1: Pelileo - Jeans Tailoring in the Ecuadoran Sierra

The rural town of Pelileo is located some 200 kms south of Quito in the Sierran province of Tungurahua. The town has a population of 26,000 and is connected by paved road to the city of Ambato, about 20 kms away.

In Pelileo there are around 400 enterprises engaged in the tailoring of jeans. This activity started in the early 1970s when an entrepreneur started sub-contracting out to households. Rapid expansion of tailoring activities took place during the 1980s. While Pelileo has specialized in jeans tailoring, other communities in Tungurahua have focused on shoe-making, knit-wear and shirt-making. In total some 3,000 people are employed in one capacity or other by the jeans economy. A few firms are large (about 15 out of the 400 in Pelileo, employing around 70 people each), but most are household based, with an average of no more than 5 members. Most of the household-based enterprises operate in a subcontracting relationship with larger firms.

Many of the smaller firms are located in the environs around Pelileo, where households combine their tailoring activities with agriculture. Agriculture in this part of Tungurahua province has stagnated in recent years, and tailoring represents an important, albeit modest, supplement to household income. In the household based enterprises, one person, using a simple sewing machine, tailors a pair of modest-quality jeans in about 45 minutes. The cost of inputs in producing such jeans is about US $5.00, and profit received per pair of jeans is approximately $0.60. For a five-member firm, with each member tailoring perhaps 9 hours per day, six days a week, total weekly profits amount to less than $220. In many of the household firms, women and children make up the workforce. For these individuals alternative income sources are often scarce.

Larger firms produce jeans of better quality in approximately 27 minutes (compared with 23 minutes per pair in the US). A pair of such jeans fetches a price of around $14 in Quito. Unlike the lower quality products produced by household firms, and usually marketed locally with crudely imitated designer-labels, these jeans are sold under their own labels and are exported to Colombia, Peru and even as far as Canada.

Government provided credit to small enterprises, through the Banco Nacional de Fomento (BNF), can be obtained in loans ranging from $1,500-5,000. This credit is available at relatively attractive interest rates (about 36 percent per annum in nominal terms), but additional transactions costs through corruption, delays and complications significantly raise the total cost of credit from BNF. A private financial institution known as INSOTEC provides loans of similar size at a rate of about 6 percent per month. All in all, credit is available but expensive. Few of the Pelileo entrepreneurs turn to such sources of finance, preferring to draw on savings and sources of informal credit.

Source: Personal interview with the head of the Pelileo Chamber of Commerce in Pelileo, Ecuador, May 1994.

Outside jobs which are regular and permanent are presumably the most attractive to rural households as such jobs reduce the exposure to fluctuations associated with cultivation. With the sole exception that a lower incidence of off-farm employment is observed, across regions, and between the poor and non-poor, the same patterns are observed when we focus on the percentage of the working population employed in a regular, permanent off-farm job.

Within the Sierra, the most important activities in the non-farm sector for both the poor and non-poor are sales, manufacturing and textiles. However, both these occupations are relatively more common among the non-poor than the poor. There appears to be no particular type of occupation in the Sierra which is more common among poor workers than non-poor workers.

In the Costa, the most important occupations outside of agriculture are sales (for both poor and non-poor), transportation (for non-poor) and the 'other' category (which includes predominantly a variety of service occupations). In the Oriente, off-farm employment occurs in virtually all the categories, with once again sales being the most important. In all cases, employment is concentrated among the non-poor.

To focus attention only on *primary* occupations is likely to understate the importance of the rural non-farm sector. The inter-relationship between the off-farm sector and agriculture is that such activities often occur precisely during periods of agricultural slack. Moreover, off-farm employment is known to be attractive for women, who try to supplement household incomes by seeking non-farm earnings on a part-time basis. In Table 19, employment in off-farm activities is examined for both primary and secondary occupations. In addition, employment in such activities is broken down between men and women. When this broader definition of employment in the off-farm sector is taken, it appears that as many as one in two of the non-poor of working age have some employment in the off-farm sector. For the poor the corresponding figure is 38 percent. More strikingly, the percentage of women employed in this sector (for both the poor and non-poor) is greater than the comparable figure for men.

While sales are the most important non-farm activity for both men and women, the percentage of women employed in such activities is nearly twice as high as for men. Other occupations which are important for women relative to men are textiles. Once again, there are few non-farm occupations in which the poor are more likely to be employed than the non-poor. Two important exceptions are construction for men and domestic service for women.

7.   Econometric Analysis

The purpose of this section is essentially threefold: first, we want to try to bring together the disparate strands of the analysis above in assessing their relation to rural poverty; second, we want to try to identify those correlates of rural poverty which are independently associated with poverty; finally, we want to step back from the focus only on the poverty incidence (implicit in the 'poor/non-poor' comparisons we have been making) to examine in addition, what factors are associated with the depth and severity of poverty. We report on the results of two types of model estimations. We estimate models for each region in turn, in light of the finding that the circumstances of poverty can vary markedly between regions (even though we have shown that efforts to rank regions in terms of the degree or extent of poverty are not very promising). The specifications reported here are restricted versions of what were originally much broader possible models (comprising the whole range of variables described in the preceding sections). As many of the variables are correlated with one another, little in terms of additional explanatory power was contributed by many of the variables. The restricted specifications reported here, are therefore those which include those variables which are independently and significantly associated with poverty (although, as we shall see, the same specification for a given region does not necessarily indicate the same degree of significance for a particular variable, across different poverty measures).

We estimate two Tobit models for the poverty gap and squared poverty gap, respectively, and a Probit model on the probability of being poor. As the poverty gap and square poverty gap are continuous for those households below the poverty line, it is of interest to investigate whether certain independent variables are more strongly associated with different degrees of poverty. Regardless of the model, it is important to stress that the results here should not be interpreted as implying a causal relationship. It is entirely possible that rather than causing poverty, poverty might indeed 'cause' an 'exogenous' variable. The value of this exercise lies in the observation that where a significant association is found between poverty and a right hand side variable this relationship holds, controlling for all other variables in the specification. As such, the explanatory variable can be interpreted as representing an association with poverty, *independent* of the association between poverty and the other explanatory variables.

In Table 20 we present results from Tobit models on the poverty gap, for the Costa, Sierra and Oriente in turn. All variables in the models to which one intuitively attributes a direction of association with poverty confirm this expected direction. In all regions the more land per capita significantly reduces the depth of poverty. This relationship seems most pronounced in the Sierra. In the Costa, if a households is engaged mainly in subsistence agriculture (i.e. selling less than 30 percent of output on the market) it is significantly more likely to be very poor. In the Sierra, the relationship between subsistence agriculture and poverty is not statistically significant beyond 80 percent confidence, but has a similar sign. In the Oriente marketed surplus did not appear to have much of a separate influence on poverty. Certain crops are related to poverty depth in the Costa, Sierra and Oriente. In the Costa, cocoa cultivators are likely to be poor, while sweet corn cultivators in the Sierra and maize cultivators in the Oriente are less exposed to poverty, controlling for all other variables. In all three regions, if the household head is not educated up to secondary school level, the household is significantly more likely to be very poor than educated households. Similarly, in all regions, the larger the proportion of family members employed in a regular off-farm job, the less likely it is that the household will appear among the very poor. Interestingly, access to some organized waste removal arrangement reduces the poverty gap, independently controlling for other variables.

An additional group of variables appears to be important in the Sierra and Oriente. There, the depth of poverty is clearly linked to whether the household head is an indigenous language speaker. In addition, in these two regions, if the households consume gas they are significantly less exposed to poverty. Households with larger homes in the Sierra and Oriente are also less represented among the very poor.

In the Sierra, whether the household benefits from technical assistance in agriculture, whether it is connected to the telephone network, or whether it benefits from some organized sewage arrangement, are additional factors which are helpful in describing the depth of poverty. In the Oriente and Costa these variables do not appear independently important. In the Oriente, in turn, access to the electricity network was of additional, independent, significance.

Tables 21 and 22 repeat the analysis, using the same specifications as above for each region, but applying the Probit model to the head count and the Tobit model to the severity of poverty, respectively. The broad conclusions obtained from Table 20 remain.

In the case of the head count measure of poverty, fewer of the right hand side variables are significant, but the analysis based on poverty severity mirrors that in Table 20 very closely.

Before completing this section, we want to briefly note that variables which are not included in the specification reported in Tables 20-22 are broadly found not to be significant. Variables such as gender of household head, ownership of productive assets and livestock, access to or use of credit, etc., are not found to correlate with poverty independently from the measures included in these specification.

8.   Concluding Comments

Poverty in rural Ecuador is widespread, intense and rural poverty is more acute than urban poverty. Regional rankings of poverty are not robust, i.e. conclusions regarding the relative poverty of one region vis-a-vis the other are sensitive to the precise location of the poverty line and the poverty measure employed.

However, the rural economy, and hence the determinants of poverty, is quite different between regions. There is great heterogeneity between Costa and Sierra in terms of how agriculture is organized, what is grown, etc. Agriculture in the rural Costa is more dynamic, with more fertilizers and pesticides being applied by Costa farmers and with more farmers selling output on the market on average than in the Sierra. However, the distribution of land in the Costa remains highly unequal, and a large number of marginal farmers exist. Moreover, a large number of households in the Costa have members employed as paid laborers in agriculture. This greater involvement by the poor in the Costa agriculture means that they are more exposed to income and consumption risk associated with harvest failures caused by drought, etc.

Land quality issues are particularly important in the Sierra - the terrain in the Andes mountains implies great heterogeneity in slope, rainfall, altitude, etc. In addition, cultivating households in the Sierra are relatively less likely to sell their output on the market. While the variable capturing subsistence agriculture was not found to be independently significant in the econometric estimations, it is quite likely that this variable in both the Sierra and Oriente is correlated with a household speaking an indigenous language. In both these regions, indigeneity was found to be very strongly linked to greater poverty.

The infrastructure variables we have examined have been limited to household connections and access, and have not permitted a study of the contribution of infrastructure to employment and household income. We have also not been able to assess the quality of infrastructure *services* which are being provided. Nonetheless, access to infrastructure appears to be closely associated with poverty in rural Ecuador. The extent to which infrastructure contributes to improved access to off-farm employment and higher agricultural productivity merits further investigation.

Land is closely linked to living standards in rural Ecuador. Households with lower per capita landholdings are at high risk of poverty and are highly represented among the extreme poor. We have also determined, based on the LSMS, that land productivity declines with farm size. This combination suggests that improving access of the poor to land could actually increase agricultural production and lower poverty. Of course, the political constraints on a concerted land reform may be quite considerable, and the experience over time with land redistribution, suggest that these are indeed important in Ecuador. However, the recent experience in Colombia offers some grounds for optimism. In a climate of economic reform, where both price and other supports to large farmers are being dismantled, the option of pulling out of agriculture altogether by such farmers and voluntarily selling their land becomes increasingly attractive. These developments may point to an opportunity to effect change in the distribution of land in Ecuador as well.

The econometric analysis has established a number of factors which are closely linked to poverty in rural Ecuador. Apart from the above mentioned per capita landholdings, levels of education, and access to off-farm employment are critically important factors in describing poverty, whether measured using the head count or using distributionally sensitive measures of poverty. Separately, in the Sierra and Oriente, indigenous households are at a high risk of poverty, while in the Costa, subsistence farmers are very exposed. Access to infrastructure services such as waste disposal, gas, telephones or electricity appear to be important, although to varying degrees in different parts of the country.

Finally, the non-farm sector in Ecuador appears to offer an important route out of poverty in rural areas. It is a particularly relevant sector for women. It is not clear what specific policy measures should be taken to encourage the expansion of this sector, with the exception perhaps of supporting rural manufacturing and commerce with appropriate infrastructure. Perhaps the best perspective on this sector is to focus on removing what impediments there might be to its expansion. Further research into possible credit and regulatory constraints will help determine the appropriate steps.

References

Atkinson, A.B. (1970), 'On the Measurement of Inequality', Journal of Economic Theory, Vol 2, No. 3.

Atkinson, A.B. (1989), Poverty and Social Security (Hemel Hempstead: Harvester Wheatsheaf).

Binswanger, H., Deininger, K. and Feder, G. (1993), 'Power, Distortions, Revolt and Reform in Agricultural Land Relations', forthcoming in Behrman, J. and Srinivasan T.N. (eds) Handbook of Development Economics, Vol III (North Holland: Elsevier).

Cabrera, Y., Martinez, J. and Morales, R. (1993), Medicion de la Pobreza en las Area Urbana y Rural del Ecuador (Quito: Instituto Nacional del Empleo).

Chaudhuri, S. and Ravallion, M. (1993), 'How Well do Static Welfare Indicators Identify the Chronically Poor?', Journal of Public Economics 53(3).

Guzman, M. (1994), Bicentralismo y Pobreza en el Ecuador (Quito: Corporacion Editora Nacional).

Howes, S. (1993), Income Distribution: Measurement, Transition and Analysis of Urban China, 1981-1990. Ph.D. dissertation, London School of Economics, University of London.

de Janvry, A. and Gillman (1991), 'Encadenamientos de Produccion en la Economia Agricola en el Ecuador', mimeo, FIDA-ICCA.

Instituto Nacional del Empleo (1990), Encuesta Permanente de Hogares (Quito: Banco Central del Ecuador).

Ravallion, M. (1994), Poverty Comparisons (Chur: Harwood).

Ravallion, M. (1995), 'Bounds for a Poverty Line', mimeo, Policy Research Department, Poverty and Human Resources Division, the World Bank.

Ravallion, M. and Bidani, B. (1994), 'How Robust is a Poverty Profile', World Bank Economic Review, 8(1).

Scott, C.D. (1987), 'Rural Poverty in Latin America and the Caribbean', mimeo, Food and Agriculture Organization, Rome.

Watts, H.W. (1968), 'An Economic Definition of Poverty', in D.P. Moynihan (ed) On Understanding Poverty (New York: Basic Books).

Whittaker, M. and Coyler D. (1990), Agriculture and Economic Survival: The Role of Agriculture in Ecuador's Development (Boulder: Westview Press).

TABLE 1. Poverty By Region in Ecuador: Summary Measures

Final Poverty Line (Sucres 45,446 per fortnight)

	Incidence	Number of Poor	Depth	Severity
Costa				
Urban	0.26	954,566	0.07	0.03
Rural	0.50	988,014	0.15	0.06
Sierra				
Urban	0.22	502,947	0.08	0.04
Rural	0.43	1,095,975	0.14	0.07
Oriente				
Urban	0.20	11,172	0.05	0.02
Rural	0.67	198,925	0.30	0.16
National				
Urban	0.25	1,468,685	0.07	0.03
Rural	0.47	2,282,914	0.15	0.07
Total	0.35	3,751,599	0.11	0.05

Food Poverty Line
(30,733 Sucres per fortnight)

	Incidence	Number of Poor	Depth	Severity
Costa				
Urban	0.09	314,406	0.04	0.02
Rural	0.22	431,018	0.11	0.05
Sierra				
Urban	0.11	258,840	0.06	0.03
Rural	0.20	504,448	0.11	0.06
Oriente				
Urban	0.07	3,885	0.03	0.02
Rural	0.50	148,320	0.27	0.16
National				
Urban	0.09	577,131	0.05	0.03
Rural	0.22	1,083,786	0.12	0.06
Total	0.15	1,660,917	0.08	0.04

Notes:

1. Expenditures across regions and sectors were adjusted with a Laspeyres price index based on the differential cost of a food basket yielding 2237 ckals per person per day (Cabrera, Martinez, and Morales, 1993, pg 95 and 98). The food basket was based on consumption patterns of the 2nd and 3rd quintile of the population (in nominal per capita expenditure terms).

2. Poverty Incidence, Depth and Severity are measured with the Foster-Greer-Thorbecke index with parameters 0,1 and 2 respectively (see Ravallion, 1994).

Source: LSMS, 1994

TABLE 2. Previous Estimates of Rural Poverty In Ecuador

Study	Reference Year	Incidence of Rural Poverty	Total Number of poor persons in Rural Areas	Share of Rural Poor in Total National Poverty
Scott (1987)	1980 - 82	65%	2,900,000	n.a.
de Janvry and Gilman (1991)	1987	75%	3,750,000	n.a.
Cabrera, Martinez and Morales (1993)	1990	88%	3,823,000	53%
Guzman (1994)	1993	92%	4,230,000	49%
this study based on LSMS 1994 poverty line	1994	47%	2,282,914	61%
this study based on LSMS 1994 vulnerability line	1994	67%	3,274,000	59%

<u>**Figure 1**</u>

Distribution Functions for Consumption
Urban Versus Rural Sector

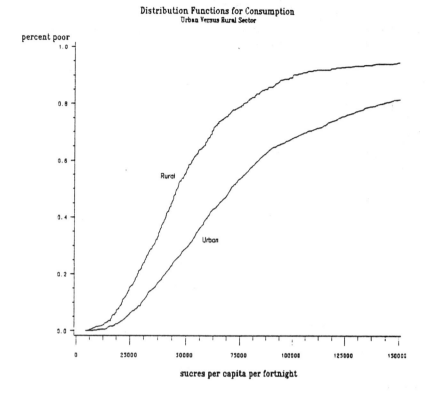

sucres per capita per fortnight

<u>**Figure 2**</u>

Distribution Functions for Consumption
Rural Regions

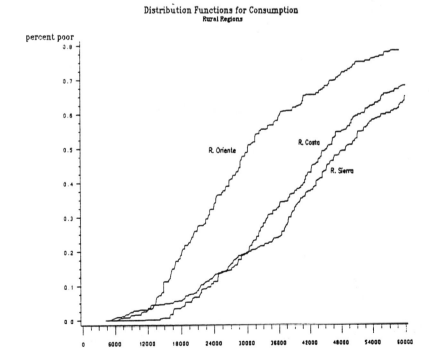

sucres per capita per fortnight

Figure 3

Deficit Curves for Consumption
Rural Regions

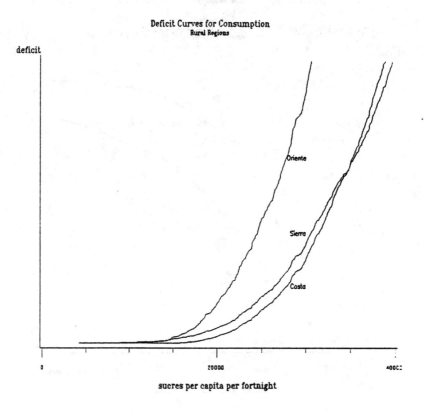

sucres per capita per fortnight

Figure 4

Deficit Curves for Consumption
Urban Versus Rural Sectors

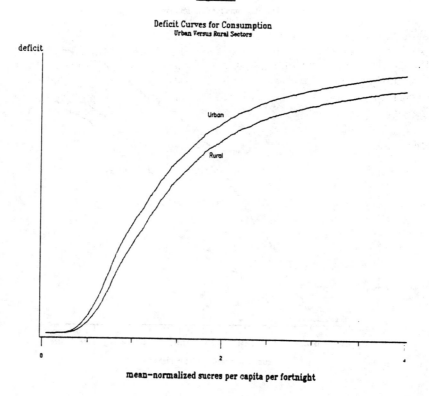

mean-normalized sucres per capita per fortnight

TABLE 3. Inequality of Consumption: Summary Measures

		Gini Coefficient	Atkinson Measure $\epsilon=1.0$	Atkinson Measure $\epsilon=2.0$
Costa				
	Urban	0.38	0.21	0.36
	Rural	0.35	0.18	0.30
Sierra				
	Urban	0.46	0.31	0.52
	Rural	0.40	0.24	0.41
Oriente				
	Urban	0.40	0.24	0.40
	Rural	0.43	0.27	0.41
National				
	Urban	0.43	0.26	0.43
	Rural	0.38	0.22	0.37
TOTAL		0.43	0.27	0.44

Note:
1.   Unit of observation is per capita consumption expenditure.
2.   Expenditures across regions and sectors were adjusted with a Laspeyres price index based on the differential cost of a food basket yielding 2237 kcals per person per day (for selection of this cut-off point, see Cabrera, Martinez and Morales, 1993, pg 95 and 98). The food basket was based on consumption patterns of the 2nd and 3rd quintile of the population (in nominal per capita expenditure terms).

Source: LSMS, 1994.

TABLE 4. Further Indicators of Poverty: Comparisons Between Rural and Urban Areas

	Ecuador		Urban		Rural	
	Poor	Non-Poor	Poor	Non-Poor	Poor	Non-Poor
Percentage of Persons with						
Access to Consumer Durables						
Refrigerator	18%	58%	32%	70%	9%	37%
Color Television	10%	49%	22%	62%	3%	26%
Black and White TV	54%	57%	66%	57%	45%	55%
Radio/Cassette Player	56%	75%	61%	79%	53%	68%
Bicycle	30%	46%	30%	51%	30%	38%
Car	2%	21%	3%	25%	1%	13%
Housing Characteristics						
Average Number of Rooms	2.6	3.4	2.5	3.6	2.6	3.1
Number of Persons Per Room	3.3	1.9	3.6	1.8	3.2	2.2
% of Houses With Mud Walls	11%	7%	8%	5%	13%	11%
% of Houses With Wood Walls	13%	6%	5%	2%	18%	13%
% of Houses with Dirt Floor	13%	5%	10%	3%	15%	9%
Access to Basic Services						
Electricity User	76%	92%	98%	99%	62%	77%
Water Connection	31%	57%	54%	76%	16%	24%
Waste Disposal	24%	50%	60%	76%	1%	6%
Sewage Connection	46%	77%	75%	92%	27%	50%
Education of Household Heads						
No Education	24%	10%	14%	5%	30%	19%
Primary School Only	63%	46%	61%	37%	64%	63%
Secondary School Only	11%	26%	21%	33%	5%	14%
Tertiary Education	2%	17%	4%	25%	0%	4%
Access to Healthcare						
Upon illness, minutes of travel before treatment	30	25	17	19	38	35
% of Households treating at least one illness informally	33%	26%	30%	22%	35%	31%
Languages Spoken						
Indigenous only	1%	0%	0%	0%	1%	0%
Indigenous	6%	1%	1%	0%	9%	3%
Consumption of Liquor						
mls per household per day	12	41	5	24	16	73
Food Consumption						
Calories Consumed per day (kcals per person)	1600	2883	1568	2792	1621	3041
Food Share	55%	46%	49%	40%	60%	55%

Source: LSMS (1994).

TABLE 5. Land Distribution in Ecuador: 1954 - 1994

Region and size (ha)	% Farms			% Total Area		
	1954	1974	1994	1954	1974	1994
1. Sierra						
0 - 5	81.7	77.1	80.2	10.8	12.7	14.1
5 - 10	8.7	10.8	8.9	5.2	8.7	8.1
10 - 20	4.0	5.3	3.2	4.8	8.7	5.5
20 - 50	3.0	4.1	5.2	7.3	16.2	20.9
50 - 100	1.4	1.3	1.0	7.6	11.0	8.4
100 - 500	0.9	1.2	1.6	16.1	22.9	42.9
500+	0.3	0.2	0.0	48.3	19.8	0.0
Total	100	100	100	100	100	100
N[1]	260	388	389	2,737	3,096	3,233
2. Costa						
0 - 5	73.1	70.3	57.9	3.0	6.6	5.1
5 - 10	10.5	21.0	12.5	3.9	6.0	3.8
10 - 20	6.2	7.5	9.9	5.1	9.1	6.1
20 - 50	5.6	6.6	11.5	12.5	18.7	16.4
50 - 100	2.4	1.8	4.3	11.0	10.6	13.5
100 - 500	1.8	1.6	3.3	23.0	26.5	33.5
500+	0.4	0.2	0.6	41.4	15.7	21.6
Total	100	100	100	100	100	100
N[1]	85	228	239	2,979	3,854	5,801

Note:
1.   Thousands of farms and ha.

Source: Scott (1987) drawing on Maletta (1984) for figures for 1954 and 1974. LSMS (1994) for 1994 figures.

TABLE 6. Distribution of Land Cultivated and Land Owned in Rural Ecuador

LAND CULTIVATED

	Sierra	Costa	Oriente	Ecuador
1. Including Non-Cultivators				
Number of Households in Sample	612	497	265	1374
Average Operational Holding(ha)	5.59	12.4	12.8	8.55
Gini Coefficient	0.87	0.87	0.78	0.87
2. Exluding Non-Cultivators				
Number of Households in Sample	390	275	168	833
Average Operational Holding(ha)	8.48	19.3	17.9	13.1
Gini Coefficient	0.80	0.80	0.69	0.81

LAND OWNED

	Sierra	Costa	Oriente	Ecuador
1. Including Landless				
Number of Households in Sample	612	497	265	1374
Average Operational Holding(ha)	5.19	11.8	12.5	8.10
Gini Coefficient	0.89	0.89	0.79	0.89
2. Exluding Landless				
Number of Households in Sample	365	234	162	761
Average Operational Holding(ha)	8.39	21.2	18.1	13.5
Gini Coefficient	0.82	0.80	0.69	0.82

Source: LSMS, 1994.

TABLE 7 Poverty and Per Capita Landholdings

Per Capita Land Holdings	Percent of Rural Population	Average Per Capita Expenditure (per month)	Incidence of Poverty	Poverty Gap	Poverty Severity (x100)
non-cultivators	32.9%	S. 62,418	43.4%	13.2%	5.6
0 - 1 hectares	46.9%	S. 55,564	51.5%	17.9%	8.9
1 - 2.5 hectares	9.3%	S. 63,921	51.5%	15.8%	7.9
2.5 - 5 hectares	4.6%	S. 58,147	33.8%	13.0%	5.8
5 - 30 hectares	5.8%	S. 88,700	39.9%	9.8%	3.6
30+ hectares	0.5%	S.371,006	0.0	0.0	0.0
Rural Ecuador	100%	S. 62,292	47.1%	15.4%	7.2

Source: LSMS, 1994.

TABLE 8. Land Tenure and Land-Use Arrangements In Rural Ecuador

	Percent of Rural Households					Percent of Poor Rural Households			
	Costa	Sierra	Oriente	Ecuador		Costa	Sierra	Oriente	Ecuador
Landless	44.1	38.2	31.2	40.2		44.8	32.1	30.3	36.9
Non-Cultivating	35.9	34.1	28.5	34.5		36.2	28.6	27.0	31.5
Landless but Cultivating	8.2	4.1	2.7	5.6		8.6	3.5	3.3	5.5
Renting Land	50.6	44.7	34.3	46.5		50.8	41.3	32.5	44.5
of which:									
Share-Tenant	9.9	25.3	12.0	18.5		14.2	29.8	12.9	22.0
Cash Rent	14.8	7.2	9.0	10.5		8.7	8.2	8.3	8.3
Labor Payment	0.9	0.7	1.2	0.8		2.4	1.0	0.0	1.6
Other/Not Available	74.1	66.7	78.4	70.3		75.0	61.0	78.8	68.1

Source: LSMS, 1994.

TABLE 9. Proportion of Gross Agricultural Output Value From Selected Crops (percent)

Cultivating Households

Crop	Costa		Sierra		Oriente	
	Poor	Non-Poor	Poor	Non-Poor	Poor	Non-Poor
Rice	49	51	1	1	1	1
Cacao	10	11	1	1	7	3
Coffee	10	9	2	5	6	4
Banana	3	2	0	0	3	3
Barley	0	0	7	3	0	0
Maiz	4	9	11	7	6	8
Potato	0	0	10	7	0	1
Tree Tomato	0	0	4	12	0	0
Maiz-Suave	1	0	9	15	1	4
Beans	2	1	7	7	1	2
Alfalfa	0	0	6	2	0	0
Vegetable (legumbre)	0	0	2	3	0	0
Morocho	0	0	3	1	0	0
Habas	0	0	2	1	0	0
Wheat	0	0	3	1	0	0
Chocho	0	0	2	0	0	0
Greens (verdura)	0	0	2	2	0	1
Garlic	0	0	0	1	0	0
Cassava (Yuca)	2	2	1	1	29	23
Plantain	4	3	0	3	23	24
Sugar Cane	2	0	0	0	0	2
Fruit (general)	9	8	17	16	19	18

Note:

1.   The average shares were obtained by averaging, across cultivating households, the value of output from a particular crop relative to total output value.

Source: LSMS (1994).

TABLE 10. Output Sold on the Market as a Proportion of Total Output Value
(Cultivating Households, percent)

	Poor	Non-Poor	All
Costa	64	73	70
Sierra	34	42	39
Oriente	37	34	36
Ecuador	45	54	50

Average Marketed Surplus And Per Capita Landholding
(Cultivating Households, percent)

Land Size Class (per capita)	Costa	Sierra	Oriente	Ecuador
<1 ha.	71	37	29	49
1-2.5 ha.	71	45	46	55
2.5-5 ha.	68	60	35	61
5-30 ha.	68	50	44	59
30+ ha.	59	84	56	65
All	70	39	36	50

Source: LSMS (1994).

TABLE 11. The Land-Size Productivity Relationship In Rural Ecuador
(Regression of (Log) Value of Gross Output on (Log) Land Cultivated)

	All Cultivators	Rice	Fruit	Maize
Land Cultivated	0.550 (20.31)	0.368 (4.210)	0.870 (4.560)	0.578 (5.530)
Intercept	12.57 (213.9)	14.08 (108.2)	12.65 (28.72)	11.45 (54.14)
R²	0.283	0.167	0.311	0.320
No. of Observations	1045	91	48	67

Notes:

1. Numbers in parentheses are *t-statistics*.
2. The regression results in the first column relate the total value of gross agricultural output to total land holdings among all farming households.
3. The regression results reported in columns 2-4 control for crop, and apply for those farmers who derive the bulk of gross output from one crop (at least 80%). It is thus assumed here that the farmers devote all their landholdings to the one respective crop. The data do not permit attributing the fraction of total landholdings to specific crops when the household cultivates more than one crop.
4. Narrowing the focus to those farmers who derive 100% of their gross output from the respective crop reduces the available number of observations (especially among fruit and maiz growers) but does not affect the parameter estimates appreciably.
5. Aggregating across similar crops, e.g. cereals, fruit and tree crops, and vegetable and tubers, increases the available number of observations. For example, rather than looking only at cultivators who derive 80% of gross output from rice, one can aggregate together cultivators deriving a similar fraction of output from barley, alfalfa and wheat. This exercise has no marked impact on the parameter estimates, but does reduce the fit of the regression.

Source: LSMS (1994).

TABLE 12. Intensity of Cultivation and Agricultural Capital Among Cultivating Households

Average Annual Expenditure on Seeds, Fertilizers and Pesicides

		Seeds	Fertilizers	Pesticides
Costa				
	Non-Poor	23791	272244	202815
	Poor	2615	40484	22823
Sierra				
	Non-Poor	36368	176819	210520
	Poor	35945	142001	150772
Oriente				
	Non-Poor	9817	5784	9499
	Poor	3053	4360	6698
Ecuador				
	Non-Poor	30441	207633	199869
	Poor	21257	94654	93145
	Total	26731	161987	156750

TABLE 13. Outstanding Debt and Proportion of Cultivating Households Borrowing

		Average Debt Outstanding	Percentage of All Households Borrowing From:			
			BNF	Money-lender	Family	Other Source
Costa						
	Non-Poor	2581238	7%	13%	2%	22%
	Poor	1126220	4%	12%	4%	13%
Sierra						
	Non-Poor	91506	2%	0%	0%	1%
	Poor	208108	2%	0%	0%	2%
Oriente						
	Non-Poor	820440	3%	0%	0%	4%
	Poor	281055	2%	0%	0%	2%
Ecuador						
	Non-Poor	1092731	4%	5%	1%	10%
	Poor	554701	3%	4%	1%	6%
Total		875357	3%	5%	1%	8%

Source: LSMS, 1994.

TABLE 14. Technical Assistance and Ownership of Farm Assets
(Cultivating Households)

Percentage of Households Reporting Having Received Technical Assistance

		Any Assistance	Private	Public
Costa				
	Non-Poor	3%	1%	2%
	Poor	1%	1%	0%
Sierra				
	Non-Poor	5%	3%	2%
	Poor	1%	1%	0%
Oriente				
	Non-Poor	6%	5%	1%
	Poor	0%	0%	0%
Ecuador				
	Non-Poor	4%	2%	2%
	Poor	1%	1%	0%
	Total	3%	2%	1%

Source: LSMS, 1994.

TABLE 15. Average Value of All Farm Assets per Household
and the Relative Frequency of Ownership, percent

		Average Value of All Assets per Household	Tractor	Vehicle	Generator	Water Pump	Other Irrigation Equipment
Costa							
	Non-Poor	1644795	0	7	1	13	5
	Poor	377223	0	0	1	17	3
Sierra							
	Non-Poor	1072818	1	3	1	1	0
	Poor	374781	0	1	0	1	1
Oriente							
	Non-Poor	660407	1	1	3	2	0
	Poor	103581	0	0	1	0	0
Ecuador							
	Non-Poor	1280800	1	5	1	6	2
	Poor	356802	0	0	1	7	1
	Total	907487	0	3	1	6	2

Source: LSMS (1994)

TABLE 16. Agricultural Labor in Rural Ecuador

	Costa		Sierra		Oriente		Ecuador	
	Non-Poor	Poor	Non-Poor	Poor	Non-Poor	Poor	Non-Poor	Poor
Percentage of Households with at least one member involved in agriculture as his/her principal activity.	86%	92%	68%	76%	64%	92%	75%	83%
Percentage of Households with at least one member involved in cultivation of the family farm as principal activity.	43%	43%	52%	55%	53%	86%	49%	52%
Percentage of Households with at least one member involved in paid agricultural labor outside the family farm as his/her main occupation.	47%	67%	14%	24%	8%	18%	27%	40%
Percentage of Households with at least one member with *some* involvement in paid agricultural labor outside the family farm.	60%	79%	20%	40%	18%	39%	36%	55%
Percentage of Households not cultivating but with one member involved in paid agricultural labor outside the family farm.	19%	28%	5%	12%	1%	7%	11%	18%

Source: LSMS, 1994.

TABLE 17. Rural Household Ownership of Livestock and Domestic Animals

Average Number of Animals Owned Per Household

Livestock and Domestic Animals	Costa Non-Poor	Poor	Sierra Non-Poor	Poor	Oriente Non-Poor	Poor	Ecuador Non-Poor	Poor
Cows	11.5	4.9	3.6	2.5	5.8	3.8	6.8	3.5
Sheep	0	0	1.6	2.4	0	0	0.9	1.4
Goats	0.2	0.2	0.2	0.1	0	0	0.2	0.1
Pigs	4.4	4.7	1.9	1.6	0.6	0.4	2.9	2.6
Guinea Pigs and Rabbits	0.8	0.2	5.0	3.2	2.1	0.3	3.3	1.9
Chickens	25.4	21.2	5.1	3.3	3.3	2.4	13.0	9.9
Turkeys	1.1	0.9	0.2	0.1	0	0	0.5	0.4
Ducks	3.4	3.0	0.7	0.1	0.4	0.4	1.8	1.2
Horses, Donkeys or Mules	1.5	1.2	0.5	0.4	0.6	0.2	0.9	0.7

Source: LSMS (1994)

TABLE 18. Non-Farm Activities in Rural Ecuador (Principal Occupations, in percent)

	Costa Non-Poor	Poor	Sierra Non-Poor	Poor	Oriente Non-Poor	Poor	Ecuador Non-Poor	Poor	Total
Percentage of Working Population With Principal Occupation In:									
Fishing	0	0	0	0	1	0	0	0	0
Mining	0	0	0	0	1	1	0	0	0
Textiles	0	1	5	2	1	0	3	1	2
Transportation	1	1	2	1	3	0	2	1	2
Construction	0	1	4	4	2	2	3	3	3
Manufacturing	0	1	6	6	3	1	4	4	4
Sales	7	3	12	7	7	3	10	5	8
Domestic Service	1	1	1	2	3	1	1	1	1
Food Processing	0	0	1	0	1	0	1	0	1
Other	6	2	7	6	21	4	7	4	6
Any Non-Agricultural Activity	15	10	38	28	43	12	31	19	27
Percentage of working population employed in a regular, permanent non-farm occupation	14	6	34	22	35	11	28	15	22

Source: LSMS, 1994.

TABLE 19. Non-Farm Activities in Rural Ecuador (Secondary Occupations, in percent)

	Males			Females			Ecuador		
	Non-Poor	Poor	Total	Non-Poor	Poor	Total	Non-Poor	Poor	Total
Percentage of Working Population With Some Involvement in:									
Fishing	0	0	0	0	0	0	0	0	0
Mining	0	1	0	0	1	0	0	1	0
Textiles	2	1	2	8	4	6	5	2	4
Transportation	6	4	5	0	0	0	4	2	3
Construction	8	9	8	1	1	1	5	6	5
Manufacturing	8	6	7	5	3	5	7	5	6
Sales	13	8	11	24	14	20	17	10	14
Domestic Service	0	0	0	3	6	4	1	2	2
Food Processing	1	0	1	3	1	2	2	0	1
Other	10	5	8	12	14	13	11	8	10
Any Non-Agricultural Activity	48	34	42	56	44	51	52	38	45

Source: LSMS, 1994

TABLE 20. Multi- Variate Analysis of Poverty
(Tobit on the Poverty Gap)

	Costa	Sierra	Oriente
Intercept	-0.107	0.151	0.208
	(0.093)	(0.043)	(0.022)
Per Capita Land	-0.020	-0.035	-0.025
	(0.000)	(0.000)	(0.000)
Subsistence Cultivator (Less than 30%	0.130	0.055	-
of Gross Output Sold on Market)	(0.039)	(0.179)	-
Share of Cocoa in Gross Output	0.247	-	-
	(0.044)	-	-
Share of Sweet Corn in Gross Output	-	-0.190	-
	-	(0.064)	-
Share of Maize in Gross Output	-	-	-0.431
	-	-	(0.026)
Household Head Having Less Than Secondary	0.110	0.127	0.188
School Education	(0.075)	(0.033)	(0.002)
Proportion of Workers	-0.906	-0.595	-0.675
in Regular Off-Farm Employment	(0.000)	(0.000)	(0.015)
Organized Waste Disposal	-0.302	-0.279	-0.217
	(0.027)	(0.058)	(0.019)
Household Head Speaking the Indigenous	-	0.138	0.214
Language	-	(0.009)	(0.000)
Gas Connection	-	-0.174	-0.139
	-	(0.000)	(0.013)
Total Number of Rooms in House	-	-0.027	-0.047
	-	(0.061)	(0.005)
Household Recipient of Agricultural	-	-0.386	-
Extension	-	(0.009)	-
Telephone Connection	-	-0.284	-
	-	(0.097)	-
Organized Sewage	-	-0.127	-
	-	(0.001)	-
Electricity Connection	-	-	-0.111
	-	-	(0.049)
Log Likelihood (M)	-228.73	-276.66	-95.75
Log Likelihood (0)	-262.60	-366.93	-179.71
Total Observations	497	612	265
Observations at 0	308	366	137
Observations > 0	189	246	128

Source: Own Calculations based on LSMS, 1994. Asymptotic probability values in parenthesis.

TABLE 21. Multi- Variate Analysis of Poverty
(Probit on the Headcount Ratio)

	Costa	Sierra	Oriente
Intercept	-0.299	0.285	0.522
	(0.122)	(0.218)	(0.144)
Per Capita Land	-0.056	-0.101	-0.073
	(0.001)	(0.000)	(0.006)
Subsistence Cultivator (Less than 30% of Gross Output Sold on Market)	0.139	0.160	-
	(0.508)	(0.227)	-
Share of Cocoa in Gross Output	0.945	-	-
	(0.019)	-	-
Share of Sweet Corn in Gross Output	-	-0.411	-
	-	(0.178)	-
Share of Maize in Gross Output	-	-	-1.011
	-	-	(0.156)
Household Head Having Less Than Secondary School Education	0.264	0.391	0.564
	(0.168)	(0.029)	(0.011)
Proportion of Workers in Regular Off-Farm Employment	-2.566	-1.514	-1.875
	(0.000)	(0.000)	(0.048)
Organized Waste Disposal	-0.796	-0.612	-0.560
	(0.046)	(0.133)	(0.076)
Household Head Speaking the Indigenous Language	-	0.334	0.680
	-	(0.072)	(0.001)
Gas Connection	-	-0.406	-0.422
	-	(0.001)	(0.061)
Total Number of Rooms in House	-	-0.061	-0.170
	-	(0.162)	(0.009)
Household Recipient of Agricultural Extension	-	-1.000	-
	-	(0.021)	-
Telephone Connection	-	-0.806	-
	-	(0.102)	-
Organized Sewage	-	-0.455	-
	-	(0.000)	-
Electricity Connection	-	-	-0.357
	-	-	(0.121)
Log Likelihood (M)	-301.98	-339.88	-122.05
Log Likelihood (0)	-330.11	-412.36	-183.53
Total Observations	497	612	265
Observations at 0	308	366	137
Observations > 0	189	246	128

Source: LSMS, 1994. Asymptotic probability in parenthesis.

TABLE 22. Multi- Variate Analysis of Poverty
(Tobit on the Poverty Severity)

	Costa	Sierra	Oriente
Intercept	-0.067	0.078	0.010
	(0.035)	(0.094)	(0.097)
Per Capita Land	-0.010	-0.022	-0.018
	(0.000)	(0.000)	(0.000)
Subsistence Cultivator (Less than 30% of Gross Output Sold on Market)	0.084	0.032	-
	(0.006)	(0.197)	-
Share of Cocoa in Gross Output	0.102	-	-
	(0.095)	-	-
Share of Sweet Corn in Gross Output	-	-0.108	-
	-	(0.091)	-
Share of Maize in Gross Output	-	-	-0.302
	-	-	(0.019)
Household Head Having Less Than Secondary School Education	0.053	0.071	0.129
	(0.086)	(0.056)	(0.001)
Proportion of Workers in Regular Off-Farm Employment	-0.455	-0.367	-0.429
	(0.000)	(0.000)	(0.022)
Organized Waste Disposal	-0.143	-0.151	-0.118
	(0.036)	(0.095)	(0.055)
Household Head Speaking the Indigenous Language	-	0.098	0.138
	-	(0.003)	(0.000)
Gas Connection	-	-0.112	-0.096
	-	(0.000)	(0.009)
Total Number of Rooms in House	-	-0.019	-0.030
	-	(0.034)	(0.007)
Household Recipient of Agricultural Extension	-	-0.234	-
	-	(0.012)	-
Telephone Connection	-	-0.158	-
	-	(0.142)	-
Organized Sewage	-	-0.073	-
	-	(0.002)	-
Electricity Connection	-	-	-0.076
	-	-	(0.039)
Log Likelihood (M)	-85.25	-139.90	-32.72
Log Likelihood (0)	-118.69	-229.39	-114.81
Total Observations	497	612	265
Observations at 0	308	366	137
Observations > 0	189	246	128

Source: Own calculations based on LSMS, 1994. Asymptotic probability values in parentheses.

Working Paper 5: Rural Qualitative Assessment
Jesko Hentschel, William F. Waters and Anna Kathryn Vandever Webb

1.   Introduction

With the Ecuador Rural Qualitative Assessment (RQA), we tried to learn about the views of rural households on poverty.[1] The World Bank started in April of 1994 a Poverty Assessment for Ecuador and one its main objectives is to examine the causes of poverty in rural and urban areas. As part of this poverty analysis, we wanted to complement statistical analysis from household surveys with qualitative information on how households themselves view their living conditions. Little such information exists for rural areas so that we concentrated the qualitative assessment on poverty in rural Ecuador.[2]

The Rural Qualitative Assessment has three main objectives with which the rural analysis under the Poverty Assessment is complemented: First, it aims to assess what poverty means to marginalized rural families. Second, it tries to determine what kind of survival strategies families employ in times of hardship. Third, it strives to learn what these households believe is necessary to alleviate poverty.

Several key messages evolve from the Rural Qualitative Assessment presented in this Paper.

- First, rural communities with the same characteristics like area, soil quality and ethnic background are actually very heterogeneous. This holds with respect to their command of land resources, definition of well-being, the range of economic activities carried out in the communities and their recommendations for what is necessary to overcome poverty.

- Second, almost all families interviewed state that the recent years have been very hard for them and they have increasingly complemented income from traditional sources (like subsistence agriculture and small animal husbandry) with earnings from new activities. Besides migration, which plays a pivotal role in all communities, piecework and weaving in the Sierra, small businesses in the Costa and increased cash crop production in the Oriente have taken their role in income generation. Families have also reduced expenditures for clothing, fiestas and food -- the latter being quite alarming as malnutrition rates in rural Ecuador are already very high.

- Third, poor rural families express very practical solutions to overcome their poverty. Demands are not directed at sweeping changes like expropriation of large farmers. Families overwhelmingly suggest measures which will increase the productivity of available land and human resources. Almost half of the recommendations are related to infrastructure and a very high share also demanded agricultural and non-agricultural training courses.

---

[1]   We gratefully acknowledge financing for the Ecuador Rural Qualitative Assessment (RQA) by the Government of the Netherlands. Special thanks are due to the Ecuadoran reserach teams for their excellent field work. They were comprised of Carlos Arcos, Silvia Arguello, Maria Gloria Barreiro, Fernando Garcia, Rosario Jacome, Nelson Nartinez and Hugo Vinueza.
[2]   For urban areas, a qualitative survey underlies part of the analysis in Working Paper 3.

This Working Paper, based on case studies conducted in May 1994 in seven rural communities, is organized as follows: Section 2 provides a short background on rural life in Ecuador's three diverse regions. In Section 3, we present the research objectives, the design, and methodology of the qualitative survey. Section 4 contains community descriptions. Location and population, the employment pattern, basic service access or community organization are some of the characteristics we look at. Sections 5 to 7 then portrait the results of the assessment: Section 5 describes the perceptions of households regarding the underlying causes of their poverty; Section 6 focuses on the specific strategies that these households employ in order to survive and Section 7 presents the household members' recommendations for actions that could be undertaken to alleviate rural poverty. We conclude with a short summary.

After the fieldwork of the Rural Qualitative Assessment had been undertaken, UNICEF Ecuador commissioned a second round of qualitative surveys in six Sierra communities to complement the analysis and examine whether the findings of the initial community studies were confirmed. We summarize the results of these additional community surveys, which relate closely with the conclusions of the Rural Qualitative Assessment, in an Addendum to this Working Paper.

2.   Living Conditions in Rural Ecuador

This section discusses two aspects of living conditions in rural Ecuador: rural heterogeneity and access to productive resources.

Rural Heterogeneity

Ecuador is indeed a country of contrasts; its heterogeneity is expressed in ecological, socioeconomic, and cultural terms not only between and within disparate areas of the country, but even within a given community.

Inter-regional heterogeneity. Ecuador's regional division in the Costa (coastal lowlands), Sierra (highlands) and the Oriente (upper Amazon basin) manifest themselves in three distinct rural structures. Since the colonial period, the predominant feature in the *Sierra* has been the bifurcated hacienda-minifundia system. Before agrarian reform in the early 1960s, the system was based on the monopoly of land and the imposition of obligatory labor services, but it subsequently experienced substantial change that revolved around the evolution of modern dairy farms and independent peasant communities. In the past decade, the nontraditional agricultural export (NTAE) sector has developed producing products such as cut flowers which provide part of the growing off-farm rural employment in the region. Other off-farm employment possibilities in the rural Sierra are textile, shoe or hat production which take place with simple machinery within the household boundary. Working Paper 3 takes a very close look at the extent and importance of these off-farm employment activities.

Development in the *Costa* began in the mid-19th century, and was based on export-oriented plantation agriculture, where wage labor systems evolved alongside commercially oriented small- and medium-scale farms. One consequence of this process was the development of intermediate cities and transportation networks dedicated to facilitating the export of traditional crops such as coffee, cacao, and since 1948, bananas. The Costa has been the engine of growth of the Ecuadoran economy for the past ten years as real economic activity expanded on average by 5 per cent, largely due to a primary export market boom for shrimps, and to a lesser extent, for bananas.

Economic activity in the *Oriente* consists of resource extraction and small-scale agriculture by the indigenous and migrant population. Extractive activities (e.g., gold and rubber) have been carried out since the colonial period. The region remains relatively isolated, however, because of poor roads and difficult terrain. Since the early 1970s, the defining elements of development in the region have been the petroleum boom and settlement of migrants which have had the effect of accelerating the production of coffee, wood, citrus crops and beef cattle not only by the settlers but also by the indigenous inhabitants.

Over-exploitation of fragile tropical resources is threatening the Amazon rainforest. The incorporation of the region into the national socioeconomic and political system has obliged the indigenous population to abandon traditional and sustainable, rotational horticulture and, like mestizo colonizers, to settle on fixed landholdings provided for in colonization legislation. On these holdings, indigenous households now grow market crops such as coffee in the tropical region, and naranjilla in the subtropical cloud forest region. To a large degree, this process has initiated a vicious circle of poverty and environmental degradation, characterized by deforestation, soil erosion, and water pollution.

The regional heterogeneity is further enhanced by ethnic factors. While there is no general agreement on the precise definition of ethnic boundaries, many Sierra and Oriente communities can be characterized as indigenous by any measure. Ethnic identity is based on many cultural factors, including community, nuclear and extended family relationships, which are reinforced by language, dress, and sets of common norms and values. Racial discrimination has historically excluded the indigenous population from the political arena.[3]

Intra-regional heterogeneity. The case studies included in the Rural Qualitative Assessment illustrate the considerable heterogeneity among apparently similar rural communities even within regions, especially in the Sierra. Historically, some communities obtained access to more or better resources than others through agrarian reform or purchase. Some communities have also started to diversify their economic activity, e.g. textile production. Further, development projects of the national government, often funded by international or bilateral donor organizations, have improved the access of a number of communities to basic services but by far not all. In sum, almost neighboring communities can exhibit considerable differences in living standards and type of economic activities.

Intra-community heterogeneity. Although we conducted the RQA in only a few communities, we observed that living standards and the distribution of income within the same community can vary significantly between households. For example, in Jatun Era, a community in the province of Cotopaxi, some families live in simple one room shacks made of grass and clay while others occupy relatively modern brick or cement houses with electricity, water and separate latrine facilities. Similarly, the distribution of land and its quality is strikingly unequal in Jatun Era.

---

[3]   Annex 1 to this Working Paper provides a short overview of the different forms of indigenous organizations.

This intra-community heterogeneity may result from unequal access to land or may be related to the family cycle. Certain families may dominate (both economically and politically) because of particularly favorable access to productive land or for their capacity to generate income from small businesses. A second source of differentiation within the community is related to the family cycle. Frequently, young people lack access to land, while their elders retain uncultivated land because grown children have left the household or as a result of widowhood. In this sense, intra-community stratification based on landownership is not necessarily permanent, but may, rather, have a cyclical component. The effects of inequality based on family cycles can, in some cases, be offset by forms of organization (as observed, for instance, in indigenous communities in the Sierra) that provide for the exchange of resources (e.g., land for labor). We will revisit this point later on.

Poverty and Productive Resources: Land, Water, Credit and Market Access

For many rural households, access to land, water and credit is limited which can lead to a vicious circle of poverty and soil destruction. Almost all rural households try to complement income from agricultural activities, which remains the most important income source for almost all families, with other earnings. But if the household is not very successful in obtaining other incomes, the pressure on maximizing agricultural production in the short run increases. Due to an increase in land pressure and stagnant productivity, smallholders then replace traditional, sustainable cultivation techniques with more intensive alternatives that increase the likelihood of soil exhaustion and erosion. Consequently, smallholders enter a vicious circle of poverty and environmental degradation that is essentially based on inadequate access to land and other productive resources.

Land. Land ownership in Ecuador has been highly concentrated since the colonial period, and unequal distribution continues to the present day. The agrarian reform process resulted in the gradual transfer of relatively small proportions of agricultural and pasture land to indigenous and peasant communities, which generally received the most unproductive and fragile lands. In particular, small land holdings in the Sierra are frequently so steeply sloped that even the most meticulous stewardship can not maintain soil fertility indefinitely, so that in many communities, soil erosion has reached alarming levels. While smallholdings undergo constant subdivision because of demographic pressure and inheritance patterns,[4] large holdings have been consolidated. As shown in Working Paper 4, the Gini coefficient of land distribution stayed relatively constant between 1954 and 1994. While the modern hacienda is more capital intensive and somewhat more compact than in the pre-reform period, it continues to control access to land, and in addition, occupies the most productive areas.

If households do not possess pasture land, domestic animals, which are a central feature of farming systems, cannot be kept. Domestic animals are a central feature of farming systems in that they both depend upon and support crop production. The possession of animals allows for the diversification of income (not only from live animals, but also from by-products, such as meat, wool, milk, eggs, and cheese). In addition, animals represent a source of savings, which can be utilized in times of emergency or special need. If households don't

---

[4]   The only two national agricultural censuses conducted in Ecuador reveal that the average size of the minifundia (holding of less than five hectares) decreased from 1.71 hectares to 1.54 hectares between 1954 and 1974.

own or cannot use pasture land, they are limited to holding small animals like sheep, pigs, and chickens which are kept in or around the house. In the Sierra, guinea pigs are kept in the house, and represent as much a ritual good as a food resource.

Credit. Poor rural households who seek credit do so in the informal sector, where interest rates are high, but where conditions are flexible. Public credit schemes by the Banco Nacional de Fomento (BNF) have traditionally been benefiting the medium- and large-scale farmers.[5] While probably more important than the public sector, the role of private financial institutions to lend to small-scale farmers has also been limited for several reasons. First, the lack of collateral is nearly universal, because many small landholdings are not titled and even when they are, their value is very low. Second, many small-scale farmers lack information on credit and face serious cultural barriers to seeking loans.[6] Third, small-scale farmers often require very small amounts of capital (usually less than $2,000 and frequently as little as $100) and flexible terms that banks are often not equipped to cope with. Nevertheless, a few pioneering private financial institutions of the formal sector have started to reach out to small and poor farmers and supply tailor-made credits.

Market Access. As shown in Working Paper 4, the capacity of the rural household and community to provide for the sustenance of their members also depends on the degree to which they are linked to or isolated from markets. This factor can be understood in terms of distance to regional and national urban centers, the quality of feeder roads, access to agricultural extension and marketing experience. The distances and the difficulties in bringing goods to market further erode the terms of trade for rural inhabitants because they must sell to intermediaries. At the same time, the cost of purchased items, including clothing, food, agricultural inputs, and medicines, is higher than in less isolated areas.

3.   Research Design, Methodology, and Data Analysis

In this section, we shortly revisit the design and methodology employed for the Rural Qualitative Assessment.

Study design. Two Non-Governmental Organizations conducted the field work for the Rural Qualitative Assessment in seven small rural communities in May 1994. Both NGOs, the 'Centro Ecuatoriano de Servicios Agricolas' (CESA) and 'Desarrollo y Autogestion' (DyA) had conducted qualitative research before and had ample experience in working with rural communities. The NGOs formed three research teams which each stayed one week in one community. Four of the communities are located in the Sierra (Chimborazo and Cotopaxi provinces), two in the Costa (Manabi) and one in the Oriente (Napo). All communities are located in cantons which are classified as very poor -- by a variety of different indicators -- in the Poverty Map by the Consejo Nacional de Desarrollo.[7] None of the communities is close to an urban center. While the NGOs had substantial experience working with the population in

---

5	See World Bank (1993), Annex 2, p.9.
6	As reported in Part 1 of this study, only about half of all farms with up to 30 hectares are properly titled.
7	CONADE (1993).

the region of the selected communities, they had not worked directly with the communities selected. This served to avoid a bias between the village population and the research teams.[8]

Methodology.   The field methodology employed in the RQA was based on the technique of triangulation, where qualitative and quantitative information is gathered from several sources, using different methods of data collection.   The principle advantage of the technique is that it permits for cross-checking and validation.

We obtained information from four sources.   First, key informant interviews were conducted with community leaders and others (e.g., school teachers and rural physicians), familiar with the principle trends and tendencies present at the local level.   Second, the researchers conducted semi-structured, household-level interviews with men and women in each community, following a thematic interview guide that was developed in a training workshop.   The research teams tested the content and length of the interview guide in the first week of fieldwork, and minor changes were made in a follow-up review meeting.   Third, focus groups discussed the general themes addressed in the assessment.   These discussions generally started with both men and women, and then divided into separate groups on the basis of gender.   This strategy was particularly useful, because these discussions showed that men and women perceive of poverty in somewhat different terms, and that they emphasize different elements of the survival strategies employed by their households.   Finally, researchers made direct observations of household facilities and community infrastructure.   This step provided information on access to basic services, types of building materials, presence of durable consumer goods, and agricultural production patterns.

Representativeness.   The seven communities do not suffice to achieve representativeness on the national or regional level but we examined a large percentage of households within each community.[9]   We are not able to estimate levels of statistical significance within the communities because we did not employ random selection procedures. Therefore, it can not be known whether the cases selected for interview are strictly representative of the communities or not.   But the methodology employed does provide reasonable certainty that the characteristics of the selected households reflect those at the community level. Specific households were not purposely selected according to previously established criteria, and the number of interviews conducted within each community was large enough to permit extrapolation to the community (but not regional or national) level.

Community approach.   It is important to note that the research teams obtained community support before field work commenced. Research teams spent at least the first day in each community with local leaders in order to explain the objectives and methodology of the analysis, and when appropriate, the community was offered a formal presentation of the results of the field work.

Data processing. Field information was processed in three steps. First, notes were taken during the conversations after permission was obtained. Second, hand-written summaries were prepared each day. Third, the summaries were computer-processed using a pre-defined

---

[8]   By profession, team members included anthropologists and sociologists, a nutritionist, and an agronomist.

[9]   In total, NGO staff conducted 176 interviews in the seven communities of which 92 were women and 84 men.

standard text-file shell, and were accompanied by information about each household. Summaries of group discussions were similarly entered into the data base.

The next step consisted of tabulating the answers for most individual sub-themes at the community level. This task was simplified by the relatively small range of responses to each question; in cases where the range was greater, answers were classified according to their underlying content. We applied two methods to quantify the qualitative data. First, we used person-based (instead of frequency-of-answer-based) aggregation for those cases where community members gave varying numbers of answers to a question. For these questions (i.e. what the most important obstacles to better life was for a family) we standardized the weight of each answer so that they total to one per person. Second, if the respondents supplied an explicit ranking in their answer (i.e. *"the most important obstacle is access to land; less important, is that we have only few animals"*), we took this ranking into account by giving the first option a higher weight than the second.

4. The Communities

Community Characteristics

Table 1 presents an overview of the seven communities in order to provide a backdrop for the perceptions expressed by their residents. The first panel presents data on basic characteristics (region, ethnicity, and size), access to health care (in terms of the presence or absence of a health center), and access to basic services (potable water system, electricity, and latrines). The second panel summarizes the household activities employed in the communities (agriculture, labor migration, commercial activities, and handicraft production). The third panel adds an educational profile of one community in each region.

Four general tendencies can be observed. First, regional location in this study is coterminous with ethnicity: the Sierra and Oriente communities are inhabited by indigenous households, while the residents of the coastal communities are mestizos. Second, the coastal communities are much larger than in the other two regions. While the tables do not reflect it, these communities are also much more complex in terms of economic and social infrastructure. Third, nearly all of the households secure their sustenance through agricultural production but migration (either permanent or temporary) plays an important role for income earning, too. Fourth, almost all primary school age children attend school. Their work responsibility in the household or on the field does hence not exclude school attendance. In contrast, large proportions of adults (particularly those over 60 years of age) never attended school.

The Sierra Communities

The clearest general characteristic of the four Sierra communities is that their households possess few resources. These communities are strictly indigenous in terms of the presence of shared cultural elements (e.g., use of the Quechua language), as well as organization at the intra- and inter-household levels. They are also remote and isolated; roads are treacherous and public transportation is usually available only on market days (once or twice weekly).

Except for primary schools, there are virtually no public services in these communities, and while potable water, electricity, and latrines are present in some cases, they are always rudimentary. Local, independent water systems are generally built by residents with the assistance of public or private development agencies, and consist of a catchment system, holding tank, and pipeline to each house. Typically, each residence has a single tap in the front yard. Latrines are sometimes constructed when water systems are installed. As is true for water systems, the installation of electricity is paid for by the community. The service is usually limited to no more than one or two lights in each house.

In terms of housing, most families continue to live in traditional *chozas*, which have dirt floors, adobe walls, and straw roofs. Only recently has this type of construction begun to be supplanted by cement block walls and zinc roofs.

Virtually all young children attend primary school, but secondary school attendance is extremely rare. Rates of functional adult illiteracy range from 70 percent to 78 percent, and tends to be higher for women and, in particularly, the elderly. There are no health centers in any of the communities, and health care can only be obtained (when transportation is available) in towns that may be several hours away.

Table 1 also shows that virtually all households depend primarily on agriculture. Corn, barley, and potatoes are the basic subsistence crops in the Sierra; potatoes are the most common market crop. Secondary crops include onions, beans, quinua, broad beans (*habas*), lentils, and native tubers (*ocas, mellocos, mashua*). The farming system combines the production of these crops using shifting sets of techniques, including rotation and intercultivation, with small animal husbandry (sheep, pigs, chickens, and guinea pigs). Labor responsibilities are commonly divided on the basis of age and sex, and may include exchanges within extended families and communities.

Because access to land is so limited, agricultural production alone (whether for consumption or sale) can not sustain the family, and other income must be obtained. The most frequently used mechanism is off-farm employment, and in these communities, up to 55 percent of households include temporary migration in their survival strategies. Handicraft production and commercial activities are also important mechanisms for supplementing household income.

Melan. The indigenous community of Melan is situated in the southern part of Chimborazo province at between 2,300 and 3,600 meters above sea level. The community is very remote, and is reached by traveling south from the market towns of Licto or Chambo for one and a half to two and a half hours on poor dirt roads. While 70 percent of households have access to a potable water system and to electricity, none possess latrines.

Landholdings in Melan range from only 1/4 to two hectares of steeply sloped, non-irrigated land. The best land and the largest landholdings in Melan are owned by persons from the neighboring community of Alao who married inhabitants from Melan, thus acquiring land there. One fourth of the households have purchased an average of two additional hectares of paramo (high Andean meadows), where they graze small numbers of horses and cows. Of 49 families in Mela, twelve own pasturage and keep large animals (1-2 cows, horses, burros). Typical households own on average five sheep, three pigs and 5-15 guine pigs. Subsistence production is supplemented by the sale of onions, potatoes, and the occasional small domestic animal. Given their limited access to land, members of over half of households migrate temporarily, usually to work in the informal construction sector in Quito. Consequently, women must assume much of the responsibility for household production, and even very young children must help out in the house and fields.

Table 1: Characteristics of Seven Case-Study Communities

A. General Characteristics and Access to Basic Needs

			Percent of households with:				
Community	Region	Ethnicity	Popu-lation	Health Center	Potable Water	Electri-city	Latrines
Melan	Sierra	Indigenous	255	No	70	70	0
Jatun Era	Sierra	Indigenous	259	No	95	95	95
Maca Chico	Sierra	Indigenous	557	No	87	90	100
Apunag	Sierra	Indigenous	378	No	95	0	98
Bellavista	Coast	Mestizo	1200	Yes	70	90	97
Membrillal	Coast	Mestizo	1240	Yes	0	90	83
Villano	Oriente	Indigenous	352	No	0	0	0

B. Economic Activities

	Percent households working in:		
Community	Agriculture	Migration	Commerce/handicrafts
Melan	100	55	15
Jatun Era	100	20	10
Maca Chico	90	53	20
Apunag	100	0	0
Bellavista	59	46	8
Membrillal	96	80	0
Villano	100	0	0

C. Educational profile of three communities.

Community	Percent of children[a] in school	Adult[b] educational levels (%)			
		None	Primary	High school	High school graduation
Membrillal	96.4	21.5	64.5	10.8	3.2
Melan	100.0	40.4	57.4	2.1	0.0
Villano	100.0	14.3	65.5	13.1	8.3

[a] Age 8 to 12.
[b] Age > 15.
Source: Rural Qualitative Assessment.

Apunag. Like Melan, the village of Apunag is reached by traveling along small roads south from Chimborazo's capital of Riobamba. Connection to Riobamba and the local center of Licto has recently improved with the completion of a road linking its neighboring community El Etén. Nevertheless, travel still takes several hours. Before, the entire distance was covered on foot or by mule, damaging crops in the process which resulted in lower prices for the produce of the families.

The small primary school lacks resources, and this community has the highest rate of adult illiteracy among the seven included in the RQA. While nearly all households are connected to the potable water system and have latrines, no household has electricity but installation has started.

Household parcels are small (averaging no more than two to three hectares), and they are highly eroded, because they are steeply sloped and their owners use them intensively. Agriculture is carried out primarily to satisfy subsistence needs, but small surpluses are sporadically sold. The average household has three pigs and ten sheep, rabbits and guinea pigs. Household income is supplemented by temporary migration, which provides on average the equivalent of US$50 per month during part of the year.

Jatun Era. Of the four Sierra communities, the situation of Jatun Era appears to be the most favorable. It is somewhat less remote than the others, and almost all households have access to basic services: potable water, latrines, and electricity. It has a primary school but no health care facility.[10]

In quantitative terms, access to land is adequate by Sierra standards. Most households own between five and ten hectares which is greater than in other communities because families who had worked at a nearby hacienda were able to purchase land from the hacienda. At present, households can not only provide for most of their own subsistence needs, but also produce a surplus for market.

Because landholdings can generally provide for family sustenance in Jatun Era, few heads of households migrate, and in only one fifth of households, younger males seek off-farm employment. Nevertheless, the productive quality of the land is limited by its elevation, topography and absence of irrigation water. In the future, this factor is likely to combine with impending subdivision of the holdings to constrain the relative well-being of the community.

Maca Chico. A large ravine bisects Maca Chico. It is difficult (and at times impossible) to cross this ravine, so that some school children find it easiest to attend school in a neighboring village, and undoubtedly, community integration suffers for the same reason. While most households have access to potable water and electricity, none have latrines, and, as in the other Sierra communities included in the RQA, health care must be obtained in the nearest town.

Maca Chico, which is the largest of the four Sierra communities, also has the clearest signs of stratification based on landownership. While a few households own around six hectares, and can therefore probably produce surpluses, others own around three hectares, and can therefore barely cover their subsistence requirements. Finally, a larger group has access to less than one hectare, which is not enough to produce enough for market or for subsistence. Consequently, members of more than half of households participate in temporary migration, while 20 percent obtain additional income from handicraft production or commercial activities,

---

[10]   *"Things are a little better now because ... we have land and animals, even though there are changes from year to year. Some years are better, in other years, you recuperate. Sometimes, there is extra work".* (Household interview #1, Jatun Era).

usually as tailors. For all households of Maca Chico, then, landownership is the defining characteristic of poverty.

Box 1. Family Case Study 1: Maca Chico[11]

Angel, age 31, lives with his wife Maria Angelina (29) and their four children, Blanca (9), Veronica (8), Nancy (6), and Luis (5 months) in Maca Chico, in the province of Cotopaxi. Angel and Maria are somewhat unusual in their community because they both finished primary school. They live in a small house constructed of cement block with a tile roof. Their's is newer than that of their neighbors, some of whom live in the more traditional house of adobe walls and straw roof. They have a faucet in the front yard, but no electricity or latrine. Meals are cooked in a fireplace, but when the family is in a hurry, they use the small gas stove. The only other substantial consumer goods the family possesses is a treadle sewing machine and an old bicycle.

On their small plot of steeply sloped land that was received from Angel's father, the family grows (not necessarily in the same cropping cycle) corn, potatoes, beans, chochos (a leguminous bean), lentils, quinua, barley, heat, onions, and two Andean tubers: oca and mashua. The family consumes most of what they produce, but they sometimes sell small quantities of corn, potatoes, chochos, and lentils. They also have three cows, three pigs, four rabbits and, inside the house, six guinea pigs. The animals are raised for sale.

Because the sale of crops and animals does not earn enough to cover the family's expenses, Angel works for two weeks at a time as a mason in Quito. He does not have a contract, though, and must obtain a new job each time he goes to the city. His wages are low, partly because there are so many other fellow *campesinos* also looking for work. Sometimes, Angel is not lucky, and he must return home empty-handed. If he becomes ill or is injured, he can not work, and must pay his own expenses. If he is fortunate, on the other hand, he can earn as much as $30 a week, and if he is careful, he can save half of that amount.

Maria Angelina used to work in a neighboring town taking care of a businessman's animals, but now that the family has grown and Angel goes to Quito, she is primarily responsible for taking care of the crops and animals. Blanca and Veronica both go to school, but only during the morning. Before they leave and after they get home, they take care of the animals and little Luis.

With their limited income, the family has a hard time earning enough to cover their expenses. They have attempted to reduce their expenditures on food to offset increasing prices; the only food items they buy are rice, noodles, salt, vegetable shortening, and oats; these are combined with the food crops they grow. They almost never consume meat, milk, fresh vegetables, or fruit. Everything they must buy is getting more expensive; for instance, although schooling is free, they must spend four dollars on each daughter for pencils, pens, notebooks, and the like, as well as 10 dollars for their uniforms and three dollars for shoes. Likewise, the cost of health care has gone up so much that home remedies are usually used. When there is not enough money, Angel's parents lend them 15 or 20 dollars without interest.

For Angel and Maria Angelina, poverty is a result of disorganization at the community level and at the household level, the lack of land and sufficient income. Their situation has worsened progressively since the early 1980s. For them, the only solution for poor families is temporary labor migration.

---

[11]   This case study, and the two that follow, are based on information given by specific households. They are not composites. Quotations included in the text on different topics were drawn from interviews conducted in the communities mentioned.

The Coastal Communities

Several characteristics of the two coastal communities included in the Rural Qualitative Assessment stand out in Table 1. First, it can be seen that they are both two to three times the size of the Sierra communities. Second, they are both inhabited by non-indigenous (mestizo) families. Third, while access to public services is somewhat better than in the Sierra (both communities have a health center), the proportion of families with access to potable water is not higher. On average, these households have more consumer durables than their Sierra counterparts: most have stoves and refrigerators, and many also own televisions and stereos. Fourth, many families engage in a variety of commercial activities besides their agricultural work. And many families receive remittances from family members who have moved on a more or less permanent basis to Guayaquil.

Membrillal. This mestizo community is situated in a transition zone between the dry *sabana* lowlands and the more humid Chongon-Colonche coastal range. The majority of the inhabitants belong to one of eight families, and many households are subdivided -- 63 per cent of the families have members who have moved permanently to urban centers, particularly Guayaquil. Membriallal actually consists of five populated centers; Membrillal Centro, which was selected for inclusion in the RQA, is the parroquia (parish) center. As such, it is the location of the community's church, school, civil registry, health subcenter, and community meeting hall. Traditionally, the area around Membrillal has produced coffee, but declining prices have led to the abandonment of substantial areas of land.

The community is relatively well endowed with basic infrastructure and families own some luxury goods. Most primary school children attend the public school, but a private school was initiated as a response to the poor quality of the public education; nevertheless, even its modest cost is beyond the reach of most families. There is a high school, but it has very few students, and does not cover the final two years. Most households have electricity and latrines, but the water supply comes from a series of wells, and is not potable. The health subcenter has few equipment or supplies and is attended by a rural doctor who is not available on weekends or holidays. In order to feed the doctor, a health financing committee was organized which charges 500 sucres per consultation (about US$0.25). In Membrillal, most families have radios and many have sewing machines; a minority has televisions and stereos.

Agricultural production and transfers from family members living in the cities are the most important sources of income for the families. Households with access to land at higher elevations are able to grow coffee and cacao, otherwise production includes plantina, avocado, lemons, corn, beans, and melons. Only a few single-parent households do not participate in agriculture, but virtually all farm families have additional income, which is obtained from family members (usually grown children) who have moved to Guayaquil, or temporary migration to the coffee plantations, or from a variety of commercial activities. The most common of these is the production of charcoal, which is recognized to be a short-term, non-sustainable strategy because it is based on increasing deforestation, which is likely to worsen the already poor quality of local soils. Other remunerative activities include small stores, ambulatory sales, services, and wage labor in a local small factory. Finally, the sale of small animals, chickens, and eggs is a common element of earning the household's income. In fact, virtually all of Membrillal's households combine several of the above-mentioned elements to make their ends meet.

Box 2. Family Case Study 2: Membrillal

Tomas (58) and Carmen (47) have 13 children, of whom 10, ranging in age from six to 21, still live with them. The other three have married, and one of them lives in Guayaquil. They live in a small house elevated above the ground on stilts; it has plank floors, bamboo walls, and a roof of corrugated zinc. They have a single water faucet in front of the house and they also have electricity. They are currently digging a latrine behind the house, and garbage is disposed of by throwing it in the nearby river. Tomas and Carmen both left school after the second grade, but they believe that education is important; all of the children from six to 16 are in school, while Roberto (21) and Alejandro (19), who now help with the farm work, both finished primary school.

Tomas is primarily a farmer; he owns only a hectare and a half, though, and because the land is so dry, he can grow very little. He is always in search of ways to earn additional income. His major source of income is coffee, but productivity is low, and prices have dropped consistently for the past three years. This year, he and Roberto went to the Oriente to work for a friend for six weeks. While Carmen considers herself to be a housewife, she harvests coffee in nearby plantations every June and July; this year three of her daughters accompanied her. Many of their neighbors own small businesses, especially shops, but Tomas and Carmen do not have time for that. Also, many neighbors produce charcoal for local markets, but Tomas does not have enough land to be able to cultivate the necessary trees or brush.

Besides buying nearly all of the food the family needs, Tomas and Carmen have a series of other expenses. For instance, they spent roughly US$100 to equip seven children for school. For them, poverty is a product of insufficient land and the unavailability of wage labor. One of the ways that they adjust to their situation is by consuming less food. Health care is another area of concern; if extra money is needed, the community has a fund that was by the parish priest from church offerings. Illnesses are usually treated at the public health center. However, there is a new young doctor every year, and the center has no equipment. Treatment is supposed to be free, as are the medicines, but usually, Tomas must purchase these in the local pharmacy.

Tomas belongs to a community church group, but he is not affiliated with either of the two local farmer groups. He believes that every family solves its own problems; he says that *"what is mine is mine, and what is yours is yours; people (in this community) are very stingy."* Because there are insufficient sources of employment, and since the community is so disorganized, Tomas thinks that the best way for households to deal with their poverty is by obtaining credit for raising small animals and cattle.

Daily household subsistence is largely the responsibility of women because many of the male household members migrate temporarily or permanently to the cities. Migration is due to many families not being able to earn enough income from agriculture. Landownership is limited and the land is unequally distributed, which is the product of the creation of the parroquia, the subsequent retention of communal land by the State, and its sale to a small number of wealthy individuals. Because of the high migration incidence, for extended periods of time (up to eight months annually) many families consist of women, children, and the elderly.

Bellavista. This community is located on a paved road about an hour's drive from the provincial capital of Jipijapa in the humid Portoviejo River valley. It is the least isolated of the seven communities included in the RQA, and public transportation is readily available. Subsistence and cash crops are rice, plantain, peanuts, corn and yuca. Some households with good land also plant coffee and cacao as cash crops. Most houses are typical of the Coast: elevated on stilts, bamboo walls, wooden floors, and palm or zinc roofs. Basic services in Bellavista are superior to those found in many rural communities because of the size and location of the community. Two private schools -- one of them a Cathlic school -- exist, an agricultural high school, and a workshop that teaches sewing to adult women. A health center is staffed by a rural doctor, nurse, and nurse's aide. Nearly all households have electricity, and 70 percent are connected to the town's water system (while the rest have wells).

As in the case of Membrillal, the households in Belavista can be grouped on the basis of landownership. While 10 families own an average of seven hectares, another group of 60 families owns less than one hectare each, and 30 families are landless, and are either obliged to rent land or to work as day laborers. All of these households share a common limiting factor: none have irrigation water, so that crops can only be grown during a few months in the winter. Consequently, only 59 percent of the households provide for their sustenance primarily through agriculture, while fully a third are locally employed in the public or private sector, and nearly half participate in either permanent or temporary labor migration.

Three constraints exist on subsistence and cash crop production. The first is lack of land for purchase. All land in the municipality is owned so new land becomes available only very seldom and if so at very high prices. Second, since land is not irrigated, agricultural production is limited to one crop per year, i.e. during the rainy season (January to May). The third is land titling. The titling process is expensive and without titles access to credit is difficult if not impossible. Animal-raising (cattle, chickens, pigs) is adversely affected by the lack of land for pasturage and to grow forage for use during the dry season.

The Oriente Community

Villano. This community was founded by Quechua-speaking residents of the Archidona-Tena corridor, who moved east two decades ago as part of a more general eastward migration that had its origin in increasing population density and impending landlessness. Community and extra-community organization are strong; Villano is one of several communities forming an agricultural cooperative. Age plays an important role in the organization. Access to land in Villano is typical of indigenous communities in the Oriente. Communal land is distributed to members, but distances between the community center and farmsteads are often considerable, and difficulties in transportation in the region make travel particularly problematic. Household landholdings average one-half to two hectares. Distance is actually a function of age because new generations are allocated more distant land.[12]

Villano, like virtually all indigenous communities in the region, has developed sedentary, relatively intensive market-oriented farming systems. In the tropical regions west of Villano, Quechua communities produce coffee; here in the subtropical cloud forest (600-1,600 meters above sea level), the major product is naranjilla which is also the main economic activity of the agricultural cooperative to which Villano belongs. But transport of the product to the market center is difficult.

As the community of Villano, like its neighbors, has become increasingly integrated into the market system, household organization has been transformed in several important respects. First, individual access to fixed landholdings has replaced traditional patterns of rotational land use. Second, males' traditional responsibilities for hunting and fishing have been replaced by activities related to the production of naranjilla and limited quantities of coffee, cocoa, and feed

[12] This process must necessarily reach a culmination within the next several generations; at some point, the reserve will be exhausted as all available land is assigned to individual households, and the impending problem of total landlessness will have to be confronted.

corn. This change represents, in some respects, an incursion into traditional female responsibilities for horticultural production.

Box 3. Family Case Study 3: Villano

Eduardo (30) and Alicia (29) have been married 13 years and they have five children; a sixth is due in a month. Eduardo is a high school graduate and while he is partly a farmer, he is also employed as the budget official for the local office of bilingual education. Like many of the young men in the community, he was active in community organization, and served as treasurer for the provincial indigenous organization Federacion de Organizaciones Indigenas de Napo (FOIN). The three older children, aged seven, eight, and eleven, all attend school. The family lives in a wooden house with a corrugated zinc roof, but they have neither electricity nor water. The consumer goods that they own are a gas stove, portable radio-cassette deck, two bicycles, and a small battery-powered television.

The family grows coffee, naranjilla, and cacao for the market, as well as cassava, plantains, bananas, beans, corn, and several varieties of native crops for subsistence. Eduardo and Alicia participate nearly equally in all of the agricultural tasks, and the older children also help. Nevertheless, Alicia undoubtedly does more agricultural work than her husband, because he has a full-time job. He can not hunt now because of the density of human settlement, and fishing is poor. Despite the fact that the community has no access to basic services, Alicia believes that the family is better off than most in the community, but they have suffered some setbacks; for instance, they used to own 15 head of cattle, but they all died. Nevertheless, they are better off than six years ago, because then, they were a young couple with no independent resources, and they received little help from their families.

The major expenses are food, medicine, clothing, and transportation. Carmen also believes that Eduardo spends too much on alcohol. When they do not have enough to cover their expenses, they ask for credit in the local store, or borrow money from friends or relatives. This is expected, and they lend to their relatives just as frequently. In her view, poverty is related principally to the relative isolation of the community; crop prices have risen somewhat in the recent past, but transportation costs are so high that net incomes are very low. The only viable strategy for overcoming poverty is, for her, to obtain more land and to work harder.

The residents of this community have no access to basic services of any kind. The only exception is a small, bilingual primary school. Health care can only be obtained (if transportation can be secured) hours away, and there are no public water or electricity networks.

5.   Perceptions of Poverty in Seven Case Studies

This section discusses how households in the seven communities view their living conditions. These vary between communities, regions and according to additional factors such as gender. A summary of the meanings of poverty for the respondents is presented in Table 2. In some cases, different options are listed jointly, reflecting that respondents viewed these as intertwined.

In six of the seven communities, limited access to land is viewed as the most important component of poverty, and when respondents were asked to compare their situation with that of their neighbors, and to compare their community with other communities, land was the most commonly-employed yardstick. In large part, access to land also defines the relationship of the individual and household to the community and to the larger society.

Table 2. The Meaning of Poverty

Rank	Melan	Apunag	Maca Chico	Jatun Era	Bellavista	Membrillal	Villano
1	land, animals: too little	land, animals: too little	land, animals: too little	land, animals: too little	land, animals, capital: too little	employment possibilities: lacking	Land, credit: too little or not accessible
2	elderly and widows: alone without help	elderly and widows: alone without help	income and debt:vicious circle	Local employment possibilities: lacking	Local employment and commerce possibilities: lacking	own business: not possible to open	Roads, services: bad
3	basic needs: unmet	food: too little	basic needs: unmet (housing)	basic needs: unmet (health)	crop prices: too low	Land, animals too little	plant diseases and human illness: rampant
4	---	destiny: born poor	---	---	Consumption goods: lacking; services: poor (transport)	Consumption goods: lacking; services: poor (health)	destiny: born poor

Source: Rural Qualitative Assessment.

The Sierra Communities

Land and animals: Little land and few animals are the most important indicators of living conditions for the Sierra communities.[13] In the Sierra, land has both cultural and economic significance to indigenous communities. The earth is regarded as a "supernatural symbol of procreation, fecundity, protector of the weak, the infirm and is propitiated accordingly".[14] Land provides the context within which community and family relations are expressed. In these communities, 'landless peasant' is a contradiction in terms. Economically, land is the primary source of subsistence; the precise manner in which the household obtains its sustenance depends on the size and productive quality of its holdings. When appropriate techniques are employed, and when the holding is of sufficient size and productive quality, a surplus can be sold. When it is not, as in case of most of the households in the four Sierra communities, other sources of non-agricultural income must be sought.

Access to land has a qualitative aspect; particularly in the Sierra, respondents identified poor soil, steep terrain, and erosion as serious limiting factors to production and productivity. In Jatun Era, for example, landownership is well above average; nevertheless, respondents observed that this factor was more than offset by the agroecological limitations that are present.

The majority of the households in the four communities own relatively few domestic animals, essentially because they do not have enough land to dedicate to pasture. In addition, access to paramos (high Andean meadows) is limited, because little or none was obtained through agrarian reform or purchase. Villagers said that animals are important as a saving

---

[13]   *"Poverty is because of the land; the person who doesn't have any must obligatorily leave to do day labor."* (Household interview Maca Chico, #1).
[14]   Gustavo Cáceres quoted in: 'Mujer Andina, Condiciones de Vida y Participación', Quito.

means for bad times and for meat consumption. Hence families without animals are generally regarded as poor.

Elderly and widows: The respondents in the Sierra communities were particularly sensitive to the relationship between landholding and the family cycle. In both Melan and Apunag, the perception that the elderly, widows, and other people left 'alone' are the poorest reflects the relative incapacity of this group to adequately exploit their land resources on their own. These households depend to a much greater degree than others on exchanges of labor and land. In particular, sharecropping is used to obtain a scarce resource (labor) in exchange for one (land) that for these households is plentiful.[15]

Basic Needs: Three of the four communities in the Sierra assigned needs as housing or health a high weight. Poor housing quality was of particular concern to the inhabitants of Maca Chico and poor health was a defining element of poverty conditions by the families asked in Jatun Era

Income and debt: Only the interviewed families in Maca Chico mentioned income to be a key determinant of poverty but they linked it not only to the obvious purchasing capacity of the household but also to the relationship between income and debt. As quite a few families are indebted in this community, the little current income what families possess has to finance the debt besides maintaining the family. If the families were not indebted, on the other hand, they could rather store sum of their produce and sell it at higher market prices later in the season.[16]

Destiny: The interviewed families in Apunag feel that they are destined to be poor. Besides ethnic reasons, this feeling could well also be a product of the distant and poor lands where many indigenous communities are located. For example, it is impossible to leave the village of Apunag if rains are heavy because the road connection is so scarce and fragile.

The Costa Communities

Land, animals and capital: As for the Sierra, the command over productive resources like land, animals and capital, is the clearest indication of a family's well-being for Costa inhabitants asked in the two communities. However, it should be taken into account that on the Coast, land is essentially a commodity, and landownership conveys a sense of community to a much lesser degree than in the other regions. Average landownership is greater in the Coast than in the Sierra, in part because in newer areas of settlement, colonization provided 50 hectares to each household. In older, more marginal communities, however (particularly in Manabi Province, where the two case study communities included in this report are located) landownership is nearly as limited as in the Sierra. Additional land is either unavailable or prohibitively expensive, and productivity is limited by the absence of irrigation.[17]

---

[15]   *"We 'widows' are left alone, because they (the men) leave in order to work."* (Household interview Membrillal, #1).

[16]   *"If the farmer had money, he could store (his products) until prices increased, but because of debts, he must sell (immediately)."* (Household interview Maca Chico, #2).

[17]   *"There isn't much income; there are no secure labor (opportunities), and we harvest only once a year."* (Household interview Bellavista, #1).

Employment and commerce: In the more commercially-based economy typical of the Coast, subsistence production is less central to the well-being of the household, and wage labor or small commercial activities are very important as reflected in the ranking of poverty definitions in the table. Many households provide seasonal plantation labor or try to open small commercial enterprises on the side. To a greater extent than in the Sierra, therefore, lacking local employment opportunities are perceived in Bellavista and Membrillal to be a defining characteristic of poverty. It is interesting to observe that women in Membrillal do not view the lack of employment opportunities as a cause of poverty because women on the coast generally do not work outside the home, with the exception of small animal husbandry activities.

Infrastructure: In general, households are better able to have adequate housing and to feed their families than in the Sierra, and poverty is viewed more in terms of lack of consumer items that few Sierra households possess. On the other hand, inadequate public infrastructure (e.g., roads) and services (particularly, health care in Membrillal) are associated with poverty.

The Oriente Community

Asked what constitutes 'poverty' or 'well-being', the inhabitants of Villano in the Ecuadoran Oriente see their limited command of land and credit as a first, bad roads and services as a second, plant and human health problems as a third and the indigenous people's 'destiny to be poor' as a fourth factor.[18] Limited land availability does not permit traditional forms of rotational slash-and-burn agriculture which, in addition, are located far from the village center. Alternative sources of income in or near the community are scarce.

The physical isolation of the community is keenly felt in Villano. Any trip, whether it be to the reserve (to carry out agricultural tasks) or to regional urban centers (to purchase inputs or food items or to sell their products) involves a huge (and costly) effort. The lack of public services would also be felt to be a product of the relative inaccessibility of the community

As outlined above, the community of Villano is typical of the region in that it lacks virtually all basic services. This situation is conceived of, in part, as a product of the above-mentioned isolation, due to the inadequacy of feeder roads and public transportation. For that reason, the virtual absence of basic public services (e.g., potable water, electricity, elimination of wastes) is seen to be a major component of the poverty that characterizes the community and the entire region.

For many indigenous inhabitants of Oriente communities like Villano, the situation is so bleak that poverty seems to be preordained.[19] This attitude, however, may reflect less the acceptance of fate than a recognition of the structural nature of poverty in a community separated from the rest of the country by much more than a few miles of bad road.

---

[18]   *"We have neither land nor work... Some of us have land in the reserve, but we can't transport our products from their, because it is so far. It is difficult to carry them, and since I don't have land here, and only in the reserve, I am poor. Sometimes, I don't have enough to make do."* (Household interview Villano, #1).

[19]   *"We have lived poor, and we have to live poor, like our parents and grandparents."* (Household interview Villano, #2).

Especially women mentioned that men's alcohol consumption and drinking habits are a big problems. Men are responsible for money management and they spend a sizable portion of earnings from naranjilla sales on fiestas, alcohol and consumer goods as opposed to agriculture or home improvements.

6.   Household and Community Strategies to Address Rural Poverty

This section describes three sets of mechanisms used by rural households in the seven communities to make ends meet in times of economic hardship.[20] First, households attempt to complement and diversify income. Second, they reduce expenditures which can largely only be achieved by limiting the already low levels of consumption. Third, households depend to varying degrees on intra-family and intra-community help and resource exchange. The resulting survival strategies should not be understood merely as the selection of separate items, as from a menu. Rather, the interaction among the various elements is very important, and as conditions change, the use of specific mechanisms and their relative importance may be substantially modified.

Table 3. Strategies to Complement Household Income

Rank	Melan	Apunag	Maca Chico	Jatun Era	Bellavista	Membrillal	Villano
1	Temporary migration	Female & child labor	Temporary migration	Female & child labor	Family assistance	Permanent migration	Cash crops
2	Female & child labor	Temporary migration	Domestic animals	Domestic animals	Domestic animals	Temporary migration	Subsistence production
3	Land/labor exchanges	Domestic animals	Piece work	Temporary migration	Permanent migration	Small business	Day labor, work harder
4	Weaving	Land/labor exchanges	Land/labor exchanges	---	Small business	Family subsistence	--
5	Day labor	Cash crops	---	---	---	---	--

Source: Rural Qualitative Assessment.

Strategies to Increase and Diversify Income

Sierra

The strategies to increase and diversify income are presented in Table 3 and as can be observed, respondents did not include subsistence production as a diversification strategy. Nevertheless, the most essential component of household reproduction (that is, its capacity to renew itself on a daily and generational basis) is subsistence production.

---

[20]   Interviewers gave the families a time-frame from 1988 to the present when they discussed these alternative strategies. Although reference to 1988 was easy for persons interviewed on the Coast and in the Oriente, it was not possible for persons in the Sierra because the communities studied had little connection with national life, and the individual's singular frame of reference was the life cycle (birth of a child, marriage, death of a family member).

The evolution of the independent, landowning peasant household has not altered the central role that subsistence production plays in the strategies developed in rural communities in the Sierra. Answers in Table 3 should therefore be viewed as 'additional' income sources.

Temporary migration. Given the limitations in agricultural production and limited local employment opportunities, the most common element to earn additional income is temporary migration of one or several family members. Usually, young men and male heads of households migrate on a temporary and often cyclical basis. Most frequently, labor is provided in urban centers, and less often, in agriculture. In both cases, migration takes place during lulls in the cropping cycle on the small holding.

The migration rate for household heads ranges from 55 percent in Melan to 20 percent in Jatun Era, and young men migrate in similar proportions. Men from Melan travel primarily to Quito to work in construction (i.e., part of the informal sector) and to a lesser degree, to rural areas in the provinces of Esmeraldas (on the Coast) and Napo (in the Oriente). Most men migrate for a total of two to three months at a time, but rarely at a single stretch. They return home briefly (usually during weekends or at the end of the month) to remit their savings to their families. Men migrate mostly to Quito, to the regional centers like Ambato or Latacunga, or to the rice-producing region around Quevedo, on the Coast.[21]

Female and child labor. Temporary male migration increases household labor and management responsibilities for women and children. The complementary nature of these two mechanisms is illustrated by their ranking as the top two mechanisms to supplement incomes in three of the four Sierra communities surveyed. Women have always played a central role in agricultural production in indigenous communities in the Sierra, and children assume increasing responsibilities as they become older. In addition, women and children are responsible for household reproduction (cooking, cleaning, fetching water and firewood, health care, and other tasks). Studies indicate that women in communities like those studied have a work day of 15 to 18 hours; culturally, leisure is considered unacceptable for women, and they may work at spinning wool even as they walk and talk.

In addition to household labor, communal labor obligations that formerly were the responsibility of men have shifted to women. In communities like Melan, women have largely replaced men in *mingas* (communal labor parties), and labor exchanges within the extended family. It is not surprising that more women than men report this component as an important part of household survival.

As already mentioned above, while parents do integrate children more in the household work, they nevertheless do not take them out of school.

Small animal husbandry. In times of hardship families rely on the functions small animal husbandry has in an integrated farming system. Animals consume crop byproducts (e.g., corn stalks), and complement crop production (e.g., by providing manure). Small

---

[21]   For some, migration begins at a very early age. *"Since I was very young, I've migrated -- beginning at age seven -- and I've started migrating again because I can't support my family staying here."* (Household #2, Melan).

animal (sheep, pigs, chickens, guinea pigs, and rabbits) husbandry is carried out in the four communities as a means of saving for emergencies (especially illness or crop loss), or for regular purchases (particularly costs related to attending school: clothing, books, and supplies). This element of the farming system nearly always falls within the province of women and, in fact, small animal raising is one of the few women's activities which does not require consultation with one's spouse, e.g. women can sell animals without their husbands' permission. It is particularly important for the four communities because they lack access to pasture land and therefore, have a very limited opportunity to raise cattle.

Day labor and land/labor exchanges. Marginal Sierra families in three of the four communities exchange land and labor more intensively in times of hardship and this can again be viewed as complementary to temporary migration. In addition to regular exchanges of land and labor between households which do not have labor (elderly, widows) or land (the very poor), increased exchange of labor and land occurs if male family members migrate temporarily to the cities. Not every family need to send one or more family members to the cities since the tasks of those who leave on the land have to be assumed by the rest of the family or -- if this does not suffice -- by other members of the community. Land and labor exchanges are now very common in these communities. In Melan, for example, 35 of 49 households engage in land or labor exchanges.

Additionally, members of the poorest households may engage in day labor on a sporadic basis in their own or in neighboring communities, and are hired by slightly more affluent peasant households. To some degree, community members are hired as a form of community assistance in very bad times.[22]

Handicrafts. In both Melan and Maca Chico families have started to weave and produce piecework for the local market which earns additional income. Several men in Melan weave ponchos, shawls, and skirts on hand looms, using wool that is spun by women. Earnings are meager, however, because the weavers do not know how to dye their cloth. For that reason, weaving is a part-time job. In Maca Chico, young men have started to sew trousers on a piecework basis, using machines purchased on credit in the provincial capital.

The Costa Communities

Permanent and temporary migration. Permanent and temporary migration is a very important additional income source for the Costa communities. It is common to encounter households with members who have permanently moved to urban centers-- usually Manta or Guayaquil--in order to obtain secondary school education or employment. For the household, their remittances are an important source of income, and are used to cover food, education, and health care expenses. An estimated 90 per cent of households in Bellavista receive such remittances.

While this form of migration involves full-time urban residence, it rarely represents a total separation from the countryside. At the national level, the rate of urban-rural

---

[22]   Labor is also provided by a limited number of rural residents on neighboring haciendas. Because of mechanization, however, there is little demand for a permanent labor force, and work may only be available for labor-intensive activities, such as sowing and harvesting, that take place at the same time as in the peasant community.

migration is fully one-half of rural-urban migration, and usually takes place when land becomes available to landless rural-urban migrants, or in cases of urban unemployment. Additionally, it is frequently the case that only part of a household moves to the city; for instance, young children may be left with grandparents or other relatives and remittances cover their expenses. In addition, when parents in the community of origin become ill, they may travel to their children's urban residence to obtain health care. In this sense, permanent migrants maintain a presence in their rural places of origin.

While less prominent, rural inhabitants of coastal communities also migrate on a temporary and usually cyclical basis. In Bellavista, men work as laborers on medium- and large-scale coffee and banana plantations during the harvest (June-July). In Membrillal, men work on neighboring large farms and ranches. These constitute an essential component of total household income.

Family assistance. Family assistance comprising work of women and children but also help from relatives in the from of work or credit constitute an important additional income source for the Costa communities as well. As in the Sierra, children constitute an important element of the household labor force, although they tend to start working at a somewhat later age. Traditionally, rural women in the Coast have not worked in the wage labor force. In the past five years, however, their participation in non-traditional crop plantations and processing plants has increased in many rural communities of the Costa but this process has not yet started in the two communities under study.

Labor exchanges within and among households are uncommon in these mestizo communities, and communal labor is a relatively rare phenomenon. Members of the nuclear and extended family assist relatives with small loans for which there is no fixed repayment period. This component illustrates that household economies are more monetarized on the Coast than in the Sierra.

Small businesses. Microenterprises are more commonly encountered in communities like Bellavista and Membrillal than in the Sierra and have become an important income source. They may include home-based garment production, shop-keeping, laundry services, small appliance repair, charcoal production, preparation of coffee sacks, and the like. Many development projects are based on local capacity to initiate and sustain this type of activity, and households that have small businesses are perceived to be better off than those that do not.

Small animal husbandry. Women in the coastal communities are primarily responsible for raising chickens and pigs as a source of savings and occasional special need.

The Oriente Community

Residents of the community of Villano report that strategies to increase income are based on three principle elements. First, and as discussed earlier, agricultural production has become more market-oriented. In the area around Villano, naranjilla production for the national market is a major income source. Smaller amounts of coffee, cacao, and hard (feed) corn are also produced and sold.

Second, families in Villano attempt to increase subsistence production of agricultural produce which traditionally has been the responsibility of women, and from hunting and fishing, which was considered to be men's work. The latter is increasingly less important, however, as environmental degradation and demographic pressures limit the availability of wild animals and fish. Consequently, tasks related to the production of corn, cassava, bananas, peanuts, and other subsistence crops is currently shared with men.

Third, the kind of temporary, cyclical migration undertaken in the Sierra and Coast is not found in the Oriente, but day labor is another way in which essential cash income can be obtained. For the most part, labor is provided in the production and packaging of naranjilla in nearby cooperative subcenters.

Strategies to Reduce Household Expenditures

It can be seen in Table 4 that households in the seven communities combine any of eight mechanisms to reduce expenditures as a response to poverty. As in the case of the root causes of poverty, some responses are multiple, because strategies to reduce spending are interlinked.

Table 4. Items for which Household Expenditures are Reduced

Rank	Melan	Apunag	Maca Chico	Jatun Era	Bellavista	Membrillal	Villano
1	Food	Clothing	Food	Clothing	Clothing	Food	Food, clothing, medicine
2	Clothing	Medicine	Clothing	Food	Food	Medicine	Alcohol, fiestas
3	Fiestas	Food	Fiestas	Number of children	Medicine	Clothing	Public transport
4	Food sharing	Fiestas	Public transport	---	Secondary school	---	-- -

Source: Rural Qualitative Assessment.

Sierra

In the Sierra, household expenditures are reduced primarily by purchasing fewer and cheaper foodstuffs and clothing. Other components of the strategy include the use of traditional medicine, limiting ritual expenses (fiestas), walking instead of using public transportation, and, in Jatun Era, planning on fewer children.

Food. Households in all four Sierra communities report that they are purchasing less food and are utilizing the most inexpensive items available. In particular, women reported this mechanism. Processed foodstuffs such as starches (especially pasta and rice), salt, sugar, and vegetable shortening are used in very small quantities to complement diets based largely on potatoes, corn, and barley. The consumption of more nutritious, but more expensive items, such as meat and milk is rare.[23]

---

[23]   This element of household survival is particularly significant given the fact that the rates of infant and child malnutrition are highest in rural communities in the Sierra. In 1990, chronic

Clothing. Households report that they purchase clothing less frequently than before and used clothing is often sought out. Women and children wear clothes for longer periods of time; children's clothing is passed down to younger siblings. In indigenous communities, women tend to wear traditional clothing more than men, but this custom still requires the purchase of manufactured items. While in communities like Melan, women sew clothing from cloth purchased in local markets, the self-production of cloth is essentially a lost art.

Community ritual. Community celebrations (fiestas) are less common and less expensive. In Apunag, some households report that they do not participate in celebrations at all, in order to dedicate scarce resources to food consumption. In Maca Chico, community ritual celebrations have been shortened considerably, while in Melan, fiesta expenditures have been converted from a community responsibility to an individual household option. While this change may be viewed in a positive light, one negative impact is that it tends to reduce community solidarity.

Medicine. Households have also reduced their expenditures for medicine. In the Sierra, they had traditionally relied upon locally-available herbs and other remedies and only seldom used government provided services. Nevertheless, these few visits to clinics and hospitals have been reduced and are now reserved only for the gravest cases.

Transportation. Another way to reduce expenditures, which was reported in Maca Chico and Apunag, is to walk rather than pay for public transportation. Maca Chico is somewhat less isolated than the other three communities, however; this mechanism is not practical for traveling to and from more isolated communities on a regular basis. In Apunag, individuals walk up to four hours to reach a neighboring community to save the transport cost of 2000 sucres (about US$1).

Family planning. A long-range mechanism mentioned by several women in Jatun Era is to limit the size of the family. This element would be related to the capacity of the family to redistribute labor responsibilities and to ensure the future care of the parents. Data aggregated at the national level indicate that fertility has decreased consistently since the 1960s, and while rural families are still larger, on average, than their urban counterparts, the demographic transition has clearly arrived in rural Ecuador.

The Coast

Food. In Membrillal, reduction in food consumption was the most important means of reducing expenditures. The standard diet is typical of the rural poor on the Coast; it consists of rice, plantain, and peanut sauce. Fish may be eaten in small quantities twice a week, while meat is rarely or never consumed. In Bellavista, the reduction of food consumption was the second most important factor mentioned. Nevertheless, the changes that have been put into effect are significant. Households report that they now eat only twice a day, and consumption has been decreased. As in the Sierra, meat consumption is relatively infrequent. Children no longer drink milk, and the consumption of fruit juices has been cut in half.

---

malnutrition of children below the age of five reached 67 per cent in the rural Sierra. This compares very high to a national average of 45 per cent. See Working Paper 1.

Clothing. Coastal households have reduced clothing expenditures by purchase ready-made items rather than those sewed by tailors and by using clothing for as long as possible. In contrast to the Sierra, women are more preoccupied with clothing purchases than men.

Medicine. As in the Sierra, many households have opted to limit visits to clinics and hospitals to the strictly necessary, and visit traditional curers and midwives. Similarly, locally-available herbs and other remedies are used instead of purchasing medicine.

Education. Most households believe that the education of their children is of utmost importance, and have tended to keep them in school longer than in the past. In addition, the traditional breach in years of school attendance between boys and girls has tended to close. Nevertheless, while school attendance is both free and obligatory, the related costs can be considerable. In times of scarce household income, when child labor is particularly important, the tendency to withdraw children from school (and/or high rates of absenteeism) can be expected. This tendency is observed, for example, in the case of Bellavista, where children are normally not sent to secondary school.

Oriente

The finding that half of respondents in Villano could not identify any particular mechanism for reducing expenses reflects less the absence of a strategy than the fact that the elements of minimizing expenditures are so common and so long-standing (i.e., not a 'new' strategy). That is, the purchase of food items, agricultural inputs and medicine has never been an important part of the household economy and can therefore not be readily reduced. Nevertheless, other respondents reported that they have, in fact, reduced the purchase of food, clothing, and medicine, that they have reduced the consumption of alcohol related to ritual activities, and travel more than before by foot.

Mutual Assistance Through the Exchange of Resources

In all three regions, households and communities have developed mechanisms by which neighbors and family members assist each other. These mechanisms do not constitute a safety net, per se, because they are not designed simply to care for those who can not care for themselves. Rather, in the traditional setting, they are an integral part of community and household membership and provide not only for the exchange of resources (e.g., land for labor), but allow for the expression and extension of community solidarity and cohesion, as well. As such, they are particularly important in indigenous communities, whose very existence is based on blood and ritual family bonds.

In the Sierra, resources are exchanged in times of family crisis, such as illness, death, or crop loss. Neighbors and, in particular, family members, can be counted on to provide food, labor, or money in such moments. This practice is simply the extension of a more general principle of exchange which, as discussed earlier, provides for different forms of sharecropping, labor exchanges, or sporadic wage labor. But the community at large also provides a form of safety net in many cases. For example, the community of Melan does not have a cemetery and when somebody dies, special transport must be hired to take the deceased and his or her relatives to the next cemetery at a cost of 100,000 sucres (US$50). The community pays one-half of this cost.

In addition, indigenous communities have a long history of communal labor, which is normally provided on a monthly basis for regular maintenance of community infrastructure, such as roads. In addition, special labor obligations may be provided if, for instance, the community votes to participate in a particular project (e.g., construction of a water system or a community meeting hall). Communal crop production is relatively rare, but communal ownership of pasture land is less so (even though this factor is limited in the four communities under discussion).

Similarly, in indigenous communities in the Oriente such as Villano, most households are bonded by family ties. Consequently, there is no clear distinction between family and community assistance. As in the Sierra, members of extended families frequently exchange labor services, and loans may be provided on an informal basis. Similarly, communal *minga* labor is convened for the maintenance or improvement of community infrastructure.

In contrast, in coastal communities like Bellavista and Membrillal, blood and ritual ties among households are weaker. Consequently, assistance is rarely afforded within the community. For example, 10 of Bellavista's 26 respondents reported that no mutual aid links community members. It is much more common to contract day labor for community works, as household members are more fully integrated into regional cash economies than in the Sierra or Oriente.

7.   Recommendations for Poverty Reduction

Residents of the seven communities were asked to recommend a response to their poverty. Several interesting lessons can be drawn from the responses summarized in Table 5. First, respondents believe that solutions are at hand, and that certain elements related to poverty can be addressed. This finding contradicts the old 'culture of poverty' theory and which argues that the poor accept their situation and transmit norms and values related to living in poverty from generation to generation.

Second, the expressed solutions are quite practical. Responses do not call for major land reforms or simply income transfers. Families do not ask for 'more land and animals' as one might have expected after their own poverty definitions showed above. Rather, families overwhelmingly suggest measures which will increase the productivity of available land and human resources. Infrastructure (48 percent) and training emerge as very important suggested solutions.

Third, the families distinguish between exogenous and endogenous factors they view as important to better living conditions and do not only expect 'help' to come from the outside. Three of the seven communities give organization of the community itself a high importance in overcoming poverty.

Sierra

The first recommendation from the four Sierra communities is related to enhancing the use of -- rather than the access to -- land. This recommendation has two interrelated parts. First, since local resources alone are insufficient, rural families ask for credit to purchase agricultural inputs and animals. Second, training is necessary for maximizing the utility of these resources. In particular, most of these households have never participated in development projects, and respondents perceive the need for extension programs that include components in crop, domestic animal, and forest management.

Table 8. Recommendations for Responding to Poverty

Rank	Melan	Apunag	Maca Chico	Jatun Era	Bellavista	Membrillal	Villano
1	Credit for land, animals, and inputs	Credit for land and animals; roads	Training	Credit and training	Employm. generation	Services (water, latrines)	Roads
2	Services (latrines, electricity, water)	Community organization	Roads, bridge, irrigation	Organiz.	Credit for land, animals, and inputs	Employm. generation	Services (water, health)
3	Communal meeting hall	More work	Services (water, latrines)	Roads, communal meeting hall, telephones	Community organization	Roads	Communal meeting hall
4	Communal store	---	Church, clinic, school	---	Improved economic conditions	Schools	Credit
5	Training	---	---	---	---	--	--

Source: Rural Qualitative Assessment.

Training is sought for both agricultural and other actives. Small farmers want to know how to recover the productive capacity of the soil, prevent soil erosion, produce and use organic fertilizers and have access to improved seeds to combat plant disease and increase yields. They also want to be trained in large and small animal health and management, e.g., parasite treatment. Inhabitants of Jatun Era recommend the establishment of an artisan workshop.

A second thread that runs through the recommendations offered in the Sierra relates to the development of infrastructure, both productive (particularly roads, bridges, and irrigation systems) and social (e.g., community meeting centers, community stores, and churches). Closely linked to training actives, residents of Melan seek the creation of a community weaving center which would provide youth with local employment so that they would not have to migrate and allow savings on clothing purchases. A third area of concern is basic services; water, electricity, latrines, telephone systems, health centers, and schools. Finally, it is felt in several communities that local organizational capacity is inadequate and that the community itself has to improve its own support system of members.

The Coast

For rural inhabitants of the Coast, employment is more of a central concern to household sustenance than in the Sierra because agriculture, which provides the main source of household income, is not a year-round occupation. Employment opportunities refer to both within the community as well as in urban centers. In Bellavista, the permanent unemployment rate among the economically active population is about 30 to 40 per cent.

In Membrillal, other concerns relate to infrastructure and services. In Membrillal, water, which is only available from wells, is of highest concern and families desire a pump and make the existing water system operationable. Latrine upgrading for the 30 percent of household which do not have this service is similarly sought. Community members also seek road upgrading to facilitate market access year-round because the 12 km dirt road which links Membrillal and Manta is impassable during the rainy season. The residents of Bellavista, like Sierra communities, find that credit for the purchase of land, domestic animals, and agricultural inputs is necessary. Finally, parents in Membrillal recommend that the Ministry of Education improve the quality of education in the primary school which has 250 students but only four professors. In addition to the high student-teacher ratio, the parents' chief complaint is teacher absenteeism to which the ministry has not responded to date.

In contrast to Membrillal, Bellavista residents do not recommend infrastructure and services but rather credit and improved community organization. Credit is needed for land and animal acquisition, agricultural inputs and storage facilities. Credit would help families to store their products and wait for better prices before selling them in the market. For example, the price of corn at harvest is 6000 sucres per 100 pounds but the price rises to 22000 sucres thereafter. Community members also feel that communal organization has seriously slipped recently, partly reflecting that many male members have migrated to the urban centers in the Coast.

Oriente

Infrastructure and basic services projects are dominant in the answers of the inhabitants of Villano. They clearly prioritize the completion of the road connecting the village to Archidona of which 1.5 km is missing. This will improve market access considerably. Services like water and health rank second -- the community is seeking assistance in the construction of a water system from the Municipal Council of Archidona and Integrated Health Program of the agricultural cooperative of which it is a member. A community center, under construction by the Federation of Indigenous Organizations of Napo, is viewed as a symbol of well-being in the community and families anxiously await its completion. Finally, credit is viewed as a fourth important item to overcome poverty.

8.   Final Comments

Our aim with this qualitative assessment was to learn about the views of poor rural households on their living conditions, strategies in times of change and recommendations for anti-poverty programs. Although the scope of this assessment was not even close to a 'representative survey', we have nevertheless obtained several very interesting insights into the rural life of seven communities which could well be indicative of the rural areas in general. Further, while the presented qualitative analysis cannot substitute for more quantitative studies using a representative survey like the LSMS, the presented results can be viewed as complementary: they can help researchers formulate questions and research subjects which can then be applied in quantitative analyses.

We found that rural life is everything but static. Almost none of the rural households in the seven very different communities survive on subsistence agriculture alone. New income opportunities are sought, ranging from traditional animal husbandry to piecework, specialization in cash crops to migration and from weaving to the start of small businesses. The choice of this array of income sources depends primarily on the family composition but also community support and mutual assistance between families.

Of most importance is that the rural poor believe that practical solutions to overcome their poverty are at hand. Families distinguish very clearly between factors they have to improve within their community from those where outside help is needed; infrastructure and training are the main categories suggested for outside assistance.

References

CEPAR (1993), Perfil Socio-Demografico del Ecuador. Quito: CEPAR.

CONADE (1993), Mapa de la Pobreza Consolidado, Quito.

Freire, W.B., H. Dirren, J.O. Mora, P. Arenales, E. Granda, J. Breilh, A. Campana, R. Paez, L. Darquea, and E. Molina (1988), Diagnostico de la situacion alimentaria, Nutricional y de Salud de la Poblacion Ecuatoriana Menor de Cinco Anos-DANS. Quito: Consejo Nacional de Desarrollo/Ministerio de Salud Publica.

ILDIS (1993), Informe Ecuador No. 1. Ajuste y Situacion Social. Quito: ILDIS.

MAG (1985), 1970- Estimacion de la Superficie Cosechada y de la Produccion, Agricola del Ecuador. Rusumen. Direccion Sectorial de Planificacion, Division de Informatica y Estadistica. Quito: MAG.

World Bank (1993), Agricultural Sector Review, Report No. 11398-EC, Washington D.C.

Annex 1: Local Organization

Rural people in Ecuador are organized at several levels. While organizational capacity varies by region and social group, the institutions mentioned here can be found throughout the country. First, the *comuna* is the legal expression of most rural communities; alternatively, they may be instituted as cooperatives. Neither alternative necessarily implies a specific form of marshalling community resources and in practical terms, there is usually no significant difference between the two.

In the Sierra, community organization is particularly strong because most members are related by blood or ritual kinship ties, which permit households to enter into different land/labor arrangements, including sharecropping (partidario) and labor exchanges (prestamanos). In addition, communal labor (minga) continues to be a standard element of community organization centuries after its introduction by the Incas. Indigenous communities in the Oriente are similarly based on kinship relations. In contrast, mestizo communities in the Oriente and in the Coast usually have weaker kinship ties and are usually poorly organized at the local level.

Additionally, communities may be linked on a regional and national basis. Their relationship to 'higher' levels, is not based on formal membership or strict lines of authority, but on representation and common interests. Thus, at the lowest level, the organizaciones *de segundo grado* (frequently called *uniones*) link as many as 20 communities in a limited area (often a single parroquia or canton). An example is UPOCAM (Union de Organizaciones Populares y Campesinas de Manabi) to which the case study community of Membrillal belongs. These organizations (as well as the individual communities) may, in turn, belong to federations that operate on a provincial basis. Examples include FICI (Federacion Indigena y Campesina de Imbabura) in the Sierra and FOIN (Federacion de Organizaciones Indigenas de Napo) in the Oriente, to which the case study community of Villano belongs.

The next level links organizations in each of Ecuador's three principle regions. For example, CONFENIAE (Confederacion de Nacionalidades Indigenas de la Amazonia Ecuatoriana) represents indigenous organizations, such as FOIN, throughout the Oriente. Finally, CONAIE (Confederacion de Nacionalidades Indigenas Ecuatorianas) represents indigenous interests at the national level. A theoretical organizational chart is complicated, first, by the fact that all levels can intersect at any point. For instance, an individual community can deal directly with CONAIE. Second, not all indigenous communities participate in this system. Most notably, those that have converted to evangelical Protestantism have developed a parallel chain of organization.

In the past decade, different levels of community organization have been strengthened, particularly within the indigenous population. In particular, as they have become more experienced in interacting with governmental and non-governmental agencies, communities have become increasingly capable of identifying specific problems, and of searching for solutions. A series of recent events have enhanced this effect. The 1987 earthquake obliged community organizations in the Sierra and Oriente to seek outside assistance and, in the process, to learn to propose and manage specific projects and programs. The 1990 'uprising' and the 1993 'march to Quito' further consolidated indigenous organizational capacity and redefined the relationship between the indigenous population and non-indigenous power blocs. The debate over the new Agrarian Law has continued that process; in this case, the participation of various indigenous groups has been decisive in the form that the law will take in its final form.

ADDENDUM

After the fieldwork for the Rural Qualitative Assessment had been undertaken, UNICEF Ecuador commissioned a second round of qualitative surveys in six Sierra communities to complement the analysis and examine whether the findings of the initial community studies were confirmed. In this addendum, we briefly compare the findings of the UNICEF field research to the results of the RQA. In general, the major conclusions of the RQA pertaining to the Sierra communities are confirmed.

Community Characteristics: The six communities analyzed in this addendum are very similar to the four studied in the RQA with respect to their command of productive resources, their heterogeneity, and their access to basic services. They are all located in Ecuador's highland or *Sierra* region. Three (Molobog, Galgualán, and Guanlur) are in the Licto region of southern Chimborazo province, not far from the communities of Melán and Apunag, which were included in the RQA. A fourth community (Chilsulchi Grande) is located in Cotopaxi province, between the capital of Latacunga and the town of Sigchos. The final two communities are somewhat different than the others because they are located in the southern highland province of Cañar, which was not covered in the first phase.

Table A1. General Community Characteristics

Community	Province	Ethnicity	Population
Molobog	Chimborazo	Indigenous	700
Galgualán	Chimborazo	Indigenous	190
Guanlur	Chimborazo	Indigenous	198
Chilsulchi Grande	Cotopaxi	Indigenous	182
Achupillas	Cañar	Indigenous	192
Palmas Pamba	Cañar	Indigenous	170 (approx.)

Source: UNICEF Qualitative Assessment.

Like the four communities included in the first phase, these six are indigenous according to nearly any definition. For instance, the Quechua language is spoken exclusively or partially by all or nearly all residents. In addition, the study reveals the presence of other sociocultural characteristics that reflect indigenous identity, including community organization and household and community labor exchanges.

The economy and social structure of all six communities, like the original four, are based on small-scale agricultural production that is oriented toward subsistence production and sporadic marketing of small surpluses. Additionally, day labor in off-farm activities is another income source. In each of the six, access to land is extremely limited, most holdings ranging in size from less to two hectares to no more than five hectares.

Access to basic services is scarce. Only in Achupillas have some households obtained potable water; all households in all communities lack sewage. Electricity is available to between 40 and 80 per cent of households in Molobog, Gulgualán, and Chisulchi Grande, but none in Palmas Pamba. While an electric system has been installed in Achupillas, it is not connected to individual homes because many families can not afford an installation fee amounting to nearly US$100.

Perceptions of Poverty: Like in the RQA, land was also of greatest concern in these six *Sierra* communities. This underscores the nature of rural poverty in Ecuador as it is experienced and perceived by indigenous peasant farmers. In particular, respondents to the survey felt that their poverty was principally due to (a) the limited access to land; (b) the poor productive quality of the land as in all communities the land is steeply sloped and highly eroded; (c) the lack of access to irrigation facilities; and (d) the limited capacity to maintain and sell large domestic animals (see Table A2).

Table A2. Definition of Poverty

Rank	Molobog	Galgualán	Guanlur	Chisulchi	Achupillas	Palmas Grande
1	Little land, irrigation	Land, inheritance	Irrigation	Poor soil	Little land, poor land	No land
2	Erosion poor land	Erosion	Little land	Poor climate	Low productivity	No animals
3	Elderly and widows; no help	--	Poor land	Low income	Poor climate	Low productivity
4	Bad organi-zation	--	Elderly and widows	Little land; few animals	--	--
5	--	--	Fate	Elderly and widows	--	--

Source: UNICEF Qualitative Assessment.

Strategies to increase and diversity income. As in the Sierra communities included in the RQA, the three most commonly mentioned possibilities to increase household income in the UNICEF study were migration, women and child labor and animal husbandry/crop diversification. Temporary male migration rates vary between 30 percent (Molobog), 70 percent (Guanlur) to 100 percent (Galgualán). This finding is consistent with the RQA and with many studies conducted in Ecuador's highland rural communities. Relating to women and child labor, the RQA and the research in the additional six communities reveal that many rural women work for wages on a sporadic basis, either within the community (e.g., assisting in agricultural tasks on larger holdings) or in nearby haciendas. Table A.3 summarizes the results.

Table A3. Strategies to Complement Household Income

Rank	Molobog	Galgualán	Guanlur	Chisulchi	Achupillas	Palmas Grande
1	Temporary migration, day labor	Temporary migration	Female & child labor	Market prod., production	Temporary migration	Animal husbandry
2	Female & child labor	Female & child labor	Animal husbandry	Animal husbandry	Female & child labor	Temporary migration
3	Animal husbandry	Day labor migration	Temporary migration	Temporary husbandry	Animal	Work in hacienda
4	Crop diversification	--	Help from children	Other	Other	Female & child labor
5	Help from family	--	Female migration	--	--	--

Source: UNICEF Qualitative Assessment.

Strategies to reduce expenditures. Respondents -- particularly women -- identified ways in which they reduce expenditures in times of economic hardship. As in the four communities studied in the RQA, households in the six communities under consideration report that in particular, they have limited consumption of food, clothing, and medicine by purchasing in lesser quantity and poorer quality.

An interesting difference with respect to the RQA is that in three of the original four communities, the reduction of expenditures on community celebrations (*fiestas*) was mentioned, but only as the third or fourth most important option. In contrast, *fiestas* were mentioned in four of the six communities under consideration here as the first option for reducing expenditures. In many Sierra communities, *fiestas* serve a series of important functions related to maintaining community cohesion and solidarity. Therefore, the decline or disappearance of these events has the potential to weaken the capacity of communities to work together to confront times of economic crisis.

Table A4. Items for which Household Expenditures are Reduced

Rank	Molobog	Galgualán	Guanlur	Chisulchi	Achupillas	Palmas Grande
1	Fiestas	Medicine	Fiestas	Fiestas	Food, clothing	Fiestas
2	Food Medicine	Food	Food	Medicine	Medicine	
3	Fewer children	Fiestas	None	Clothing	Fiestas	Clothing
4	Medicine	--	Medicine	Food	--	Food
5	Clothing	--	Clothing	Transportation	--	--

Source: UNICEF Qualitative Assessment.

Mutual assistance through the exchange of resources. The RQA demonstrates that one of the defining characteristics of highland indigenous communities and families has long been the implementation of different forms mutual assistance, which consists of two different sets of practices. First, extended families and neighbors exchange labor both on a regular basis and in times of special need. Second, in moments of extreme crisis, people may obtain loans or gifts of money or goods.

Findings form the six communities under study here underscore an important dimension of this feature of collective action. In four of the six, most respondents indicated that they rely principally on family, friends, and neighbors, while only two (Achupillas and Palmas Pamba) identified the community itself as the primary source of assistance. Many respondents felt that community solidarity is declining because they are poorly organized and because individual households are obliged to ensure their own survival, often through the frequent absence of household heads and others. In these circumstances, family members and neighbors find it hard to honor labor exchange commitments.

Table A5. Sources of Mutual Assistance through the Exchange of Resources

Rank	Molobog	Galgualán	Guanlur	Chisulchi	Achupillas	Palmas Grande
1	Family	Family	Friends, neighbors	Family	Community	Community
2	Institutions	Friends, neighbors, community	Family	Institutions, community	Family	Family, neighbors
3	Friends, neighbors	--	Community	Neighbors	Neighbors	Hacienda, institutions
4	Community	--	Institutions	Other communities	Institutions	--

Source: UNICEF Qualitative Assessment.

Recommendations for Poverty Reduction. Responses from the six communities under study display substantial agreement with the four highland communities analyzed in the RQA with respect to the concrete nature of recommendations for addressing poverty. As in the RQA, these communities do not consider structural measures such as redistribution of land or income as realistic options. Clearly, since these communities have been essentially defined by poverty for generations, it is impossible for them to visualize the possibility for broad, sweeping change. Nevertheless, as in the communities covered in the RQA, they readily identify specific actions that can be taken to improve conditions in their communities. The recommendations shown in Table A6 confirm the emphasis on infrastructural investment (especially in irrigation, potable water) and agricultural extension/training to raise the productivity of land. Credit is also given a prominent role by the respondents, although to a somewhat lesser extent than in the RQA communities.

Conclusions. The study of the six highland indigenous communities of Molobog, Galgualán, Guanlur, Chisulchi Grande, Achupillas, and Palmas Pamba further illustrate perceptions of rural poverty, the means by which it is addressed on a daily basis, and the actions that the poor believe can and should be taken. These six additional case studies confirm to a large degree the findings portrayed in the RQA relating to the Sierra communities.

Table A6. Recommendations for Responding to Poverty

Rank	Molobog	Galgualán	Guanlur	Chisulchi	Achupillas	Palmas Grande
1	Credit	None	Irrigation	Community organization	Irrigation & pot. water	Irrigation & pot. water
2	Irrigation	Irrigation	Training	Improve crop productivity	Training	Community organization
3	Community organization	Improve soil	Improve crop diversity	Reforestation	Community infrastructure	Credit
4	Improve agroecology	Others	Potable water	Animal husb.	Latrines	Latrines

Source: UNICEF Qualitative Assessment.

Working Paper 6: Subsidies, Social Expenditures, and the Poor
Haeduck Lee, Jesko Hentschel and Norman Hicks

1.   Introduction

The public sector can have a major impact on the level of poverty and social welfare in a country. The power to tax and spend resources carries with it the power to redistribute income, improve social welfare, and provide basic public services to those who would otherwise do without. The objective of this chapter is to examine the impacts of certain public sector activities on the welfare of the population. We will focus our attention on two major activities which are most likely to have important redistributive impacts in the Ecuadoran society, which are subsidies and social sector expenditures.

We examine the incidence of subsidies and social expenditures by expenditure quintiles. We calculate the distribution of subsidies for water, electricity, cooking gas and urban transport in proportion to the quantities consumed of these commodities or services. In contrast, we allocate the benefits of public expenditures according to the access (and not actual consumption) to public services as we do not have information on the quality of these services.[1] As a reference for the reader, Table 1 contains some consumption characteristics of the Ecuadoran population important for the incidence analysis. Poorer households tend to have a larger family and the distribution of consumption is highly skewed as the population in the highest quintile consumes about 10 times more than the population in the lowest expenditure quintile.

Table 1. Distribution and Characteristics of Households by Expenditure Quintile, 1994

	Consumption Expenditure Quintile					
	1st	2nd	3rd	4th	5th	Overall
% Individuals	20.0	20.0	20.0	20.0	20.0	100.0
Household size	6.1	5.5	5.1	4.6	3.5	4.8
% Households	15.6	17.6	18.7	20.7	27.4	100.0
% Consumption Exp.	5.5	9.5	13.3	19.5	52.3	100.0

Source: LSMS (1994).

Overall, the non-poor in Ecuador are the major beneficiaries from subsidies and public social expenditures. Contrary to popular belief, the poor benefit little from subsidies, especially not from the ones for electricity and gas. Public expenditures in the social sectors are also tilted towards the more fortunate in society, largely owing to a striking maldistribution of secondary and higher education expenditures.

Before turning to the subsidy distribution, one short remark about 'progessivity' and 'regressivity' is important. We will avoid these terms in the discussion of subsidies and expenditures as they can be misleading. For example, a subsidy can be theoretically

---

[1]   We base all calculations on the 1994 Living Standard Measurement Survey (LSMS), which was conducted by the Servicio Ecuatoriano de Capacitacion Profesional (SECAP).

termed 'progressive' if its distribution is better than the income (or expenditure) distribution in society -- or in other words if the removal of the subsidy would worsen the overall income distribution in society. But should this be the benchmark against which we measure the effectiveness of subsidies and expenditures? As observed in Working Paper 1, Ecuador has a very unequal distribution of income so that it is actually not difficult for a subsidy to be 'progressive'. Rather, we will look at which part of society obtains the largest share of the subsidy as our benchmark is that the poor should be the major beneficiaries of the subsidies and expenditures.

2.   Subsidies

From an efficiency and equity perspective, subsidies have to fulfill two conditions to justify their existence. First, from an efficiency perspective, subsidies should induce only minimal shifts in the consumption of goods and resources in society (unless they are introduced in order to reflect the existence of positive externalities associated with the consumption of the subsidized good). Hence, subsidized goods should display very low substitution and income elasticities. Second, from an equity perspective, the poor should be the main beneficiaries from subsidies and leakage to higher income groups should be small. Inferior goods -- with a negative income elasticity -- will fulfill such a condition.

Over the past couple of years, the Government of Ecuador has eliminated major direct and indirect subsidies which had catered to the rich. The most prominent subsidies to be eliminated were the ones for petroleum products. Previously, the price of petroleum had been fixed at the cost of domestic production and not at its international opportunity value.

But a number of major subsidies remain in place. The most important ones are electricity, water, cooking gas, urban transport and housing. Except for the housing subsidy, which is very difficult to allocate across consumer groups, we can analyze the distribution of the other subsidies using information from the LSMS. Table 2 shows the behavioral pattern of households in the use of electric power, water, and cooking fuel by consumption quintile. The access to basic services is highly correlated with the consumption level. It should be noted that urban residency is often times a precondition for gaining access to public water supply or electricity and hence for enjoying subsidized goods and services.

Table 2. Uses of Utilities by Expenditure Quintile, 1994

Utilities Category	Consumption Expenditure Quintile					
	1st	2nd	3rd	4th	5th	Overall
Electricity (%)	71.5	82.2	87.1	90.6	97.6	87.4
-- of which % public	99.8	99.4	99.2	98.9	99.3	99.2
-- electricity consumption (kWh/household/month)	72.7	83.2	106.0	140.5	225.8	141.9
Water from public source (%)	30.4	37.4	44.3	54.2	75.1	51.4
Cooking gas (%)	59.1	76.2	83.4	85.9	88.6	80.3

Source: LSMS (1994).

Electricity. INECEL, the Ecuadoran electricity company, adopted a complicated tariff scheme in June 1993 which subsidizes the residential sector but roughly covers long-run marginal costs in the commercial sector. For residential users, INECEL applies a graduated tariff structure with the unit price per kWh progressively increasing from 7.5 sucres to 240 sucres in 12 steps. Most unit prices are lower than the long-run marginal cost, estimated by INECEL to be 189 sucres per kwh. Only the extremely intensive users of more than 1000 kwh pay a price which is above long-run marginal cost. As seen in Table 2, with consumption of the richest quintile of the population at 225 kwh on average (1994), even these consumers are subsidized, although at a lower per-kwh rate than the poorer quintiles.

We calculate the subsidy per household based on the information of total electricity expenditures per household. While the Living Standard Measurement Survey only provides us with the total expenditures per household, we can recursively deduce the total household subsidy by applying the tariff structure because we can determine the threshold levels for which households have to pay a specific marginal tariff rate. We make two important assumption in this exercise: that households are billed for what they actually consume and that household declare the actual amount of payment correctly.

We estimate the monthly residential electricity subsidy at around US$14 million. While we applied the same long-run marginal cost estimate than INECEL, our total subsidy estimate calculated from the household data is higher than the total subsidy estimate by INECEL itself (US$9 million per month). Several factors might account for this discrepancy. First, our monthly electricity consumption estimate is higher than the one INECEL had applied which can be due to seasonal fluctuation or rationing. Second, our consumption estimate would be inflated if households declared a higher expenditure for electricity than they actually had, especially those with an illegal electricity connection.

As expected, the electricity subsidy does not reach the poor. Only about 20 percent of the subsidy goes to the lowest two expenditure quintiles (Table 3). This unfavorable distribution is due to two factors: First, far less poor than rich families -- especially in the rural areas -- are connected to electricity which restricts their access to the subsidy. Second, the rate of increase of electricity consumption with expenditures overcompensates the lower 'average' subsidy rate per kwh paid by heavy consumers. Or in other words, while the rich get a lower subsidy rate per hour of electricity use, they consume so much that the total subsidy amount is much higher for them than for the poor.

Water. Due to the decentralized distribution system of water, it is almost impossible to calculate the explicit amount of water subsidies in Ecuador. According to the Banco del Estado, there are some 189 entities supplying potable drinking water to households in Ecuador. Costs to supply the water, water tariffs and the collection rate differ substantially between the companies so that it would be necessary to evaluate the balance sheet for every single company, conduct individual calculations of the long-run marginal costs and derive company-specific subsidies. Such an endeavor goes beyond the scope of this analysis.[2]

---

[2]   To provide the reader with a benchmark, we shortly list the main components of the earning statement for the water company for Quito (EPAP-Q) for FY93: operating revenue (33.4 billion

Alternatively, we use imputed water expenditures -- which evaluate the actual consumption of water at its marginal value to the consumer -- to derive the distribution of an implicit water subsidy. Less than half of all households in Ecuador are connected to the public water network, and the connection rate varies positively with household expenditures. Prices charged for water and the marginal value to the consumer diverge widely for those connected as water shortages are a fact of life. In fact, the LSMS records that 74 percent of those who are connected do not pay for the services at all -- for them, the subsidy rate is 100 percent. The social optimum would hence be to equalize the marginal value of water across consumers by auctioning of the available water. As explained in Working Paper 1, we can impute water expenditures by evaluating actual water consumption at the free market price. We can hence use the difference between imputed and actual water expenditures as an estimate of the water subsidy.

As Table 3 shows, we estimate the overall water subsidy at around US$36 million for 1994, much smaller than the electricity subsidy. Nevertheless, almost half of this subsidy goes to the richest 20 percent in the Ecuadoran population. This is largely due to the unequal access to the public water net. It turns out that the water subsidy is actually the most unequally distributed subsidy examined here.

Gas. Cooking gas is heavily subsidized in Ecuador today. In 1994, consumers paid only about 25 percent of the import price of cooking gas, having a strong fiscal impact as most of Ecuador's gas consumption stems from foreign sources. The Government planned several times to remove the subsidy and substitute it with a targeted income support but these plans never materialized.

The largest part of the subsidy benefits the residential sector as only gas in small bottles is subsidized. The Government estimates the total subsidy to have reached US$120 million in 1994, a figure which we almost exactly reproduce when we use the Living Standard Measurement Survey and derive subsidies per household as three times the household expenditures. However, the past years have shown that gas consumption grows very fast at the current low price as gas is not only used for cooking but also heating or car fuel.

We find that, once again, the rich in Ecuador benefit the most from the subsidy (30 percent) but that the subsidy has the most 'egalitarian' distribution of all the four ones looked at here, owing to a moderate income elasticity of gas consumption. Average household consumption actually varies very little with expenditure class although per capita consumption increases due to the smaller household size of richer families.[3] Use is another determining factor of the subsidy distribution. While a simple gas stove does not represent extraordinary high fixed costs as an investment, the remoteness of many rural areas combined with the bulkiness of the gas bottles limits access for many of the rural poor.

Sucres) of which 66.8 per cent was for the sale of water and connection for residential households, other income (2.3 bil.), earmarked taxes (8.0 bil.) on the revenue side, and operating expenses (35.6 bil.), administrative expenses (13.9 bil.), financial costs (8.1 bil.) and net loss (1.2 bill). Source: EPAP-Q, *Estado de perdidas y ganancias*, Oct 1994.
[3] Compare UNDP et al (1994).

Urban Transport. The objective of the urban transport subsidy is to keep low bus fares for the urban poor. Subsidies are channeled through the Consejo Nacional de Transito y Transporte Terrestres to owners of buses, while the bus owners in turn charge only a fare of 150 sucres per ride. This subsidy program is administered in 21 cities of 16 provinces, and 4,176 buses were being operated under this program as of March of 1994. In order to receive subsidies, bus owners have to operate the bus 18 days per month and complete at least 4 rounds of the designated route each day. Upon satisfying the above conditions, the Consejo grants lump-sum subsidies of 1,000,000 sucres per month to owners of gasoline-operated buses, and 700,000 sucres to diesel fuel-operator vehicles.[4]

According to the Consejo Nacional de Transito, the program cost the government approximately 4,000 million sucres per month. Based on budget information from the Consejo, the estimated annual subsidy for 1994 has been 38,547 million sucres (US$16.5 million). We assume here that these subsidies ultimately benefit the intra-urban bus users (as only those buses qualify for the program). Even though the fuel subsidies are given directly to the operators, they are eventually passed on to the riders by fixing the bus fares.

We estimate urban transport subsidies to be similarly distributed than the cooking gas subsidy, hence mildly tilted towards the wealthier classes of the population. The LSMS provides us with exact information on the amount of trips per day of the urban employed and we use this information as a proxy for the overall distribution of the subsidy hence excluding other trips as for shopping or pleasure. Although the overall subsidy is small compared to electricity and cooking gas, the result that the public transport subsidy leaks substantially to the richer quintiles is somewhat surprising as the general opinion in Ecuador appears to be that the ones who can afford to avoid public transport will do so.

Housing Subsidies by the Ecuadoran housing bank, the Banco Ecuatoriana de Vivienda (BEV), are difficult to estimate but it can be safely assumed that they do not reach the poor. Two types of subsidies currently exist: First, not all housing loans are recovered; the non-recovery rate in 1994 was 4.46 percent. Second, a large share of current debtors benefit from a long period in which interest rates were subsidized. BEV only raised the interest rate to market levels in 1991 and before that fixed interest rates were below market level and the implicit subsidy grew in an inflationary environment.

These 'hidden' subsidies are not shared by the poor but the middle class. As a longtime policy, BEV has required a minimum household income as a precondition for loan approval, being a function of the salario minimo and the loan size. We estimate the absolute lower bound of monthly income which would qualify a family for loan eligibility at US$335 per month. A comparison of average monthly household expenditures for the households in the lowest quintile (US$121) or the second quintile (US$185) reveals that

---

[4] The government intends to phase out the urban transport subsidies program by allowing the bus operators to charge higher fares for the new fleet of buses. For instance, a new bus service called executive class (clase ejecutiva) charges 500 sucres per ride and is operated without any subsidy from the government. The government encourages the bus operators to replace the old polluting buses with new imported buses through tax incentives (exemption of import duties).

without any doubt, poor families in Ecuador have not qualified for such BEV loans and have hence also not been the beneficiaries of the subsidies.[5]

Overall Assessment. None of the above described subsidies fulfills the 'classifying' criteria we outlined above: none of them caters to the poor and at least two of them are from a efficiency perspective highly distortive. Although calculated as relatively small, the implicit subsidy for water is the most unequally distributed, followed by the largest subsidy, electricity. The two largest subsidies, for electricity and gas, are also the ones which are the most distortive from an economic perspective. Studies from other countries have shown that both price and income elasticities for these energy sources can be quite substantial, especially if leakage from residential to commercial users is possible.

Table 3. Distribution of Subsidies by Expenditure Quintile, 1994

Subsidy Category	Consumption Expenditure Quintile					Overall
	1st	2nd	3rd	4th	5th	
	million sucres (% in parentheses)					
Population Share	(20.0)	(20.0)	(20.0)	(20.0)	(20.0)	(100.0)
Household Share	(15.7)	(17.2)	(18.6)	(21.5)	(27.0)	(100.0)
Household Expenditure Share	(5.6)	(9.4)	(13.4)	(19.8)	(51.8)	(100.0)
Electricity	32,191	45,987	62,850	89,676	152,143	382,847
	(8.4)	(12.0)	(16.4)	(23.4)	(39.7)	(100.0)
Water	6,309	9,643	12,175	18,860	33,082	80,069
	(7.9)	(12.0)	(15.2)	(23.6)	(41.3)	(100.0)
Cooking Gas	28,930	42,613	49,362	62,359	76,729	259,993
	(11.1)	(16.4)	(19.0)	(24.0)	(29.5)	(100.0)
Urban Transport	4,517	4,712	6,781	7,431	8,682	32,123
	(14.1)	(14.7)	(21.1)	(23.1)	(27.0)	(100.0)
OVERALL	71,947	102,955	131,168	178,326	270,636	755,032
	(9.5)	(13.6)	(17.4)	(23.6)	(35.8)	(100.0)

Source: LSMS (1994); Consejo Nacional de Transito y Transporte Terrestres.

While tackling the electricity and gas subsidies has to be of highest priority for the government from an economic and social point of view, this has to be done with care. Electricity is the easier one to tackle. Restructuring the tariff system to introduce a simple two or three stage tariff schedule protecting low-volume consumers can considerably improve both efficiency and equity while reducing the total subsidy to about US$35 million.[6] Electricity is an income-elastic good which a very large percentage of the non-poor consume beyond a certain level. While we find today that even a fair amount of the

---

[5] We can make such a statement as poor families typically save very little, if at all, so that family income and expenditures will not differ substantially.

[6] The total subsidy and its distribution depends on the price elasticity for electricity for the different consumer groups. If all households in the two lowest expenditure quintiles would consume 80 kWh in order to be eligible for the lifeline rate, the total subsidy would be around US$35 million (without any charge for the lifeline rate).

poor consume above these levels due to a very low price of electricity, their demand behavior would likely change if a simple lifeline tariff scheme were introduced. Such a tariff scheme would consist of (a) a low fixed-cost rate for consumers of electricity up to about 80 or 90 kWh; (b) a different charge rate once consumers go beyond the lifeline quantity, also retroactively billing the initial 80 or 90 kWh at the charge rate.[7] If desired, this charge rate could be broken up into several progressive rate increases. Such a schedule would be economically efficient since it would signal to the heavy consumers the true economic cost of electricity consumption. While part of the subsidy would continue to flow to the non-poor -- because electricity consumption is only imperfectly correlated with household expenditures -- the poor's share in the total subsidy would significantly increase. With a total subsidy amount of around US$35 million, such a scheme would free considerable resources to finance poverty alleviation programs.[8]

The gas subsidy is more difficult to tackle. A complete and once-and-for-all removal of the gas subsidy, without accompanying compensation measures, will inflict a sizable welfare loss on the poor, and especially the very poor gas users. The extremely poor households using gas (85 percent in urban and 50 percent in rural areas) spend on average 2.5 percent[9] of their total budget on gas purchase. Assuming a relatively modest price elasticity for gas (-0.2), a tripling of the gas price -- which would be necessary to eliminate the subsidy, would lead to a welfare loss of more than 5.3 percent[10] for the very poor. A once and for all removal without compensating measures would also worsen expenditure distribution in Ecuador since the poor spend a much higher proportion of their budget on cooking gas than the rich.

Several alternative options can be studied. A phasing out of the gas subsidy while introducing targeted benefits might be the best, and politically most viable, option. Such phasing out could follow pre-determined and pre-announced steps. Another alternative would be an attempt to target the subsidy by only selling the subsidized gas (in special containers) in low-income neighborhoods. Leakage of such a scheme would depend on the degree to which this self-targeting mechanism works and the non-poor avoid either the transaction costs or the 'social blame' of using marked containers for low-income neighborhoods. This self-targeting scheme could be combined with a mechanical device that hooks up the subsidized gas bottles only to certain, very simple one-or two flame stoves which most of the non-poor will avoid. Finally, and economically most efficient,

---

7   Such a tariff scheme introduces a steep kink in the expenditure curve of electricity since for the consumer, the marginal cost of the 81st unit is not only the new charge rate but also the cost of the first eighty kWh times the new charge rate. However, few better-off households would be deterred by this kink since the level of 80 kWh is incompatible with their style life.

8   It would be better to raise the remaining subsidy from general tax revenues rather than to introduce a cross-subsidization scheme in the tariff schedule.

9   This estimate is somewhat lower than in the UNDP/World Bank study 'Energy Pricing, Subsidies and Interfuel Substitution' (1994) which estimated the budget share of all households in the lowest expenditure quintile to be 3.9 per cent. The difference in the measurement of total expenditures is likely responsible for this discrepancy as we have included rent, consumption of consumer durables etc.

10 This calculation measures the welfare loss as the reduction in the consumer surplus, assuming linearity of the Marshallian demand curve in the respective range. See Hope and Singh (1995), p.29.

the subsidy could be redirected entirely from the variable input to the fixed inputs, the stove. However, with 90 percent of the urban poor and almost 50 percent of the rural poor owning gas stoves today, the extent of shielding the poor from the price increase will be minimal.

3.   Public Expenditure in the Social Sector

The provision of necessary social services by the government is another area in which the government can have a positive effect on the welfare of its people. Cost recovery of social services in Ecuador is very low as school tuition and health fees are minimal or absent. Social expenditures are hence financed by general taxation.

While we outlined that subsidies should not leak substantially to the non-poor, the case is somehow different for social expenditures. Basic social expenditures such as primary health and primary education are universal programs, exclusion of the wealthier parts of the Ecuadoran society can hence not be an aim. Rather, it is important for the Government that these expenditures also reach the poor. The same holds, although to a lesser degree, for secondary and higher education and health care. For example, if we find that these expenditures are largely benefiting the rich in society, the Government has to think about recovering costs of these services and / or expanding access to these services also to the poor in society. Before examining the incidence of health and education expenditures, we briefly review trends in social expenditure allocation over the past years.

Trends in Public Expenditures by Sector. Real per capita social expenditures of the Central Government have declined significantly over the past years. Since the early 1980's, Ecuador has experienced a decline in government revenues due mainly to declining income from petroleum production. In order to maintain government expenditures at their high levels, Ecuador attempted to replace declining tax revenues with increased borrowings, which eventually raised the debt service, both internal and external. Consequently, total government expenditures have remained more or less constant as a share of GDP (about 14-15 percent), but social sector expenditures have declined as a share of both the budget and as a percent of GDP. As shown in Table 4, social sector expenditures gradually declined to about 28 percent of the budget by 1993. One of the important factors responsible for the decline in the social sector share (especially during the middle eighties) has been the rise in the share of the budget devoted to interest expenses.

Real per capita social expenditures also declined. Population growth continued to exceed 2 percent per annum, faster than the average GDP growth. Consequently, per capita social expenditures of the Central Government between 1990 and 1993 alone declined by 8 percent. While real per capita education expenditures stayed constant during this time span, real per capita health expenditures fell by 35 percent. On the other hand, 'general' and 'other' expenditures increased strongly and -- although there is no information on the type of expenditure reductions by sector -- overall there has been a significant decline in capital spending.

Table 4. Central Government Expenditures By Sector

Year	1980	1985	1988	1990	1993
Budget Shares (% of total expenditures)					
Social	41.0	32.7	34.4	28.6	27.5
-- education	33.1	24.5	23.6	18.5	19.9
-- health & Comm. Dev.	6.9	7.3	9.7	8.2	5.4
Interest	8.9	21.4	18.2	26.2	12.7
Economic	18.9	19.8	17.4	14.6	13.8
General	23.9	24.4	27.8	24.8	30.7
Other	7.4	1.7	2.2	5.9	15.4
Total current & capital	100.0	100.0	100.0	100.0	100.0
Total Expenditures/GDP	14.2	15.1	13.8	14.7	14.0
Social Sectors/GDP	5.8	4.9	4.8	4.2	3.9
Real Spending Per Capita (1985 constant thousand sucres)					
Social Sectors	7.2	5.8	5.5	4.8	4.4
-- education	5.8	4.4	3.8	3.1	3.2
-- health & comm. dev,	1.2	1.3	1.6	1.4	0.9
Interest	1.6	3.8	2.9	4.4	2.0
Economic	3.3	3.5	2.8	2.5	2.2
General	4.2	4.4	4.5	4.2	4.9
Other	1.2	0.4	0.4	0.9	3.1
Total Government	17.5	17.9	16.1	16.8	16.6

Source: Ministry of Finance.

Naturally, many expenditures listed as 'economic' or 'general' can be important for the poor. The establishment of the social investment fund (FISE) in the Office of the President, for example, accounts for a large increase in the 'general' category. At the same time, many social expenditures, such as for tuition-free public universities and large urban curative care hospitals, may not necessarily be beneficial for the poor. Nevertheless, we see a clear trend for declining social sector expenditures, in the face of rising expenditures for interest, defense and other areas, which would seem to have diminished the ability of the government to attend to welfare needs.[11]

Education: Unit Cost Estimates, Quality and Incidence of Expenditures. Declining real education expenditures occurred at a time when enrollment rates increased, which lead to a decline in the quality of education. Total primary school enrollment increased by 27 percent between 1980 and 1991, while secondary school enrollment jumped by 51 percent. Enrollment in higher education doubled. At the same time, resources for primary education fell by 58 percent, and per pupil primary expenditures fell by 67 percent.[12] For higher education, while enrollment went up 50 percent between 1985 and 1991, expenditures declined by 5 percent in real terms. The result was a severe deterioration in the quality of education, including the complete absence of books and materials in many schools, lower teacher salaries, and an inability to maintain existing

---

[11]   See also: World Bank (1990, p.30).
[12]   Calculations based on data from EB/PRODEC.

structures. Indicative of the latter is that the largest part of the Ministry of Education's budget goes to pay salaries of teachers and employees. In 1994, over 80 percent of the budget, excluding transfers, is earmarked for salaries.

Table 5. Education Expenditures and Education Efficiency Indicators, 1994

Education Level	Public Spending on Education (1994) (A)	Number of Students Enrolled (1994) (B)	Unit Cost (Sucres) (C)=(A)/(B)	Unit Cost (Dollars)	Student/Teacher Ratio
	(million sucres)				
Primary	342,356 (35.9%)	1,900,000	180,187	81.9	30.4
Secondary	363,526 (38.2%)	643,702	564,743	256.7	13.4
Higher	245,443 (25.8%)	215,268	1,140,174	518.3	--
Overall	951,325 (100.0%)	3,029,516	289,010	123.7	--

Source: Pfister, E. (1995).

The developments over the past decade, although affecting all parts of the education system, have increased the unbalanced distribution of education finance to dramatic levels. Table 5 shows per unit cost estimates of students based on the 1994 Ministry of Education budget. According to these estimates, unit costs for higher education are about six times higher than for primary education and three times higher than for secondary education.

Calculating the incidence of public education expenditures in 1994 shows that financing of primary school expenditures reaches the poor but that this is less so for secondary and especially higher education financing. As presented in Table 6, the poorest quintile of the population benefit overproportionally from primary education expenditures (27.2 percent). This incidence is calculated as an 'access' variable -- we assume that children attending school benefit equally from the public outlays. The finding for primary education can easily be explained: school attendance of primary school is close to universal by now (compare Working Paper 1) but many more richer families send their children to private schools. Hence, public expenditures benefit the poor overproportionally. But already for the distribution of secondary expenditures the picture changes: benefits are already largely realized by the upper expenditure classes because secondary school attendance of children in richer households far exceeds the one in poorer households, overcompensating the tendency for the higher expenditure groups to send their children to private education facilities (compare Working Paper 1). The most unequitable distribution is associated with higher education expenditures. The poorest 40 percent of the population only obtain 12 percent of these expenditures.

Public Health. The basic Ecuadoran health care system consists of the public system and private providers. In the public sector, the Ministry of Health and Social Security Institute (IESS) are the main actors, complemented by the Armed Forces Health Services and small programs under the responsibility of other public agencies. As shown in Table 4, there has been a significant decline in real per capita health expenditures (-35 percent) of the 1990-93 period. These data, however, only cover the programs of the Ministry of Health (MOH), which serves about 27 percent of the population. Another 11 percent are covered under the social security program (IESS), which is comprised of the General System and the Seguro Social Campesino program (SSC). Because of its historically low and declining quality, many people rely on the private sector for health services. Even among the poorest groups, large numbers attend private clinics.[13]

The overall constraint on resources has meant diminishing funds for all types of expenditures. As a result, salaries are low, and there are little or no funds for medicines, supplies and equipment repairs. In many hospitals, particularly in rural areas, it is common for nurses to give patients a list of items to be purchased in the private sector, which they must bring with them to the hospital. Even so, there is a substantial bias in expenditures toward the larger, curative care hospitals in the urban centers. About 45 percent of total resources support 32 large urban hospitals, while only 35 percent is allocated for primary care facilities.[14] About 80 percent of the MSP personnel are located in urban areas. Overall, there are 537 people per doctor in urban areas in Ecuador, but 3142 people per doctor in rural areas.[15] Despite having a surplus of trained doctors and other medical personnel, there remains a deficit of medical professionals in rural areas.

Yet despite these problems, there have been substantial improvements in health status of the population over the decade of the 1980s. Infant mortality decreased from 72 to 53 per 1,000 births, the total fertility rate declined from 5.4 to 3.8 (1979-89), and overall mortality from communicable diseases fell by 45 percent.

Within the social security system (IESS), only the affiliates, not even their family members, are allowed to seek medical attention in the IESS-run hospitals. On the other hand, the IESS hospitals are over-crowded by the rural population who are allowed access through the Seguro Social Campesino. The contribution to social security funds by the rural population, on the other hand, is negligible. A large number of IESS members and their family members in turn find it convenient to visit MOH hospitals. The link between contributions and benefits in the social security system in Ecuador is blurred because of this peculiar dynamics.

Health expenditures of the Ministry of Health are mildly pro-poor while expenditures of the IESS largely go to the non-poor. To calculate the incidence of health expenditures, we use information from the LSMS about the *last* visit to a public health facility. This can obviously be only a rough indicator of actual benefits received because we can neither control for the quality of the health services provided nor for the quantity of visits because this information is not contained in the LSMS. Nevertheless, the obtained pro-poor bias stems from a comparatively higher proportion of the poor to visit

---

[13]   See Working Paper 1.
[14]   Enriquez (1994).
[15]   ILDIS (1994).

public health facilities than the rich. Including the quality aspect of the service might change the estimates considerably as quality of service in poor neighborhoods, and especially in the rural areas, is likely to be worse than in higher income neighborhoods. The U-shaped benefit curve relating to IESS expenditures is purely due to access to the system: The first quintile population benefits mainly through the affiliation of part of the rural poor with the Farmers Security Scheme -- again, we cannot assess the quality of the service. But the close link between formal sector employment and affiliation with the General Security Scheme tilts the overall distribution in favor of the non-poor.

Overall Assessment. Overall, the incidence of social public expenditure is shown to be mildly tilted to the rich. While this bias is much less pronounced for expenditures than for subsidies, it is nevertheless not desirable. Tuition for higher education, which could finance access for poorer groups in society to secondary education, could be one of the means to obtain a more equal distribution of public social expenditures.

Table 6: Distribution of Social Public Expenditures by Expenditure Quintile, 1994

Expenditure Category	Consumption Expenditure Quintile					
	1st	2nd	3rd	4th	5th	Overall
	million sucres (percent in parentheses)					
Population Share	(20.0)	(20.0)	(20.0)	(20.0)	(20.0)	(100.0)
Household Share	(15.7)	(17.2)	(18.6)	(21.5)	(27.0)	(100.0)
Household Expenditure Share	(5.6)	(9.4)	(13.4)	(19.8)	(51.8)	(100.0)
Public Education						
Primary	93,121	90.381	72,579	57,173	28,758	342,012*
	(27.2)	(26.4)	(21.2)	(16.7)	(8.4)	(100.0)
Secondary	46,531	61,072	85,056	93,426	77,431	363,516*
	(12.8)	(16.8)	(23.4)	(25.7)	(21.3)	(100.0)
Higher	13,990	15,217	41,970	68,969	105,295	245,441*
	(5.7)	(6.2)	(17.1)	(28.1)	(42.9)	(100.0)
Public Health						
MOH	60,207	71,550	65,442	58,752	34,904	290,855*
	(20.7)	(24.6)	(22.5)	(20.2)	(11.9)	(100.0)
IESS	32,131	17,491	27,801	38,469	47,114	163,006*
	(19.7)	(10.7)	(17.1)	(23.6)	(28.9)	(100.0)
OVERALL	245,980	255,711	292,848	316,789	293,502	1,404,830*
	(17.5)	(18.2)	(20.8)	(22.5)	(21.0)	(100.0)

Source: LSMS (1994); Pfister (1995); Ministry of Finance. The expenditure estimates for the IESS, and both the Ministries of Health and Education are provisional.

4.   Conclusion

This Annex has shown that a large part of Government subsidies and expenditures do not reach the poorest groups in the Ecuadoran society. We first looked at the distribution of the major subsidies. While we were not able to quantify the (implicit) housing subsidy, we found that especially the electricity subsidy needs to be redesigned quickly. As stands, the Government encourages excess electricity consumption through a huge subsidy of about US$160 million which benefits to 60 percent the richest 40 percent of the population. Next on the agenda is a redesign of the gas subsidy. Although much more difficult to tackle than electricity, Ecuador cannot afford to prolong a reform as consumption grows rapidly which will cause a higher and higher burden in the budget. Nevertheless, an elimination of the subsidy has to go hand in hand with a targeted support scheme to the poor in society.

Health and education expenditures, theoretically 'universal' programs, also reach the poor underproportionally. This is less the case for primary education but pronounced for both secondary and especially higher education finance which directly cater to the needs of the already fortunate in society. The coverage of health care is dismal forcing even the very poor to seek help in private clinics. Expenditures in the system are very low. While we find them to be relatively homogeneously distributed, this can hardly be interpreted as a positive development as they clearly fall short of providing a basic health net for the poor in Ecuador.

References

Banco Central del Ecuador, <u>Egresos Iniciales P.G.E.</u>, 1980-1993, Quito.

Banco Central del Ecuador, <u>Ingresos Efectivos P.G.E.</u>, 1980-1993, Quito.

Banco Central del Ecuador (1995), <u>Informacion Estadistica Mensual</u>, Quito.

Enriquez, Francisco (1994), <u>La Reforma del Ministrio de Salud: Algunos Elementos</u> (draft), Quito.

Hope, E. and B. Singh (1995), <u>Energy Price Increases in Developing Countries</u>, Policy Research Working Paper 1442.

IESS (1994), <u>Servicio Medico de la Seguridad Social</u>, Quito.

ILDIS (1994), <u>Informe Social</u>, Quito.

INECEL (1993), <u>Empresas Electricas del Pais: Estimacion de los Precios Medios para 1993</u>, Quito.

Ministerio de Finanzas (1993), <u>Presupuesto del Estado</u>, Quito.

Pfister, E. (1995), <u>El Presupuesto de Educacion, Algunos Indicadores</u>, EB/PRODEC, Quito.

SECAP (1994), <u>Encuesta Sobre Condiciones de Vida</u>, Quito.

UNDP, the World Bank, and ESMAP (1994) <u>Ecuador: Energy Pricing, Poverty and Social Mitigation</u>, Report No. 12831-EC, Washington D.C.

World Bank (1990), <u>Ecuador: A Social Sector Strategy for the Nineties</u>, Washington D.C..

World Bank (1993), <u>Ecuador: Public Expenditure Review: Changing the Role of the State</u>, Report No. 10541-EC, Washington D.C..

Working Paper 7: Targeting Social Programs to the Poor
Armando Godinez and Julie van Domelen

1.   Context

As part of its poverty alleviation strategy, the Government of Ecuador has developed a number of social programs that seek to expand access to or improve the quality of basic services. Most of the more recent social programs have explicitly stated objectives of reaching the poor and targeting elements built into their design. However, to date there has been little analysis or monitoring of whether these objectives are being met. In short, are the benefits of social programs reaching the poor?

The issue of targeting has taken on increasing importance to the Government of Ecuador in recent years. Macroeconomic constraints on public spending have made it all the more important that scarce resources be spent efficiently and with the greatest incidence and impact on the poor. Basic information has improved, including the development of several poverty maps and provision of new data from the 1990 Census and the 1994 Living Standards Measurement Survey, allowing for more accurate identification of the poor.

This Working Paper reviews the experience with targeted social programs in Ecuador. First, we describe the framework of analysis in Section 2, followed by a brief summary of the major social programs in Ecuador in Section 3. Several Annex tables contain information about these programs. Section 4 then presents case studies of seven targeted social programs. The case study approach allows for a more detailed treatment of targeting mechanisms. This assessment includes analysis of the costs of targeting and administering targeted programs, potential incentive effects, and political considerations. The Working Paper concludes with a consolidated view of targeting accuracy and a summary of the lessons from targeted social programs in Ecuador.

Our assessment of the seven social programs falls short of determining the targeting accuracy, i.e. the extent to which each of the programs reaches the poor. None of the reviewed programs monitored its beneficiary group by means of continuous evaluation or surveys. To enable an evaluation of the targeting accuracy, such assessments would have to record expenditures (or at least incomes) of the beneficiary households. Alternatively, if we were able to rely on a large household survey which recorded program access by household type, this would also suffice to evaluate the targeting accuracy. However, beneficiary numbers are generally too small to permit us extrapolation of information contained in the available Living Standard Measurement Survey.

2.   Framework of Analysis[1]

<u>Universal versus Targeted Programs</u>. Targeted social programs seek to deliver benefits to a selected group of participants, in particular the poor and vulnerable. Targeted social programs are distinguished from universal services which in theory are accessible by all, such as public primary health and education services. Such universal

---

[1]   The framework of analysis is drawn from Grosh (1994).

services do not attempt to explicitly screen out potential participants. However, in practice, these services tend to be uneven in terms of quality and equitable coverage.[2]

There is often a direct relationship between targeted and universal social programs. Examples include nutrition programs that piggyback onto public health services or a targeted school lunch program administered through the public education system. Some of the targeted programs reviewed in this chapter have been designed specifically to improve access to and quality of these universal services toward the poor. For instance, several of the targeted social programs in Ecuador are designed to improve the quality of universal health and education services as delivered to low-income or high-risk groups.

Targeting Mechanisms. Within targeted programs, a variety of mechanisms exist for identifying potential beneficiaries. A useful taxonomy divides these mechanisms into three types:

- *individual assessment mechanisms* that require program managers to decide whether or not to accept individual applicants (e.g., based on means tests, social worker evaluations, or nutritional status);

- *group or geographic targeting mechanisms* which use location, usually as a proxy for poverty level, to determine program eligibility (e.g., by school, by canton, parroquia, or health area); and

- *self-targeting mechanisms* which rely on the individual decision of a potential candidate to participate or not (e.g., employment programs with emphasis on unskilled labor and subsidies on products consumed by the poor).

The choice of mechanism depends largely on the type and scale of benefits involved. For instance, access to social infrastructure is usually defined geographically by catchment area. General employment creation programs often seek self-targeting mechanisms due to their scale and the cost and logistics involved in identifying individual beneficiaries. Many programs use more than one kind of targeting instrument, either explicitly or implicitly.

In the analysis of the accuracy and costs of these targeted programs, we considered several points. Accuracy can be viewed in several ways, including the incidence of benefits according to criteria determined by the program itself, incidence of benefits determined according to a standard measure of poverty, and finally through external measures of the participation rate (i.e., what fraction of the population benefits from a program). Where possible, costs have been disaggregated between the overall costs of administering targeted programs and the costs of targeting itself (i.e., incremental costs of identifying potential beneficiaries). Possible disincentive effects (relocation, substitution, unproductive behavior) are discussed but not quantified. In practice, both the accuracy and efficiency of targeting is largely dependent on administrative and political considerations, which are also discussed.

---

[2]   See our analysis of the incidence of public expenditures for education and health in Working Paper 6.

3.   Short Overview of the Major Social Programs in Ecuador

There are numerous social programs in Ecuador. They vary by sector, executing agency, size and coverage. The Government and UNICEF have made attempts to catalogue these programs, or at least consolidate information about them.[3] These programs focus largely on health, education, and early child development impacts and account for almost US$100 million of annual investment, although the consolidated financial information on these programs is not very complete.

Only about a third of the major social programs operate with an explicit targeting mechanism. Of the twenty-four programs identified, over half intend to reach a national level of coverage, with the remainder oriented to selected provinces, cities or local areas. In addition, 15 out of the 24 purport to be targeted programs in the sense of explicit objectives to reach poor and/or at-risk populations, however only 8 of these specify targeting mechanisms. The lion's share of these programs is executed by central Ministries or agencies, such as the ministries of health, education and the National Institute for Children and the Family. Other executing agencies include the President's Office, local government and NGOs.

We chose seven case studies for this review, two from the education sector, two child development programs, one health program, the school lunch program, and the intersectoral Social Investment Fund. We selected the case studies based on their primary focus on key vulnerable groups, the scale of the program (national coverage and size of investment), and availability of data. While we also chose the cases with the intention of comparing programs, differences in scale, sector, and kinds of benefits limit the applicability of these comparisons. Each case study includes a description of the program and the targeting mechanism employed, an assessment of targeting accuracy as defined by the program itself, and an analysis of the administrative and targeting costs of delivering program benefits.

As mentioned above, our assessment of seven social programs falls short of determining the targeting accuracy because none of the reviewed programs monitored its beneficiary group by means of continuous evaluation or surveys.

4.   Case Studies

Case Study 1: Operation Child Rescue (Operación Rescate Infantil - ORI)
Description of Program

In the late 1970's, the Government of Ecuador initiated programs to offer access to childcare centers, first under a UNICEF sponsored program that was subsequently incorporated into the Ministry of Social Welfare. Based on this experience, the Community Network ('Red Comunitaria') program was launched in 1989 to provide a system of basic care services for the daily needs of children through the establishment of childcare centers and small-scale daycare providers. The program operated until 1993, with an average annual financing of about US$11 million. The official coverage at the

---

[3]   UNICEF (1994).

height of the program was estimated at about 200,000 children (although other estimates put the effective coverage at 120,000). Several administrative and bureaucratic factors constrained the full and effective implementation of the program. In addition, the high visibility and identification with the outgoing administration were factors in the decision taken by the new administration to terminate the program in 1993.

In 1994, the Government replaced the Community Network with the Child Rescue Operation (ORI), aimed at providing services to children aged 0-6 through Community Child Development Centers. ORI uses in part infrastructure remaining from the Community Network. The day care services include early education and nutrition programs.

ORI is structured as an autonomous entity under the Ministry of Social Welfare, with regional offices in all provinces except Galapagos. Initially to be financed from the proceeds of an earmarked tax through the National Child Fund (FONIN), in March 1994 the earmarked tax was eliminated and the program is currently being financed from the General Budget, which has severely constrained implementation. Actual coverage estimates for 1994 total 46,524, which represents half of the initial target of 100,000, for which a budget of s/54,000,000,000 was approved by the Ministry of Finance, though actual disbursements have fallen short of the approved amounts.

Targeting Mechanisms

The ORI program has developed a targeting scheme as a combination of geographical and individual targeting. The proposed targeting system, which ORI developed in early 1994, is quite complex and entails three levels. *At the regional and provincial level*, fund allocation is based on a number of indicators including (a) number of children under 5 years old, (b) nutritional status, (c) coverage of the area with health services, PRONEPE and Child Development. Data sources include the CONADE consolidated poverty map, INEC's basic services maps, and the coverage figures from the respective programs. This process is then repeated using much of the same information to determine priorities at the *parroquial and community* levels, with priorities assigned 1-4, with '1' designating highest priority. Finally, at the level of the *daycare center*, staff from the provincial office are to take weight and height data as well as social information (e.g., number of hours accompanied by the mother during the day) on children pre-selected by the centers. This worker assessment leads to a priority rank assigned to each child (1 = malnourished and without daycare, 2 = malnourished and with daycare, and 3 = at nutritional risk and without daycare).

As designed, the system would allow for an objective screen to allocate resources. However, the system is not being used, in part due to the complexity of data required and the introduction of other considerations. For instance, according to the Director of ORI many of the requests to open centers come from less priority locations though are deemed to reach a very low-income population. In addition, priority has been placed on using existing infrastructure, which limits the flexibility of opening new centers in hitherto unserved areas and has resulted in skewed service in favor of the Guayas and Pichincha urban areas. At the individual level, screening at the door to allow only those with malnutrition has been viewed with skepticism by ORI staff in terms of discriminating between members of the same family and/or children from the same poverty level as well as creating potential disincentive effects which would lead to the creation of malnutrition to qualify for program benefits.

Targeting Results

Assessing targeting accuracy of ORI is difficult. While ORI has applied parroquia rankings of 1-4 based on a variety of indicators, including malnutrition from the 1990 Height and Weight Census, access to basic services, housing conditions and level of instruction of mothers, the weighting given to each factor is not transparent and there appears to be corrections made based on community rather than parroquia level conditions. Moreover, several parroquias participating in the ORI program have not been assigned a ranking. To illustrate the potential range of malnutrition conditions found under ORI's parroquial ranking system, the following table matches parroquial malnutrition levels as determined by the 1990 Weight and Height Census with ORI's parroquia-level rankings by ORI (1-4). While the average malnutrition rates are slightly higher in parroquias designated with a high priority for intervention under ORI's ranking system, we detect a wide variation among parroquias of the same rank. For instance, for the highest priority parroquias (group 1) malnutrition rates range from 100 percent to 21 percent.

Table 1. ORI Ranking

ORI Ranking of Parroquias	Average Parroquial Malnutrition Rate (percent)	Range of Malnutrition Rates (percent) Among Parroquias in Group
1	56.2	21-100-
2	53.6	13-85-
3	46.8	18-78-
4	35.9	17-74-

Table 2 presents the incidence of program participants based on ORI's own ranking. Over half of all ORI program beneficiaries are located in parroquias deemed by ORI to have the highest levels of needs.

Table 2. ORI: Share of Beneficiaries

Parroquial Ranking	Share of Program Beneficiaries (percent)
1	30
2	23
3	9
4	18
Unranked	20

Information is not available to evaluate targeting accuracy at the individual level, i.e., the poverty or malnutrition levels of children entering daycare centers. Although growth monitoring is part of the essential service package of ORI, such data are not transmitted for overall monitoring by the central ORI unit.

Cost Analysis

Administrative Costs. The approved 1994 budget for ORI was US$23.7 million for a target coverage of 100,000 children by the end of 1994, increasing from 16,000 at the start of the year. The principle cost components of the program include: food (56 percent), payments to day care mothers (16 percent), debt and transfers (12 percent) and administrative costs (16 percent). Salaries of program personnel account for 25 percent of administrative costs, training, seminars and workshops and publicity accounts for 18 percent, utilities (rent, insurance) 16 percent, transportation 12 percent, equipment replacement in day care centers 11 percent, with the remainder for other office expenses.

While administrative expenses appear quite high at 16 percent (or 15 percent net of replacement of day care equipment), they are quite sensitive to scale of the program. For instance, ORI presented a budget for 1995 of US$68.9 million to increase coverage to 320,000 children by the end of 1995. At this scale, administrative costs would fall to 8 percent.

Targeting Costs. Potential targeting costs of the ORI program include expenditures in setting up and monitoring its geographical targeting system and costs associated with site visits and selection of individual beneficiaries of its day care centers. The cost of the geographical targeting system is zero as the information used to identify priority areas is freely available. The cost of identifying and/or screening beneficiaries at the local level is difficult to estimate accurately as the personnel in charge of targeting activities also carry out training, supervision and administration of day care centers.

To arrive at an estimate of these targeting costs, we assume that the costs are borne primarily in the use of staff time. Of the 331 staff of ORI, 96 are located in the central and regional zone offices, representing 40 percent of the ORI wage bill, and can be assumed to carry out largely management, administrative and supervision functions. The staff of the local offices can be divided between technical functions which imply direct contact with beneficiaries (nurses, social workers and nutritionists) and administrative staff consisting of managers, accountants, drivers and other support personnel. ORI local offices have 98 such technical positions, representing 29 percent of the wage bill structure of the agency. As a theoretical upward limit, if these personnel spent all of their time on targeting functions (selection of day care sites, interviewing of families, and nutritional screening of children), overall targeting costs of the program would amount to about 1.2 percent. Since it is unlikely that any more than 20 percent of their time is spent on these activities, we estimate that targeting costs do not exceed 0.2 percent of total program costs.

Case Study Two: The Emergency Social Investment Fund (FISE)

Description of Program

In March 1993, the Government of Ecuador created the Emergency Social Investment Fund (FISE) as a temporary and autonomous agency under the Office of the President. FISE provides financing for small-scale social investments aimed at poverty alleviation based on an institutional design similar to social funds operating in other LAC countries. FISE appraises, finances and monitors projects in the areas of: (i) social infrastructure (health posts, dispensaries, primary schools, training centers, day care centers, orphanages and shelters, and latrines); (ii) socio-economic infrastructure (water supply and sewerage, tertiary and feeder roads, micro-irrigation, drainage, street rehabilitation and erosion control); (iii) social services (equipment, materials and training services for health campaigns, community pharmacies, nutrition programs, primary education and informal training programs); and (iv) productive community investments in support of small-scale programs in agriculture and agricultural processing, handicrafts, fishing and manufacturing. FISE was planned as a demand-driven mechanism in that it relies on project proposals generated and executed by a wide range of institutional actors, including ministries, local governments, NGOs and community-based organizations.

FISE was established as a temporary agency, with a target program of US$120 million over the four and a half year life of the fund, slated to close at the end of 1997. As of the end of February 1995, over 8,000 project proposals had been received by FISE, with over 3,000 approved. The value of the projects approved amounted to US$60.5 million or about half of the target program total and reaches approximately 3.2 million beneficiaries. Of note for its potential effect on targeting accuracy, NGOs and grassroots organizations account for 56 percent of FISE's portfolio of committed resources, with sector ministries representing 24 percent and other governmental authorities (provincial and municipal councils and autonomous entities) 20 percent. In addition, resources have been very evenly divided between rural and urban areas, at 49 percent and 51 percent, respectively.

Targeting Mechanisms

FISE uses a combination of geographical, group and self-targeting mechanisms. One of the principle objectives of FISE is to reach the poor and vulnerable groups with basic social infrastructure and services. To ensure that benefits reach the intended population, FISE has adopted a three-pronged poverty targeting strategy. First, the types of projects eligible for FISE financing, such as latrines, feeder roads and standpipes for water supply, by their nature tend to be oriented to the needs of the poor. Second, priority beneficiaries are identified, for instance women, children and informal sector workers. And finally, FISE uses a map to provide geographical targeting of priority areas. Further, there is a self-targeting mechanism in the distribution of employment benefits during the execution of the small-scale works themselves. All small-scale infrastructure projects are carried out by private sector contractors which apply market prices for unskilled laborers. As studies have demonstrated in other social funds, the use of market-based wages for unskilled labor is a 'costless' and highly effective self-targeting mechanism for the distribution of the employment benefits derived from FISE investments.

Of particular interest to this analysis, FISE's geographical targeting mechanisms were designed to ensure a fair distribution on a national level and to limit leakage to better-off areas. During the establishment of FISE's system, the Consolidated Poverty Map developed by CONADE in 1992 was used to provide overall poverty coefficients on a canton scale based on a consolidation of eight different poverty maps. Target allocations were ascribed to each canton. However, it was determined that the canton level was too large of an area and too heterogeneous to ensure that benefits reached the poor within cantons. However, the CONADE map provided poverty coefficients only for rural and not for urban parroquias.

An initial attempt was made using Census data on basic needs indicators to determine poverty at the parroquial level. However, this data aggregated all the parroquias of major urban centers into one canton-level unit. The first analysis of targeting accuracy revealed that this aggregation problem resulted in lower poverty levels throughout the major urban areas and effectively masked more vulnerable neighborhoods, particularly in Quito and Guayaquil.[4] To correct this situation, FISE used malnutrition data from the 1990 Height and Weight Census which was the only information available which disaggregated urban areas into parroquias. For rural areas, a composite poverty index was used based on malnutrition, literacy, infant mortality and access to basic services.

To render the use of these indicators more operational, parroquias were arranged in groups of 1 - 5, with 1 denoting the most vulnerable parroquias. FISE then established resource allocation targets for each zone (see Table 3). While grouping parroquias into ranges makes it easier to manage overall resource allocations to the over one thousand parroquias in Ecuador, how these ranges are established provides an element of subjectivity to the targeting process.[5]

Because FISE projects are very small in scale (average project amount US$20,000), there is a risk of rejecting projects that would reach pockets of poverty in otherwise better-off parroquias if all resources where assigned to only the 'poorest' parroquias. In the appraisal process for each project, a site visit by a FISE evaluator assesses the overall socio-economic conditions on a local basis. For instance, one project located within an urban parroquia with a '4', or lower priority ranking, consists of providing water supply and day care for a neighborhood of very low-income workers who tend the local dump.

Targeting Results

The experience of the first year and a half of FISE operations is sufficient for an initial evaluation of FISE targeting. However, it can be assumed that poverty targeting of a social fund improves over time for two reasons. First, as the initial period is dedicated to building up a pipeline, there is very little indication of screening out demand from less poor regions. Rather, target allocations for less poor areas are filled first. For instance, no canton to date has received more than its overall program allocation in absolute terms despite apparent 'overfunding' of some cantons on a percentage basis during the start-up period. Second, initial demand is often from those areas most organized and able to present projects, with an inherent lagtime in response to promotion efforts aimed at generating project proposals from the poorest and most isolated regions.

---

[4]   It should be noted that even the parroquia level is not a sufficient geographic targeting base in the larger cities. Several parroquias in Guayaquil and Quito have several hundred thousand inhabitants and span poor and wealthy areas alike.

[5]   For rural parroquias, ranges were established based on a composite poverty index (zone 1 - 100-65 percent index, zone 2 - 65-60 percent, zone 3 60-45 percent, zone 4 - 45-40 percent and zone 5 40-0 percent). For urban areas, zone 1 corresponds to parroquias with malnutrition rates of 45-100 percent, zone 2 - 35-45 percent, zone 3 - 20-35 percent, zone 4 - 15-20 percent, and zone 5 - 0-15 percent.

As for most other programs here we are only able to examine whether the overall allocation of funds matches FISE's own targeting map and hence the geographical distribution of funds but not to what degree benefits really reach the poor or leak to the non-poor. As mentioned above, geographical targeting is an important means to guide overall resource distribution of the programs. But individual beneficiary assessments (or large LSMS type household surveys covering programs) are necessary to evaluate whether projects really reach the poor within each geographical area as the FISE projects are relatively small and tend to cover only a fraction of the population in a parroquia, especially in urban areas.

Overall Targeting Performance Based on Poverty Zones. Through the end of January 1995, FISE's performance based on the poverty zone is depicted in Table 3. Based on the findings above, the poverty targeting experience of the FISE thus far is mixed. In general, rural projects appear to be better targeted than urban projects, a surprising result given the perceived weakness and isolation of poorer rural communities and the institutional capacity in these zones. There is evidence of leakage, or resources going to less poor parroquias, however, this 'leakage' should be interpreted with caution. Given the small scale of FISE projects, resources going to less poor parroquias may in fact be financing activities within pockets of poverty in these parroquias.

Table 3. FISE

Poverty Zone - Rural	% of Committed $	Original Target (%)
1	47	40
2	17	30
3	11	20
4	24	10
5	0	--
Poverty Zone - Urban		
1	21	40
2	11	30
3	58	20
4	8	10
5	2	--
Poverty Zone - Total		
1	34	40
2	14	30
3	35	20
4	16	10
5	1	--

A further consideration is the indicators themselves. The largest distortion in the observed targeting outcome versus the original goal is in the urban parroquias ranked '3', where 58 percent of FISE urban resources are going versus a program goal of only 20 percent. To analyze this case in particular, a listing of these parroquias was reviewed. Over 30 percent of the resources in the urban '3' group are allocated to six urban parroquias - Ximena, Tarqui and Febres Cordero in Guayaquil; Tarqui and Andres de Vera in Manabi; and Santo Domingo de los Colorados in Pichincha. These parroquias are quite densely populated. In Guayaquil, these areas are known to be the poorest in the city;

however, the average parroquial malnutrition rates are not that low, and hence they have received a '3' ranking. Therefore, in urban areas, going down to the parroquial level in targeting mechanisms still leaves significant problems of heterogeneity within parroquias and difficulties in determining real leakage.

As a demand-driven agency, FISE relies on project proposals from a variety of organizations. As noted previously, NGOs and grassroots organizations account for over half of FISE's current portfolio. Figure 1 shows the amount of projects by type of institution for each of the poverty zones of the country. FISE's ability to reach the poorest, or '1', parroquias is a function of the open access to grassroots organizations.

Figure 1. Committed FISE Resources by Poverty Zone (Total) Sponsoring Agency (in US$)

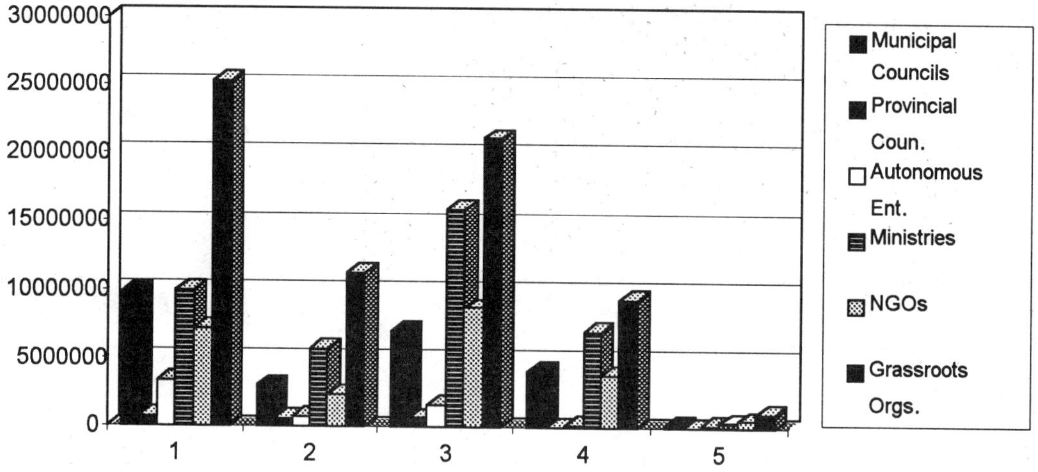

Cost Analysis

Administrative Costs. Of FISE's overall program target of $120 million, administrative costs were estimated at $9.7 million or 8 percent of total program amount. These administrative costs were defined broadly to encompass all expenditures not related to financing of projects, including salaries, operating expenses, capital expenditures on vehicles, computers, equipment, and external technical assistance. The capital expenditures, the bulk of which are applied to setting up this new agency, amount to about 25 percent of administrative costs and are costs not faced by the other programs analyzed since these rely extensively on existing institutional infrastructure.

FISE's administrative costs tend to decrease over time as scale of operations expands, capital investments are amortized, and disbursements are made against projects which have generated administrative costs during promotion and appraisal. For instance, as of December 31, 1994, administrative costs represented 17 percent of disbursements, a ratio which will decline to an overall of 8 percent by the end of 1997.

Costs of Targeting. FISE incurs potential targeting costs on two levels. First, the identification of project types and the geographical targeting system have been virtually costless as they have used existing personnel and information. The second type of targeting cost relates to the demand-driven nature of FISE. If FISE simply opened its doors and relied on demand from any region on a first come first serve basis, there would be no targeting costs. However, to get sufficient demand from poorer, less organized areas, the Promotion Department was established to ensure that FISE reached its target population. As such, the costs of the Department can be considered a cost of targeting. To the extent that the Promotion Department undertakes other activities, such as project reformulation and programming functions, attributing all the costs of the department inflates slightly the estimate of targeting costs.

Nonetheless, to arrive at an overall estimate, we include the actual expenditures of the Department for 1993 and 1994, US$26,673 and US$90,574 respectively including salaries and travel expenses, and assume that the full functioning of the Department would continue through 1995, then be scaled down to one half in 1996, with full phasing out in 1997, since by the end of 1995 FISE should have accumulated a bank of project proposals well in excess of its financing capabilities. Under this assumption, total costs of the Promotion Department would amount to US$250,000, or 0.2 percent of the total program amount.

Case Study Three: School Lunch Program

Description of Program

The School Lunch Program ('Colaciones Escolares') has been operated by the Ministry of Education since January, 1990 with support of the World Food Program. The objectives of the program are to provide nutrition supplements to primary schools considered at risk for their socio-economic conditions as a stimulus to school participation and academic achievement. Analysis of the program can be divided in two phases, the first corresponding to 1990-93 and the second beginning in 1994 when the program was substantially restructured based on the findings of the first three years.

During the first phase, rations of bread were to be provided to 300,000 children located in 1,200 public primary schools covering nineteen of the twenty-one provinces of the country. The total cost of this phase was US$16.3 million. Although the intent of the program was to provide rations only to those public schools where children came from disadvantaged families, several design and operational flaws limited its effectiveness. A politically motivated expansion in the number of children receiving rations to 1 million in over 8,000 schools resulted in insufficient ration amounts (117 children per school versus an original estimate of 250 per school), irregular distribution, and a reduction in the number of days each child was to receive a ration from the initial 190 days to 90 days. Several design features biased against participation of the poorest schools, including a requirement that all schools be located within a 25km radius of the bakeries, and that parents would have to pay for the transport costs to the school. In addition, administrative controls were deficient, with significant levels of corruption suspected in the processing and distribution of the rations and a lack of effective monitoring of the poverty targeting objectives of the program.

An evaluation of the program in 1993 called for its restructuring, keeping in mind the overall importance of the objectives and the widespread poverty conditions of the country. Centrally-processed, fortified biscuits along with powdered milk are to be distributed to 500,000 children for a total program cost of US$22.7 million over the 1995-

97 period. Transport costs are included in the program to avoid excluding poor and more remote beneficiaries. In selected cases where transport costs were considered prohibitive, for instance in remote communities in the Amazon Basin, funds rather than food are to be provided.

Targeting Mechanisms

The new program designed a transparent targeting methodology which generated a pre-selected list of schools to participate in the program. Data was collected on: (i) malnutrition levels through the National System of Food and Nutrition Monitoring (SISVAN), (ii) population by age structure from the Census, and (iii) school enrollment data from the Ministry of Education. A ranking of schools was then determined based on the parroquial-level malnutrition data. Individual schools were selected based on the following criteria: all schools in parroquias with a malnutrition level over 45 percent, and for schools located in parroquias with less than 45 percent all schools with only one teacher (unidocente) or fewer than 30 students as a proxy for identifying schools which are typical in poorer rural areas. Based on these criteria, an estimated 61 percent of the nation's public primary schools will be participating in the program. An information system is being established to provide effective monitoring of the targeting system.

Targeting Results

Based on the list of 7560 primary schools selected, 73 percent of the students benefiting from the program are in rural areas. In addition, with an average number of students per school of 67, compared to 117 experienced in the first phase, the redesigned program reflects a commitment reaching the rural poor. Overall, two-thirds of the programs participants are from parroquias with over 45 percent malnutrition. The remaining one-third represents schools with less than 30 students or with only one teacher. There are very few exceptions to these criteria, although some individual cases exist.

Cost Analysis

Administrative Costs. Of the total three-year program cost of US$22.7 million, purchase, processing and transport of food accounts for 94 percent, with the remaining 6 percent absorbed by administrative costs of the program, including personnel, materials, procurement administration and other operating expenditures. This relatively low administrative cost is in part due to the nature of the benefit (delivery of a standard ration), the scale of the program and the effect of 'piggybacking' the program onto the existing structure of the Ministry of Education, and as such does not factor in the added effort by school administrators and teachers in delivering the benefit to students.

Costs of Targeting. Since the targeting mechanism chosen is based on the use of geographical information freely available, there are no incremental costs of identifying participating schools. There are some additional costs in actually delivering the program benefits to a largely rural, dispersed population. As seen in the data, the program has a preferential incidence on rural school children. The necessity of transporting rations from the center of each parroquia to dispersed rural schools combined with the attention placed on including small schools as recipients implies a greater logistical effort and increased transportation costs than if the program had chosen participating schools on a strictly random basis. Assuming a national distribution of rural/urban schools of 53:47 percent, versus the targeted program outcome of 74:26 percent rural/urban, the incremental local transport costs of the targeted approach are about 20 percent of local transport costs, or less than 0.5 percent of the total program cost.

Case Study Four: The Basic Health Project FASBASE

<u>Description of Program</u>

In the early 1990's, the Government began discussions with the World Bank regarding support to Ecuador's community and family health care program. These discussions culminated in the preparation of the US$102.2 million Second Social Development Project: Health and Nutrition (FASBASE) to support the Government's planned investment programs for the expansion and strengthening of basic health and nutrition services, including basic sanitation. The specific objectives of the project are to: (a) gradually expand basic health care, nutrition and sanitation coverage to reach the poorest population groups, (b) improve the quality of basic health care services already provided to the poor, and (c) strengthen decision-making and management of public institutions involved in the delivery of basic health, nutrition and sanitation programs.

The project consists of four main components, including improvements in basic health care coverage and quality (US$69.8 million), introduction of nutrition interventions as part of the basic primary health care package (US$6.4 million), investments in basic sanitation and safe water supplies (US$13.2 million), and sectoral policy development and institutional strengthening of the Ministry of Health (US$12.8 million). The planning of project activities is based on the Ministry of Health's long-term health sector development plan. To this end, the Ministry of Health has divided the country into 195 local health service areas. A medium-term investment program covering the 71 poorest areas was established to concentrate investment resources initially. This medium-term plan covers a target population of about 3.2 million Ecuadorans representing about 30 percent of the total population. The Bank-financed project covers 40 of these health areas, with the remaining 31 areas to be financed eventually by the IDB and/or other donors. The project was initiated in 1993 and has a seven-year timeframe.

<u>Targeting Mechanisms</u>

FASBASE mainly uses a geographic targeting mechanism. Given its objective of reaching Ecuador's poor, FASBASE established a targeting system to allow for a selection of priority health areas. Developed in 1991, the methodology is based on a system of classifying Ecuador's cantons according to a taxonomy of critical 'poverty'. Three studies were used to build the classifications.[6] Each study classified cantons on a 1-6 or 1-4 range. The ranges established in each study were then standardized into a summary classification of 1-4 with 1 denoting cantons with the highest need for intervention. Using this methodology, 5 percent of the country's population was found to be located in cantons with a '1' ranking, 20 percent in category '2', 53 percent in category '3', 15 percent in category '4' and 7 percent in cantons that were unranked.

The canton level was selected due to: (a) the nature of a health service area which establishes a global health network, including reference hospitals, requiring a minimum

---

[6]   Suarez, J. (1988), Briehl, J. (1990), Freire, W. (1989).

population, and, (b) to a certain extent, the lack of disaggregated data at the parroquial level. However, the canton as a unit of analysis presents several problems, most notably the lack of consistency between a canton and a health service area. In several rural areas, health service areas are larger than canton boundaries. Conversely, cantons which encompass large urban areas, such as the cantons of Quito and Guayaquil, have many health service areas inside them and a large degree of heterogeneity of socio-economic conditions.

FASBASE attempted to refine the methodology using the 1988 INEM Household Survey to assess what share of each canton's population lived under poverty conditions in order to estimate the number of poor which would be covered by the health service system. However, this survey covered only *urban* Ecuador. Applying this standard urban-based poverty coefficient across all cantons, be they rural or urban, was methodologically inconsistent and did little to increase FASBASE's ability to distinguish poverty levels between health areas. Additional considerations were used to select the 40 health areas under FASBASE, including regional distribution and variety in the types of areas between rural, peri-urban and metropolitan areas. An additional health area was included in 1994 due to a natural disaster which occurred in one rural area. There were no allocative targets set by poverty level.

The water and basic sanitation component of the project is oriented to investments on a smaller geographical scale than the health area, and as such developed a separate targeting methodology. The basic criteria to be applied include: (a) only areas covered by the health component and (b) only communities between 250 - 2,000 inhabitants, although smaller and more dispersed may be included later. These criteria were expected to generate a list of 700 communities as candidates, of which 165 would be selected based on: (a) representative range of communities in terms of size, location and socio-economic characteristics due to the pilot nature of the component, (b) preference on population of 250-1,000, (c) incidence of water-borne diseases, (d) status of existing water and sanitation facilities, and (e) a participatory assessment to judge demand and willingness to pay. It is too early to assess the application of these criteria as the final 165 communities have yet to be determined.

Targeting Results

Table 4 presents the distribution of FASBASE beneficiaries according to the classification used by the project. Compared with total population figures, both FASBASE and the overall Ministry of Health medium-term plan present a slightly favorable bias towards health areas located in the highest priority (category 1) cantons. However, approximately 80 percent of FASBASE beneficiaries are located in cantons characterized by lower average levels of need (categories 3 and 4), which is above the overall population share of 68 percent for these cantons. This is largely a function of the canton-based classification, where average 'poverty' levels are much lower for urban cantons, effectively disguising the urban poor. Indeed, 40 percent of FASBASE beneficiaries are in urban areas and a further 40 percent in health areas characterized as urban-rural.

Table 4. FASBASE

Category	% of Total Population	% of 'Poor' according to FASBASE	% of MOH Medium-Term Plan	% of FASBASE Beneficiaries
1	4.9	4.9	7.8	7.8
2	20.0	20.5	23.4	11.9
3	53.1	56.2	54.0	64.8
4	15.0	14.9	13.5	15.6
Unranked	7.0	3.5	1.3	0
Total	100.0	100.0	100.0	100.0

Cost Analysis

An analysis of administrative and targeting costs is generally not applicable to this type of program for several reasons. Since FASBASE is in effect 'piggybacked' onto existing health services it is not possible to estimate the actual costs of carrying out activities such as health promotion campaigns, nutritional monitoring and pre-natal screenings which use MOH personnel already in place in the health areas. In addition, the wide range of objectives, including institutional strengthening of the MOH and the development of health policies, call for expenditures not directly associated with service delivery. In terms of targeting costs, the use of geographical targeting based on existing data reduces to virtually zero the cost of identifying participating health areas.

The administrative costs of the water and sanitation component alone are more applicable to analysis. Of the US$11.8 million budget (base cost) to implement 165 water and latrine projects and upgrade 42 existing water systems, US$8.7 million (74 percent) represents the cost of the water and sanitation investments, design of the systems and training of users; US$0.55 million (5 percent) will finance sector studies, and US$2.57 million (22 percent) represents administrative costs in the form of program personnel and consultants, equipment and materials, monitoring and evaluation, coordination and supervision. This relatively high share of administrative costs is due to the pilot nature of the program and the extensive use of technical consultants, both national and international. It is not possible to estimate the costs devoted to selecting participating communities, and hence targeting costs of this component can not be determined.

Case Study Five: INNFA: Child Development Program

Description of Program

The National Institute of Children and the Family (INNFA) is an autonomous agency of the Government dedicated to addressing the most pressing problems of Ecuador's children and their families. To this end, INNFA operates a Child Development Program (PDI) which includes child development centers, public feeding and school support centers, and early education units. In addition, INNFA runs five shelters which serve 182 orphaned and abandoned children. Efforts are being made to orient INNFA's activities to the most needy segments of Ecuadorian society.

As of mid-1994, the PDI program worked with a network of 45 public feeding and school support centers reaching 3,520 children aged 5-12 and 967 child development centers for children aged 0-5 distributed throughout the country. Coverage is estimated at about 33,000. At these centers, children receive day care, early education and nutritional supplements equivalent to seventy percent of daily caloric requirements. Communities provide the physical facilities and administration of the centers is arranged through contracts with grassroots organizations and parents' committees. INNFA trains, evaluates and supervises the mothers providing the services as well as the developmental path of the children.

Targeting Mechanisms

INNFA has recently introduced a more narrowly focused targeting framework which is a combination of geographic targeting plus an individual assessment. The network of INNFA's PDI centers has developed over time and in response to local demand as well as INNFA's own criteria of regional distribution, administrative factors and other considerations of how resources should be allocated. In 1993, INNFA began to place more attention to the targeting of its program, attempting to locate any new centers in marginal areas. To determine these locations, INNFA has utilized CONADE's Consolidated Poverty Map to identify priority cantons and parroquias. The methodology used by INNFA does not assign targets or cut-off points to guide resource allocation decisions. In addition, once the priority locations are selected, an individual screening mechanism is used based on malnutrition, as measured by height and weight for age, of the children applying for entry to the centers.

Targeting Results

Overall, 54 percent of children attended by INNFA are located in rural parroquias, with the remaining 46 percent located in urban areas. While no specific targets have been set against which performance can be compared, we can examine the distribution of funds using parroquial-level malnutrition data. Table 5 shows the incidence of INNFA participants. While one-third of program participants are in the parroquias with the highest malnutrition levels, in this case above 45 percent, there appears to be a significant amount of leakage into less needy areas. One reason for these results include a lack of flexibility in allocating resources since once a center is funded it tends to continue to be funded; any improvements in targeting efficiency are on the margin in terms of new centers that can be opened. In addition, because of the small scale of the benefit delivered, with the average number of 35 children per center, it is quite possible that actual participants are poorer than a parroquial average would suggest.

Table 5. INNFA

Parroquial Malnutrition Levels (percent)	Share of INNFA Participants (percent)
Over 45	37.3
35.1 - 45	16.7
20.1 - 35	44.3
15.1 - 20	0.8
Under 15	1.0

Regarding the second level of targeting, screening individual children for entrance to centers, in practice this methodology was *not* used as a filter. Rather, baseline information about the malnutrition levels of participants was collected for growth monitoring purposes. To program staff, rejecting children that did not satisfy malnutrition criteria was deemed not feasible in the local context.

Cost Analysis

The total budget of INNFA for 1995 was approximately US$29 million. This total includes the central operations of INNFA (US$9 million) as well as the costs of the three programs it runs: the Child Development Program outlined above (US$15 million), the program for working children (US$2 million) and the health services program (US$3 million). Since the overhead of INNFA is shared between these programs, this distorts slightly the analysis of administrative costs of the Child Development Program. Nevertheless, overall, administrative costs account for 24 percent of INNFA's total budget. As such, INNFA is one of the least efficient of any of the targeted social programs reviewed. Administrative costs of the Child Development Program itself are estimated by INNFA at about 2 percent, however this does not include any of the administrative costs of the central operations of INNFA and as such is not a valid reflection of the cost structure.

The targeting costs of identifying potential beneficiaries can be divided into two parts. First, INNFA has begun to use CONADE's poverty map to identify high risk geographical areas. As a public good, this information has not generated any internal costs. Second, screening of individual beneficiaries is based on the same methodology employed by ORI. Existing staff in local offices promote the opening and monitor the operations of child development centers, one function of which is to screen potential beneficiaries. While data are not available, we can assume that the targeting costs of INNFA would be about the same as those ORI, which were estimated at well under one percent of total program costs.

Case Study Six: The Rural Basic Education Project PROMECEB

Description of Program

In 1990, the Program for Improving the Quality of Primary Education (PROMECEB) was initiated with funding from the Inter-American Development Bank and the Government of Ecuador. The program is executed by the Ministry of Education and seeks to improve rural primary education through curriculum development, provision of textbooks and educational materials, infrastructure improvements and teacher training. The project supports the Government's efforts at spatial planning and organization of the educational system around hub schools which would be centers of excellence to provide both models of high quality education and nuclei for networks of surrounding schools. Total project costs are estimated at US$48.9 million and would cover the establishment of 80 such rural networks encompassing 1300 rural primary schools in 18 provinces of the country. This accounts for roughly 9 percent of all primary schools and about 24 percent of the projected number of rural networks needed to cover the country.

Targeting Mechanisms

The planning and selection of the networks to be included in the project were based on a number of considerations. Although no explicit social indicators were discussed, overall socio-economic conditions and community cohesion were listed as factors in determining selection of networks. The lack of specific social or poverty criteria is explained in part by the view that the risk of program benefits being captured by the non-poor is extremely limited in a program that focuses on public primary schools in rural areas. In determining the location of the hub school several criteria were applied. First, to be designated as a hub, a school must be a 'complete' school with all grades of basic education. It should also serve as a central point for schools which are located no further than 15 kilometers away. These networks should be as homogenous linguistically and culturally as possible, although several networks encompass both rural and urban areas due the local conditions in certain zones.

Based on a school facilities map generated by the Department of Rural Education of the Ministry of Education, a suggested list of 80 networks was developed at the early stages of the project. Subsequently, about one-fourth of the original candidate networks have been changed. Reasons range from shifting populations to initial oversights (i.e., no schools from the Oriente zone were included in the first round).

Targeting Results

Of Ecuador's 21 provinces, 15 participate in PROMECEB. No specific indicators were used to define priority sites and -- again -- due to lacking poverty data on a geographic basis, we can only compare the incidence of program benefits against the malnutrition map. Over half of PROMECEB's program beneficiaries are located in parroquias with malnutrition rates of 45 percent and above.

Cost Analysis

Because PROMECEB is 'piggybacked' onto the existing education system and has objectives beyond service delivery, including institutional strengthening of the Ministry of Education, analysis of administrative and targeting costs is not very applicable. Nonetheless, the salary and operating costs for the project implementation unit represent 7.8 percent of the total project cost net of financial charges. There were no incremental costs of targeting associated with the selection of the participating networks.

Case Study Seven: The Urban Basic Education Project EB/PRODEC

Description of the Program

In 1992, the Government supported by the World Bank launched the First Social Development Project: Education and Training (EB/PRODEC). The six-year US$118.7 million project has two main areas of intervention: improving access to and quality of urban primary education, particularly in low-income areas, and support for adult literacy and training activities. For the purposes of this analysis, only the first component will be analyzed. Support for urban primary education (US$76.9 million) consists of: providing quality-enhancing inputs through a system of school networks similar to PROMECEB, developing a national student assessment system, and improving the Ministry of Education capacities in budgeting and sectoral management. The quality-enhancing investments in local school systems include infrastructure upgrading, in-service teacher training, the addition of pre-school classes to existing primary schools, provision of textbooks and educational materials, and improvements in special education services. The project is intended to cover 55 urban-based school networks reaching an estimated 482,000 students.

Targeting Mechanisms

Selection of participating school networks is based on an identification of marginal urban zones. These marginal zones (of cities with more than 15,000 inhabitants) are identified by computing a service indicator from Census data. The service indicator comprises indexes relating to the quality of housing, crowding, sewerage access, hygiene facilities, the school attendance level of minors and the 'economic capacity' of the zone.[7] Second, within the so defined marginal urban areas, case by case studies of schools are conducted which lead to the exact definition of the investment area. The defined investment area, hence, need not correspond exactly to the marginal urban area defined by the Census; in several cases it covers the whole city or even (in one case) the whole Canton.

Targeting Results

As of October 1994, 47 cantons had been identified, including 27 locations for the establishment of networks, with an average of 18 schools per network. It is difficult to assess whether the project is reaching the poorest urban areas of the country for a number of reasons. First, due to the rolling nature of network selection, it is not possible to judge overall targeting effectiveness as only about half of the eventual networks participating have been selected. More importantly, the spatial planning of urban networks does not correspond necessarily to the parroquial division which is the basis for most of the existing social indicator data. Overlapping boundaries between networks and parroquias renders ineffective the use of standardized poverty indicators across parroquias. While the canton level information is available, for urban cantons, the high degree of heterogeneity with the canton leaves it a poor guide for poverty targeting in urban areas.

Cost Analysis

Like PROMECEB, EB/PRODEC is 'piggybacked' onto the existing education system and has objectives beyond service delivery, including institutional strengthening of the Ministry of Education, as well as improving adult literacy and training. Hence, analysis of administrative and targeting costs is not very applicable. Nonetheless, for comparative purposes, the salary and operating costs (not including investment costs of equipment and vehicles) for the project implementation unit represent 7.0 percent of the total project cost. There are no incremental costs of targeting associated with the selection of the participating networks.

5.   A Consolidated View of Targeting Accuracy

In developing targeting mechanisms, each program has used a variety of indicators and methodologies to identify geographical target areas and several programs have combined this with individual assessment and self-targeting mechanisms. The differences in criteria arc oftcn justified due to the types of benefits each program delivers. For

---

[7]   The economic capacity variable is constructed from data on age and education level of household heads and the number of family members without an occupation.

instance, criteria regarding enrollment rates, school size and other planning variables are appropriate to use in selecting areas in the two education projects reviewed, EB/PRODEC and PROMECEB. In a similar fashion, health indicators for health projects and malnutrition indicators for both the school lunch program and child development projects are used to more closely link the characteristics of the beneficiaries with the service to be provided.

For none of the above-discussed projects are we able to calculate targeting indicators such as coverage or leakage rates. Programs do not monitor or periodically evaluate their beneficiary population. As mentioned above, it is not possible to employ the Living Standard Measurement Survey to provide us with data on the targeting accuracy of individual social projects because too few beneficiaries are reached by the household survey.

It might be, nevertheless, interesting to compare the geographic distribution of program funds using a common yardstick. As we don't have a poverty map based on expenditure measures in Ecuador, we limit ourselves to comparing the geographic distribution of funds to the incidence of benefits for programs that could be identified at the parroquial level (ORI, FISE, School Lunch, INNFA, PROMECEB) with the parroquial level malnutrition map. As Table 6 shows, for all programs a significant share of program benefits are reaching the parroquias with the highest malnutrition rates. There is virtually no leakage of benefits to parroquias with less than 20 percent malnutrition rates. The school lunch program and PROMECEB on average have higher incidence in zones of most severe malnutrition than INNFA, FISE and ORI.

Table 6. Program Incidence According to Malnutrition Rates
(Percent)

Malnutrition Level	School Lunch	INNFA	ORI	FISE	PROMECEB
Maln +45%	66	37	46	46	51
Maln 35.1 - 45	16	17	14	11	14
Maln 20.1 - 35	18	44	38	43	30
Maln 15.1 - 20	0	1	1	1	5
Maln 0 - 15	0	1	0	0	0
Maln. +70%	21	15	18	17	26

In the case of PROMECEB, this outcome is largely a result of its exclusive concentration in rural areas, where the average malnutrition is 51 percent compared with 39 percent for urban parroquias. Indeed, when only rural areas are analyzed using the same breakdown of malnutrition rates, the incidence of program benefits for rural parroquias with over 45 percent malnutrition rate is as follows: school lunch - 70 percent, ORI - 69 percent, FISE - 68 percent PROMECEB 54 percent and INNFA - 51 percent.

The outcome of the school lunch program is largely a reflection of the methodology used to select participating schools. All schools in parroquias with malnutrition rates of over 45 percent were selected, with exceptions made for schools either under 30 students or with only one teacher in parroquias with malnutrition rates under 45 percent. Therefore, the 34 percent of participants which are from parroquias with lower levels of malnutrition represents the program's attempt to get at pockets of poverty amid generally 'better off' regions.

For FISE, INNFA and ORI a number of criteria were used to determine resource allocation only one of which was parroquial level malnutrition rates. In the cases of ORI and INNFA, reliance on existing infrastructure reduces flexibility in selecting beneficiary communities. In the case of FISE, the demand-driven nature of a social fund makes the agency dependent on the motivation and capacity of communities and sponsoring agencies to apply for FISE grants. In addition, for all three programs, the scale of benefit is quite small for each individual investment. Therefore, for the program benefits going to less poor parroquias, it is quite possible that communities receiving support are well below the parroquial malnutrition averages if local promotion and screening activities are being carried out well.

Political discussion in Ecuador regarding incidence of program benefits has largely been a debate about regional and provincial distribution. This issue cuts across poverty considerations and begs the question of, in addition to whether the poor are being reached, to what extent is there a 'fair' distribution of program benefits on a national level. Although the poor are not evenly distributed across regions, all regions contain significant numbers of Ecuador's poor. Even if a social program fulfilled its objective of reaching only poor beneficiaries, if all of these beneficiaries were concentrated in a given region, the outcome would be less than optimal from a national perspective. The following graph presents the distribution of program benefits by the main ecological regions of the country. The distribution of the poor (headcount index, compare Working Paper 1) and the population shares are given for comparison. Based on the distribution of the poor, the Costa should receive most of the expenditures, followed by the Sierra and the Oriente.

Figure 2: Distribution of Social Program Benefits by Region

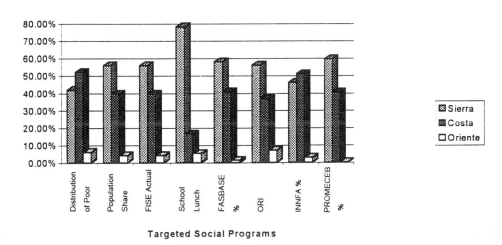

Targeted Social Programs

As seen in Figure 2, with the exception of INNFA, all of the targeted social programs reviewed 'overspend' in the Sierra region, compared to either straight population shares (column 2) or shares adjusted for poverty levels (column 1). Partly, this is due to most programs using malnutrition data as the only (or at least as one important) base for their geographical targeting. The most striking example for this 'overspending' is the school lunch program, with almost 80 percent of its benefits going to the Sierra region. Yet, as shown above, the school lunch program has the most accurate targeting in terms of the incidence of its benefits in zones of greatest malnutrition. Since the program uses principally malnutrition data to determine school selection, the fact that average malnutrition in Sierra parroquias is 55 percent, versus 33 percent in the Coastal region and 49 percent in the Amazon Basin, tends to direct benefits toward the Sierra.

Looking only at the distribution on a regional level can conceal important differences in incidence between provinces. For instance, the skewing toward the Sierra region could be interpreted as an effect of centralization around the capital, Quito, particularly since all of the programs reviewed are headquartered in Quito. However, as shown in Table 7 below, the province of Pichincha, where Quito is located, receives less than its population share of all major programs with the exception of FASBASE. Instead, other Sierra provinces such as Chimborazo and Cotopaxi consistently receive a greater share of program benefits than their population. These provinces are usually associated with the rural Andean poverty of Ecuador.

While there is a need to seek a fair regional distribution, there is the danger that debates about regional distribution will obscure the issue of whether poor are being reached or not. In certain instances, poverty targeting objectives are being met but not optimal regional distribution. The opposite is also possible, with optimal regional distribution cloaking significant leakage to the non-poor.

Table 7. Provincial Distribution of Program Benefits

Province	Population Share	FISE %	FISE Target %	School Lunch	FASBASE %	ORI	INNFA %	PROME CEB%
Azuay	5.3	6.9	5.4	10.4	3.6	5.0	10.5	4.2
Bolivar	1.6	1.3	1.6	4.9	3.7	2.7	0.0	6.4
Canar	2.0	1.4	2.2	6.3	2.1	5.0	0.9	5.5
Carchi	1.5	1.1	1.6	4.5	1.4	3.0	0.8	4.1
Cotopaxi	2.9	5.9	4.6	7.9	3.2	3.5	3.7	9.2
Chimborazo	3.8	8.2	5.8	10.0	6.8	8.3	7.0	4.3
El Oro	4.3	4.7	3.4	1.0	3.3	4.0	2.2	9.1
Esmeraldas	3.2	2.3	3.3	2.2	6.6	5.9	4.7	8.2
Guayas	26.3	17.6	21.4	3.8	19.5	17.8	24.7	7.6
Imbabura	2.8	6.9	3.1	6.2	5.2	4.5	1.8	3.8
Loja	4.0	6.4	4.1	10.1	6.9	12.8	3.0	5.5
Los Rios	5.5	4.3	5.3	2.2	5.4	3.8	5.1	8.7
Manabi	10.8	10.7	11.2	7.4	5.9	5.4	14.2	6.9
Morona S.	0.9	1.4	2.2	0.8	0.0	1.8	2.1	0.0
Napo	1.0	1.0	3.4	2.1	0.0	1.2	0.0	0.0
Pastaza	0.4	0.2	0.4	1.0	0.0	1.7	0.7	0.0
Pichincha	18.4	13.2	12.1	10.2	18.6	10.0	17.9	9.0
Tungurahua	3.8	4.5	3.6	7.7	6.4	1.4	0.5	7.7
Zamora Ch.	0.7	0.9	1.5	0.7	0.0	0.7	0.0	0.0
Galapagos	0.1	0.5	0.1	0.0	0.0	0.0	0.0	0.0
Sucumbios	0.8	0.8	3.5	0.8	1.3	1.6	0.0	0.0
	100.0	100.0	100.0	100.0	100.0	100.0	100.0	100.0

Summary of Cost Analysis. Based on this review, the administrative and targeting costs of the major targeted social programs in Ecuador are in line with international experience. As shown in Table 8 below, overall administrative costs range from 6 to 15 percent, excluding the 22 percent overhead for the pilot water and sanitation component of FASBASE. However, these figures should be interpreted with caution. Estimates of costs associated with project implementation units of internationally financed programs (e.g. FASBASE, PROMECEB, EB/PRODEC) suffer distortions for the following reasons: (a) a portion of the administrative cost is related to the financing source itself (i.e., personnel to handle procurement and disbursement matters) rather than delivery of program benefits, (b) these programs tend to piggyback most extensively onto existing universal services (health and education) which blurs identification of true program costs, and (c) the variety of objectives beyond service delivery (building institutional capacity and developing sectoral policies) makes a comparison difficult. In addition, definitions of what is included as an administrative expense vary widely between programs, such as the inclusion of investment costs (e.g., purchase of vehicles and equipment) under administration and differences in the treatment of monitoring and supervision costs. And finally, administrative costs are affected to varying degrees by the scale of program, type of benefit, and managerial efficiency. For instance, an expected tripling of ORI coverage would halve the share of administrative costs from 16 to 8 percent.

Table 8. Summary of Administrative and Targeting Costs of Social Programs

Program	Primary Targeting Mechanism	Administrative Cost (as % of Total Cost)	Targeting Costs (as % of Total Cost)
ORI	Geographical/ Individual Assessment	15%	0.2%
FISE	Geographical/ Self	8% (including invest-ment - equipment, TA) 6% (net of investment)	0.2%
School Lunch	Geographical	6 %	0 (to identify poor) 0.5% (incremental cost of reaching poor)
PROMECEB	Geographical	8%	0
EB/PRODEC	Geographical	7%	0
FASBASE Total Water/Sanitation Component	Geographical	N/A 22%	0 - N/A N/A
INNFA	Geographical/ Individual Assessment	N/A	N/A
Grosh ranges:	Programs with Individual Assessment Mechanisms	0.4 - 29%	0.4 - 8%
	Programs with Geographic Targeting	4 - 16%	0 - 2%
	Programs with Self-Targeting	3 - 10%	0

The costs of targeting itself are quite low, and in all cases represent well under 1 percent of total program costs. This result is also in line with similar experiences in Latin

America as presented by Grosh (1994). This cuts against the general impression that in a country with widespread poverty, it is not worth the time and expense establishing mechanisms to identify potential program beneficiaries. In fact, the costs are quite marginal and, based on the results of targeting accuracy, can have a significant effect of improving the incidence of program benefits to the poorest segment of society.

Potential Incentive Effects and Other Considerations. In theory, targeting schemes may generate incentive effects. The principal of these effects, as outlined in Grosh (1994), are related to leisure-labor choices, relocation, and unproductive behavior. The leisure-labor issue occurs in programs which use income as a means test for access to benefits. If benefits are sufficient, people may chose to work less to quality for the program. This does not apply to any of the social programs reviewed. The relocation problem may occur in geographically targeted programs, where access to geographically determined benefits affects potential participants' decision on where to live, where to send children to school, which health post to visit, etc. In this case, the non-poor would seek access to services located only in poorer areas. To date, no program has analyzed this risk. Given the relative scale of program benefits and the degree of associated negative incentives of moving into poorer areas (lack of access to water and sanitation facilities, lower quality schools, social stigma, rural isolation) it is doubtful that relocation is a serious consideration in program design. And finally, there is a potential problem of unproductive behavior in programs like INNFA and ORI that screen individual participants using malnutrition criteria. In such cases, mothers may be tempted to underfeed their children to guarantee access to program benefits. In both INNFA and ORI local staff have dropped the use of malnutrition as a screen for not only the potentially unproductive behavior of mothers but the social and family level conflicts that might ensue.

A further consideration in overall program effects are political and stakeholder interests which may affect program design and implementation. For instance, regional politics may affect benefit patterns either in addition to or in place of other geographical poverty targeting mechanisms. Indeed, the selection of which indicators to use in defining poverty may have political implications.

6.   Lessons From Targeted Social Programs in Ecuador

The experience of the main targeted social programs in Ecuador demonstrate that social investments can effectively and efficiently reach poor populations. The experience also shows that a certain level of leakage does occur and improvements can be made in program design, targeting methodology and program implementation to heighten the impact on the poor and reduce the chance of leakage. Since the social programs reviewed all rely primarily on geographical targeting, the lessons regarding targeting are more specific to this type of mechanism. These lessons can be summarized as follows:

- *The costs of running these programs and identifying potential beneficiaries are within reasonable expectations.* These costs are more a function of program design and managerial efficiency than the efforts to reach poor beneficiaries. Strategies such as increasing the scale of pilot-types programs, controlling unit costs and improving managerial efficiency could further reduce the overhead spent on delivering program benefits.

- **Scale of targeting matters tremendously.** To reduce leakage and other forms of mistargeting, the scale of the geographical unit selected should be as closely aligned as possible to the scale of the potential benefits. For instance, using the canton level for large urban areas is ineffective in allocating resources to poor urban areas due to the heterogeneity of socio-economic conditions within the canton. Parroquial level indicators improve the chances of identifying poor areas, though flexibility should be allowed for programs to reach poor within better-off parroquias. Examples of this include individual daycare centers and other small-scale social investments. Clearly, no reliable targeting can be done on a provincial or regional level.

- **Program design affects outcome independent of targeting mechanism.** Focusing exclusively on methodologies for selecting beneficiaries misses important issues in overall program design which in the end may have more relevance for the impact on the poor. Each program should be analyzed to identify elements in design and procedures which would either promote or reduce participation by the poor. For instance, ORI and INNFA's reliance on existing infrastructure limits flexibility in assigning resources to priority areas. FISE's demand-driven nature which relies on the ability of communities and intermediary organizations to present project proposals may hamper its performance in terms of targeting outcomes. Criteria used by EB/PRODEC and PROMECEB in defining school networks, including the requirement that the hub be a complete school, minimum number of students, and other educational system planning criteria, are correct given the overall objectives of these programs. However, they tend to bias against inclusion of the poorest, most remote dispersed populations.

- **Although geographical targeting is accepted as a guideline for allocating resources, a consolidated map has to be developed.** Each program uses a different set of indicators to define priority areas. The majority have used elements of CONADE's Consolidated Poverty Map. The CONADE information is not sufficiently disaggregated to allow for targeting at the parroquial level in urban areas. Moreover, the validity of the map itself is subject to discussion as it is built from several different poverty maps which vary in the degree of coverage, reliability and timeliness of the statistics used (e.g., the Census data from 1990 are not incorporated in the map). Several programs have based targeting to a greater degree on malnutrition data but this is obviously only an imperfect poverty indicator. The unmet basic needs indicators developed by INEC from the 1990 Census, despite the timeliness of the information, did not allow for a disaggregation of urban cantons and could probably be improved as indicators of poverty (compare Working Paper 1 and Annex 2 to Working Paper 1). In addition, there is some debate as to whether certain indicators can be applied consistently across regions or between rural and urban areas. The decision on which map and which indicators to use is not simply technical; there are political ramifications in terms of regional distribution of resources which must be taken into account.

- *Geographical targeting mechanisms appear deceptively simple, but in fact can be methodologically quite complex.* Related to the previous point, selecting criteria and building operational targeting mechanisms can be difficult. In several instances, the relative weights of criteria and the screening processes were not transparent. In other cases there were flaws in methodology. Even using transparent indicators with solid methodology may not be sufficient. For instance, to render these indicators more operational, rankings are often assigned. However, the definitions of the group rankings are arbitrary and inject an element of differentiation which may overstate reality (i.e., little difference between a high '2' and a low '3').

- *Initial emphasis on setting up targeting mechanisms is usually not followed by consistent monitoring of performance.* Despite the efforts to establish targeting mechanisms, in the end most programs are not able to say to what extent they are reaching the poor. In part this is due to inherent weaknesses in the targeting mechanisms. However, there is a general lack of monitoring of targeting performance, particularly at the central Government level. While each program usually keeps information on where it reaches, the degree to which this information is fed back into the agency to determine future actions varies. In addition, rarely are adjustments made to methodology or new poverty data incorporated as it is made available. The central role of CONADE in orienting public investments and INEC in providing basic statistical information have not been used to fullest advantage. To this end, CONADE and INEC should provide the necessary technical guidance and general monitoring, including updating information on poverty conditions. This monitoring effort should go beyond statistically tracking regional investment patterns. The Living Standards Measurement Survey can generate data on the consumption and income profiles of program beneficiaries. Participatory beneficiary assessments can provide insights into the appropriateness and impact of the services being delivered.

- *In general, coordination between programs should be increased, particularly at the operational level.* Most of these programs operate in the same locations, with limited interaction. At the least, this coordination will avoid duplication of programs. Improved coordination would also help the Government maximize synergies between programs. Some examples include: (a) FISE financing of daycare centers to address the targeting constraint faced by ORI in terms of lack of resources for new infrastructure; (b) nutrition screening of children entering daycare assisted by health programs operating in the area to reduce program costs; and (c) EB/PRODEC and PROMECEB financing main infrastructure and FISE small satellite schools under the network umbrella. Such coordination can only be carried out effectively at the local level and may help to lower overall program costs and increase impact.

References

Briehl, J. (1990), <u>Deterioro de la Vida</u>, Quito

Freire, W. (1989), <u>Diagnostico Alimentario Nutricional y de Salud del Ecuador</u>, CONADE.

Grosh, M. (1994), <u>Administering Targeted Social Programs in Latin America</u>, World Bank Regional and Sectoral Studies, Washington.

Jordan (1994), <u>Informacion Sobre Proyectos y Programas de las Instituciones de Gobierno, Organismos Internacionales y Organizaciones no Gubernamentales</u>, UNICEF, Quito.

Suarez, J. (1988), <u>La Situación de Salud en el Ecuador</u>, Ministry of Health, Quito.

Annex 1

Table A.1: Social Programs in Ecuador

Name of Program	Executing Agency	Beneficiary Type A	Beneficiary Type B	Beneficiary Type C
Programa materno Infantil	Ministry of Public Health	Women	Children	Adolecents
Programa ampliado de inmunizaciones	Ministry of Public Health	Pregnant Women	Under 5 Years of Age	–
Programa de control de enfermedades diarreicas	Ministry of Public Health	–	Under 5 Years of Age	Cholera Victims
Lactancia materna	Ministry of Public Health	Women	Children	–
Programa nacional de control de crecimiento	Ministry of Public Health	–	Children	–
Programa de alimentación complementaria mat. inf.	Ministry of Public Health	Pregnant Women	Under 5 Years of Age	–
Programa de educación alimentaria y nutricional	Ministry of Public Health	–	–	General Population
Lucha operacional contra el bocio endémico	Ministry of Public Health	–	–	Population at Risk
FASBASE	Ministry of Public Health	Pregnant Women	Under 4 years of Age	Rural Population
Salud materna y planificación familiar	Ministry of Public Health	Cancer Risk Fertile Women	–	–
EBPRODEC	Ministry of Education	–	Under 10 Years of Age	Adults without Education
Educación basica de adultos y formación profesional	Ministry of Education	Minors	–	–
Operación rescate infantil	Ministry of Social Welfare	–	Mothers	–
Fondo de Inversión Social de Emergencia	Presidencia	Children Under 6	Under 6 Years of Age	Poor People
Programa de desarrollo infantil	INFA	–	–	–
Programa nacional de discapacidades	INFA	–	–	Affected Population
Programa trabajadores prematuros	INFA	–	Minors 6-17 Years of Age	–
Programa médico social	INFA	Women	Children	General Population
Atención primaria en salud y mejoramiento del saneamiento	Ministry of Public Health	Pregnant Women	Lactating Women	Pre-Schoolers at Risk
Mejoramiento de la educación primaria en zonas prioritarias	Ministry of Education	Under 14 Years of Age	–	–
Ayuda integral para el sector urbano marginal de Quito	Municipio	Low Income Families	–	–
Defender el medio ambiente	PMT-BCE	Children	Adolecents	–
Chicos de la calle	Salesianos	Street Children	–	–
Programa nacional de educación preescolar	Ministry of Education	High Risk Children 4-6 yrs.	–	–

Source: Jordan (1994) and World Bank.

Note: Projects and programs without direct beneficiaries or substantial investments are not included.

Table A.1 (Cont.): Social Programs in Ecuador

Name of Program	Benefits/Services	Coverage	Universal/Group
Programa materno Infantil	Health Care	Women	Specific Group
Programa ampliado de inmunizaciones	Vaccines	National	Universal
Programa de control de enfermedades diarreicas	Health Care	National	Universal
Lactancia materna	Nutritional Education	National	Specific Group
Programa nacional de control de crecimiento	Health Care	National	Universal
Programa de alimentación complementaria mat. inf.	Food Rations & Health Care	National	Specific Group
Programa de educación alimentaria y nutricional	Nutritional Education	National	Universal
Lucha operacional contra el bocio endémico	Iodine Rations	Rural Sierra	Universal
FASBASE	Health, Nutrition, Sanitation	Various Provinces	Specific Group
Salud materna y planificación familiar	Health Care	Various Provinces	not identified
EB/PRODEC	Basic Education Services	Urban Areas in 10 Provinces	Specific Group
Educación basica de adultos y formación profesional	Basic Ed. & Training	National	Specific Group
Operación rescate infantil	Basic Care Services	National	Specific Group
Fondo de Inversión Social de Emergencia	Infra. & Social Services	National	Specific Group
Programa de desarrollo infantil	Basic Care Services	Urban/Rural Various Prov.	Specific Group
Programa nacional de discapacidades	Disabled Care & Prevent.	National	not identified
Programa trabajadores prematuros	Educational Assistance	20 Cities	not identified
Programa médico social	Health Care Subsidies	National	Specific Group
Atención primaria en salud y mejoramiento del saneamiento básic	Health & Sanitation Services	Health Areas of 5 Provinces	Specific Group
Mejoramiento de la educación primaria en zonas prioritarias	Food Supplements	Children of Selected Schools	Specific Group
Ayuda integral para el sector urbano marginal de Quito	Basic Services	Quito	Specific Group
Defender el medio ambiente	Training	National	Universal
Chicos de la calle	Misc. Services	Quito	Specific Group
Programa nacional de educación prescolar	Teaching Services	National	Specific Group

Source: Jordan (1994) and World bank.

Note: Projects and programs without direct beneficiaries or without substantial investments are not included.

Table A.1 (Cont.): Social Programs in Ecuador

Name of Program	Targeting Mechanism	Beneficiaries/Year	Annual Cost
Programa materno Infantil	* Targeted by Program	n.a.	n.a.
Programa ampliado de inmunizaciones	not speficied	n.a.	$270,000
Programa de control de enfermedades diarreicas	not speficied	n.a.	$116,000
Lactancia materna	* Targeted by Program	n.a.	n.a.
Programa nacional de control de crecimiento	not speficied	n.a.	n.a.
Programa de alimentación complementaria mat. inf.	not implemented	n.a.	$4,332,981
Programa de educación alimentaria y nutricional	not speficied	n.a.	$259,420
Lucha operacional contra el bocio endémico	not speficied	n.a.	
FASBASE	* Targeted: Geographic	n.a.	$10,000,000
Salud materna y planificación familiar	not implemented	n.a.	$1,500,000
EB/PRODEC	* Targeting: Geographic	n.a.	$13,000,000
Educación basica de adultos y formación profesional	not implemented	n.a.	$1,450,000
Operación rescate infantil	* Targeted: Geographic / Indiv.	100,000	$2,400,000
Fondo de Inversión Social de Emergencia	* Targeted: Geographic / Self	1,001,127	$30,000,000
Programa de desarrollo infantil	* Targeted: Geographic / Indiv.	32,000	$1,204,155
Programa nacional de discapacidades	not implemented	n.a.	$2,400,000
Programa trabajadores prematuros	not implemented	n.a.	$1,539,247
Programa médico social	n.a. (by survey)	12,500	$950,580
Atención primaria en salud y mejoramiento del saneamiento básic	not implemented	6,000	$3,840,000
Mejoramiento de la educación primaria en zonas prioritarias	* Targeted: Geographic	36,740	$7,556,128
Ayuda integral para el sector urbano marginal de Quito	not implemented	503,778	$1,475,353
Defender el medio ambiente	not speficied	51,997	$114,300
Chicos de la calle	not implemented	31,000	$296,300
Programa nacional de educación prescolar	not implemented	1,396	$126,921

Source: Jordan (1994) and World Bank.

Note: Projects and programs without direct beneficiaries or substantial investments are not included.

Working Paper 8: Determinants of Hourly Earnings in Ecuador:
The Role of Market Regulations
Alejandra Cox Edwards

1.   Introduction

Ecuador has a cumbersome labor legislation.   There are several mechanisms through which the government interferes with wage setting in the private sector, including the national minimum wage, specific minimum wages determined by sectors and by occupations within sectors, and both minimum and mandatory wage adjustments to compensate for increases in the cost of living.   There is also a whole array of mandated benefits, each of them determined according to a specific rule and paid at a different point in time.   Some of these benefits are proportional to the base wage of the worker, while others are set as a lump sum; some are paid monthly, while others are due either one or several times a year.   Finally, firms willing to downsize or restructure may end up paying a severance equivalent to many yearly salaries to each of the displaced workers.

Besides causing efficiency problems, labor market segmentation has a direct link to equality and poverty.   In terms of efficiency, by precluding labor to be allocated optimally across the different sectors of the economy, the private sector's international competitiveness is undermined.   This will especially weaken the export base.   But such regulation can be a major source of increasing inequality in society and this is the main reason we want to study labor market segmentation in this Poverty Report.   The benefits regulations create favor generally only a few, and the resulting segmentation of the labor market can put a heavy toll on informal sector workers: their wage rate is not only artificially reduced but entry into the 'protected' regulated sector is hindered so that it is much more difficult for the poor to grow out of poverty by using their own labor.   The growth of this informal sector in Ecuador in recent years is viewed by many as a consequence of this segmentation.

However, in the Ecuadoran case, several factors exist which might weaken the alleged direct link between labor market legislation and segmentation.   First, the weakness of enforcement capabilities, as described below in more detail.   As an example, the enforcement agency at the Ministry of Labor does not have a single car of its own to inspect firms suspected of not abiding by the law.   Second, even if regulations were enforced, private contracts could still undo part of the potential distortions.   For instance, if there are mandated benefits to be paid in addition to the base earnings, then the latter can be adjusted downwards, so that take-home pay (including the benefits) remains equal to the relevant alternative wage.   Third, some firms in the modern sector of the economy may be willing to pay wages above market-clearing levels even if not forced to do so, for efficiency reasons.   High wages can be used to attract the best workers, to reduce turnover, to improve morale, and to elicit high levels of effort.   Fourth, wages can also be high because of union activities, and there are other variables, apart from labor market legislation, affecting union strength.   Particularly, unions tend to be powerful in the government and in sectors characterized by limited competition in product markets.

The goal of this paper is to take a fresh look at labor market segmentation in Ecuador, and to assess the role of labor regulations in accounting for this segmentation.

Such a fresh look is necessary because the existing evidence on the distortive impact of labor market regulations in Ecuador is not conclusive, as we will argue in detail below. And the fact that we can take a fresh look is made possible by the availability of a new data set, the recently completed *Living Standards Measurement Survey* (LSMS), which covers both urban and -- for the first time in Ecuador -- rural areas. The LSMS is much more detailed than previous Ecuadoran household surveys, both regarding earnings (including all of the mandated benefits) and individual characteristics such as unionization, or social security enrollment. These data allow to compare the hourly earnings associated with different jobs, depending on whether these jobs are actually subject to labor legislation, on whether they are in the modern sector of the economy, and on whether they are in unionized firms. The richness of the questionnaire allows us to control for a large set of individual characteristics.

The paper shows that labor market regulations do raise labor costs, but less than claimed by previous studies. Individuals who earn the benefits mandated by law enjoy a higher take-home pay than their otherwise identical fellows. But in the private, modern sector of the economy, the gap (about 18 percent) is much smaller in practice than it looks on paper. In fact, most of the impact of the mandated benefits is outweighed by a sharp reduction (roughly 39 percent) of the base earnings upon which mandated benefits must be paid. This downward shift is facilitated by both the low level and weak enforcement of minimum wages. Moreover, the impact of mandated benefits on labor costs is even smaller than suggested by the 18 percent increase in take-home pay. This is because mandated benefits, unlike base earnings, are not subject to social security contributions and payroll taxes. Thus, total labor *costs*, including social security contributions and payroll taxes, increase by only 8 percent for an employer complying with labor regulations.

This Working Paper is organized as follows. Section 2 presents the main features of the Ecuadoran labor market legislation, regarding wage setting mechanisms, mandated benefits, payroll taxation and job security. It also discusses the enforcement capabilities of the Ministry of Labor and the *Instituto Ecuatoriano de Seguridad Social* (IESS), and the role of labor unions in both enforcement and wage setting. Section 3 analyzes the available evidence on the extent of labor market segmentation as well as on the role of labor market regulations in explaining this segmentation. The available evidence is made of qualitative surveys of large firms, and of econometric studies using previous household data sets. Section 4 employs the LSMS to provide a typology of jobs: whether they are actually subject to labor market regulations, whether they belong to the modern, private sector of the economy, and whether they are unionized. The degree of overlap between these classifications is analyzed in detail, to the extent that it is crucial to disentangle the role of different sources of labor market segmentation. Section 5 deals with the measurement of hourly earnings, taking all benefits (mandated or not), bonuses and allowances into account. Distributions of take-home pay are constructed according to the typology of jobs discussed in Section 4. Section 6 estimates earnings functions, explaining the take-home pay and base earnings of individuals as functions of their own characteristics, but also of the type of job they hold (regulated, modern, unionized). In the case of take-home pay, the coefficients associated with the job type variables can be seen as indicators of labor market segmentation. Section 7 analyzes the robustness of the results, by replicating the regression analysis for specific sub-sets of observations, and by modifying the criteria used to decide whether a job is in the regulated, the modern or the unionized sector of the economy. Section 8 concludes.

2.   Labor Market Distortions

Ecuadoran labor market regulations may distort the labor market through several, largely independent, mechanisms. The government interferes with wage setting in the private sector of the economy by deciding on both minimum wages and across-the-board wage increases. Labor market regulations also impose an impressive number of mandated benefits, whose total amount represents roughly twice the base wage for someone earning the national minimum wage. In addition, firms and workers are supposed to pay contributions to a social security system which, everybody agrees, is technically bankrupt. Finally, legislation determines a high cost of workers' separation.

The national minimum wage, or *Salario Mínimo Vital General* (SMVG), is set by the *Consejo Nacional de Salarios* (CONADES), a body composed of seven members, five from government, one representing employers and one representing labor. Base wages at the sectoral level, as well as for each occupation within each sector, are decided by the *Comisiones Sectoriales de Salarios*. These are tripartite commissions, composed of three members, one each from government, employers and employees. There are 119 commissions, one per sector. Their decisions are made with some reference to changes in the SMVG. In addition, the government, by decree, periodically grants nation-wide wage increases.

On top of base wage, there are many mandated benefits. The list includes the thirteenth, fourteenth, fifteenth and sixteenth salaries, the cost-of-living compensation, the complementary bonus and the transportation bonus (see Sánchez Carrión, 1994, for details). Some of these are defined as a function of the SMVG, some are a function of the base wage (which varies by individual worker), and some are lump-sum amounts. The calculation and timing of payment varies from item to item, making administration and budgeting complex. This complexity can be illustrated by briefly describing each of the 'teen' salaries. The thirteenth salary is equal to the sum of all the salaries (base wage plus overtime) received by the worker between December and November (excluding mandated benefits) divided by twelve; it is paid in December. The fourteenth salary is equivalent to two monthly national minimum wages, and is paid in September of each year. The fifteenth salary is equal to 50 thousand sucres for all workers in the public and private sectors, and to 30 thousand for domestic service workers, per year; it is paid in equal amounts in February, April, June, August and October.[1] The sixteenth salary is equivalent to 1/8 of the base wage; it is paid every month.

Both the employee and the employer have to make contributions to the social security system. These contributions represent a tax on labor, rather than a delayed payment, as the expected benefits are weakly linked to contributions, if at all. The poor financial situation of the IESS (due to the negative yield of its investments, the government's failure to pay its share, and mounting administrative expenditures) force a

---

[1]   As of September 1994, the exchange rate was roughly 2,300 sucres per dollar.

recognition of future default. The perceived link between benefits and contributions is further weakened by the substantial degree of discretion the government has exercised over the determination of social security benefits over the years. Total labor taxes, including employer and employee contributions to IESS, but also to SECAP and IECE, amount to 21.5 percent of the base wage in most cases. Mandated benefits, such as the teen salaries, are not subject to social security contributions.

Job security provisions represent yet another potential source of labor costs. A minimum compensation must be paid to workers in cases of dismissal with 'just cause' (major misconduct) or voluntary separation, and an additional compensation in cases of dismissal 'without just cause'. If the dismissal is justified, the employer must pay 0.25 monthly salaries per year of service. If it is not, there is an additional compensation of three monthly salaries for employees with less than three years of service, or one month per year of service (up to 25 months) for those with more than three years of service.

Enforcement capabilities are weak regarding minimum wages.[2] The *Inspección del Trabajo*, belonging to the Ministry of Labor, has quite limited resources. Its Quito branch, which has authority over roughly half of the country's labor force, has 26 inspectors in all. Most of the time and effort of these inspectors is spent in the arbitration of labor disputes, such as judging whether a dismissal is justified or not. Consequently, they only carry out inspections when requested to do so by workers or, more often, by trade unions. In this case, the worker or union pays the cab for the inspector to visit the firm, because the *Inspección del Trabajo* has no vehicle of its own. Only when the firm is located out of town do the inspectors grab a car belonging to the Ministry. In addition, should firms be penalized, the punishment for non-compliance with labor legislation is relatively low. It cannot exceed five national minimum wages regardless of the severity of the fault or the number of workers affected. As a result, the total amount of fines collected by the Ministry of Labor in the fiscal year 1993-94 was only 9 million sucres. The enforcement of labor regulation may therefore be viewed as ineffectual.

Enforcement is somewhat more effective regarding payroll taxation. The *Departamento de Fiscalización Patronal* of IESS, which has around 80 inspectors and a few vehicles of its own, concentrates its efforts on the 30 thousand largest firms. Those firms with less than ten employees are not targeted, both because of a strong focus on revenue maximization, and because of the fear that employment would suffer from strict enforcement. Complaints from employees still play the main role in identifying the firms to inspect. Overall, the IESS estimates that roughly 22 percent of the yearly contributions due by the private sector are not paid (arrears by the public sector are much higher). However, this figure is based on money amounts, not on workers or firms. In fact, only 28 percent of the labor force is affiliated with the IESS. Compliance is higher in the Sierra than in the Costa; it is almost nil in the agricultural sector.

The above description of enforcement mechanisms leads to the suggestion that trade unions may play a significant role in compliance with labor law. In fact, nearly one fifth of labor-management disputes within unionized firms arise from their failure to

---

[2]   The description of enforcement capabilities and practices is based on personal interviews with officers at the Ministry of Labor and IESS.

comply with the payment of legal minimum wages. However, there are two important and related caveats. First, collective bargaining between firms and unions is usually associated with earnings well above the national minimum wage. Second, unions are authorized only in large firms, which are likely to pay above the minimum anyway. In practice, only 350 thousand workers, or about 10 percent of the labor force, are unionized. Moreover, trade unions are particularly strong and pugnacious in the public sector. For instance, there are 104 different unions in the IESS, and these unions are not even enrolled with the same central organization. The membership rate in the private sector is therefore much smaller than suggested by the nation-wide average.

Some would argue that in spite of its very limited coverage, private sector unionism has a significant capacity to affect labor market practices. In the case of Ecuador, union shops are allowed, that is, union membership may be required to be eligible employee. Also, labor is legally entitled to regular pay during strike periods and allowed to occupy the plant during those periods. Yet, there has been an undeniable decline of union strength over time. In November 1991, a labor market reform raised the threshold to form a union from 15 to 30 employees. At that time, the right to strike while wages are negotiated was limited, and an automatic arbitration mechanism was set up in case no agreement is reached after one month of negotiations. Not surprisingly, most of the recent strikes and work stoppages have been in the public sector.

3.   The Available Evidence

To assess whether excessive regulation raises labor costs and distorts the allocation of resources, a first possibility is to check the managers' view on the issue. In this respect, it is useful to refer to a survey of firms carried out by the World Bank (1994). The aim of the survey was to identify the impact of the most burdensome government regulations in Ecuador on private sector firms, and to quantify the overall costs associated with the regulatory framework. The survey covered a total of 68 firms from Quito, Guayaquil and Cuenca. Firms were randomly selected from a register of the thousand largest companies in the country, by the *Superintendencia de Compañías*. Firms with 50 and more employees accounted for 86 percent of the sample.

The primary finding of the survey was that political stability and inflation dominated the concerns of firm managers. Constraints related to the regulatory framework appeared to be relatively less important, although they still imposed substantial costs on firms in terms of management time and money. But contrary to expectations, the labor regime was not identified as the most difficult government regulation. The World Bank report does not provide any explanation for this disturbing finding. However, it is worth noting that nearly three fourths of the interviewed firms were paying extra benefits, as increments to those offered by the IESS, at an average cost of 7 percent of each employee's nominal monthly salary. The size of these voluntary benefits suggests that minimum wages and mandated benefits may not be binding in the case of large firms.

A more casual survey of firms carried out by Hachette and Franklin (1991) led to similar results. Private sector managers interviewed in this survey said that labor market regulations do not represent a major obstacle for their firm's operations. If economic incentives were there for production, these managers believe they could do well within the current legal framework. Hachette and Franklin conclude that employers have learned how to evade labor market regulation, or at least how to live with it.

There is however one reason why private sector managers could prefer not to complain about labor market legislation even if the latter was highly distortive, and that reason is tax avoidance. None of the teen salaries or mandated benefits is subject to social security contributions and payroll taxes. If the SMVG is raised to compensate for inflation, then roughly one fifth of the increase goes to the IESS; but if compensation is achieved by creating a new teen salary, or by raising the amount of any of the mandated benefits, then the marginal social security contribution on the wage raise is zero. In spite of this loss of revenue, the government also has a good reason to favor mandated benefits over wage increases. The budget deficit is linked to the national minimum wage. For each increase of one thousand sucres in the SMVG, annual government wage expenditures go up by about 20 billion sucres or, in elasticity terms, a one percent increase in the SMVG raises the government's wage bill by about 2.4 percent (World Bank, 1994, p. 14). This explains why, in spite of the consensus about the absurdity of the current system, no one really wants to change it.

As firm surveys are inconclusive regarding the effects of labor market regulations, it is preferable to complement these studies with an analysis of individual earnings, which controls for the characteristics of the workers. If the labor market was efficient, individuals with the same characteristics (such as schooling, experience and the like) would get similar earnings across different sectors and activities. If, on the other hand, excessive labor market regulation created labor market segmentation, then the earnings would differ depending on whether or not the employer abides by the law. Put differently, those who benefit from minimum wages, mandated benefits and job security can be expected to earn more than those who do not.

Two econometric studies explicitly or implicitly assess the extent of labor market segmentation based on micro-data. They both rely on urban household surveys from the *Instituto Nacional de Empleo* (INEM). The most detailed of these studies, by Griffin and Roberts (1994), estimates earnings functions for the years 1988 through 1992. After excluding persons employed as domestic workers or in agriculture, the study finds that formal sector workers earn, on average, 28 percent more than their informal sector counterparts. However, much of the wage gap is explained by the significantly higher education levels of formal sector workers over those in the informal sector: 10.26 years as compared to 7.41 years. The coefficient of the formal sector (dummy) variable in the earnings function is quite low: 18.4 percent in 1989, only 7.5 percent in 1992. Similar results are obtained by Samaniego (1995), using the 1989 urban household survey of INEC. Samaniego finds that the coefficient associated with the formal sector variable is not only low (3.9 percent): it is not even significant at the 10 percent level.

As for firm surveys, these econometric exercises could be seen as evidence that in spite of all their absurdity, labor market regulations do not represent a major source of dualism. Still, this second piece of evidence is not conclusive either, for two reasons. First, the income variables reported in the INEM surveys are ill defined, particularly regarding the mandated benefits which could be one of the main causes of labor market segmentation. In each survey, the respondent is asked to report total earnings in the previous month; in some years (1989 and 1990) the respondent is also asked to report his or her base earnings. But the nature of the benefits, bonuses and allowances included in the answers to these two questions remains unclear. Although INEM creates a variable that is meant to measure total earnings, there are serious reservations about whether it successfully does so. In some years, no adjustment is made to the reported earnings; in others, there is an adjustment ranging from 25 to 35 percent. Sometimes, the adjustment is made across the board; at other points, domestic workers are excluded from it. Despite this variability in the criteria, Griffin and Roberts (1994) use last month earnings as reported, but this may lead to an underestimate of the earnings gap between formal and informal sector workers. Samaniego (1995) uses the income variable created by INEM.

The second problem with these estimates concerns the definition of the formal sector variable. INEM surveys do not ask whether the respondent receives the teen salaries, is enrolled with the IESS, or has a written contract. Therefore, the formal sector dummy variable is constructed based on information on the occupation of the respondent and, more importantly, on the size of the firm he or she works in. For Griffin and Roberts (1994), the formal sector comprises professionals and workers in establishments with a personnel of six or more. For Samaniego (1995), the size boundary is the same but professionals are not included in the formal sector. The problem with these definitions is that large firms are more likely to comply with labor market legislation, but also more likely to be unionized, and more likely to pay efficiency wages. It is thus impossible to identify the role of labor market regulations in accounting for labor market segmentation.

4. A Typology of Jobs

To measure the extent of segmentation, jobs can be classified according to three dimensions: sector of activity, compliance with labor regulations and unionization. Fortunately, the LSMS is rich enough to allow using several alternative criteria in order to capture each of these dimensions. The jobs classified in this paper are the main occupations of the LSMS respondents in the week preceding the survey, provided that these occupations were remunerated, and that the data on individual characteristics associated with them are detailed and consistent enough. However, all agricultural jobs held by farmers working on their own land are set aside, for reasons that will be explained in the next section of the paper. These criteria left us with a sample of 7,281 observations.

The first dimension of the jobs, sector of activity, is captured by assigning all observations into one of four groups: the modern (private) sector, the public sector, the informal (urban) sector and the agricultural sector. Classifying the jobs according to this first dimension is quite straightforward, except for the distinction between the modern and the informal sectors. Following the standard practice, the modern sector is defined in this study so as to include all workers in establishments with a personnel of six or more, as well as all professionals. However, the resulting sector is labeled as modern, not formal, to avoid misunderstandings. Having a personnel of six or more does not guarantee that the employer complies with regulations. The salient feature of larger firms and activities deployed by professionals is rather the importance of efficiency wage considerations. In this respect, the six personnel cutoff point is of course arbitrary. It is chosen here to facilitate comparisons with the other studies based on Ecuadoran micro-data, which were briefly reviewed in the previous section. The consequences of modifying this cutoff point are analyzed in Section 7, when dealing with the robustness of the results.

Compliance with labor market regulations, which is the second dimension of the job classification, can be assessed based on three different criteria. The LSMS asks whether the respondent is entitled to teen salaries because of his or her main occupation, whether he or she is affiliated with the IESS, and whether the main occupation is backed by a written contract. An affirmative answer to any of these questions can be seen as evidence that the employer plays by the rules. But in practice, the first question turns out to be inclusive of the other two. More than 80 percent of those who receive teen salaries are affiliated with IESS and have a written contract, while only a few of those who are affiliated with IESS or have a written contract are not paid their teen salaries. The first question is therefore chosen to classify the main occupations in terms of compliance. The consequences of using the other two instead are explored in Section 7.

The third dimension, unionization, can be dealt with in two ways. The LSMS asks whether the respondent is unionized, but also whether he or she works in a unionized establishment. In practice, the latter question encompasses the former, i.e. all union members work in unionized establishments, but these establishments also employ non-unionized workers. Therefore, jobs are classified according to the second question. As for the other two dimensions, the consequences of changing the criterion are explored in Section 7. It is worth noting that with the chosen criterion, the relationship between unionization and compliance is as expected: almost all unionized employees receive teen salaries, are affiliated with IESS and have a written contract. However, the reciprocal relationship does not hold true: most of the respondents who enjoy mandated benefits do not work in unionized firms.

The distribution of the sample according to the three dimensions which characterize the jobs of the respondents is summarized in Table 1. As expected, both compliance and unionization are highly uncommon in the informal sector, and totally absent from the agricultural sector. At the other end, compliance is widespread in the public sector, where more than half of the employees are unionized. The modern sector occupies an intermediate position, with roughly half of the jobs paying the mandated benefits, but less than 10 percent of them being held by unionized workers. Overall, the union membership rate in the sample is about 8 percent. Similarly, only one out of four jobs in the overall sample pays the benefits mandated by law, which confirms that labor market regulations protect only a small share of the labor force.

The relationship between labor market regulations and inequality can be further explored by comparing the consumption levels of individuals holding jobs with different characteristics. Based on LSMS data it is possible to estimate quite accurately the level of consumption per capita, in comparable purchasing power units, for each of the households in the sample (see Working Paper 1). Table 2 uses these levels of consumption to classify the jobs in the sample according to the consumption quintile of their holder. The cutoff points delimiting the quintiles are those of the whole Ecuadoran population, after expanding the results of the LSMS. Therefore, Table 2 is a good indication of how rich or how poor, in Ecuadoran terms, the holders of different types of jobs are.

The nature of the jobs held by Ecuadorans changes as they become richer. Public sector jobs are more prevalent both at the lower and upper ends of the consumption scale, while salaried employment in agriculture is more concentrated in the intermediate quintiles. On the other hand, jobs in the modern sector of the economy, jobs that pay the benefits mandated by labor law and unionization are all more common as per capita consumption increases. Finally, the share of informal sector jobs in the sample is largely independent from consumption levels, and fluctuates around 40 to 45 percent.

5.   Hourly Earnings

Estimating the hourly earnings associated with each job in the sample is a trying task, because of the wide variety of wages, bonuses and benefits that have to be taken into account. This section provides a brief presentation of the results. To clarify matters, the hourly labor cost is disaggregated into a series of components, as indicated in Table 3. Also, to facilitate the discussion of the regression results in the next section, the first column in Table 3 reports what the legal minimum would be, as of September 1994, for a worker whose employer abides by the law. One of the striking features of this first column is the relative importance of mandated benefits (row B), which should account for more than three quarters of take-home pay (row C) for someone earning the national minimum wage. As a result of this bias, social security contributions and payroll taxes, which are both proportional to the base wage (row 1), become quite minor components of total labor cost.

Average hourly earnings in the sample, as of September 1994, are reported in the second column of Table 2. When interpreting the figures in this column it is worth keeping in mind that for most jobs in the sample the base wage is the only component of the labor cost. Also, it is important to stress that the reported hourly earnings are those associated with the main occupation of the respondent, not his or her average hourly income. Earnings from other sources (including secondary occupations) are set aside because the aim of this paper is not to assess whether some individuals earn more than others but rather whether some jobs pay more than others. The criteria used to construct the data on earnings based on the LSMS questionnaire, and to convert these data into comparable September 1994 figures when warranted, are described in detail in Annex 1.

Earnings figures were not constructed for farmers, for two reasons: one practical, the other conceptual. The practical reason is that the estimates would be of dubious quality. There is an important seasonality in the selling of harvests, as well as in the number of hours of work. Moreover, the cost of inputs, like seeds, which has to be subtracted from gross earnings, is difficult to assess. The conceptual reason is that even if this calculation was feasible, it would not necessarily fit the requirements of this study. The focus here is on the efficiency of the labor market to equalize the labor incomes of similar workers. But the earnings of farmers include land rent and returns to capital, in addition to labor income, so that they are not comparable to the take-home pay of salaried workers.

It could be argued that returns to capital plague the earnings of informal sector workers too. Although this is a valid remark, many informal sector workers are actually engaged in short-run (e.g. day to day) salaried relationships. What makes them different from salaried workers is that the relationship is short-lived, rather than sustained over time. As regards those informal sector workers who actually are independent, their capital stock is very limited. A survey of informal sector entrepreneurs in the cities of Guayaquil, Machala and Manta found that more than two thirds of them started their activities with a capital of less than 50 dollars, and roughly half of them had a capital stock of less than 100 dollars (see Ponce 1992). Assuming a real rate of return of ten percent per year, a capital of 100 dollars would yield a return of less than 0.5 cents of a dollar per hour of work (about 11 sucres, as of September 1994), which should not affect much the estimated hourly earnings.

Average hourly earnings in the sample are much higher than required by law. Take-home pay (row C in Table 3) is more than 50 percent higher than the corresponding legal minimum. The base wage (row 1) is about five times as high as the minimum. But in spite of a much higher base wage, social security contributions by workers are lower than the legal minimum. For a base wage of 1,908 sucres, the worker's contribution to IESS (row D) should be 178 sucres. The comparison with the actual average contribution indicates a compliance rate of roughly 20 percent, much below the IESS estimate for the private sector. The comparison between the two columns in Table 3 also highlights the different composition of earnings on paper and in practice. The difference is partly due to the fact that only one out of four jobs in the sample pays these benefits.

The legal minimum are not binding for the vast majority of workers. This hypothesis, already suggested by the comparison between actual earnings and legal minimum, can be assessed in a more rigorous manner by considering the whole distribution of hourly earnings, instead of the mere averages. The distribution is depicted in Figures 1, 2 and 3, which split the sample by sector of activity, payment of mandated benefits and unionization, respectively. The most salient feature of these figures is the absence of any spike at or around an hourly earning of 1,593 sucres. This result may seem surprising in the case of jobs which actually pay the mandated benefits (see Figure 2). The smoother distribution makes sense if the payment of benefits affects the composition of take-home pay rather than its level.

6.   Earnings Functions

The level of hourly earnings can be explained as a function of individual and job characteristics. Individual characteristics are intended to capture labor productivity, while job characteristics account for differences in wage setting mechanisms. As usual, individual characteristics include years of schooling and years of work, which provide information on the human capital stock. For each of these two variables a quadratic specification is chosen, so as to allow for non-linearities in the returns to education and experience. Individual characteristics also include gender, marital status and indigenous background. The ethnic variable is constructed based on the declared fluency in either Quechua or Shuar. The specification is completed by adding dummy variables for the location of the household (urban or rural; in the Costa, the Sierra or the Oriente) and for the characteristics of the job, as defined in Section 4.

Earnings functions, based on the individual and job characteristics listed above, were estimated for both the log of take-home pay and the log of base earnings. Regression results are reported in Tables 4 to 7; the means of all variables are presented in Annex 2. In addition to the full sample estimates, the Tables present regression results for each of the four sectors of activity considered in this paper (modern, public, informal and agriculture) as well as for unionized and non-unionized workers and firms. Splitting the sample according to the sectoral classification is warranted because of potential obstacles to labor mobility between sectors, leading to different earnings patterns in each of them. Similarly, the way labor legislation is applied may vary significantly depending on whether or not there are unions. The econometric results confirm that both the sector of activity and the union status affect the shape of the earnings functions, particularly regarding returns to education, gender gaps, and wage differentials between individuals with and without an indigenous background.

Marginal returns to education increase with the number of years of schooling in both the modern and the informal sector, but they are constant in the public sector, and nil in agriculture. Similarly, there are increasing returns to schooling for workers who either are non-unionized or work in non-unionized firms, but constant returns to schooling for the rest of the workers. Increasing returns are reflected in the parabolic shape of the earnings function: the coefficient multiplying the schooling years is not statistically significant, whereas the coefficient multiplying the square of the schooling years is. Constant returns are associated with a linear earnings function, where the statistical significance of the coefficients on schooling and schooling squared is reversed. Finally, the coefficients multiplying both schooling variables are not statistically significant in the case of agriculture. This result can be seen as evidence that salaried workers in this sector tend to perform heavy physical tasks, with relatively low requirements in terms of intellectual activity. The lack of significance of the coefficients multiplying the experience variables in agriculture provides support to this interpretation.

The econometric results also show significant earnings differentials by gender, ethnic background, and geographical region. The size of these differentials depends on the sector of activity and the union status, though. Not surprisingly, the gender gap is much narrower in the public sector than in the rest of the economy. It is also narrower where unions are active than where they are not. Equal pay usually characterizes collective bargaining outcomes, and is a salient feature of meritocratic organizations such as the civil service. At the other end of the spectrum, gender and ethnic background are highly relevant in agriculture and in non-unionized activities. Part of the gender gap in earnings could be explained by the requirements, in terms of physical strength, of some better paying agricultural tasks. However, the earnings differentials against women and people of indigenous background are also likely to reflect a great deal of discrimination.

From the perspective of this paper, the most interesting results are those related to the dummy variables summarizing the job characteristics. Tables 4 to 7 show that, on average, hourly earnings in the public sector are not significantly different from those in the informal sector. Wages may be higher for low-skill workers, and lower for managers and technical staff, as reflected in the shape of the returns to schooling, but in the aggregate these differences cancel out. Hourly earnings in agriculture, by contrast, are 30 percent lower than in the informal sector.[3] This gap cannot be attributed to regional differences in consumer prices, hence in the purchasing power of hourly earnings, because the regressions already control for the location of the household. The gap cannot be attributed to the regulatory setting either, since there are no institutional barriers to entry into the informal sector. The most likely explanation for the earnings gap, apart from measurement error, is that migrating out of agriculture entails a cost (objective, subjective or both) for workers and their families.

Workers in the modern sector, those protected by labor market regulations and those in unionized firms all get a higher take-home pay than otherwise identical workers. The increase in take-home pay is estimated at 9 percent for jobs in the modern sector, at 21 percent for jobs complying with labor law, and at 8 percent for jobs held by unionized workers. Note that the coefficient multiplying the union dummy variable is barely significant, which could be consistent with the weakening of the labor movement in recent years. The coefficient multiplying the modern sector dummy variable, in turn, is within the range found for formal sector dummies in previous studies. This similarity is not surprising, because the definition of the formal sector variable in such studies was close to that of the modern sector variable in this paper (see Section 3 above). Finally, the impact of compliance on take-home pay varies across sectors. It is very high in the public sector, but nil in the informal sector; it is about 18 percent in the modern sector of the economy. Similarly, the impact of compliance is much higher where unions are active than when they are not.

It may seem surprising that compliance with labor regulations raises take-home pay by only 18 percent in the modern sector, when on the other hand mandated benefits are supposed to represent such a big addition to base earnings. The answer to this puzzle is relatively straightforward: those workers who are paid the benefits mandated by law also get much lower base earnings. Indeed, the most striking feature, when comparing Tables 4 and 6, or 5 and 7, is the change in the sign of the coefficient multiplying the compliance dummy. On average, the base earnings of the workers who are entitled to mandated benefits are 39 percent lower than those of otherwise identical workers. This shift is mostly driven by changes in the composition of take-home pay in the private sector. The compensating decrease of base earnings is roughly the same in the modern sector as in the sample as a whole; it is much higher in the informal sector, but not statistically significant for public sector workers and unionized workers.

The change in the composition of take-home pay induced by compliance with labor regulations would not be possible if base earnings were prevented to adjust downwards by a binding minimum wage. But this does not appear to be the case, for two reasons. First, base earnings in the sample are much higher than the minimum wage. The average base earnings of workers who get the mandated benefits is 1,908 sucres per hour, as compared to a legal minimum of 373 sucres (see Table 3). And second, the minimum wage is only weakly enforced anyway. The density functions drawn for take-home pay in Section 5

---

3   Keep in mind that a coefficient c multiplying a dummy variable can be interpreted as a percent change in the endogenous variable only as long as c is close to zero. For larger values, in absolute terms, the percent change in the endogenous variable is given by $100 [\exp(c) - 1]$.

made it clear that there was no spike at or around the legal minimum, which in turn was consistent with the description of enforcement capabilities at the Ministry of Labor, in Section 2. Only in the public sector and where unions are active is the downward adjustment of base earnings unfeasible.

7.   Robustness

The econometric results in the previous section could well be driven by the particular definition of the dummy variables used to classify the jobs in the sample, or by particular sub-sets of observations. To assess the robustness of the obtained results, the regression analysis was therefore replicated for different sets of explanatory variables, as well as for different partitions of the sample. Regarding the explanatory variables, alternative criteria were chosen to allocate jobs into sectors of activity, to judge whether these jobs comply with labor market regulations and to decide whether they are affected by union activities. The LSMS questionnaire allows to define the modern sector so as to exclude establishments with less than 11 or 31 employees (instead of 6), to assess compliance through affiliation to IESS or existence of a written contract (instead of entitlement to teen salaries), or to define the unionized sector so as to include only those individuals who work in unionized firms (instead of those who actually are union members). Regarding the sample, the regression analysis was replicated for each of the main regions in the country (Costa, Sierra and Oriente). Regressions were also produced for a sub-set of workers which excluded those whose take-home pay is in the upper or lower 5 percent-tails of the earnings distribution. Observations falling in any of these two tails are indeed likely to be subject to measurement errors either in the size of earnings or in the number of hours worked and therefore more prone to include outliers.

The main results of the analysis are unaffected by either the sub-sample used or the definition chosen for the dummy variables. Depending on the criteria used to decide whether a job is covered by labor market regulations, the impact of compliance on take-home pay ranges from 15 to 22 percent (see Table 8). Base earnings, in turn, decline by 21 to 39 percent (Table 9). The estimates remain roughly the same when the 5 percent tails of the earnings distribution are set aside, which suggests that results are not driven by outliers (see Tables 10 and 11). From a regional perspective, however, the Oriente seems to differ from the rest of the country. This is the only region where mandated benefits lead to an increase of take-home pay without any significant compensating decline of base earnings.

8.   Conclusion

This paper shows that Ecuadoran labor market regulations do raise labor costs, but to a much lesser extent than suggested by the vast array of benefits mandated by law. On average, and after taking into consideration the different criteria that can be used to classify jobs, it is safe to conclude that take-home pay is about 18 percent higher for private sector jobs complying with labor regulations than for otherwise identical jobs. The impact of mandated benefits on take-home pay is drastically attenuated by the companion decrease of the base earnings on top which mandated benefits have to be paid. This compensating decrease, of about 39 percent, is in turn facilitated by the low level and weak enforcement of minimum wages. Furthermore, the increase of labor costs induced by compliance with labor regulations is smaller than the corresponding increase in take-home pay. This is because mandated benefits are not subject to social security contributions or payroll taxes.

To illustrate the point, consider the following example, which refers to an employer willing to pay his or her employee a total of 1,000 sucres per hour, net. Total labor cost, from the employer's perspective, would be 1,215 sucres per hour, because of contributions to IESS, SECAP and IECE, at a rate of 21.5 percent. What would be the consequences of complying with mandated benefits? According to the econometric results above, take-home pay would increase to about 1,180 sucres per hour, while base earnings would drop to roughly 610 sucres. Since only base earnings are subject to social security contributions and payroll taxes, total labor cost would be now 1,311 sucres per hour (add 21.5 percent of 610 to take-home pay). This represents an increase of 8 percent over the total labor cost in case of non compliance. The increase could be somewhat higher, if transaction costs associated with compliance, and interest on the present value of firing costs (if any), were taken into account. However, the example suggests that the burden created by labor market regulations is not as heavy as it may look at a first glance. This could explain why managers do not complain much about these regulations.

A simplification and streamlining of the intricate and confuse set of labor market regulations currently in force would be welcome but the results we presented in this paper should caution policy makers to believe that a liberalization of the labor market alone will improve the living conditions of the poor. As shown in Working Paper 10, a reform of the Ecuadoran labor market will indeed lead to a reallocation of jobs from the 'unprotected' and lower paying informal sector to the currently 'protected' and higher paying modern or formal sector. But given that private contracts offset a large part of the mandated benefits to workers in the regulated sector, such static efficiency gains are going to be moderate.

References

Griffin, P. and J. Roberts (1994), 'An Exploratory Analysis of Ecuadoran Labor Markets', unpublished, California State University, Long Beach, CA, October.

Hachette, D. and D. Franklin (1991), 'Empleo e Ingresos en el Ecuador: un Contexto Macroeconómico', unpublished, Agency for International Development, Quito, February.

Ponce, M. (1992), 'Economía Informal y Empleo en Ciudades Grandes e Intermedias: Casos de Guayaquil, Machala y Manta', unpublished, Centro de Investigaciones Económicas (CIE), Universidad Católica de Guayaquil, Guayaquil, May.

Samaniego, P. (1995), 'El Ingreso y la Educación en el Ecuador: Análisis por Niveles de Instrucción', Cuestiones Económicas 24, pp. 135-155, Banco Central del Ecuador, Quito.

Sánchez Carrión, G. (1994), *Remuneraciones Adicionales y Beneficios Sociales a que Tienen Derecho los Trabajadores*, Ediciones Edype, Quito.

World Bank (1994): *Ecuador: Private Sector Assessment*, Green cover draft, The World Bank, Washington, DC, June.

Annex 1

Estimation of Hourly Earnings

The simplest case is that of independent workers, because no additions or subtractions to the declared earnings are required. The declared earnings represent in this case both the base wage (row 1 in terms of Table 3) and the take-home pay (row C). Although one individual declared to be entitled to old-age pension because of his or her main occupation, the LSMS reports *net* earnings, so that no adjustment is warranted. The declared earnings are adjusted for inflation though, to get their equivalent as of September 1994. The assumption here is that earnings of independent workers increase in line with consumption prices, at a rate of roughly two percent per month. This rate is cumulated over the time period going from the last declared earnings to September 1994.

The number of hours of work associated with the declared earnings is estimated based on a series of questions in the LSMS survey. These questions concern the frequency of the earnings, the number of hours worked per day and the number of days worked per week. In all three cases, the answers refer specifically to the main occupation of the respondent, not to all of his or her activities. However, the calculation of the number of hours worked is less straightforward when the declared earnings correspond to a quarter, a semester or even a year. If this is so and, in addition, the main occupation is said to be either occasional or temporary, the declared earnings are prorated by the number of months a year the respondent declares to work in the main activity.

Additions and subtractions to the declared earnings make the case of salaried workers more complicated than that of independent workers. Because of the way the LSMS questionnaire is structured, the declared earnings correspond to the sum of the base wage (row 1), the social security contribution (row D), if any, and the mandated benefits (rows 5 to 8), if any, with the exception of the 13th to 15th salaries. For those who declare to receive teen salaries, full compliance with the law is assumed. Therefore, all the mandated benefits, as set by labor regulations in force, are deducted from the declared earnings in order to estimate the base wage (row 1). Contributions to the IESS are subtracted from this basic wage when the respondent declares to be entitled to old-age pension or to unemployment benefits because of his or her main occupation.

The declared earnings of salaried workers need also be adjusted for a whole array of bonuses and extra payments (rows 2 to 4). Concerning bonuses (row 3), all payments for the anniversary of the firm or institution, for Christmas and for vacation purposes are added up. The resulting total is divided by 12 to obtain its monthly equivalent. Other additions are the average monthly earnings associated with tips and overtime (row 2), and the monthly value of food, clothing, transportation and housing provided by the employer (row 4). In the case of workers receiving teen salaries, the mandated transportation allowance is not added up to the total, because it is already included in the declared earnings. All the earnings components are divided by the number of hours worked per month in the main occupation, following the same criteria as in the case of independent workers.

Only a few of the items included in the take-home pay of salaried workers are adjusted for inflation. Indeed, during the period covered by the LSMS there were no adjustments of the SMVG, and no mandatory wage raises across the board either. Monthly earnings in September 1994 should therefore be the same as in the previous months. It can be argued that those jobs which are not actually subject to labor regulation, or those whose earnings are determined by collective bargaining might have experienced wage raises during the few months when the LSMS was carried out. But there is no way to assess this possibility and to correct the declared earnings accordingly. Regarding other earnings, such as the Christmas bonus, the LSMS questionnaire is too ambiguous to warrant any adjustment. The respondent is indeed asked to report either the actual amount of the last bonus or the expected amount of the next one. Therefore, it is unclear whether this amount has to be inflated or deflated. When needed, the purchasing power of the teen salaries is corrected for inflation, though. This is feasible because labor legislation clearly specifies the point in time where these teen salaries have to be paid. For instance, the thirteenth salary is due by the end of December. Consequently, to estimate its present value as of September 1994 we multiply it by a factor of 0.942, resulting from cumulating an inflation rate of two percent per month over three months.

Table 1. Job Distribution
(Sample size)

	Sector				
	Modern	Public	Informal	Agric.	Total
Teen salaries	986	790	101	0	1877
No teen salaries	1143	46	3149	1066	5404
Enrolled with S.S.	788	750	74	0	1612
Not enrolled	1341	86	3176	1066	5669
Written contract	910	777	79	0	1766
No written contract	1219	59	3171	1066	5515
Total	2129	836	3250	1066	7281
Unionized firm	282	568	17	0	867
Non-unionized firm	1847	268	3233	1066	6414
Union member	138	438	6	0	582
Non member	1991	398	3244	1066	6699
Total	2129	836	3250	1066	7281

Source: Own calculations based on LSMS (1994).

Table 2. Job Characteristics by Consumption Levels
(Sample size)

	Consumption per capita (quintiles)				
Job Characteristics	1st	2nd	3rd	4th	5th
Sector					
Modern	313	364	396	470	586
Public	44	88	142	234	328
Informal	597	625	657	667	704
Agriculture	382	277	204	132	71
Total	1336	1354	1399	1503	1689
Teen salaries					
Yes	172	245	324	469	667
No	1164	1109	1075	1034	1022
Total	1336	1354	1399	1503	1689
Union member					
Yes	44	62	96	147	233
No	1292	1292	1303	1356	1456
Total	1336	1354	1399	1503	1689

Note: The consumption per capita cutoff levels correspond to the whole Ecuadoran population, according to the 1994 LSMS, and not only to the sample in this paper.
Source: Own calculations based on LSMS (1994).

Table 3. Earnings Composition (Sucres per hour, as of September 1994)		
Component	Legal Minima	Sample Average
1) Base wage	373	1908
2) Tips and overtime	0	20
3) Voluntary bonuses (vacation, Christmas, firm anniversary ...)	0	32
4) Voluntary allowances and payments in kind (food, housing, clothing ...)	0	177
A) Basic earnings (=1+2+3+4)	373	2137
5) Teen payments	196	102
6) Compensation bonus	294	68
7) Cost-of-living bonus	659	152
8) Mandatory transportation allowance	71	6
B) Mandated benefits (=5+6+7+8)	1220	328
C) Take-home pay (=A+B)	1593	2464
D) Social security contribution by worker	39	35
E) Payroll taxes	50	?
F) Total labor cost (=C+D+E)	1682	?

Note: In the calculation of the legal minima, a month was supposed to include 170 hours of work and no overtime. All legal figures correspond to the most general regime.

Source: Own calculations based on LSMS (1994).

Table 4. Determinants of Take-Home Pay (in Log)					
Variable	Sector				Full
	Modern	Public	Informal	Agric.	Sample
Schooling	-0.0126 (-0.876)	0.0878 (3.664)	-0.0009 (-0.073)	0.0085 (0.373)	0.0011 (0.151)
Schooling^2	0.0042 (6.883)	-0.0005 (-0.509)	0.0038 (5.353)	-0.0001 (-0.059)	0.0034 (9.602)
Experience	0.0250 (6.127)	-0.0302 (5.718)	0.0285 (8.264)	0.0029 (0.471)	0.0249 (11.123)
Experience^2	-0.0003 (-4.251)	-0.0004 (-3.823)	-0.0005 (-7.481)	-0.0002 (-1.772)	-0.0004 (-10.286)
Male	0.2145 (5.709)	0.1143 (2.768)	0.2871 (8.712)	0.6167 (6.678)	0.2886 (13.079)
Married	0.1672 (4.129)	0.0626 (1.464)	0.1138 (3.120)	-0.0940 (-1.330)	0.0900 (3.915)
Indigenous	-0.0201 (-0.185)	0.0308 (0.295)	-0.0279 (-0.315)	-0.2997 (-2.615)	-0.1676 (-3.266)
Urban	0.0587 (1.267)	-0.0080 (-0.129)	0.0861 (2.113)	0.2092 (2.445)	0.0768 (2.856)
Costa	0.1157 (1.382)	0.0218 (0.371)	0.1872 (3.082)	0.2120 (1.895)	0.1761 (4.623)
Sierra	0.1188 (1.428)	0.1059 (1.958)	0.0031 (0.052)	-0.0130 (-0.120)	0.0513 (1.384)
Modern					0.0887 (3.059)
Public					0.0466 (0.924)
Agriculture					-0.3696 (-10.518)
Compliant	0.1680 (4.727)	0.5116 (5.739)	0.0836 (0.890)		0.1884 (5.507)
Unionized	0.0881 (1.256)	0.0311 (0.774)	-0.3244 (-0.858)		0.0809 (1.710)
Intercept	6.3658 (50.763)	5.6970 (31.757)	6.1254 (64.223)	6.0916 (36.306)	6.2442 (103.041)
Adj. R^2	0.2822	0.2814	0.1262	0.1173	0.2673
n	2129	836	3250	1066	7281

Note: t-values are in parentheses.
Source: Own calculations based on LSMS (1994).

Table 5. Determinants of Take-Home Pay (in Log)				
	Union member		Unionized firm		Full
Variable	Yes	No	Yes	No	Sample
Schooling	0.0575 (2.265)	-0.0054 (-0.695)	0.0847 (3.492)	-0.0087 (-1.092)	0.0011 (0.151)
Schooling^2	0.0007 (0.693)	0.0038 (9.878)	-0.0003 (-0.315)	0.0040 (9.965)	0.0034 (9.602)
Experience	0.0263 (4.228)	0.0247 (10.458)	0.0246 (4.415)	0.0248 (10.266)	0.0249 (11.123)
Experience^2	-0.0003 (-2.820)	-0.0004 (-9.901)	-0.0003 (-2.738)	-0.0004 (-9.809)	-0.0004 (-10.286)
Male	0.0723 (1.440)	0.3098 (13.113)	0.1241 (2.743)	0.3133 (12.861)	0.2886 (13.079)
Married	0.0203 (0.396)	0.0978 (3.974)	0.0904 (1.962)	0.0925 (3.648)	0.0900 (3.915)
Indigenous	0.1590 (1.208)	-0.1882 (-3.451)	0.1720 (1.443)	-0.1947 (-3.479)	-0.1676 (-3.226)
Urban	0.0450 (0.587)	0.0791 (2.795)	0.0908 (1.310)	0.0750 (2.594)	0.0768 (2.856)
Costa	0.0224 (0.299)	0.1852 (4.451)	0.0812 (1.192)	0.1841 (4.267)	0.1761 (4.623)
Sierra	0.0872 (1.293)	0.0506 (1.240)	0.1097 (1.750)	0.0467 (1.101)	0.0513 (1.384)
Modern	0.3363 (1.387)	0.0796 (2.653)	0.1436 (0.902)	0.0847 (2.758)	0.0887 (3.059)
Public	0.2091 (0.867)	0.0568 (0.989)	0.0433 (0.266)	0.0751 (1.136)	0.0466 (0.924)
Agriculture		-0.3742 (-10.321)		-0.3790 (-10.332)	-0.3696 (-10.518)
Compliant	0.5815 (4.273)	0.1713 (4.763)	0.5099 (6.375)	0.1570 (4.139)	0.1884 (5.507)
Unionized					0.0809 (1.710)
Intercept	5.6860 (19.377)	6.2537 (96.385)	5.6266 (25.330)	6.2713 (94.225)	6.2442 (103.041)
Adj. R^2	0.2662	0.2445	0.2951	0.2347	0.2673
n	582	6699	867	6414	7281

Note: t-values are in parentheses.
Source: Own calculations based on LSMS (1994).

Table 6. Determinants of Base Earnings (in Log)					
	Sector				Full
Variable	Modern	Public	Informal	Agric.	Sample
Schooling	-0.0166 (-0.969)	0.1283 (3.920)	-0.0016 (-0.123)	0.0085 (0.373)	-0.0033 (-0.416)
Schooling^2	0.0049 (6.781)	-0.0013 (-0.992)	0.0038 (5.371)	-0.0001 (-0.059)	0.0039 (10.361)
Experience	0.0294 (6.110)	0.0404 (5.610)	0.0302 (8.584)	0.0029 (0.471)	0.0277 (11.492)
Experience^2	-0.0004 (-4.388)	-0.0004 (-3.337)	-0.0005 (-7.816)	-0.0002 (-1.772)	-0.0004 (-10.494)
Male	0.2621 (5.858)	0.1866 (3.315)	0.2865 (8.571)	0.6167 (6.523)	0.3083 (12.950)
Married	0.1944 (4.288)	0.1123 (1.938)	0.1065 (2.876)	-0.0940 (-1.330)	0.0942 (3.816)
Indigenous	-0.0369 (-0.294)	0.0963 (0.667)	-0.0304 (-0.338)	-0.2997 (-2.615)	-0.1719 (-3.130)
Urban	0.0244 (0.442)	-0.0129 (-0.150)	0.0869 (2.100)	0.2092 (2.445)	0.0700 (2.415)
Costa	0.1577 (1.613)	-0.0172 (-0.214)	0.1826 (2.964)	0.2120 (1.895)	0.1805 (4.410)
Sierra	0.1091 (1.126)	0.1041 (1.411)	-0.0008 (-0.013)	-0.0130 (-0.120)	0.0409 (1.026)
Modern					0.0926 (2.971)
Public					0.0074 (0.134)
Agriculture					-0.3663 (-9.757)
Compliant	-0.4958 (-11.643)	-0.2568 (-2.165)	-0.8571 (-7.714)		-0.4962 (-12.980)
Unionized	0.1402 (1.657)	-0.0036 (-0.074)	-0.1633 (-0.427)		0.0805 (1.549)
Intercept	6.2470 (42.345)	5.1914 (21.287)	6.1767 (67.236)	6.0916 (36.306)	6.1962 (95.232)
Adj. R^2	0.2601	0.2060	0.1337	0.1173	0.1914
n	2023	793	3223	1066	7105

Note: t-values are in parentheses.
Source: Own calculations based on LSMS (1994).

Table 7. Determinants of Base Earnings (in Log)				
	Union member		Unionized firm		Full
Variable	Yes	No	Yes	No	Sample
Schooling	0.0950 (2.630)	-0.0102 (-1.232)	0.1067 (3.220)	-0.0105 (-1.245)	-0.0033 (-0.416)
Schooling^2	0.0000 (0.028)	0.0043 (10.570)	-0.0001 (-0.086)	0.0043 (10.135)	0.0039 (10.361)
Experience	0.0339 (3.978)	0.0274 (10.898)	0.0304 (4.092)	0.0275 (10.727)	0.0277 (11.492)
Experience^2	-0.0004 (-2.463)	-0.0005 (-10.193)	-0.0003 (-2.260)	-0.0005 (-10.129)	-0.0004 (-10.494)
Male	0.0960 (1.401)	0.3286 (13.032)	0.1642 (2.751)	0.3284 (12.715)	0.3083 (12.950)
Married	0.1162 (1.680)	0.0951 (3.638)	0.1903 (3.167)	0.0853 (3.185)	0.0942 (3.816)
Indigenous	0.1739 (0.975)	-0.1920 (-3.325)	0.1729 (1.119)	-0.1962 (-3.330)	-0.1719 (-3.130)
Urban	0.0147 (0.138)	0.0728 (2.416)	0.0739 (0.790)	0.0691 (2.257)	0.0700 (2.415)
Costa	0.0110 (0.107)	0.1922 (4.351)	0.0789 (0.874)	0.1894 (4.166)	0.1805 (4.410)
Sierra	0.0383 (0.417)	0.0441 (1.019)	0.0721 (0.873)	0.0371 (0.831)	0.0409 (1.026)
Modern	0.3432 (1.069)	0.0844 (2.644)	0.1280 (0.630)	0.0937 (2.880)	0.0926 (2.971)
Public	0.0642 (0.201)	0.0463 (0.741)	-0.1303 (-0.628)	0.0786 (1.099)	0.0074 (0.134)
Agriculture		-0.3716 (-9.692)		-0.3765 (-9.755)	-0.3663 (-9.757)
Compliant	-0.1002 (-0.554)	-0.5204 (-13.045)	-0.1679 (-1.632)	-0.5453 (-12.967)	-0.4962 (-12.980)
Unionized					0.0805 (1.549)
Intercept	5.2958 (13.327)	6.2112 (90.179)	5.2963 (18.094)	6.2298 (88.684)	6.1962 (95.232)
Adj. R^2	0.2125	0.1919	0.2410	0.1888	0.1914
n	553	6552	818	6287	7105

Note: t-values are in parentheses.
Source: Own calculations based on LSMS (1994).

Table 8. Sensitivity of Take-Home Pay Regressions to Changes in Job Classification
(Full Sample)

Variable	Specification					
	(1)	(2)	(3)	(4)	(5)	(6)
Modern (6 and +)	0.0887 (3.059)			0.1123 (4.016)	0.1115 (3.898)	0.0883 (3.037)
Modern (11 and +)		0.0762 (2.377)				
Modern (31 and +)			0.0771 (2.259)			
Teen salaries	0.1884 (5.507)	0.1939 (5.495)	0.2010 (5.877)			0.1931 (5.588)
S.S. affiliation				0.1608 (4.594)		
Written contract					0.1415 (4.077)	
Union member	0.0809 (1.710)	0.0799 (1.689)	0.0767 (1.618)	0.0842 (1.773)	0.0939 (1.986)	
Unionized firm						0.0292 (0.695)
Adj. R²	0.2673	0.2669	0.2669	0.2678	0.2673	0.2670

Note: All other explanatory variables in the regressions are the same as in Tables 4 and 5.
t-values are in parentheses.
Source: Own calculations based on LSMS (1994).

Table 9. Sensitivity of Base Earnings Regressions to Changes in Job Classification (Full Sample)						
	Specification					
Variable	(1)	(2)	(3)	(4)	(5)	(6)
Modern (6 and +)	0.0926 (2.971)			0.0040 (0.131)	-0.0072 (-0.231)	0.0907 (2.904)
Modern (11 and +)		0.0994 (2.863)				
Modern (31 and +)			0.1111 (2.991)			
Teen salaries	-0.4962 (-12.980)	-0.5023 (-12.706)	-0.4976 (-12.962)			-0.4970 (-12.865)
S.S. affiliation				-0.3027 (-7.766)		
Written contract					-0.2320 (-6.003)	
Union member	0.0805 (1.549)	0.0790 (1.520)	0.0741 (1.425)	0.0388 (0.738)	0.0129 (0.246)	
Unionized firm						0.0599 (1.297)
Adj. R^2	0.1914	0.1913	0.1914	0.1791	0.1763	0.1913

Note: All other explanatory variables in the regressions are the same as in Tables 6 and 7.
          t-values are in parentheses.
Source: Own calculations based on LSMS (1994).

	Regions			Excluding 5 % tails	Full sample
Variable	Costa	Sierra	Oriente		
Modern	0.0269 (0.715)	0.1811 (3.815)	0.0831 (0.736)	0.0244 (1.131)	0.0887 (3.059)
Public	-0.0771 (-1.038)	0.1141 (1.462)	0.0038 (0.022)	0.0406 (1.089)	0.0466 (0.924)
Agriculture	-0.1667 (-3.335)	-0.4643 (-7.710)	-0.5580 (-5.921)	-0.1720 (-6.395)	-0.3696 (-10.518)
Compliant	0.1951 (4.285)	0.1576 (2.946)	0.4172 (2.773)	0.2271 (8.917)	0.1884 (5.507)
Unionized	0.0544 (0.710)	0.0633 (0.910)	0.0313 (0.243)	0.1057 (3.035)	0.0809 (1.710)
Adj. R^2	0.2205	0.3131	0.2520	0.2531	0.2673
n	3428	3032	821	6550	7281

Table 10. Sensitivity of Take-Home Pay Regressions to Changes in the Sample

Note: All other explanatory variables in the regressions are the same as in Tables 4 and 5. t-values are in parentheses.
Source: Own calculations based on LSMS (1994).

Table 11. Sensitivity of Base Earnings Regressions to Changes in the Sample

	Regions			Excluding 5 % tails	Full sample
Variable	Costa	Sierra	Oriente		
Modern	0.0385 (0.951)	0.1767 (3.434)	0.0511 (0.430)	0.0313 (1.287)	0.0926 (2.971)
Public	-0.1728 (-2.109)	0.1168 (1.360)	-0.0667 (-0.355)	0.276 (0.645)	0.0074 (0.134)
Agriculture	-0.1676 (-3.111)	-0.4539 (-7.039)	-0.5616 (-5.769)	-0.1771 (-5.893)	-0.3663 (-9.757)
Compliant	-0.4389 (-8.579)	-0.5813 (-9.716)	-0.2269 (-1.345)	-0.4977 (-16.695)	-0.4962 (-12.980)
Unionized	0.0639 (0.754)	0.0552 (0.720)	0.0418 (0.306)	0.1088 (2.713)	0.0805 (1.549)
Adj. R^2	0.1530	0.2354	0.1297	0.1496	0.1914
n	3346	2958	801	6391	7105

Note: All other explanatory variables in the regressions are the same as in Tables 6 and 7. t-values are in parentheses.
Source: Own calculations based on LSMS (1994).

Figure 1

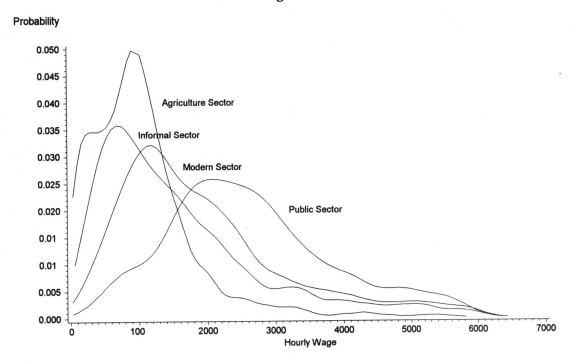

Figure 2

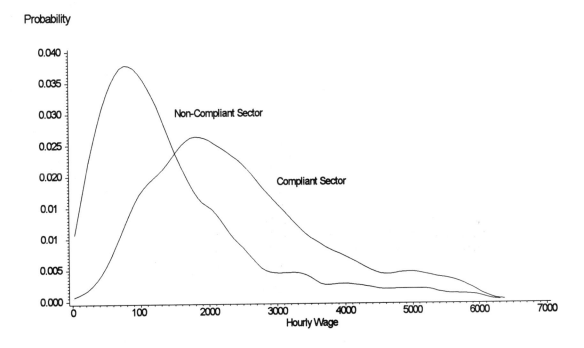

Figure 3

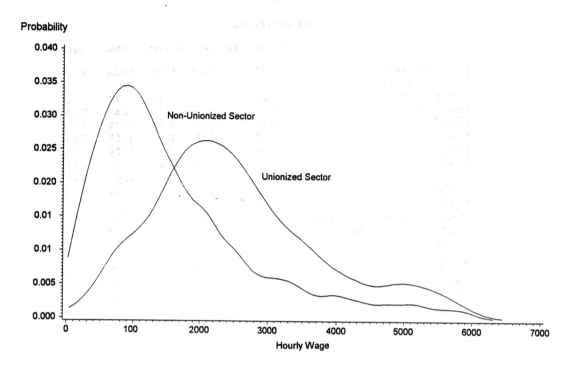

Annex 2

Individual Characteristics

	Modern	Agricultural	Informal	Public	Total
Hourly Wage (Sucres)	3088.5	1202.8	2118.6	3362.8	2411.0
Educational Attainment	–				
Schooling (Years)	11.0	4.9	7.8	13.5	8.9
Less than Primary	10.1%	50.7%	23.7%	3.6%	21.3%
Primary	22.3%	31.5%	31.5%	13.0%	26.7%
Some Secondary	21.3%	10.0%	25.3%	13.5%	20.5%
Secondary	17.6%	1.5%	9.1%	20.0%	11.7%
College	2.6%	0.2%	0.5%	8.3%	2.0%
University	24.0%	0.4%	6.3%	40.8%	14.6%
Post Graduate	1.1%	0.0%	0.0%	1.3%	0.5%
Work Experience					
Experience in Current Occupation (Years)	6.6	19.7	8.5	11.3	9.9
Total Work Experience (Years)	15.5	24.6	20.8	20.3	19.8
Age (Years)	32.6	38.8	35.8	39.3	35.7
Job Typology					
Public Sector	0.0%	0.0%	0.0%	100.0%	11.5%
Rural Sector	0.0%	100.0%	0.0%	0.0%	14.6%
Informal Sector (less than 6 employees)	0.0%	0.0%	100.0%	0.0%	44.6%
Modern Sector (6 plus employees)	100.0%	0.0%	0.0%	0.0%	29.2%
Informal Sector (less than 10 employees)	21.9%	0.0%	89.1%	0.0%	46.2%
Modern Sector (10 plus employees)	78.1%	0.0%	0.0%	0.0%	22.8%
Informal Sector (less than 30 employees)	39.8%	0.0%	89.1%	0.0%	51.4%
Modern Sector (30 plus employees)	60.2%	0.0%	0.0%	0.0%	17.6%
Teen Salaries	46.3%	0.0%	3.1%	94.5%	25.8%
IESS Member	37.0%	0.0%	2.3%	89.7%	22.1%
Written Contract	42.7%	0.0%	2.4%	92.9%	24.3%
Unionized Firm	13.2%	0.0%	0.5%	67.9%	11.9%
Union Member	6.5%	0.0%	0.2%	52.4%	8.0%
Permanent Job	84.4%	90.8%	84.4%	96.2%	86.7%
Occasional Job	12.4%	5.3%	12.2%	2.6%	10.2%
Seasonal Job	3.3%	3.9%	3.4%	1.2%	3.2%
Characteristics					
Male	70.8%	86.5%	56.5%	58.4%	65.3%
Household Head	47.9%	59.2%	45.1%	58.7%	49.6%
Married	46.5%	40.1%	41.9%	63.2%	45.4%
Location					
Urban	81.0%	16.3%	77.2%	85.4%	70.3%
Costa	51.9%	46.5%	48.1%	31.5%	47.1%
Sierrra	42.9%	35.6%	41.7%	45.8%	41.6%
Oriente	5.2%	17.8%	10.2%	22.7%	11.3%
Language					
Unilingual - Spanish	89.1%	85.3%	94.7%	87.8%	90.9%
Unilingual-Indigenous	0.0%	1.7%	0.1%	0.0%	0.3%
Any Indigenous Language	3.0%	14.2%	4.0%	4.2%	5.2%
Occupation					
Armed Forces	1.3%	6.6%	2.3%	6.3%	3.1%
Executives, Managers and Administrators	6.0%	0.1%	9.0%	6.8%	6.6%
Professionals	13.7%	0.1%	0.0%	27.5%	7.2%
Technicians and Mid-level Professions	17.5%	0.0%	0.0%	21.2%	7.6%
Clerks	6.8%	0.1%	1.9%	10.4%	4.0%
Merchants and Salespeople	6.2%	0.0%	23.9%	8.6%	13.5%
Agricultural Workers	6.3%	68.2%	6.2%	0.6%	14.7%
Skilled Industrial Workers	21.4%	1.3%	24.6%	3.7%	17.8%
Unskilled Industrial Workers	7.5%	0.4%	7.6%	5.7%	6.3%
Not Classified	13.3%	23.2%	24.6%	9.1%	19.3%

	Teen Salaries		Union Member		
	No	Yes	No	Yes	Total
Hourly Wage (Sucres)	2103.7	3295.5	2331.5	3325.9	2411.0
Educational Attainment					
Schooling (Years)	7.7	12.6	8.6	13.1	8.9
Less than Primary	27.0%	5.2%	22.7%	5.8%	21.3%
Primary	30.8%	14.9%	27.8%	14.3%	26.7%
Some Secondary	21.6%	17.5%	21.1%	13.7%	20.5%
Secondary	8.2%	21.9%	11.1%	18.9%	11.7%
College	0.7%	5.6%	1.6%	6.0%	2.0%
University	7.9%	33.7%	12.4%	39.5%	14.6%
Post Graduate	0.2%	1.2%	0.4%	1.9%	0.5%
Work Experience					
Experience in Current Occupation (Years)	10.4	8.5	9.7	11.7	9.9
Total Work Experience (Years)	20.6	17.5	19.7	20.7	19.8
Age (Years)	35.7	35.7	35.4	39.4	35.7
Job Typology					
Public Sector	0.9%	42.1%	5.9%	75.3%	11.5%
Rural Sector	19.7%	0.0%	15.9%	0.0%	14.6%
Informal Sector (less than 6 employees)	58.3%	5.4%	48.4%	1.0%	44.6%
Modern Sector (6 plus employees)	21.2%	52.5%	29.7%	23.7%	29.2%
Informal Sector (less than 10 employees)	59.0%	9.2%	50.1%	1.4%	46.2%
Modern Sector (10 plus employees)	13.8%	48.7%	22.8%	23.4%	22.8%
Informal Sector (less than 30 employees)	63.2%	17.6%	55.7%	2.2%	51.4%
Modern Sector (30 plus employees)	9.7%	40.3%	17.2%	22.5%	17.6%
Teen Salaries			19.6%	96.7%	25.8%
IESS Member	1.6%	81.1%	16.0%	92.3%	22.1%
Written Contract	3.7%	83.4%	18.2%	93.8%	24.3%
Unionized Firm	1.4%	42.2%	4.3%	100.0%	11.9%
Union Member	0.4%	30.0%			8.0%
Permanent Job	83.7%	95.1%	85.6%	98.5%	86.7%
Occasional Job	12.5%	3.5%	10.9%	1.0%	10.2%
Seasonal Job	3.8%	1.4%	3.4%	0.5%	3.2%
Characteristics					
Male	66.2%	62.8%	65.7%	60.1%	65.3%
Household Head	48.2%	53.5%	48.5%	62.2%	49.6%
Married	41.6%	56.2%	43.7%	64.8%	45.4%
Location					
Urban	64.9%	85.9%	68.9%	86.8%	70.3%
Costa	49.0%	41.6%	48.6%	29.0%	47.1%
Sierrra	39.9%	46.6%	40.8%	51.2%	41.6%
Oriente	11.1%	11.9%	10.5%	19.8%	11.3%
Language					
Unilingual - Spanish	92.0%	87.6%	91.1%	88.1%	90.9%
Unilingual-Indigenous	0.4%	0.0%	0.3%	0.0%	0.3%
Any Indigenous Language	6.1%	2.8%	5.4%	3.6%	5.2%
Occupation					
Armed Forces	2.9%	3.7%	3.1%	3.3%	3.1%
Executives, Managers and Administrators	6.3%	7.5%	6.6%	6.7%	6.6%
Professionals	3.1%	19.0%	5.6%	25.1%	7.2%
Technicians and Mid-level Professions	4.0%	17.8%	6.6%	18.2%	7.6%
Clerks	1.4%	11.5%	3.3%	12.2%	4.0%
Merchants and Salespeople	15.9%	6.5%	14.1%	6.2%	13.5%
Agricultural Workers	18.7%	2.9%	15.8%	1.7%	14.7%
Skilled Industrial Workers	20.8%	9.2%	18.8%	6.5%	17.8%
Unskilled Industrial Workers	5.5%	8.6%	6.1%	9.0%	6.3%
Not Classified	21.4%	13.3%	20.0%	11.0%	19.3%

Source: LSMS, 1994.

Working Paper 9: Towards a Labor Market Reform in Ecuador
Alejandra Cox Edwards

1.   Introduction

Ecuador has a population of about 11 million, and an income per capita or around US$1,200.   After a decade of oil boom, the 1980s began with serious macroeconomic imbalances -- external debt had risen from US$330 million in 1974 to US$2.6 billion in 1979, while the exports sector failed to diversify, traditional agriculture stagnated, and non-tradables boomed.   A first serious signal came in 1982 with a devaluation of the sucre, but a full scale orthodox stabilization plan did not start until 1984. A slow process of adjustment followed.   Due to a significant reduction in the relative price of non-tradables, particularly right after the devaluation, production of non-tradables rendered lower real incomes. Activities in the tradables sector picked up, particularly those related to agriculture. Yet, investment, and therefore labor demand, have been sluggish, resulting in severely depressed real wages for almost a decade.

Demographic forces, which were in place long before the crisis unraveled, generated an increase in the labor force of 4.5 percent per year on average between 1982 and 1990. This meant adding 1.3 million workers to a labor force of 2.3 million in eight years. More than half of this addition to the labor force is explained by demographics -- that is by the increase in the working age population (at an annual rate of 2.8 percent), the rest is due to behavioral changes -- that is, by the increase in the labor force participation rate, especially of females.

The rapid increase in labor supply, particularly in urban areas, was not matched by an equally rapid increase in demand for labor in the formal sector, and resulted in a rising degree of informality and a decline in average productivity of labor for the economy as a whole.   It is important to note that changes in the working age population of this magnitude are not unprecedented in the world economy, nor are they necessarily a disadvantage for developing countries. Malaysia, one of the fast growing economies of the 1980s, saw its working age population double between 1965 and 1990 and created employment for 3.8 million additional workers during the same period. (The working age population and the labor force grew at 3.2% per year.) But Ecuador could not make an asset of the availability of labor resources in the 1980s. The economy had entered a crisis which called for a major adjustment program. When the large cohort of workers arrived into the labor force, what could have been an opportunity, turned into a burden for the economy.

While Ecuador has recognized that macroeconomic stability is a precondition to investment and an essential component of employment creation, it is now very important to also reform the labor market. With most of the poor of today being employed in the informal sector, an important step out of poverty is to create incentives for formal sector employment. Labor market reform can play an important role in reducing entry barriers to formal sector employment.   As we have seen in Working Paper 8, labor market segmentation is relatively modest in scope but nevertheless present in Ecuador today.

This Working Paper outlines important labor market reforms. While the current labor law promises a minimum wage, wage adjustments every six months, job security, pensions, access to credit, and more, these laws reach only a minority today. The necessary revisions would entail a simplification of the wage formula, a social security system reform including accidence insurance and a reform of job security legislation. A reform needs to establish rules which are enforced primarily by those affected by them; that is employers and workers. Inspectors, courts and authorities in general, would play a substantive role as witness of rule violations, or as enforcers of penalties.

We begin by shortly talking about the role of the labor legislation in a market economy. Section 3 points out the measurable problems of the Ecuadoran labor market today, namely low productivity growth and increasing informality. We outline the main areas in which labor market reform is important in Section 4. We end by summarizing the main points of the paper.

2.   The Role of Labor Legislation

Ecuador's policy makers have long intervened in the labor market, primarily in the wage determination process. This was often done in the name of protecting the poor. But labor market interventions can have a perverse effect on the creation of formal sector employment if they create a labor market segmentation by artificially increasing the cost of labor. We have observed in Working Paper 8 that segmentation does indeed raise labor costs, by around eight percent. A more effective approach to help workers is one that encourages employment creation in the private-formal sector. If employment creation is encouraged, then labor market conditions will tend to push wages to higher levels, benefiting workers in general. Employment creation requires either the expansion of previously existing economic activities or the establishment of new ones. Ecuador is an open economy and the expansion of economic activity is not constrained by the demand side. Rather, the expansion of economic activity is the result of entrepreneurs' decisions to choose Ecuador as a production center. In the case of non-tradable goods, this decision is very much linked to domestic demand projections, and cost considerations. In the case of tradable goods, the decision is linked to comparative advantages. Both involve the decision of entrepreneurs to invest.

In a market-oriented economy, labor legislation plays a central role. It has the potential to improve the operation of the labor market by reducing transactions costs, or dispute-resolution costs. The labor legislation, by establishing or failing to establish clear rules, is one important determinant of the degree of risk associated to an investment, which is so important in guiding investment decisions (Dixit and Pyndick, 1994). The labor legislation may affect the cost of labor, and thus, the level of employment. In short, the labor legislation is one of the fundamental factors that affect labor demand and supply, and the equilibrium level of employment and real wages.

3.   Labor Market Performance

The recent performance of the labor market has been dismal in Ecuador and this is why labor market reform is important today. While the labor force grew significantly over the past fifteen years or so due to demographic patterns and behavioral changes, employment in the modern sector has stagnated. Average labor productivity growth has been negative between 1982 and 1990 and the urban informal sector has grown over the past years. The economy and with it the labor market have to become more efficient -- labor market reform is one of the tools to achieve this end.

The Growth of Labor Supply: Demographic Forces and the Participation Rate. Over the past decade, the Ecuadoran labor supply increased strongly due to both demographic pressures and an increase in the labor force participation rate. During the period from 1982-90, the working age population grew at an annual rate of 2.7 percent but the labor force, at an annual rate of 4.6 percent (Table 2). The labor force participation rate jumped from 43 percent in 1982 to over 50 percent in 1990. Besides demographic forces, the increase in the labor force participation rate is largely due to much more women entering the work force. Illustrative, in the urban areas, we find that the female labor force participation rose from 34 percent in 1988 to 46 percent in 1993.

Table 1. Labor Force Participation, 1982 to 1990

	1982	1990	Change
Working Age Population ('000)	5,396	6,708	1,312
Labor Force ('000)	2,346	3,359	1,013
Participation Rate (%)	43.5	50.1	6.6

Source: Census 1982 and 1990.

Productivity Developments. While the labor force increased dramatically between 1982 and 1990 in an otherwise stagnant economy, average labor productivity plummeted. Table 2 shows the evolution of employment, output and average productivity by sector based on Census data. In the 1970s, employment growth concentrated in the services and industrial sectors while the agricultural sector lost employment in absolute numbers. Due to the shift in employment towards the industrial and service sectors of the economy, the average labor productivity increased between 1974 and 1982. The above observed surge in the labor force in the 1980s went hand in hand with a fall in average labor productivity, most notably in the services and industrial sectors. The fast structural change of the Ecuadoran economy in favor of the service industries continued.

Table 2. Employment and Productivity, 1982 to 1990

		1974	1982	1990
Employment ('000)		1812	2221	3163
of which:	Agriculture (%)	49.3	35.3	32.7
	Industry (%)	18.1	20.9	19.0
	Services (%)	32.6	43.9	48.3
Productivity (1987 sucres, '000)		633.8	788.1	642.9
	Agriculture	212.6	296.0	301.3
	Industry	1319.7	1351.7	1121.9
	Services	891	916	686

Source: Census 1974, 1982 and 1990.

Besides the impact of cumbersome labor market legislation, the observed low labor productivity growth in Ecuador is also partly the consequence of a development strategy that had long biased incentives against investments in labor-intensive industries. For a long time the growth of industry was due to active intervention by the state to promote Import Substituting Industrialization. "Subsidies to industry were implemented through overvalued exchange rates, protective tariffs and quotas on competitive imports, food import subsidies, preferential interest rates, and tax exemptions. These subsidies led to installation of a capital-intensive industrial sector principally concentrated in the two largest cities, Quito and Guayaquil." (de Janvry et al, 1991). Economies not favoring capital over labor generally experience rising average productivity in all sectors, and a reallocation of labor from lower productivity to higher productivity sectors.

Informality. With a strong increase in the labor supply and low absorptive capacity of the formal sectors, the Ecuadoran economy became increasingly informalized, especially in urban areas. The higher role the informal sector plays for employment can be gauged from the share of wage income in total GDP which fell from an average of 47 percent in the 1970s, to 35 percent in the early 1980s, 27 percent in the late 1980s, and 15 percent in the early 1990s. This decline cannot be explained by reductions in real wages alone. It indicates that the proportion of workers that can be classified in the 'wage employment' category in the formal sector has fallen. Lacking dynamism in such sectors as manufacturing is responsible for pushing workers into the informal sector.

Examining recent urban employment surveys, we find that urban informality also increased in the past couple of years, between 1990 and 1993. As shown in Table 3, urban informality increased by 3 percent between these two years and stands now at 48 percent of all urban employment. As expected, informality is highest in commerce with around 80 percent of all employment in this sectors being of an informal nature. Informality is larger in the Costa and Oriente urban areas, which matches the historical pattern of migration flows: rural-urban migration between 1982 and 1990 was about 70,000 per year which is equivalent to 1.8 percent of the urban population and 1.5 percent of the rural population of 1982. Outmigration was highest for the rural Sierra and inmigration highest for the urban Costa.

Table 3. Urban Informality, 1990 to 1993 (% of Work Force)

	1990	1991	1992	1993
Costa	47.0	49.0	51.0	50.0
Sierra -- North	42.0	46.0	44.0	42.0
Sierra -- South	45.0	50.0	48.0	45.0
Oriente	52.0	53.0	50.0	56.0
Total National Urban	45.0	48.0	49.0	48.0

Source: INEM, Encuesta Permanente de Hogares, 1990-1993.

We find that the probability of working in the informal sector is linked to age and education. Based on the INEM employment surveys, we estimate Probit-regressions for the likelihood of employment in the informal sector. We find that the probability of informal sector employment first falls and then rises with age; the turning point for males is 42 years of age, and the turning point for females is 28 years of age. This means that for a 'representative male', informalization declines with age, while for a 'representative female', informalization increases with age. Formal sector jobs are reserved for young women and prime age males. Education reduces the probability of urban informalization for males and females. Conversely, having no education raises the probability of being in agriculture relative to all education categories. Estimation results are included in the Annex.

4.   Critical Areas of Labor Market Reform

With lacking productivity growth and an increasing informalization of the economy, it is important to make employment in the formal, dynamic sectors more attractive. A reform of several key labor market legislation is one of the tools.

Wage Determination

The Wage Determination Process. The wage determination process in Ecuador is difficult and cumbersome. A large number of regulations govern the wage setting process in Ecuador, not only in the public but also in the private sector. CONADES determines the minimum wage and the minimum adjustment of all wages. The 'Comisiones Sectoriales' determine the basic salary in each sector. On top of the basic salaries, eight additional components are levied, some of which are defined as a function of the minimum wage, some as a function of the basic salary and some are fixed amounts (such as the Compensation for Cost of Living). Table 4 summarizes the regulated wage components and Box 1 shortly reviews the calculation of the 'teen' salaries. Further, for the interested reader to visualize how many of these regulations exist and how they impact on the payment of a salary, Annex Table 2 computes the effective salary and the labor cost for the basic salary in the years 1988 to 1992.[1]

Table 4. Regulated Wage Components

Regarding Basic Salary	Additional Compensations
* minimum wage - all workers (SMVG) - small enterprises - farm laborers - craft workers - domestic workers * basic salaries - determined by Sector Commissions by sector of economic activity (1992: 117 Commissions)	* thirteenth salary * fourteenth salary * fifteenth salary * sixteenth salary * cost of living compensation * complementary bonus * paid vacations * transportation bonus * Reserve Fund * Profit Sharing (limits refer to basic salary

Source: Ministry of Labor.

---

[1]   We have to restrict ourselves to the calculation for one month only as the compensations vary on a monthly basis.

Problems. This system creates two classes of problems for the functioning of the labor market. First, the system increases information and management costs which already become visible if one tries to calculate the impact of a change in the basic salary on the real earnings of a worker. As a consequence of this cumbersome wage determination process, the administrative cost associated with wage setting, accounting and reporting are unnecessarily high. Further, it is very difficult for an employer to estimate her or his labor costs over the period of a year, even if all her workers earn above the basic salary because adjustments in the additional components can be announced at any time. But even for the workers the mechanism entails a high degree of transactions costs: A worker that wants to organize her or his budget on the basis of the monthly salary has a hard time computing the expected cash-flow because compensations vary from month to month. This task is especially difficult because the quotation of compensations are generally made in reference to the basic salary which only applies to a fraction of the workers.

The second class of problems this policy creates is associated with diminishing the role of wages in the allocation of labor across sectors and regions. The transaction and information costs alone hinder the efficient distribution of labor across sectors since they artificially raise the cost of labor in the regulated sector, thereby creating entry barriers for workers to move to this kind of employment. Further, if the basic wage is actually binding, the allocation of labor in the economy is seriously hindered. For example, a region might experience an excess supply of labor at the basic wage, but the wage floors eliminate labor market incentives to prefer that region over others. Workers must resort to migration or to self-employment in this case. In the absence of wage floors, wage variations across regions are a signal to attract investment to labor abundant areas which would be equalized over time. While we find that the minimum wage is currently not binding (Working Paper 8), this problem might well arise in the future.

Box 1. The 'TEENS'

The *thirteenth salary* was established in 1962 and originally favored only those workers that were affiliated with the Social Security System. Its application was slowly extended to all workers. The amount of the thirteen salary is determined by the sum of all the salaries received by the worker between December and November, exclusive of additional compensations, and divided by twelve. It is paid in December. The thirteenth salary is not considered taxable income, thus it is not considered income for the purpose of calculating social security contributions or income tax.

The *fourteenth salary* was established in 1968. It is equivalent to two monthly minimum wages (SMVG) and it is paid in September of each year.

The *fifteenth salary* was established in 1979 and modified in 1990. It is paid to workers that have completed a minimum of one year of continuous employment with one employer. It is equal to 50,000 sucres for all workers in the private and public sectors, and 30,000 for domestic service workers, per year. This additional salary is paid in equal amounts in February, April, June, August, and October.

The *sixteenth salary* was established in 1992 and is equivalent to 1/8 of the basic salary applicable to the moment is due. It is paid every month.

Simplifying the Basic Wage Formula. For the above reasons, a rationalization of the minimum wage policy is very important. A reduction of the degree of intervention can be accomplished by (a) unifying the various components of the minimum wage, and (b) adjusting the minimum wage to one level for the country as a whole. That minimum wage could be placed somewhere between today's basic salary (salario minimo vital) and the basic salary plus additional compensations. To move in that direction, CONADES can begin a practice of adjustment of sectorial wages that is inversely proportional to the current minimum wage of the sector. After some time, all basic salaries would converge to a unique minimum wage.

The basic salary has been used as a unit of account and there are a number of social benefits, and perhaps contracts that have been set in terms of basic salary units (SMVG). Yet, a more appropriate solution is to set a unit of account (of constant purchasing power) to be used as a reference in all transactions that involve unknown future quantities. The government can announce, along with the wage harmonization, the equivalency between the old SMVG and a new UVC (unit of constant value). That would protect all previous contracts relative to the rate of inflation, and at the same time, allow the wage policy to be corrected.

Social Security

The most important component of the payroll tax is the contribution towards Social Security, equivalent to 20.5 percent of the basic salary in most cases.[2][3] The contribution makes affiliates eligible to workers' compensation in case of accidents on the job, public sector health care benefits, and a pension. The benefits coverage for the affiliate's dependents is the most limited in Latin America, after Haiti. Health care coverage does not extend to spouses, or the children of affiliates, except infants in the case when the mother is an affiliate. The IESS may also administer workers' Reserve Fund, which consists of 1/12 of the annual salary deposited in a special account in the individual's name. According to the law, affiliates can borrow from their own fund for housing loans, and the repayment is to be discounted from the payroll.

Due to the fact that the IESS obligations and contributions are set by law, with no strict attention to actuarial balances, there has been a significant amount of cross-subsidization across programs in the 1980s. The weak link between contributions and benefits renders the IESS contribution to be seen as an entry ticket to the IESS lottery of benefits. Individuals, not knowing the amount of benefits they will derive from the system, hence try to make the smallest contribution they can manage. Pensions are a good example to show that IESS members cannot rely on the system as a social insurance. Figure 1 shows the high fluctuation and recent dramatic decline in the real value of IESS pensions. But in spite of the declining value of pensions, employers are compelled to affiliate all their workers because the IESS provides insurance coverage against liabilities associated with accidents on the job, and old age pensions.

---

[2] The contributions are calculated over total wages, including overtime, profit sharing, commission, etc. But the 'teens', the cost of living compensation, and the other additional payments are not included.

[3] There are two additional (minor) components to the payroll taxes, adding up to 1 percent of the basic salary. These are the contribution of .5 percent to SECAP (public training institute) and IECE.

Figure 1. Real Pension Developments, 1970 to 1992

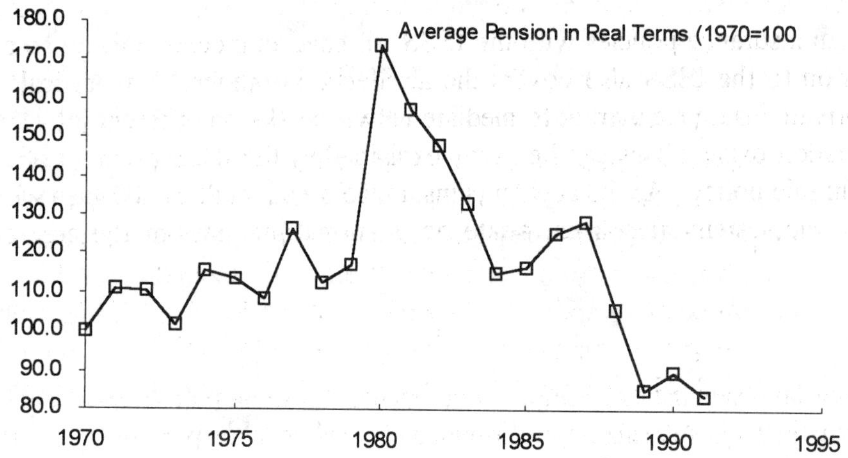

Source: IESS data.

Further, the current operation of the system is financially unsustainable (Mesa-Lago 1993). Given the expected pressures coming from the rising proportion of survivors eligible for pension benefits, a rationalization of the program is unavoidable.

The current operation of the Social Security System increases labor costs. First, the obviously unsustainable operation of the system reduces expected benefits of today's contributors to almost zero, making the contribution operate like a tax. The high degree of non-pension benefit variability (such as health or accidence insurance) adds to this assessment. Second, the law does not establish with clarity the limits to employees and employers obligations relative to that of the IESS. Moreover, in the past the degree of discretion the government has exercised over the determination of social security benefits has been significant. This experience has encouraged rent-seeking behavior among interest groups, again increasing the costs associated to labor employment.

One way to reduce the extent of rent-seeking behavior is through the establishment of clearly enforceable rules based on an actuarial balance. In the case of social security, the minimum condition for enforceability of a rule is actuarial balance between required contributions and guaranteed benefits. Since pensions are paid in the future, for an unknown period of time, actuarial balance can be attained by a combination of a life insurance policy and a savings account. Individuals cannot be promised a given wage replacement rate at the time they are making contributions to IESS. The program's benefits must be a function of the net present value of contributions plus their yield. The annuity that can be purchased with that amount would vary with the number of years the retiree is expected to live, and the rights of heirs to the pension. In short, the individual benefits from mandated savings for retirement, are going to depend on the real interest rate and on the difference between expected survival rates at the time of retirement and the actual survival rate of the individual.

Work Accidents. A further problem connected to the functioning of the social security system is that the work accidence insurance scheme subsidizes unsafe occupational practices at the cost of safer ones. The current law establishes a minimum compensation in case of on-the-job injuries of various kinds but does not distinguish the contribution to the scheme between jobs of different accident risk. While employers are not required to take up insurance policies with the IESS, all have an incentive to do so as the general contribution to the IESS also covers the accidence insurance. Theoretically, we would expect a private insurance market to mediate between risks on different jobs but no private insurers market exists. This can be partly explained by the IESS pricing policy which acts like a tie-in sale policy. As the accidents insurance premium does not vary with the risk of accidents, the system subsidizes unsafe occupational practices at the cost of safer ones.

Job Security

Ecuador's labor law establishes a minimum compensation to be paid to workers in case of dismissal with 'just cause' (major misconduct) or voluntary separation, and an additional compensation in case of dismissal without 'just cause'. A 1991 reform established very steep penalties for dismissals (the maximum compensation was 12 months of wages in the old legislation). The amounts involved are high by international standards, and even within the Latin American region, where job security legislation has been part of the tradition.

If the dismissal is justified, the employer must pay .25 monthly salaries per year of accumulated service. If the dismissal is not justified, there is an additional compensation that ranges from:

- 3 monthly salaries with less than 3 years of service;

- 1 month per year of service (up to 25 months) with more than 3 year of service;

- 80 percent of pension if the dismissed worker has more than 19 years of service and less than 25.

The current law helps to create an environment where employers become cautious with respect to hiring new workers and hence contributes to the creations of a dual labor market where only a minority is able to obtain formal sector jobs.[4] Furthermore, the discontinuity in the severance payment creates perverse incentives for employers and employees. An individual with 20 years of experience, has an additional incentive to be dismissed without 'cause'. Similarly, an employer has an additional incentive to fire an employee just before he/she completes 20 years with the firm. Workers with 19 years of experience in one firm are likely to be at risk of loosing their jobs.

A reform of article 189 is an essential element towards encouraging the establishment of a better working environment within firms. Returning to the maximum of 12 months, as had been the law until 1991, can be a start. A radical reform may be the most effective approach, introducing the notion of 'economic cause' for dismissal, and transforming the severance formula into a 'contribution defined' benefit. (See Cox Edwards (1993) for discussion).

---

[4]   For a detailed analysis of the economic impact of this type of job security legislation, see Cox Edwards (1993).

Further, the law would better serve a larger fraction of the population if it recognized the merits of a larger variety of labor contracts. Particularly in a country like Ecuador, where many workers take jobs in various cities, move back and forth from the rural to the urban areas, the law should be ample enough to make temporary work in agriculture and other sectors, a voluntary choice of employers and workers. Article 16 (and the extension introduced by Law 133) introduce job security to temporary jobs in agriculture. If the employer fails to recall the same worker, a dismissal without 'cause' is presumed. The likely impact of such legislation is an informalization of the working relationship.

Collective Bargaining and Dispute Resolution

One of the responsibilities of governments in market oriented economies is that of eliminating sources of market failures. To that aim, governments must assign property rights, protect the economic system from the possible effects of monopoly or monopsony power, and provide public goods. In a market oriented economy, unions function as institutions of collective voice. They can play an important role in reducing transactions costs, to the extent that employers negotiate wages and working conditions for a group, rather than with each individual worker. Granting workers the right to organize and bargain collectively can reduce transaction costs and enhance efficiency. Yet, that right has to be given at the same time as competition is preserved in the labor market. The labor legislation is key in balancing or failing to balance these two objectives.

In Ecuador, as in a number of developing countries, market oriented reforms have rendered the labor legislation somewhat inadequate. Workers' organizations as well as entrepreneurs are searching for a more appropriate framework where agreements can be reached and conflicts can be resolved. One of the most important bargaining tools used by unions is the strike. In an ideal scenario, a strike is a mechanism through which the seriousness of the petition is ascertained against the seriousness of the employer's refusal. Each part is risking something to put pressure on the other. Yet, under Ecuador's law, employees' costs associated to strikes are very uncertain. Currently they are a function of a number of minimum requirements that define due process. If the strike is declared illegal, workers would not get their wages. From the employers' point of view, the costs are also uncertain. If the strike is legal, wages are paid and employers are forced to a stoppage since temporary replacement of workers is not allowed.

After a period of serious conflicts and general strikes, it became clear in Ecuador that the framework for its conflict resolution was inadequate. The solution chosen in 1991, was that of requiring arbitration in all cases where there are disagreements. Legal strikes can only proceed if due process is violated. This solution has worked relatively well in the private sector, if one uses the number of strikes as an indicator of conflict. Nevertheless, it has not been an adequate solution for the public sector, nor is it necessarily adequate in the long run.

The opinion of many workers, employers and labor lawyers in Ecuador is that, at the enterprise level, labor-management relations are cordial. Among medium-size enterprises, there is less experience with collective bargaining, and a non-surprising reluctance to the notion of dealing with unions. The labor reform of 1991, has successfully reduced the incidence of conflicts between employers and organized labor. The unions have a very important role to play in the process of reforms. In particular, they can be essential in establishing an environment that encourages investment and that facilitates on-the-job training. In short, labor-management relations can improve if there is a consistent attempt from all parts to generate an environment of cooperation. The reform process is ultimately designed to encourage economic growth, and this is the most important determinant of job creation and thus real wage gains.

5.   Conclusions

In this Working Paper, we have examined some features of the Ecuadoran labor market and the policy dilemmas that it presents today. Declining average labor productivity and increasing informalization of the economy signal the importance the labor market has today, for both growth and poverty alleviation. While the current labor law promises a minimum wage, wage adjustments every six months, job security, pensions, access to credit, and more, only few poor workers are employed in the regulated sector. A labor law revision is in order. Such revision, is to establish a set of labor laws compatible with markets. Rules are to be enforced, primarily by those affected by them; that is employers and workers. Inspectors, courts and authorities in general, would play a substantive role as witness of rule violations, or as enforcers of penalties. But, on a day to day basis, it must be the parties interested, the ones that accept and agree to comply with the regulations.

A rationalization of the basic wage policy is very important. A reduction of the degree of intervention can be accomplished by (a) unifying the various components of the minimum wage, and (b) adjusting the minimum wage to one level for the country as a whole. That minimum wage can be placed somewhere between today's basic salary (salario minimo vital) and the basic salary plus additional compensations. To move in that direction, CONADES can begin a practice of adjustment of sectorial wages that is inversely proportional to the current minimum wage of the sector. After some time, all basic salaries would converge to a unique minimum wage.

The most important component of the payroll tax is the contribution towards Social Security, equivalent to 20.5 percent of the basic salary in most cases. The contribution makes affiliates eligible to workers' compensation in case of accidents on the job, public sector health care benefits, and a pension. But, the law does not establish with clarity the limits to employees and employers obligations relative to that of the IESS. Moreover, in the past, the degree of discretion the government has exercised over the determination of social security benefits has been significant, encouraging rent-seeking behavior among interest groups. One way to reduce the extent of rent-seeking behavior is through the establishment of an enforceable rule.

In the case of pensions, the minimum condition for enforceability of a rule is actuarial balance between required contributions and guaranteed benefits. Since pensions are paid in the future, for an unknown period of time, actuarial balance can be attained by a combination of a life insurance policy and a savings account. Individuals cannot be promised a given wage replacement rate at the time they are making contributions to

IESS. The program's benefits must be a function of the net present value of contributions plus their yield.

The current labor law establishes minimum compensation in case of on-the-job injuries of various kinds which does not vary with the risks of accidents. Normally, this would create a demand for workers' accidents insurance from the part of employers, and the price for that insurance will be set by market conditions. Free entry to the insurance market, accompanied by an appropriate regulatory framework for insurance companies, would establish an insurance market organized around specific sectors or areas of economic activity. Moreover, insurance programs are likely to induce safer working environments through their pricing policies. Yet, the absence of private insurers in this area may be partly explained by the IESS pricing policy which includes a tie-in sale policy. Further, the accidents insurance premium does not vary with the risk of accidents. A cross-subsidization of safer for unsafer jobs takes place.

Ecuador's law establishes a minimum compensation to be paid to workers in case of dismissal with 'just cause' (major misconduct) or voluntary separation, and an additional compensation in case of dismissal without 'just cause'. The 1991 reform established very steep penalties for dismissals (the maximum compensation was 12 months of wages in the old legislation). The amounts involved are high by international standards, and even within the Latin American region, where job security legislation has been part of the tradition. The current law leaves much to be desired in terms of acceptability or enforceability. It creates an environment where employers become extremely cautious with respect to hiring new workers. The discontinuity in the severance payment creates perverse incentives for employers and employees. A reform of article 189 in the labor law is an essential element towards encouraging the establishment of a better working environment within firms. Returning to the maximum of 12 months, as had been the law until 1991, can be a start. A radical reform may be the most effective approach, introducing the notion of 'economic cause' for dismissal, and transforming the severance formula into a 'contribution defined' benefit.

The law would better serve a larger fraction of the population if it recognized the merits of a larger variety of labor contracts. Particularly in a country like Ecuador, where many workers take jobs in various cities, move back and forth from the rural to the urban areas, the law should be ample enough to make temporary work in agriculture and other sectors, a voluntary choice of employers and workers. Article 16 (and the extension introduced by Law 133) introduces job security to temporary jobs in agriculture. If the employer fails to recall the same worker, a dismissal without 'cause' is presumed. The likely impact of this is an informalization of contracts.

References

Banco Central, <u>Cuentas nacionales 1969-92.</u>

CIE (1992), 'Economia Informal y Empleo en Ciudades Grandes e Intermedias: Casos de Guayaquil, Machala y Manta', Universidad Catolica De Santiago de Guayaquil, Centro de Investigaciones Economicas.

CEOSL-INEL (1987), <u>Cuadernos Sindicales # 5,</u> El Contrato Colectivo.

CEOSL-INEL (1989), <u>Cuadernos Sindicales # 6,</u> La Salud Ocupacional.

CEOSL-INEL (1989), <u>Cuadernos Sindicales # 7,</u> Los Salarios del Trabajador y Sus Derechos en el Seguro Social.

Cox Edwards, A. (1993), <u>Labor Market Legislation in Latin America and the Caribbean</u> Latin America and the Caribbean Technical Department, Regional Studies Program, Report # 31, The World Bank.

de Janvry, A., E. Sadoulet, and A Fargox (1991), <u>Adjustment and Equity in Ecuador,</u> Paris: OECD.

Dixit, A. and Pindyck, R.S. (1994), <u>Investment under Uncertainty.</u> Princeton: Princeton University Press.

Ecuador, Registro Oficial. (1991), Ley # 133 Ley Reformatoria al Codigo del Trabajo (1978) # 650 Codigo del Trabajo.

Griffin, P. and R. Judith (1994): 'An Exploratory Analysis of Ecuadoran Labor Markets', unpublished draft, California State University, Long Beach.

INEL - CEOSL   <u>Manual Sindical de Legislacion del Trabajo</u>

INEC   <u>V Censo de Poblacion y IV de Vivieda 1990</u> (Nov. 1991)

INEC   <u>Empleo, Desempleo y Subempleo en el Sector Urbano a Julio   1993.</u>

ILDIS   <u>Informe Social 1,</u> Ajuste y Situacion Social, 1993.

ILDIS   <u>Ecuador. Analisis de Coyuntura,</u> Perspectivas 1993.

                Mesa-Lago, C.(1993) <u>Instituto Ecuatoriano de Seguridad Social,</u>   Evaluacion Economica y Opciones Para Reforma. Incae.

Annex 1

Table A.1. Probability of Informal Employment: MALES

Informal	Coef.	Std. Err.	z	P>|z|	[95% Conf. Interval]	
age	-.0079487	.0005542	-14.342	0.000	-.009035	-.0068625
age2	.000093	6.89e-06	13.504	0.000	.0000795	.0001065
sch16	.2362826	.0060752	38.893	0.000	.2243755	.2481897
sch712	.0347709	.0062719	5.544	0.000	.0224782	.0470637
sch13p	-.4705808	.0068253	-68.946	0.000	-.4839582	-.4572034
head	.2359477	.0044495	53.028	0.000	.2272268	.2446685
spouseu	-.1516613	.0092594	-16.379	0.000	-.1698094	-.1335131
spousep	-.1294783	.0051693	-25.048	0.000	-.1396099	-.1193467
syed	-.0125821	.0003729	-33.743	0.000	-.0133129	-.0118513
dumreg2	-.114829	.0023678	-48.497	0.000	-.1194697	-.1101882
dumreg3	.0076418	.0042168	1.812	0.070	-.000623	.0159066
dumreg4	.0893731	.0058989	15.151	0.000	.0778115	.1009346
cons	.0259846	.0112062	2.319	0.020	.0040207	.0479484

Table A.2. Probability of Informal Employment : FEMALES

Informal	Coef.	Std. Err.	z	P>|z|	[95% Conf. Interval]	
age	-.0084471	.0007648	-11.044	0.000	-.0099462	-.0069481
age2	.0001485	9.95e-06	14.920	0.000	.000129	.000168
sch16	-.1753344	.008031	-21.832	0.000	-.1910749	-.159594
sch712	-.3407776	.0083952	-40.592	0.000	-.357232	-.3243233
sch13p	-.921674	.009139	-100.851	0.000	-.9395861	-.9037619
head	.1984595	.0045159	43.947	0.000	.1896086	.2073104
spouseu	-.9540672	.0100121	-95.291	0.000	-.9736906	-.9344439
spousep	.7532406	.0067626	111.383	0.000	.7399861	.7664951
syed	-.0359952	.0005686	-63.302	0.000	-.0371097	-.0348807
dumreg2	-.1342925	.00298	-45.065	0.000	-.1401332	-.1284518
dumreg3	-.1722718	.0051105	-33.709	0.000	-.1822882	-.1622553
dumreg4	.2202199	.007413	29.707	0.000	.2056908	.2347491
cons	.3144872	.0149886	20.982	0.000	.28511	.3438645

Table A3. Labor Income and Labor Costs

	October 88	October 89	October 90	October 91	October 92	October 93
BASIC SALARY (monthly)	22000.00	27000.00	32000.00	40000.00	60000.00	66000.00
13th salary	1833.33	2250.00	2666.66	3333.33	5000.00	5500.00
14th salary	3666.67	4500.00	5333.33	6666.67	10000.00	11000.00
15th salary	833.33	833.33	833.33	4166.67	4166.67	4166.67
16th salary						11000.00
Reserve Fund	1833.33	2250.00	2666.66	3333.33	5000.00	5500.00
Cost of Living	1500.00	1500.00	2500.00	2500.00	30000.00	67000.00
Bonus	500.00	500.00	1000.00	1000.00	1000.00	1000.00
Transportation	1360.00	1360.00	2400.00	3200.00	4000.00	12000.00
SALARY RECEIVED IN OCTOBER						
.9065*basic	19943.00	24475.50	29008.00	36260.00	54390.00	59829.00
15th (october)	2000.00	2000.00	2000.00	10000.00	10000.01	10000.01
16th						11000.00
Cost of Living	1500.00	1500.00	2500.00	2500.00	30000.00	67000.00
Bonus	500.00	500.00	1000.00	1000.00	1000.00	1000.00
Transportation	1360.00	1360.00	2400.00	3200.00	4000.00	12000.00
RECEIVED	25303.00	29835.50	36908.00	52960.00	99390.01	160829.01
TRUE SALARY MONTHLY AVERAGE	32780.90	39238.36	48341.65	62979.17	118288.20	184370.49
CORRECTION (TRUE SALARY/RECEIVED)	1.30	1.32	1.31	1.19	1.19	1.15
IESS (9.35%+11.15%)	4510.00	5535.00	6560.00	8200.00	12300.00	13530.00
SECAP (0.5%)	110.00	135.00	160.00	200.00	300.00	330.00
IECE (0.5%)	110.00	135.00	160.00	200.00	300.00	330.00
LABOR COST	37510.90	45043.36	55221.65	71579.17	131188.20	198560.49
PAYROLL TAX %	14.43	14.79	14.23	13.66	10.91	7.70
TRUE SALARY IN CONSTANT VALUE	32780.90	25442.58	20968.60	18333.78	21521.70	25033.31
INDEXED	100.00	77.61	63.97	55.93	65.65	76.37

Working Paper 10: Ecuadoran Poverty Revisited:
The Impact of Education, Growth and Deregulation
Martin Rama

1.   Introduction

Poverty alleviation efforts can be grouped in distinct categories. A first approach emphasizes sound economic policies, including macroeconomic stabilization and trade liberalization. If these policies succeed in spurring investment and raising labor demand, then new jobs are created and earnings increase, in a context where labor is the main asset of the poor. A second approach focuses on targeted investments in human capital and social services. If earnings increase only for those who are already better off, and prosperity does not trickle down, or does it too slowly, then it is necessary to help the poor directly. Finally, a third approach stresses the importance of labor market reform. If the earnings of informal sector workers are low because of regulations depressing labor demand in the modern sector, then the deregulation of the labor market may improve the well-being of the poor.

Although each of these approaches is based on compelling arguments, their actual payoffs in terms of poverty alleviation are unclear. For instance, the employment effects of an investment outburst will be affected by the sectoral specialization of the economy, as well as by the depth of its inter-sectoral linkages. Similarly, the wage effects of an increase in the human capital of the poor will depend on the returns to education and on the sectoral and regional mobility of workers. Finally, labor market deregulation may have little impact on both employment and earnings if there is not much segmentation, or if segmentation is due to reasons which are largely independent from the labor code. These examples suggest that the actual payoffs to the poverty alleviation approaches considered may differ from country to country.

This paper evaluates the effectiveness of the different approaches to poverty alleviation in the case of Ecuador. The specific features of this country make the analysis particularly relevant in terms of economic policy. Poverty is widespread, and affects roughly 35 percent of the population. In addition, 17 percent of the population were vulnerable to be poor. The depth of poverty is greatest in the rural Sierra, a region inhabited by people of indigenous background who have benefited little from economic progress. But poverty is also prevalent in urban areas, where a large fraction of the population works in the informal sector. Earnings in this sector are lower than in modern economic activities, and excess labor market regulation is partly responsible for the earnings gap. Last but not least, in spite of major advances in macroeconomic stabilization and trade liberalization, economic growth does not seem to be picking up, and income per capita remains 25 percent below its 1980 level.

The effectiveness of the approaches to poverty alleviation is analyzed from a macroeconomic perspective. A small computable general equilibrium (CGE) model is constructed building on previous studies on both the characteristics of poverty and the determinants of labor market segmentation in Ecuador. The model is used to assess the consequences of four scenarios on employment and earnings across sectors. The first scenario assumes that macroeconomic stability and policy reform succeed in attracting a larger inflow of foreign capital, which impacts on the labor market through physical capital accumulation and real exchange rate appreciation. In the second one, the consequences of a marginal increase in the human capital of low-skilled workers are examined. The third scenario combines the first two as growth and additional education finance can be viewed as complementary. Finally, in the fourth one, distortive labor market regulations are softened, so that the gap between earnings in the modern and the informal sector diminishes.

The idea of using CGE models to evaluate the consequences of economic policies on poverty or income distribution is hardly new (see Bourguignon, Branson and de Melo, 1992). Moreover, this idea has already been applied to the Ecuadoran case (see de Janvry, Sadoulet and Fargeix, 1991). This paper differs from previous exercises in several respects, though. First, it focuses on the labor market, rather than on the input-output linkages between sectors. Particularly, it does not derive labor demand from a fixed-coefficients technology, but use micro-econometric evidence to model the determinants of sectoral earnings and labor market segmentation instead. Second, the paper analyzes the consequences of policies aimed at alleviating poverty, not at stabilizing the economy. Previous exercises analyzed the potentially adverse effects of fiscal and monetary adjustment on income distribution in the short- to medium-run, while this one deals with the longer-run consequences of structural policies. Finally, the model in this paper is derived from first principles and kept small enough to understand the mechanisms at work, while standard CGE models are much more detailed and therefore much more realistic, but they also tend to operate like 'black boxes'.

The paper is organized as follows. Section 2 presents the CGE model, describing in detail the way features such as mobility between rural and urban jobs, returns to education and the segmentation resulting from labor market regulations are taken into account. Regarding the latter, we use results presented in Working Paper 8 ('Determinants of Hourly Earnings: The Role of Labor Market Regulations'). Section 3 calibrates the model using data from the Ecuadoran economy including, particularly, the results of previous studies on poverty and the labor market. This section is relatively arid, and can be skipped by a reader interested in results, rather than technicalities. The CGE model is used in Section 4 to evaluate the consequences of the poverty alleviation approaches on employment and earnings.

Before presenting the model, we shortly want to look at the link between poverty and the labor market. Poverty in urban areas is strongly linked to informal sector activities; in the rural sector to agricultural activities. Earnings in these sectors are considerably lower than in the modern sector of the economy so that a 'modernization' or 'formalization' of the economy is an important vehicle for poverty alleviation (see Table 1).

2.   The Model

Because of their importance in terms of employment and earnings, five sectors of activity are considered in the model. These are the public sector, identified with the letter G, the modern urban sector (F), the informal urban sector (I), agriculture in the Sierra (S) and agriculture in the Costa (A). The sectors considered differ in the characteristics of their product market. Output by the modern sector (Z_F) is sold both at home and abroad, but the volume of exports is relatively marginal. Output by the informal sector (Z_I) is sold in the domestic market only. Output Z_A by the coastal agriculture is mostly exported, at given world prices. Output Z_S by the rural Sierra is used for self-consumption, and therefore has no market price. Finally, the public sector produces a public good for which, by definition, there is no market.

The informal sector uses unskilled labor L_I as its only production factor. It is assumed that this sector consists of self-employed workers, such as street vendors, who have all the same physical productivity. Under this assumption, the production function of the informal sector can be written as:

$$Z_I = \alpha_I L_I \qquad\qquad (1)$$

where a_I is the physical productivity of labor. Let W_I be the earnings in the informal sector, expressed in dollar terms. Perfect competition in the product market implies that W_I/a_I is the price of the consumption good produced by the informal sector.

The productivity of informal sector workers depends on individual characteristics such as age, education and experience. Since one of the goals of the paper is to assess the consequences of targeted investments in human capital, the model highlights the role of schooling as a determinant of productivity. Education is indeed more likely to be modified by public policies than the average age or experience of workers. Previous studies on the determinants of earnings in Ecuador indicate a non-linear relation between earnings and schooling (see Griffin and Roberts, 1994, and Working Paper 8). Based on these studies, the following specification is used for labor productivity in the informal sector:

$$\text{Log } \alpha_I = \beta_0 + \beta_1 H_I + \beta_2 H_I^2 \qquad\qquad (2)$$

where H_I measures the average human capital of unskilled workers, and the ß-s can be interpreted as the coefficients of a Mincerian equation.

Agriculture in the Sierra uses both land and labor. For a given land surface, there are decreasing returns to the amount of labor L_S employed:

$$Z_S = \sigma_0 L_S^{\sigma_L} \qquad\qquad (3)$$

Estimates based on micro-level data indicate that individual earnings in agriculture do not increase with education (see Working Paper 8). The factor productivity parameter s_0 is therefore treated as being independent from the average schooling of workers in the Sierra. But earnings can still increase with education, due to labor mobility between sectors.

There is evidence that many households in the rural Sierra have at least one member who temporarily migrates either to the informal urban sector or to the coastal agriculture. Because of free entry into the informal sector and perfect competition in the labor market of the coastal agriculture, the alternative wage of these workers is W_I. However, many of these workers have an indigenous background, and some observers believe separation from the land, family and traditions entails a welfare loss for them and their families.

The optimization problem faced by farmer households in the Sierra is to determine temporarily migration so as to maximize welfare. Let N_S be the labor force in the rural Sierra, and m the cost of migration. The problem is thus:

$$\underset{L_S}{\text{Max}} = Z_S + (N_S - L_S)(\frac{W_I}{V} - \mu)$$

subject to $L_S \pounds N_S$. In this expression, V stands for the general price index, to be defined below. Therefore, W_I/V measures the purchasing power of monetary earnings. To keep the problem simple, it is implicitly assumed that self-consumption is a perfect substitute for monetary earnings. For interior solutions of this problem, the first-order condition is:

$$L_S = [\frac{(\frac{W_I}{V}) - \mu}{\sigma_L \sigma_0}]^{\frac{1}{1-\sigma_L}} \qquad (4)$$

Earnings per worker in the agricultural Sierra are equal to the average (not marginal) labor productivity, Z_S/L_S. To facilitate comparisons between sectors, define earnings per worker as W_S/V. Equations (3) and (4) imply:

$$W_S = \frac{(\frac{W_I}{V}) - \mu}{\sigma_L} V \qquad (5)$$

which means that earnings in the Sierra may be either higher or lower than those in the informal urban sector, in spite of free entry into the latter.

Agriculture in the Costa includes traditional crops, such as bananas, as well as fish and shrimp production. This sector applies capital, unskilled labor and intermediate inputs on a given endowment of natural resources. While there is substitutability between capital and labor, intermediate inputs (such as fertilizers and chemicals) are supposed to be complementary to output, much the same as in the input-output framework. Assuming no rationing in input markets, and with obvious notations, the output volume can be written as:

$$Z_A = \alpha_0 K_A^{\alpha_K} L_A^{\alpha_L} \qquad (6)$$

For the same reasons as before, it is assumed that the total factor productivity parameter a_0 is independent from the average schooling of agricultural workers.

By appropriately choosing units, the international price of the goods produced by sector A can be set equal to one dollar. The small country assumption would imply that this price is independent from the volume of Ecuadoran exports. It has been argued that for coffee and bananas, which constitute two of the main exports of this sector, consumers tend to differentiate products by origin. Available estimates of the price elasticity of the demand for exports faced by Ecuador are strikingly low indeed (see Hentschel, 1994). However, in order to focus on the labor market mechanism and minimize the role of second-best considerations, the small country assumption is adopted in what follows.

Firms in the coastal agriculture set their employment level so as to maximize profits, for given prices and a given wage W_I of unskilled labor:

$$\underset{L_A}{\text{Max}} \ \{ \ Z_A - W_I L_A - \alpha_A Z_A - \alpha_F Z_A - \alpha_M Z_A \ \}$$

In this expression, a_A, a_F and a_M are technical coefficients relating the use of inputs to the output volume. Units are chosen in such a way that the prices of imported inputs and of goods produced by the modern sector are equal to one dollar each. These prices are exogenous to the model under the assumption that the world demand for goods produced by sector F and the world supply for imported inputs are infinitely elastic. The first-order condition of the optimization problem faced by firms in sector A determines the following labor demand schedule:

$$L_A = \{ \ \alpha_0 K_A^{\alpha_K} [\frac{W_I}{\alpha_L (1-\alpha_A-\alpha_F-\alpha_M)}]^{-1} \ \}^{1/(1-\alpha_L)} \qquad (7)$$

The analysis is similar in the case of the modern urban sector, except that the latter uses skilled labor and no land. As before, capital and labor are assumed to be substitutes, whereas intermediate inputs are complementary to production. Assuming no rationing in the markets for inputs, the production function of the modern sector can be written as:

$$Z_F = \phi_0 K_F^{\phi_K} L_F^{\phi_L} \qquad (8)$$

The total factor productivity parameter f_0, in turn, is supposed to increase with the average human capital per worker in the sector, H_F. Estimates based on Ecuadoran micro-data indicate that returns to education are very similar in the modern and the informal sectors (see Working Paper 8). Accordingly, the following specification is chosen for the total factor productivity parameter:

$$\text{Log} \phi_0 = \beta_3 + \beta_1 H_F + \beta_2 H_F^2 \qquad (9)$$

Firms in the modern sector set employment so as to maximize profits, for given prices and a given wage level W_F of skilled workers:

$$\underset{L_F}{\text{Max}} \ \{ \ Z_F - W_F L_F - \phi_A Z_F - \phi_F Z_F - \phi_M Z_F \ \}$$

The first-order condition of this problem is:

$$L_F = \left\{ \phi_0 K_F^{\phi_K} \left[\frac{W_F}{\phi_L (1 - \phi_A - \phi_F - \phi_M)} \right]^1 \right\}^{1/(1-\phi_L)} \qquad (10)$$

Labor costs are higher in the modern than in the informal sector. The gap is partly due to different human capital endowments. Workers in the modern sector have on average two to three more years of schooling than their informal sector counterparts. But there are also other reasons underlying the difference in labor costs. First, because of efficiency wage considerations, some modern sector firms pay wages above market-clearing levels. Higher wages allow them to attract better workers, to boost morale, to reduce turnover and to avoid shirking. These considerations are much less relevant in small establishments, and totally irrelevant in the case of the self-employed. Second, labor costs may be raised by trade union activities. But this is not likely to happen in the informal sector because the Ecuadoran law does not authorize unionization in firms with less than thirty workers. And third, and more importantly from the point of view of this paper, labor costs can also be higher due to government regulations. In the Ecuadoran case, they include minimum wages, mandated benefits and payroll taxes. Modern sector firms, unlike their informal sector counterparts, have difficulties in evading or avoiding these regulations.

The different sources of wage inequality across sectors are summarized in the following specification:

$$\text{Log } W_F = \text{Log } W_I + \beta_1 (H_F - H_I) + \beta_2 (H_F^2 - H_I^2) + \tau_0 + \tau_U + \tau_G \qquad (11)$$

If there were no labor market imperfections, the wage gap between the modern and the informal sectors would be determined by sectoral differences in human capital only. However, the gap is widened because of efficiency wage considerations (t_0), union activities (t_U), and distortive labor market regulations (t_G).

For the economy to be in equilibrium, seven markets have to clear: the markets for goods produced by the modern sector, the informal sector and the coastal agriculture, the market for imported goods, the exchange rate market, the capital market and the labor market. However, the equilibrium of the markets for goods produced by the modern sector and the coastal agriculture, as well as the equilibrium of the market for imported goods are implicit in the small country assumption. Note also that no equilibrium condition is needed in the case of the agricultural Sierra, because of the assumption that all goods produced by this sector are for self-consumption. Similarly, in the case of the public good only an equilibrium condition between resources (genuine taxes or else) and expenditures is imposed. Therefore, only five markets need to be explicitly considered.

To analyze the conditions under which these markets clear, some additional behavioral hypotheses are needed. Let Y be the national monetary income. The monetary income is equal the value added of all the sectors, with the exception of subsistence output by agriculture in the Sierra, plus government transfers, G, plus all other earnings from abroad, R:

$$Y = (\frac{W_I}{\alpha_I}) Z_I + (1 - \alpha_A - \alpha_F - \alpha_M) Z_A + (1 - \phi_A - \phi_F - \phi_M) Z_F + G + R \qquad (12)$$

Variable R includes both oil revenue and net capital inflows, measured in foreign currency.

The monetary income Y is used to buy consumption goods, to invest and to pay for government expenditures:

$$Y = C + I + G \qquad (13)$$

Households buy consumption goods produced by the modern sector, by the informal sector, by the coastal agriculture and by the rest of the world. Again, the list does not include goods produced by agriculture in the Sierra, because these are for self-consumption.

Since the informal sector produces final goods for domestic consumption only, its equilibrium condition is:

$$Z_I = \theta_I \frac{C}{V} (\frac{W_I}{\alpha_I V})^{-\delta} \qquad (14)$$

The right-hand side in this expression represents the demand for informal sector goods. This demand is derived under the assumption of a constant elasticity of substitution between consumption goods (see Dixit and Stiglitz, 1977). The parameter Q_I represents the share of real consumption that would be devoted to purchasing informal sector goods if their price W_I/a_I was equal to the consumption price index V. This index, in turn, is defined as:

$$V = [\theta_I (\frac{W_I}{\alpha_I})^{1-\delta} + (1 - \theta_I)]^{\frac{1}{(1-\delta)}} \qquad (15)$$

and represents the price of the consumption basket measured in dollar terms.

The equilibrium of the foreign exchange market is equivalent to that of the balance of payments. Export prices being given for Ecuador, the volume of exports is equal to the difference between domestic supply and domestic demand in each of the sectors. In the case of agricultural goods, the volume of exports X_A is determined as:

$$X_A = Z_A - \theta_A \frac{C}{V} (\frac{1}{V})^{-\delta} - \alpha_A Z_A - \phi_A Z_F \qquad (16)$$

where domestic consumption is derived from the same analytical framework as before. In the case of modern sector goods, the volume of exports X_F can be represented as:

$$X_F = Z_F - \theta_F \frac{C}{V}\left(\frac{1}{V}\right)^{-\delta} - \alpha_F Z_A - \phi_F Z_F - (1-\Phi)I \qquad (17)$$

where F is the fraction of capital goods that needs to be purchased abroad.

The equilibrium of the balance of payments obtains when the import level M is such that:

$$M = X_A E + X_F + R \qquad (18)$$

The level of variable R, which includes capital inflows from abroad, is supposed to reflect the investors' confidence in the country. If there was perfect international capital mobility, the level of capital inflows would be endogenously determined so as to fill any gap between investment demand and domestic savings. The rate of return on investment, in turn, would always be equal to the real interest rate in world markets. But the perfect mobility hypothesis is not the best suited to analyze the effects a change in the investment climate would have on employment and earnings across sectors. For this reason, both net earnings from abroad and total investment are treated as exogenous variables whose level is significantly raised by sound economic policies.

As long as there are no obstacles to capital mobility within the country, the rates of return on investment should be the same across sectors. Therefore, the equilibrium of the capital market obtains when the marginal productivity of capital is the same in sectors A and F:

$$\alpha_K(1-\alpha_A-\alpha_F-\alpha_M)\frac{Z_A}{K_A} = \phi_K(1-\phi_A-\phi_F-\phi_M)\frac{Z_F}{K_F} \qquad (19)$$

This equilibrium condition determines the sectoral allocation of capital. The total capital stock, in turn, verifies:

$$K_A + K_F = K_0(1-\Omega) + I \qquad (20)$$

where K_0 represents the initial capital stock and W is its depreciation rate.

Last but not least, the labor market is in equilibrium when total employment equals the labor force, N.

$$L_G + L_F + L_I + L_A + L_S = N \qquad (21)$$

In this equation, L_G represents the (exogenous) level of employment in the public sector. Since some of the segments of the labor market are flexible, there is no unemployment. Note that the full employment assumption is not unrealistic in the case of Ecuador, where underemployment is seen as a much more relevant problem than open unemployment.

3.   Calibration

The labor market being the link between economic policies and poverty, special attention is given to the calibration of the variables and parameters relating to employment and earnings. Figures on employment at the sectoral level are constructed based on data from the 1990 population census, the 1993 urban household survey, and the 1994 Living Standard Measurement Survey (see Table 1 at the end of the paper). The shares of agricultural and non-agricultural employment are taken from the census, but the employment structures within each of the two sectors are adjusted using the two surveys. Absolute employment levels are updated assuming exogenous growth rates for total labor force on the one hand, and for the rural labor force on the other hand. The resulting values of the L and N variables are reported in Table 2 at the end of this paper.

Data on the level and determinants of labor income across sectors are mostly drawn from Working Paper 8, where earnings functions are estimated based on individual data. According to this study, earnings in the informal sector averaged 2308 sucres an hour as of September 1994, which corresponds to 2087 dollars a year. This is thus the value of the income variable W_I. By appropriately choosing units, this is also the value of the productivity variable a_I. The estimated functions show that earnings increase quadratically with the number of years of schooling in both the informal and the modern sector. The average years of schooling H in Table 2 and the parameters β_1 and β_2 in Table 3 are taken from this analysis.

The same source is used to calibrate the parameters t determining earnings differentials between the modern and the informal sector. The earnings functions estimated in Working Paper 8 indicate that unionized firms pay on average 8 percent more than their non-unionized counterparts, after controlling for individual characteristics. Compliance with labor market regulations, in turn, increases labor costs also by about 8 percent. This increase captures the effect of minimum wages and mandated benefits, as well as the cost in terms of payroll taxes, none of which are enforced in the informal sector. The increase in labor costs is smaller than most observers believe, for two reasons. First, complying firms partly compensate the impact of mandated benefits by lowering the base earnings on top of which benefits have to be paid. And second, mandated benefits, unlike base earnings, are not subject to payroll taxes. The estimated earnings functions also show that modern sector firms pay approximately 9 percent more than their informal sector counterparts, after controlling for individual characteristics, unionization and compliance. This differential may reflect efficiency wage considerations. Taking into account all three sources of earnings inequality across sectors, as well as the sectoral difference in schooling, the labor cost per modern sector worker W_F can be put at 3058 dollars per year. This figure is higher than the corresponding take-home pay, because it includes social security contributions and payroll taxes.

There is evidence that earnings in agriculture in the Sierra are not only below modern sector wages, but also below earnings in the informal sector. The earnings functions estimated in Working Paper 8 indicate that take-home pay in agriculture is 36 percent lower than in the informal sector, while take-home pay in the Sierra is 12 percent lower than in the Costa. The compounded effect of these two differentials can be in the range of 35 to 40 percent, which would imply earnings W_S around 1300 dollars per year. This figure refers to salaried or independent workers only, not to farmers working on their own land. However, a similar result is obtained when W_S is estimated based on the average labor productivity of sector S. According to national accounts, the value added by agriculture in the Sierra is approximately 633 million dollars (see Annex A), implying an average labor productivity of 1462 dollars per year. This is the figure used in calibrating the model. It may under-estimate actual earnings if self-consumption is not appropriately taken care of by national accounts.

Production figures for all but one of the other sectors are also drawn from national accounts. Data correspond to 1992, which is the last available year. Although these output data are not as recent as the employment and earnings data, the general perception is that neither the level nor the structure of economic activity has changed much in recent years. In Annex A, national accounts are rearranged to match the sectoral structure of the CGE model. Basically, the thirty four sectors considered in the Ecuadoran input-output matrix are regrouped in five clusters, including sectors A, S, F and G, but also the oil and mining production, designated by the same letter R as earnings from abroad. The resulting production figures are reported in Table 2.

The only output figures not drawn from national accounts are those of the informal sector. Most of the economic activities in this sector are not captured by official statistics indeed. The only exception is sector 33 in the input-output matrix (domestic service), but even in this case the comparison between national accounts and household survey data suggests a significant under-estimation. A more accurate figure for output Z_I results from multiplying the employment level L_I by the average earnings W_I. This calculation yields an informal sector output of 2909 million dollars a year, which represents slightly more than a quarter of the value added accounted for in official statistics.

Rearranged national account data are used to calibrate the consumption and balance-of-payments variables of the CGE model. In the case of consumption, two adjustments are needed. First, the consumption of goods produced by sector S is not included in variable C, because the model assumes that these goods are for self-consumption, thus not leading to money transactions. This is a minor adjustment, given that goods produced by sector S account for less than 3 percent of the consumption expenditures recorded by national accounts. The second adjustment consists of including the output of the informal sector Z_I in variable C. Regarding balance-of-payments data, exports of goods produced by sector S are treated as an exogenous foreign exchange revenue, and therefore included in variable R, much the same as the exports of oil and mining products. Note also that import figures are slightly different from official balance-of-payments data because they are measured at consumer prices, rather than producer prices. The discrepancy is included in the exogenous variable R.

Having chosen units in such a way that all initial prices are equal to one dollar, the calibration of parameters Q_i, which describe the structure of consumption, and of parameter e_0, which sets the volume of exports by the coastal agriculture, is a straightforward exercise. The calibration of the price elasticity of consumption (parameter d) is less obvious though. The value reported in Table 3 for this elasticity is in fact arbitrary, although it lies within the range of values usually assumed in CGE modeling. Because of this arbitrariness, the sensitivity of results to changes in parameter d has to be checked.

The calibration of production function parameters is a difficult task too, particularly regarding the capital and labor shares of value added (parameters a_K, a_L, f_K and f_L). National accounts are not of much help in this respect, because they dramatically under-estimate the labor share. The latter is roughly 10 percent in official statistics, which is clearly unrealistic. National accounts are more reliable when it comes to intermediate transactions (parameters a_A, a_F, a_M, f_A, f_F and f_M). In Annex B, a methodology is designed to use this information, jointly with the market equilibrium conditions and the first-order conditions of profit maximization in sectors A and F, to calibrate all of the production function parameters. The only exception are the parameters of the production function in the Sierra (s_0 and s_L). the latter are set based on educated guesses, so that the sensitivity of the results to changes in their levels needs also to be checked.

The methodology used to calibrate the parameters of the production functions in sectors A and F provides, by the same token, an estimate of the capital allocation between sectors. The total capital stock is the one reported in official estimates, based on the permanent inventory method. The depreciation rate W is set so as to ensure a constant capital stock in the initial equilibrium. The implicit assumption is that the Ecuadoran economy is in a steady-state situation. Although this assumption may not be very realistic, it greatly facilitates the interpretation of the policy simulations.

4.   Policy Simulations

Policy simulations entail modifying the level of selected exogenous variables of the model and evaluating the resulting impact on selected -endogenous variables and, more specifically, on employment and earnings across sectors. Four simulations are considered. In the first one, capital inflows to Ecuador are supposed to increase; these inflows can finance either additional investment or additional consumption. In the second one, education levels are raised; this improvement in the human capital of the labor force can take place in the modern sector only, in the rest of the private sector, or in both. The third simulation then combines the first two by jointly modeling the impact of growth and education because these can be viewed as complementary to each other: Growth will lead to higher resource availability for the public sector which can then be invested in education. Finally, in the fourth one, the wedge between sectoral earnings created by labor market regulations is reduced. Each of these four simulations corresponds to one of the poverty alleviation approaches described in the introduction.

The changes assumed for the level of the exogenous variables are relatively marginal, because the model is not well suited to analyze the consequences of major shocks. Particularly, the specifications chosen to deal with the heterogeneity of human capital and earnings across sectors are drawn from the available empirical evidence, not derived from first principles. It is therefore hazardous to use the model to evaluate how the economy would operate far off the initial equilibrium which served as a basis for the calibration exercise. For instance, the wedge between sectoral earnings, which is treated as an exogenous real rigidity in the model, could itself be modified if the sectoral structure of labor demand changed dramatically. Consequently, the aim of the simulation exercises is limited to identifying the direction and intensity of changes in employment and earnings, not to fully describe what the equilibrium of the economy would be under different circumstances.

Since all the shocks considered tend to raise the share of the modern sector in total employment, the average human capital in this sector cannot be treated as given in the policy simulations. Modern sector firms have to hire their new employees from the pool of workers in the rest of the economy, and these are less qualified than incumbent workers. The drop in the average human capital of workers, in turn, reduces the productivity of the modern sector. Therefore, the model used in the policy simulations includes the following additional equation:

$$H_F = \frac{L_{F0} H_{F0} + (L_F - L_F 0) H_I}{L_F} \qquad (22)$$

where L_{F0} and H_{F0} represent the initial employment and human capital of the modern sector respectively.

The results obtained indicate that the different approaches to poverty alleviation yield substantially different payoffs. The results are summarized in Tables 4 to 7, which show the impact of each of these approaches on employment and real earnings by sector, on the aggregate real monetary income and on the average human capital of the modern sector. The real income variable is not to be misinterpreted as the domestic GDP, because it includes net transfers from abroad, in addition to factor earnings from domestic economic activities. The human capital variable incorporates both the effect of schooling policies and of the change in the skill mix of the modern sector.

Increased capital inflows alone raise the real monetary income at the aggregate level quite significantly, but have relatively little effect on employment and earnings at the sectoral level. The exercises presented in Table 4 correspond to a one-and-for-all increase of capital inflows ranging from 100 to 300 million dollars; in the left-hand-side of the panel the additional resources are used for consumption, whereas in the right-hand-side they are invested. The resulting increase in real monetary income is larger in the case where the additional resources are invested. Although the gains for labor are modest in both cases, they benefit the poorest workers (those in sectors S, A and I), not modern sector workers. However, very few among the poor gain access to the modern sector. The largest sectoral movement of labor is towards the informal sector, because increased capital inflows create a the real exchange rate appreciation, which in this case is equivalent to a higher relative price of the goods produced by sector I.

The sectoral reallocation of labor is much more dramatic when the poverty alleviation strategy is based on increased education. In our second simulation shown in Table 5, the average schooling increases by either half a year or a full year; the additional human capital can accrue to workers in the modern sector, to workers in the rest of the private sector, or to both. The main effect of increased schooling is to raise the productivity or urban jobs in sectors F and I, while the productivity of agricultural jobs in sectors A and S remains unchanged. As a result, there is a large out-migration from the agricultural Costa, and a substantial 'formalization' of the labor market. The pattern is the same regardless of who are the workers whose human capital is accrued. The impact on real earnings is different though. If poor workers get more education, their real earnings increase, while those of modern sector workers decrease; the opposite holds true when modern sector workers are the ones benefiting from additional schooling. In both cases the aggregate real income increases considerably; but unlike the previous policy simulation, this increase is due to productivity gains.

We now combine the two scenarios outlined above into a 'growth-cum-education' simulation. It is composed of a strong increase in investment over a five-year period. The improved investment performance itself will be a function of macroeconomic stability raising investor confidence. In order to show that the effects of growth will translate not only directly into higher labor demand but also enable the public sector to raise a higher (absolute) amount of resources, we combine the 'physical' investment scenario with a 'human capital' investment.

Labor demand and growth effects of this 'growth-cum-education' scenario are strong (Table 6). In the high case -- corresponding to an investment rate increase of 2.5 percent of GDP over a five-year period and an addition to the education stock of one half year -- we see real income of the economy to grow by almost 6% and a net inflow of workers into the modern sector in the order of a quarter million, improving their real income by 40 percent. This movement of workers puts a downward pressure on the real wage in the modern sector (4 percent) which shows an important trade-off policymakers have to be aware off: while a growth and education strategy promises to reduce the lot of today's poor, labor movements between sectors can impact on the real wages of the non-poor today. The stronger the growth environment, however, the smaller will this adjustment be.

Finally, the deregulation of the labor market (fourth simulation shown in Table 7) also leads to a reallocation of labor towards the modern sector of the economy. Real earnings within each of the sectors fall, but a large number of poor workers improve their condition because they get jobs in sector F, where earnings are above the average. Conversely, incumbent workers in the modern sector experience a significant reduction in their real earnings. Note that this approach to poverty alleviation appears to be basically redistributive, while having little effect on the aggregate real income. In spite of reducing the earnings gap between sectors, therefore increasing the overall efficiency of the economy, the aggregate real income declines slightly. This is because of the distorted nature of the initial equilibrium, where workers in some sectors earn the average product of labor while the earnings of the others are determined by the marginal product of labor.

5.   Conclusions

This paper used a simple General Equilibrium Model to evaluate the impact of different poverty reduction scenarios in Ecuador: The model started from a detailed description of the labor market, distinguishing among a modern (regulated) urban sector, an informal urban sector, a commercial agricultural sector, and a subsistence agricultural sector. We modeled labor as a production factor in all four sectors and capital as a production factor only in commercial agriculture and the modern sector. Further, we included the educational level of workers employed in the informal sector, commercial agriculture, and the modern sector as a crucial determinant of labor productivity and equilibrium wages in the different sectors. Wage differentials among sectors are hence due either to the difference in educational levels or to the segmentation of labor markets (compare Working Paper 8).

We simulated four different policy scenarios which all lead to a reallocation of the labor force to the modern, non-poor sector of the economy but to greatly varying degrees. The four scenarios we considered were (a) a higher inflow of foreign capital; (b) an increase in the human capital of low-skilled workers; (c) a combination of the investment and education scenario; (d) and a reduction in the degree of labor market segmentation. Higher inflows of foreign investment over a period of five years increased growth rates of the economy but achieved relatively little change in the structure of the labor force due to an accompanying revaluation of the exchange rate which made the informal sector more profitable. This result emerged largely independent of the size of the capital inflow we simulated. Higher education, on the other hand, had a pronounced impact on the size of the modern sector. Even more striking were the results when we combined the investment and education scenarios. For example, we calculated that an increase of 0.5 years in the mean educational level of workers together with a rise in investments of 2.5 percent of GDP over a five year period would draw more than a quarter million workers into the modern, non-poor sector of the economy. These workers would realize a real income gain of 40 percent. Finally, reducing some of the burdensome regulation in the labor market also reduces poverty. Decreasing labor market segmentation, e.g., from eight to four percent would shift about 100,000 workers from the (poor) informal to the (non-poor) modern sector of the Ecuadoran economy. But while labor market reform can be an important component of a pro-poor policy because it raises labor demand in the modern sector and increases overall efficiency in the economy, it emerges that labor market deregulation alone cannot be relied on to improve the living conditions of the poor.

References

Bourguignon, F., W. Branson and J. de Melo (1992), 'Adjustment and Income Distribution: a Micro-Macro Simulation Model', *Journal of Development Economics*, 38(1), p. 17-39, January.

De Janvry, A., E. Sadoulet and A. Fargeix (1991), *Adjustment and Equity in Ecuador*, OECD, Paris.

Dixit, A. and J. Stiglitz (1977), 'Monopolistic Competition and Optimum Product Diversity', *American Economic Review*, 67, p. 297-308, June.

Griffin, P. and J. Roberts (1994), 'An Exploratory Analysis of Ecuadoran Labor Markets', California State University, unpublished draft, October.

Hentschel, J. (1994), 'Trade and Growth in Ecuador: a Partial Equilibrium View', *Policy Research Working Paper*, 1352, the World Bank, Washington DC, August.

Rama, M. (1990), 'Politica Salarial y Equilibrio Macroeconómico en Ecuador', *Documentos de Trabajo*, 353, PREALC (ILO), Santiago de Chile.

Annex A

Aggregate Variables

Data on production, consumption and foreign trade are drawn from the 1992 input-output matrix. Sectors in this matrix are regrouped so as to match the sectoral structure of the CGE model, as follows. The coastal agriculture includes sectors 1, 3, 4, 5, 9 and 16 in the matrix (bananas, coffee, cocoa, livestock, forestry, meat production, fish and seafood production, and wood products). Agriculture in the Sierra is represented by sector 2 (other agricultural productions). The oil and mining activities, designated by letter R, include sectors 6, 7, 8 and 19. The public sector is represented by sector 32, while the modern sector includes all of the remaining sectors in the matrix, with the exception of 33 (domestic service).

Domestic service is assumed to be the only informal economic activity recorded in national accounts. Even in the case of domestic service, official output figures clearly under-estimate its economic importance, thus suggesting the need to evaluate informal sector output based on different sources. In this paper, household surveys are used to evaluate both total employment and earnings per worker in the informal sector. Output in this sector obtains by multiplying these two variables, under the assumption that the earnings of informal sector workers are equal to the average (rather than the marginal) productivity of labor.

In rearranging the 1992 input-output matrix, a few simplifying assumptions were needed. To estimate supply at consumer prices, indirect taxes and distribution margins had to be added to figures reported at consumer prices. Tariffs and other import taxes were added to foreign supply. Distribution margins and VAT revenue were prorated between domestic and foreign suppliers. Put differently, it was assumed that neither tax agencies nor dealers are able to distinguish domestic products from their imported counterparts. A similar assumption was used to disaggregate intermediate transactions between domestic and foreign suppliers. For each of these transactions, the imported share was supposed to be the same as for the total supply of the good used as an input. For example, 12.4 percent of the supply by sector 17 (paper) originates abroad; therefore, all intermediate sales by sector 17 are treated as including 12.4 percent of imported goods and 87.6 percent of goods produced at home.

The rearranged 1992 input-output matrix is presented in Table A-1. In the process of reorganizing the data according to the sectoral classification in the model, all unclassified transactions were prorated across sectors based on the sectoral structure of their classified counterparts. For example, exports which were not classified by sector of origin were added to those which were, proportionally to the level of the latter. As a result of this prorating of unclassified transactions, aggregate supply and demand do not necessarily match at the sectoral level. The resulting differences between supply and demand were treated as variations in the level of inventories and, as such, were algebraically added to the investment figures.

(Table A-1)

Annex B

Production Function Coefficients

The calibration of the production function parameters is done in two steps. The first step focus on the use of intermediate inputs, while the second one deals mostly with the marginal productivity of capital and labor. Although the first step is based on the 1992 input-output matrix, the latter cannot be used as such for the calibration exercise, because there are other sectors, apart from A and F, which buy and sell intermediate inputs. The chosen approach consists of finding the values of a_A, a_F, a_M, f_A, f_F and f_M that would satisfy the equations in the CGE model, given the level of macroeconomic aggregates in Table A-1. According to this Table, the total values of intermediate inputs provided by the modern sector, the coastal agriculture and the rest of the world are 4463, 1441 and 2084 million dollars respectively. Therefore, the following relationships have to be verified:

$$\alpha_F 4084 + \phi_F 12181 = 4463 \qquad \text{(B-1)}$$

$$\alpha_A 4084 + \phi_A 12181 = 1441 \qquad \text{(B-2)}$$

$$\alpha_M 4084 + \phi_M 12181 = 2084 \qquad \text{(B-3)}$$

An additional set of three equations results from imposing that the relationship between any two input-output coefficients a_j and f_j has to be the same as in the input-output matrix, which implies:

$$\frac{\alpha_F}{\phi_F} = \frac{0.0608}{0.2992} \quad , \quad \frac{\alpha_A}{\phi_A} = \frac{0.2616}{0.0324} \quad , \quad \frac{\alpha_M}{\phi_M} = \frac{0.0343}{0.1320} \qquad \text{(B-4)}$$

The values of the input-output coefficients that solve the system of equations (B-1), (B-2), (B-3) and (B-4) are reported in Table 3.

The second step in the calibration process makes use of the estimated input-output coefficients. The value of parameter a_L can be calculated by plugging these coefficients into equations (6) and (7). Similarly, the value of parameter f_L can be calculated using equations (8) and (9). Given the lack of any reliable source to estimate the value of parameter s_L, the latter is supposed to be equal to a_L, which implicitly assumes that the output elasticity with respect to the labor input is the same in agriculture in the Sierra as in agriculture in the Costa. Given the value of parameter s_L, equation (3) allows to calculate parameter s_0.

The remaining production function parameters are set simultaneously with the sectoral capital stock. Official data indicate a total capital stock, excluding housing, of about 34242 million dollars. Therefore, the sectoral allocation of this capital must verify:

$$K_A + K_F = 34242 \qquad\qquad \text{(B-5)}$$

This allocation is driven by the equalization of the rates of return to investment across sectors (equation (19) in the model). For tractability, assume that the production functions in sectors A and F are characterized by constant returns to scale. It follows that $a_K = 1 - a_L$ and $f_K = 1 - f_L$. Equation (19) can therefore be written as follows:

$$\frac{956}{K_A} = \frac{3346}{K_F} \qquad\qquad \text{(B-6)}$$

The values of K_A and K_F can be inferred from equations (B-5) and (B-6). Replacing these values in equations (6) and (8), in turn, yields the values of parameters a_0 and f_0. The results are reported in Table 3.

Table 1. Employment and Earnings

	Employment (in thousands)				Hourly earnings (in sucres)
	Population census 1990	Household survey 1993	LSMS 1994 (in %)	Estimate as of 1994	LSMS, 1994
Labor force in the rural Sierra (Ns)	756			802	
Employment in the rural Sierra (Ls)			5.3	433	
Employment in the rural Costa (La)			9.5	778	
Employment in agriculture (Ls + La)	1035		14.8	1211	1209
Employment in the informal sector (Li)		1324	47.7	1394	2308
Employment in the formal sector (Lf)			26.3	769	2908
Employment in the public sector (Lg)			11.2	327	3351
Non-agricultural employment (Li + Lf + Lg)	2128	2721	85.2	2490	
Total employment	3163		100.0	3701	
Total labor force	3360			3931	

Note: The appropriate exchange rate for figures in sucres is 2,300 per dollar.
Source: LSMS (1994).

Table 2. Baseline Level of Aggregate Variables

ENDOGENOUS VARIABLES	EXOGENOUS VARIABLES

Labor force (thousands)

$L_S = 433$
$L_A = 778$
$L_I = 1394$
$L_F = 769$

Earnings (thousand $ per year)

$W_I = 2.087$
$W_F = 3.058$
$W_S = 1.462$

Prices (dollars)

$W_I/\alpha_I = 1$
$V = 1$

Production (million $ per year)

$Z_S = 633$
$Z_A = 4084$
$Z_I = 2909$
$Z_F = 12181$

Income and consumption (million $ per year)

$Y = 14599$
$C = 11049$

Foreign trade (million $ per year)

$X_A = 1450$
$X_F = 772$
$M = 4754$

Sectoral capital stock (million $)

$K_A = 7609$
$K_F = 26633$

Labor force (thousands)

$N = 3701$
$N_S = 802$
$L_G = 327$

Schooling (years)

$H_I = 8.2$
$H_F = 10.5$

Other expenditures (million $ per year)

$G = 884$
$I = 2666$

Exchange revenue (million $ per year)

$R = 2532$

Initial capital stock (million $)

$K_0 = 34242$

Source: LSMS (1994).

330

Table 3. Initial Parameter Values

Earnings

$\beta_0 = 0.467$
$\beta_1 = 0.000$
$\beta_2 = 0.004$
$\beta_3 = 0.241$

$\tau_0 = 0.060$
$\tau_U = 0.030$
$\tau_G = 0.120$

$\mu = 1.167$

Consumption

$\Theta_A = 0.108$
$\Theta_I = 0.263$
$\Theta_F = 0.502$

$\delta = 2.500$

Production

$\alpha_A = 0.258$
$\alpha_F = 0.070$
$\alpha_M = 0.041$

$\phi_A = 0.032$
$\phi_F = 0.343$
$\phi_M = 0.157$

$\alpha_0 = 2.253$
$\alpha_K = 0.371$
$\alpha_L = 0.629$

$\phi_0 = 1.977$
$\phi_K = 0.587$
$\phi_L = 0.413$

$\sigma_0 = 13.87$
$\sigma_L = 0.629$

Investment

$\Phi = 0.475$
$\Omega = 0.078$

Source: LSMS (1994).

Table 4. Increased Capital Inflows

Effects on	R + 100 I + 0 K₀ + 0	R + 200 I + 0 K₀ + 0	R + 300 I + 0 K₀ + 0	R + 100 I + 100 K₀ + 500	R + 200 I + 200 K₀ + 1000	R + 300 I + 300 K₀ + 1500
Employment (thousands)						
L_A	-12	-25	-38	-8	-17	-27
L_S	-1	-2	-4	-6	-12	-17
L_F	2	5	7	13	26	39
L_I	11	23	34	2	4	6
Real earnings (%)						
W_S/V	0.10	0.20	0.30	0.51	1.03	1.53
W_F/V	-0.02	-0.03	-0.04	-0.08	-0.15	-0.23
W_I/V	0.05	0.09	0.13	0.23	0.45	0.67
Real income (%)						
Y/V	0.69	1.38	2.07	1.19	2.38	3.57
Schooling (years)						
H_F	-0.01	-0.01	-0.02	-0.04	-0.07	-0.11

Source: LSMS (1994).

Table 5. Increased Human Capital

Effects on	H_I + 0.25 H_F + 0	H_I + 0.5 H_F + 0	H_I + 0 H_F + 0.25	H_I + 0 H_F + 0.5	H_I + 0.25 H_F + 0.25	H_I + 0.5 H_F + 0.5
Employment (thousands)						
L_A	-72	-167	-95	-188	-173	-375
L_S	-8	-12	19	37	11	26
L_F	48	108	45	88	96	208
L_I	32	71	32	63	66	141
Real earnings (%)						
W_S/V	0.66	1.06	-1.55	-3.02	-0.95	-2.10
W_F/V	-2.31	-4.58	0.24	0.48	-2.07	-4.07
W_I/V	0.29	0.47	-0.69	-1.33	-0.42	-0.93
Real income (%)						
Y/V	0.48	1.06	0.47	0.93	0.98	2.10
Schooling (years)						
H_F	-0.12	-0.21	0.11	0.21	0.00	0.02

Source: LSMS (1994).

Table 6. Increased Capital Inflows and Education

Effects on	R + 200 I + 200 K₀ + 1000 H₁ + 0.5 H_F + 0.25	R + 200 I + 200 K₀ + 1000 H₁ + 0.25 H_F + 0.5	R + 200 I + 200 K₀ + 1000 H₁ + 0.5 H_F + 0.5	R + 300 I + 300 K₀ + 1500 H₁ + 0.5 H_F + 0.25	R + 300 I + 300 K₀ + 1500 H₁ + 0.25 H_F + 0.5	R + 300 I + 300 K₀ + 1500 H₁ + 0.5 H_F + 0.5
Employment (thousands)						
L_A	-306	-294	-408	-323	-306	-424
L_S	-3	18	15	-7	13	10
L_F	195	172	243	212	187	261
L_I	114	104	149	118	107	153
Real earnings (%)						
W_S/V	0.25	-1.52	-1.26	0.65	-1.06	-0.86
W_F/V	-4.46	-1.97	-4.21	-4.52	-2.05	-4.28
W_I/V	0.11	-0.67	-0.56	0.29	-0.47	-0.38
Real income (%)						
Y/V	2.74	3.91	3.00	5.27	5.12	5.81
Schooling (years)						
H_F	-0.16	0.04	-0.04	-0.18	0.01	-0.07

Source: LSMS (1994).

Table 7. Labor Market Deregulation

Effects on	$\tau_G =$	$\tau_G =$	$\tau_G =$	$\tau_G =$	$\tau_G =$
Employment (thousands)					
L_A	-30	-62	-96	-132	-170
L_S	3	5	9	12	16
L_F	26	54	83	113	146
L_I	1	3	5	7	9
Real earnings (%)					
W_S/V	-0.21	-0.46	-0.72	-1.00	-1.24
W_F/V	-1.65	-3.27	-4.87	-6.44	-7.93
W_I/V	-0.10	-0.20	-0.32	-0.44	-0.52
Real income (%)					
Y/V	-0.11	-0.22	-0.33	-0.44	-0.51
Schooling (years)					
H_F	-0.07	-0.13	-0.20	-0.27	-0.33

Source: LSMS (1994).

Table A-1. Rearranged Input-Output Matrix

Billion sucres, as of 1992 (*)

Sector	Intermediate demand						Final demand				Total demand
	A	S	F	G	R	Total	C	G	I	X	
A	1688.1	4.0	624.0	21.2	15.8	2353.1	1888.5	-	-79.7	2291.0	6452.9
S	24.8	38.0	604.2	10.4	-	677.4	348.4	-	60.7	110.2	1196.8
F	392.2	74.4	5758.8	409.3	411.0	7045.8	8769.0	-	2210.5	1220.0	19245.3
G	-	-	-	-	-	-	-	1396.3	-	-	1396.3
R	187.2	19.1	1465.2	47.0	1904.0	3622.5	395.8	-	-189.7	2414.5	6243.1
Total	2292.2	135.5	8452.3	487.9	2330.9	13698.8	11401.7	1396.3	2001.9	6035.7	34534.4
Imports	221.4	60.6	2540.3	151.6	537.8	3511.7	1808.5	-	2191.4	-	
Val.added	3939.2	1000.7	8252.7	756.8	3374.5	17323.9					
Supply	6452.9	1196.8	19245.3	1396.3	6243.1	34534.4					

Note: All figures are in consumer prices. The appropriate exchange rate is 1,580 sucres per dollar.
Source: LSMS (1994).

Distributors of World Bank Publications

Prices and credit terms vary from country to country. Consult your local distributor before placing an order.

ALBANIA
Adrion Ltd.
Perlat Rexhepi Str.
Pall. 9, Shk. 1, Ap. 4
Tirana
Tel: (42) 274 19; 221 72
Fax: (42) 274 19

ARGENTINA
Oficina del Libro Internacional
Av. Cordoba 1877
1120 Buenos Aires
Tel: (1) 815-8156
Fax: (1) 815-8354

AUSTRALIA, FIJI, PAPUA NEW GUINEA, SOLOMON ISLANDS, VANUATU, AND WESTERN SAMOA
D.A. Information Services
648 Whitehorse Road
Mitcham 3132
Victoria
Tel: (61) 3 9210 7777
Fax: (61) 3 9210 7788
URL: http://www.dadirect.com.au

AUSTRIA
Gerold and Co.
Graben 31
A-1011 Wien
Tel: (1) 533-50-14-0
Fax: (1) 512 47-31-29

BANGLADESH
Micro Industries Development
  Assistance Society (MIDAS)
House 5, Road 16
Dhanmondi R/Area
Dhaka 1209
Tel: (2) 326427
Fax: (2) 811188

BELGIUM
Jean De Lannoy
Av. du Roi 202
1060 Brussels
Tel: (2) 538-5169
Fax: (2) 538-0841

BRAZIL
Publicações Tecnicas Internacionais
  Ltda.
Rua Peixoto Gomide, 209
01409 Sao Paulo, SP.
Tel: (11) 259-6644
Fax: (11) 258-6990

CANADA
Renouf Publishing Co. Ltd.
1294 Algoma Road
Ottawa, Ontario K1B 3W8
Tel: 613-741-4333
Fax: 613-741-5439

CHINA
China Financial & Economic
  Publishing House
8, Da Fo Si Dong Jie
Beijing
Tel: (1) 333-8257
Fax: (1) 401-7365

COLOMBIA
Infoenlace Ltda.
Apartado Aereo 34270
Bogotá D.E.
Tel: (1) 285-2798
Fax: (1) 285-2798

COTE D'IVOIRE
Centre d'Edition et de Diffusion
  Africaines (CEDA)
04 B.P. 541
Abidjan 04 Plateau
Tel: 225-24-6510
Fax: 225-25-0567

CYPRUS
Center of Applied Research
Cyprus College
6, Diogenes Street, Engomi
P.O. Box 2006
Nicosia
Tel: 244-1730
Fax: 246-2051

CZECH REPUBLIC
National Information Center
prodejna, Konviktska 5
CS - 113 57 Prague 1
Tel: (2) 2422-9433
Fax: (2) 2422-1484
URL: http://www.nis.cz/

DENMARK
SamfundsLitteratur
Rosenoerns Allé 11
DK-1970 Frederiksberg C
Tel: (31)-351942
Fax: (31)-357822

EGYPT, ARAB REPUBLIC OF
Al Ahram
Al Galaa Street
Cairo
Tel: (2) 578-6083
Fax: (2) 578-6833

The Middle East Observer
41, Sherif Street
Cairo
Tel: (2) 393-9732
Fax: (2) 393-9732

FINLAND
Akateeminen Kirjakauppa
P.O. Box 23
FIN-00371 Helsinki
Tel: (0) 12141
Fax: (0) 121-4441
URL: http://booknet.cultnet.fi/aka/

FRANCE
World Bank Publications
66, avenue d'Iéna
75116 Paris
Tel: (1) 40-69-30-56/57
Fax: (1) 40-69-30-68

GERMANY
UNO-Verlag
Poppelsdorfer Allee 55
53115 Bonn
Tel: (228) 212940
Fax: (228) 217492

GREECE
Papasotiriou S.A.
35, Stournara Str.
106 82 Athens
Tel: (1) 364-1826
Fax: (1) 364-8254

HONG KONG, MACAO
Asia 2000 Ltd.
Sales & Circulation Department
Seabird House, unit 1101-02
22-28 Wyndham Street, Central
Hong Kong
Tel: 852 2530-1409
Fax: 852 2526-1107
URL: http://www.sales@asia2000.com.hk

HUNGARY
Foundation for Market
  Economy
Dombovari Ut 17-19
H-1117 Budapest
Tel: 36 1 204 2951 or
36 1 204 2948
Fax: 36 1 204 2953

INDIA
Allied Publishers Ltd.
751 Mount Road
Madras - 600 002
Tel: (44) 852-3938
Fax: (44) 852-0649

INDONESIA
Pt. Indira Limited
Jalan Borobudur 20
P.O. Box 181
Jakarta 10320
Tel: (21) 390-4290
Fax: (21) 421-4289

IRAN
Kowkab Publishers
P.O. Box 19575-511
Tehran
Tel: (21) 258-3723
Fax: 98 (21) 258-3723

Ketab Sara Co. Publishers
Khaled Eslamboli Ave.,
6th Street
Kusheh Delafrooz No. 8
Tehran
Tel: 8717819 or 8716104
Fax: 8862479

IRELAND
Government Supplies Agency
Oifig an tSoláthair
4-5 Harcourt Road
Dublin 2
Tel: (1) 461-3111
Fax: (1) 475-2670

ISRAEL
Yozmot Literature Ltd.
P.O. Box 56055
Tel Aviv 61560
Tel: (3) 5285-397
Fax: (3) 5285-397

R.O.Y. International
PO Box 13056
Tel Aviv 61130
Tel: (3) 5461423
Fax: (3) 5461442

Palestinian Authority/Middle East
Index Information Services
P.O.B. 19502 Jerusalem
Tel: (2) 271219

ITALY
Licosa Commissionaria Sansoni SPA
Via Duca Di Calabria, 1/1
Casella Postale 552
50125 Firenze
Tel: (55) 645-415
Fax: (55) 641-257

JAMAICA
Ian Randle Publishers Ltd.
206 Old Hope Road
Kingston 6
Tel: 809-927-2085
Fax: 809-977-0243

JAPAN
Eastern Book Service
Hongo 3-Chome,
  Bunkyo-ku 113
Tokyo
Tel: (03) 3818-0861
Fax: (03) 3818-0864
URL: http://www.bekkoame.or.jp/~svt-ebs

KENYA
Africa Book Service (E.A.) Ltd.
Quaran House, Mfangano Street
P.O. Box 45245
Nairobi
Tel: (2) 23641
Fax: (2) 330272

KOREA, REPUBLIC OF
Daejon Trading Co. Ltd.
P.O. Box 34
Yeoeida
Seoul
Tel: (2) 785-1631/4
Fax: (2) 784-0315

MALAYSIA
University of Malaya Cooperative
  Bookshop, Limited
P.O. Box 1127
Jalan Pantai Baru
59700 Kuala Lumpur
Tel: (3) 756-5000
Fax: (3) 755-4424

MEXICO
INFOTEC
Apartado Postal 22-860
14060 Tlalpan,
Mexico D.F.
Tel: (5) 606-0011
Fax: (5) 606-0386

NETHERLANDS
De Lindeboom/InOr-Publikaties
P.O. Box 202
7480 AE Haaksbergen
Tel: (53) 574-0004
Fax: (53) 572-9296

NEW ZEALAND
EBSCO NZ Ltd.
Private Mail Bag 99914
New Market
Auckland
Tel: (9) 524-8119
Fax: (9) 524-8067

NIGERIA
University Press Limited
Three Crowns Building Jericho
Private Mail Bag 5095
Ibadan
Tel: (22) 41-1356
Fax: (22) 41-2056

NORWAY
Narvesen Information Center
Book Department
P.O. Box 6125 Etterstad
N-0602 Oslo 6
Tel: (22) 57-3300
Fax: (22) 68-1901

PAKISTAN
Mirza Book Agency
65, Shahrah-e-Quaid-e-Azam
P.O. Box No. 729
Lahore 54000
Tel: (42) 7353601
Fax: (42) 7585283

Oxford University Press
5 Bangalore Town
Sharae Faisal
PO Box 13033
Karachi-75350
Tel: (21) 446307
Fax: (21) 454-7640

PERU
Editoral Desarrollo SA
Apartado 3824
Lima 1
Tel: (14) 285380
Fax: (14) 286628

PHILIPPINES
International Booksource Center Inc.
Suite 720, Cityland 10
Condominium Tower 2
H.V. dela Costa, corner
Valero St.
Makati, Metro Manila
Tel: (2) 817-9676
Fax: (2) 817-1741

POLAND
International Publishing Service
Ul. Piekna 31/37
00-577 Warzawa
Tel: (2) 628-6089
Fax: (2) 621-7255

PORTUGAL
Livraria Portugal
Rua Do Carmo 70-74
1200 Lisbon
Tel: (1) 347-4982
Fax: (1) 347-0264

ROMANIA
Compani De Librarii Bucuresti S.A.
Str. Lipscani no. 26, sector 3
Bucharest
Tel: (1) 613 9645
Fax: (1) 312 4000

RUSSIAN FEDERATION
Isdatelstvo <Ves Mir>
9a, Kolpachniy Pereulok
Moscow 101831
Tel: (95) 917 87 49
Fax: (95) 917 92 59

SAUDI ARABIA, QATAR
Jarir Book Store
P.O. Box 3196
Riyadh 11471
Tel: (1) 477-3140
Fax: (1) 477-2940

SINGAPORE, TAIWAN, MYANMAR, BRUNEI
Asahgate Publishing Asia
  Pacific Pte. Ltd.
41 Kallang Pudding Road #04-03
Golden Wheel Building
Singapore 349316
Tel: (65) 741-5166
Fax: (65) 742-9356
e-mail: ashgate@asianconnect.com

SLOVAK REPUBLIC
Slovart G.T.G. Ltd.
Krupinska 4
PO Box 152
852 99 Bratislava 5
Tel: (7) 839472
Fax: (7) 839485

SOUTH AFRICA, BOTSWANA
For single titles:
Oxford University Press
  Southern Africa
P.O. Box 1141
Cape Town 8000
Tel: (21) 45-7266
Fax: (21) 45-7265

For subscription orders:
International Subscription Service
P.O. Box 41095
Craighall
Johannesburg 2024
Tel: (11) 880-1448
Fax: (11) 880-6248

SPAIN
Mundi-Prensa Libros, S.A.
Castello 37
28001 Madrid
Tel: (1) 431-3399
Fax: (1) 575-3998
http://www.tsai.es/mprensa

Mundi-Prensa Barcelona
Consell de Cent, 391
08009 Barcelona
Tel: (3) 488-3009
Fax: (3) 487-7659

SRI LANKA, THE MALDIVES
Lake House Bookshop
P.O. Box 244
100, Sir Chittampalam A.
  Gardiner Mawatha
Colombo 2
Tel: (1) 32105
Fax: (1) 432104

SWEDEN
Fritzes Customer Service
Regeringsgaton 12
S-106 47 Stockholm
Tel: (8) 690 90 90
Fax: (8) 21 47 77

Wennergren-Williams AB
P. O. Box 1305
S-171 25 Solna
Tel: (8) 705-97-50
Fax: (8) 27-00-71

SWITZERLAND
Librairie Payot
Service Institutionnel
Côtes-de-Montbenon 30
1002 Lausanne
Tel: (021)-341-3229
Fax: (021)-341-3235

Van Diermen Editions Techni
Ch. de Lacuez 41
CH1807 Blonay
Tel: (021) 943 2673
Fax: (021) 943 3605

TANZANIA
Oxford University Press
Maktaba Street
PO Box 5299
Dar es Salaam
Tel: (51) 29209
Fax (51) 46822

THAILAND
Central Books Distribution
306 Silom Road
Bangkok
Tel: (2) 235-5400
Fax: (2) 237-8321

TRINIDAD & TOBAGO, JAM.
Systematics Studies Unit
#9 Watts Street
Curepe
Trinidad, West Indies
Tel: 809-662-5654
Fax: 809-662-5654

UGANDA
Gustro Ltd.
Madhvani Building
PO Box 9997
Plot 16/4 Jinja Rd.
Kampala
Tel/Fax: (41) 254763

UNITED KINGDOM
Microinfo Ltd.
P.O. Box 3
Alton, Hampshire GU34 2PG
England
Tel: (1420) 86848
Fax: (1420) 89889

ZAMBIA
University Bookshop
Great East Road Campus
P.O. Box 32379
Lusaka
Tel: (1) 213221 Ext. 482

ZIMBABWE
Longman Zimbabwe (Pte.)Ltd.
Tourle Road, Ardbennie
P.O. Box ST125
Southerton
Harare
Tel: (4) 6216617
Fax: (4) 621670